Violence against Women

Understanding Social Problems
An SSSP Presidential Series

Understanding Social Problems is a textbook series published in collaboration with the Society for the Study of Social Problems, under the direction of the SSSP Editorial and Publications Committee. The anthologies introduce students to the principles for assessing social problems and to exemplary research studies in the field. Articles selected from the society's leading journal, *Social Problems*, are chosen for their coverage, their relevance, and their accessibility to students. Introductions written by each book's editors situate the issues raised by the articles into a broader sociological perspective.

All royalties from this series go to support the SSSP and its activities.

Titles in the Series

Social Problems across the Life Course
    Edited by Helena Z. Lopata and Judith A. Levy

Drugs, Alcohol, and Social Problems
    Edited by James D. Orcutt and David R. Rudy

Health and Health Care as Social Problems
    Edited by Peter Conrad and Valerie Leiter

Violence against Women
    Edited by Claire M. Renzetti and Raquel Kennedy Bergen

Forthcoming

Social Problems, Law, and Society
    Edited by William J. Chambliss, Richard A. Dello Buono, and A. Kathryn Stout

Violence against Women

Edited by Claire M. Renzetti
and Raquel Kennedy Bergen

ROWMAN & LITTLEFIELD PUBLISHERS, INC.
Lanham • Boulder • New York • Toronto • Oxford

ROWMAN & LITTLEFIELD PUBLISHERS, INC.

Published in the United States of America
by Rowman & Littlefield Publishers, Inc.
A wholly owned subsidiary of The Rowman & Littlefield Publishing Group, Inc.
4501 Forbes Boulevard, Suite 200, Lanham, Maryland 20706
www.rowmanlittlefield.com

PO Box 317, Oxford OX2 9RU, UK

Copyright © 2005 by the Society for the Study of Social Problems

All rights reserved. No part of this publication may be reproduced, stored in a retrieval system, or transmitted in any form or by any means, electronic, mechanical, photocopying, recording, or otherwise, without the prior permission of the publisher.

British Library Cataloguing in Publication Information Available

Library of Congress Cataloging-in-Publication Data

Violence against women / edited by Claire M. Renzetti and Raquel Kennedy Bergen.
   p. cm. — (Understanding social problems)
   Includes bibliographical references and index.
   ISBN 0-7425-3054-X (cloth : alk. paper) — ISBN 0-7425-3055-8 (pbk. : alk. paper)
   1. Women—Violence against—United States. 2. Women—Crimes against—United States.
I. Renzetti, Claire M. II. Bergen, Raquel Kennedy. III. Social problems. IV. Series.
HV6250.4.W65V5657 2005
362.82'92'0973—dc22

                                                  2004014487

Printed in the United States of America

∞™ The paper used in this publication meets the minimum requirements of American National Standard for Information Sciences—Permanence of Paper for Printed Library Materials, ANSI/NISO Z39.48-1992.

Contents

List of Tables	vii
Introduction: The Emergence of Violence against Women as a Social Problem *Claire M. Renzetti and Raquel Kennedy Bergen*	1

Part I Forms of Violence against Women

1	"Riding the Bull at Gilley's": Convicted Rapists Describe the Rewards of Rape *Diana Scully and Joseph Marolla*	15
2	The Myth of Sexual Symmetry in Marital Violence *Russell P. Dobash, R. Emerson Dobash, Margo Wilson, and Martin Daly*	31
3	Safe Conduct: Women, Crime, and Self in Public Places *Carol Brooks Gardner*	55
4	On Being Stalked *Robert M. Emerson, Kerry O. Ferris, and Carol Brooks Gardner*	77
5	The Locker Room and the Dorm Room: Workplace Norms and the Boundaries of Sexual Harassment in Magazine Editing *Kirsten Dellinger and Christine L. Williams*	109

Part II Institutional Responses to Violence against Women

6	Prosecutorial Justifications for Sexual Assault Case Rejection: Guarding the "Gateway to Justice" *Cassia Spohn, Dawn Beichner, and Erika Davis-Frenzel*	131
7	Gender, Accounts, and Rape Processing Work *Patricia Yancey Martin*	167
8	Policing Woman Battering *Kathleen J. Ferraro*	191

9	Emergency Department Responses to Battered Women: Resistance to Medicalization *Demie Kurz*	207
10	The Social Construction of Deviance: Experts on Battered Women *Donileen R. Loseke and Spencer E. Cahill*	223

Part III   Feminist Activism and Social Change

11	The Battered Woman Movement and the Creation of the Wife Beating Problem *Kathleen J. Tierney*	243
12	Identity, Strategy, and Feminist Politics: Clemency for Battered Women Who Kill *Patricia Gagné*	261

Sources	281
Index	283
About the Editors	297

Tables

6.1	Disposition of Sexual Battery Cases in Miami, 1997	138
6.2	Prosecutorial Justifications of Case Rejection	139
6.3	Case Outcomes and Case Characteristics for Sexual Battery Cases: Cases Rejected/Dismissed and Cases Prosecuted	152
6.4	The Effect of Victim, Suspect, and Case Characteristics on the Decision to Prosecute: Miami, 1997	155
7.1	Justificational Accounts: Gender and Rape Processing Work	173

Introduction

THE EMERGENCE OF VIOLENCE AGAINST WOMEN AS A SOCIAL PROBLEM

Claire M. Renzetti and Raquel Kennedy Bergen

Over the past three decades, violence against women has been recognized as a serious and pervasive problem. Recent national, random-sample surveys show that more than one quarter (25.5%) of American women are violently victimized at some time during their lives. These victimizations include physical assaults, attempted and completed sexual assaults, and stalking. Nearly 2 percent of American women are violently victimized in a 12-month period (Tjaden and Thoennes, 2000). Although men—especially young and poor men of color—are more likely than women to be the victim of a violent crime at some point in their lives (89 percent of males currently 12 years or older compared with 73 percent of females 12 years or older), women's fear of crime is greater than men's fear of crime (Rennison, 2001; Stanko, 2001).

While women are taught from the time they are little girls to be wary of strangers, they are more likely to be victimized by an intimate partner, a friend, or an acquaintance than by a stranger. Fifty-four percent of the violent victimizations reported by women are perpetrated by someone they know (i.e., an intimate partner, another relative, a friend, or an acquaintance) compared with 45 percent perpetrated by strangers. For men, the numbers are nearly identical, but reversed: 44 percent of the violent victimizations reported by men are perpetrated by someone they know compared with 54 percent perpetrated by strangers (Rennison, 2001). Nevertheless, as shocking as these figures are, most experts maintain that they are *underestimates* of the actual incidence of violence against women, since many women are uncomfortable or fearful of reporting their victimization—especially victimization by an intimate or friend—to the police or researchers (Greenfeld, 1997; Rennison, 2001).

Despite the extent and seriousness of women's violent victimization—which many experts have concluded is primarily intimate-partner violence (Tjaden and Thoennes, 2000)—it has only been within the past 30 years, as noted earlier, that violence against women has been recognized as a social problem. In fact, it was not until 1989 that the U.S. Department of Justice began including in the National Crime Victimization Survey (NCVS)—the major source of official data on criminal victimization in the United

States—questions to more accurately estimate the incidence of rape and violence perpetrated by intimates and other family members (Bachman, 2000).

What accounts for this oversight? Certainly, it is not the case that violence against women is a "new" problem. Indeed, social scientists have documented that the physical and sexual abuse of women by intimates has occurred for centuries (Dobash and Dobash, 1979; Pleck, 1987). But as C. Wright Mills pointed out in 1959, a problem does not become a *social* problem until it is no longer seen as a "personal trouble" and instead is viewed as a *public issue*. Until the 1970s, wife abuse was viewed as a private matter, a problem of a few dysfunctional couples. And sexual assault was a crime committed by mentally unstable men or men who were provoked by women who led them on, dressed provocatively or, worse, consented to sex and then changed their minds afterward. Terms such as "wife rape" and "date rape" didn't even exist (Bergen, 1998).

The resurgence of the women's movement in the late 1960s and early 1970s was a major impetus in raising public awareness of the extent and seriousness of violence against women. Feminists organized speak-outs so that women could talk openly in a supportive environment about their victimizations—the victimization at the hands of the perpetrator and the second victimization at the hands of the police and the courts, who often dismissed their cases as "unfounded" or released offenders with little or no punishment. Feminists also opened crisis lines for victims to call for counselling and support, and shelters to house women and their children fleeing abusers (Schechter, 1982). And it was feminist social scientists who, during the early 1970s, began systematically collecting data on intimate partner violence and sexual assault, reframing the research questions from "What's wrong with women who get raped or abused?" and "What's wrong with men who abuse or kill women they claim to love?" to "How do our society's gender norms contribute to the high rate of violence against women?" and "Does the differential power that males and females have in our society contribute to the problem of violence against women?"

This work has expanded exponentially over the past three decades to influence practice and policy at the local, state, and federal levels. Consider, for example, that since the first shelters for battered women opened in the United States in 1973, they have grown from individuals sharing private apartments and space in their homes to agencies that buy or build their own facilities and offer a multitude of services, including children's therapeutic programs, help in obtaining a restraining order, job training, and primary prevention programs in collaboration with other social service providers such as prosecutors' offices, hospitals, and schools. Rape crisis centers, which began in the 1970s through the grassroots efforts of women who often opened hotlines in their basements, now number over 1,200 and offer a broad range of services, including legal and medical advocacy, counselling services, and anti-rape educational programming and activism (Campbell and Martin, 2001). Consider as well that in support of passage of the Violence Against Women Act in 1994, and in reauthorizing it in 2000 while doubling funding for prevention and intervention efforts to $3 billion over five years, congressional sponsors cited numerous studies by feminist social scientists that have documented the widespread and serious nature of violence against women.

Certainly, it is not an overstatement to say that violence against women is now a major subfield of social science research that has matured to the point of having a critical body of literature serving as the foundation upon which researchers currently build. Moreover, much of the most influential research in this subfield has been published in *Social Problems*, the journal of the Society for the Study of Social Problems. This book brings these articles together in a single core text covering the areas of sexual assault, wife abuse, sexual harassment, and stalking, as well as institutional and feminist responses to violence against women.

In compiling this collection, we reviewed 32 articles published in *Social Problems* between 1970 and 2002. The 12 articles selected for inclusion were chosen because of the extent to which they are cited by researchers working in the area of violence against women, indicating their influence on the development of this subfield. Each article focuses on a different dimension of the problem of violence against women, but what the articles share in common is their challenge to taken-for-granted knowledge. The authors of these articles do not reiterate what is "known" or replicate what has already been done. Rather, they change the research lens and ask us to look at an issue in a whole new way, often in the process debunking commonly held assumptions that their research unveils as myths.

In chapter 1, for instance, Diana Scully and Joseph Marolla call into question the popular idea that rape is "a nonutilitarian act committed by a few 'sick' men." In their groundbreaking work, Scully and Marolla interviewed more than 100 incarcerated men convicted of rape to learn how the men themselves viewed their behavior: What did they see as the "function" or objective of rape? What did they get out of it?

The often-chilling words of the rapists reveal a number of motivations for rape. Some of the men used rape as an act of revenge or punishment. These men became angry with a woman and took their anger out on another woman by raping her. Other men raped women as a "bonus" while committing a robbery or burglary. Still others used rape as a form of access to women they perceived as sexually unavailable to them or who had refused to have sex with them. Finally, other men, especially young men who had engaged in gang rapes, described the rape as an "adventure," a kind of recreational activity they carried on with friends.

Regardless of their specific motivations, however, Scully and Marolla show that the rapists shared a sense of entitlement to women, whom they objectified, and they enjoyed the dominance over women that rape gave them. For the vast majority of the rapists, rape gave them a feeling of satisfaction and accomplishment. Thus, by asking us to look at rape from the perspective of convicted rapists, Scully and Marolla debunk the commonly held notion that a tiny group of irrational, psychopathic men rape to satisfy their sexual appetites. Instead, they reveal the complex motivations behind this form of violence against women and, in doing so, have spurred future researchers to continue their quest to understand why men rape.

In chapter 2, Russell Dobash and his colleagues take on another popular myth: the idea that women are as violent as men are toward their intimate partners. This notion stems from a number of research reports that show that women are as likely—some say women are slightly more likely—to assault their intimate partners than men are (Archer, 2000; Fiebert, 1997; Straus, 1999). In their chapter, Dobash et al. systematically examine the data upon which this claim is based as well as the primary research instrument used to collect these data. They call into question the reliability and validity of the questionnaire checklist—the Conflict Tactics Scales (CTS)—pointing out that male and female couples frequently provide different accounts of their own and their partner's behavior.

Importantly, subsequent research has shown that men are more likely than women to underreport both the frequency and the severity of the intimate partner violence they inflict (Crowell and Burgess, 1996; Dobash, Dobash, Cavanagh, and Lewis, 1998). Dobash et al.'s central criticism of the CTS—i.e., that this research instrument decontextualizes violence by ignoring gendered differences in motives, meanings, and consequences—became the springboard for a significant body of subsequent research that further challenges the gender symmetry hypothesis (see, for example, Bible, Das Dasgupta, and Osthoff, 2002; Osthoff, Das Dagupta, and Bible, 2002; Das Dasgupta, Bible, and Osthoff, 2003).

In addition, they presented data to contradict the gender symmetry argument—e.g., women are more likely than men to be injured by an intimate partner and to require medical attention or hospitalization as a result. These findings have been consistently supported by subsequent studies (Archer, 2000; Tjaden and Thoennes, 2000) and are buttressed by additional research that shows that men are more likely than women to kill an intimate partner (Fox and Zawitz, 2000; Greenfeld, 1998).

Dobash et al.'s call for research on the gendered meanings and motives of intimate partner violence has led to studies that document, for instance, that men are more likely to use violence to punish or control women, especially when women challenge their authority. Women, however, are more likely to use violence, particularly severe violence, in self-defense, when they perceive they are in imminent danger of being attacked, or to fight back when being attacked (Abel, 1999; Barnett, Lee, and Thelan, 1997; Miller, 2001).

The crime prevention advice reviewed by Carol Brooks Gardner in chapter 3 would be humorous were it not for the fact that when women are attacked, they are often held culpable for having failed to heed such warnings. The traditional crime prevention literature for women that Gardner analyzed depicts women as weak in both mind and body. It encourages them to rely on others—usually men—for protection and to use rather contrived "security measures" to prevent victimization. The latter include yelling out to a fictitious male companion on the street or in their homes before answering the door and putting men's clothing or other masculine items in their cars or on display in their homes. Many of the women Gardner interviewed noted that they engage in this sort of behavior, but admitted feeling some shame because it seems "crazy" or "bizarre."

Gardner astutely observes the contradictory messages women receive about their appearance: magazines with sexy models on the cover and numerous articles and advertisements for make-up and clothing to make women attractive in public simultaneously advise women to dress so as not to "stimulate interest." As Gardner reports, such tactics amount to a "profaning of the self," and other strategies designed to prevent attack by repulsing the aggressor are even more humiliating. Gardner's article not only captures the contradictions imposed on women—e.g., be alluring to men, but if you provoke them, it's your fault—but also highlights our society's sexual double standard. As she wrote, "Thus, a woman's time in public can be altered in ways unfamiliar to male citizens; in fact, with strategies unfamiliar to most males." Can you even imagine suggesting to a man that he put his money in his underwear before he goes out, that he get off an elevator if a woman he doesn't know gets on, or that he quack like a duck in public to ward off an attacker?

The advice analyzed by Gardner reinforces women's fear of "stranger danger," when, as we have already noted, women are at greater risk of being assaulted by someone they know (Madriz, 1997; Stanko, 1996). This point is underlined in chapter 4, where Robert Emerson and his colleagues examine the phenomenon of stalking. Emerson et al. note that stalking was not identified as a social problem until the late 1980s, largely as a result of media attention given to cases involving celebrities.

Emerson et al. cite data showing that more than three quarters of stalking victims are women and nearly all of these women are stalked by men, the majority of whom were current or former intimate partners or acquaintances. Since the primary motive in most stalking cases is to establish or reestablish a relationship with an unwilling or resistant other, Emerson et al. focus their attention on what they call "relational stalking." As their data indicate, relational stalking involves a variety of behaviors that at first may seem annoying, but nevertheless nonthreatening or inconsequential. However, as the victim's resistance becomes stronger, the behaviors—following, persistent phone calls and letters, leaving unwanted gifts—escalate over time, becoming more intrusive and hostile, inducing more fear, and inflicting greater harm on the victim. One of the most significant aspects of Emerson et al.'s research is that it shows how a woman can leave an unhappy or abusive relationship, but the abuse may continue. As they put it, "while leaving might appear to be an individual, unilateral act, in fact its accomplishment depends upon the other's acceptance or acquiescence."

Emerson et al.'s research is enlightening because it shows how the reality of stalking can be, at least initially, considerably different from the public's conception of the problem. Stalking is a form of violence that is often perceived as non-threatening or not very serious in its consequences for women. Emerson et al.'s work is important in that they emphasize the definitional process as central to both the victim and the stalker.

In chapter 5, Kirsten Dellinger and Christine Williams also examine the definitional process with regard to sexual harassment, another form of violence that some may perceive as non-threatening or relatively "harmless." In their intriguing comparison of two similar yet disparate work settings, the authors demonstrate the importance of context—specifically, the normative culture of the workplace—in defining and responding to sexual harassment. As their research shows, even in highly sexualized workplaces—the editorial departments of a male pornographic magazine and a feminist magazine—boundaries are established that separate appropriate from inappropriate behavior. These boundaries, however, grow out of and reflect the organizational culture of the workplace.

Dellinger and Williams's research invites us to reconsider the usefulness of a unidimensional definition of sexual harassment. Not all sexual behavior in the workplace, they argue, is harassment, nor is it necessarily harmful to women. From this perspective, even if the behavior is unwanted, it is not sexual harassment unless it blocks employment opportunities or causes some other form of gender discrimination. Surely there are readers who will take issue with this position, but Dellinger and Williams's chapter epitomizes the kind of thought-provoking work that has been a hallmark of *Social Problems* over its many years of publication.

The remaining chapters in the book focus on two forms of violence against women—sexual assault and intimate partner abuse—with an examination, first, of the institutional responses to these forms of violence, and, second, of feminist activism focused on these two forms of violence. In chapter 6, Cassia Spohn and her colleagues look at factors that influence prosecutors' decisions to pursue or reject sexual assault cases. Their research confirms earlier findings that showed that prosecutors often use extralegal factors, particularly those related to the credibility of the victim based on stereotypes of "real" rape victims, to decide whether or not to prosecute a case. Prosecutors appear primarily concerned with getting a conviction and anything that tarnishes a victim's credibility in the eyes of a jury lowers the probability of that outcome.

Spohn et al. also discovered that most of the cases rejected for prosecution in the jurisdiction they studied were rejected because the victim failed to appear for a pre-file interview or could not be located by the prosecutor's office, the victim would not cooperate or asked that charges be dropped, or the victim recanted. Many of these were cases with evidentiary problems, but prosecutors explained that sometimes women come to believe that prosecution is not in their best interest. In cases involving intimates or relatives, women may decide to accept the offender's apology and forgive him. In cases involving strangers, women may decide that going through the legal process just isn't worth it: It is lengthy and difficult, requiring them to recount to strangers many times the humiliating circumstances of their victimization. They may also perceive that their credibility, for whatever reason, is being questioned. Other research shows that their concerns are not unfounded (see, for example, Konradi, 1997).

While Spohn et al. emphasize that the prosecution of sexual assault cases continues to be problematic, they also note that their findings reflect the effects of rape reform legislation that have helped to improve sexual assault prosecution for victims. In comparing their work, published in 2001, with that of the authors of subsequent chapters whose work appeared in earlier volumes of *Social Problems*, we can see how Spohn et al.'s findings, though certainly not ideal, depict an improvement for rape victims seeking to prosecute their assailants.

One of the changes in sexual assault case processing that feminists have long called for is increasing the number of women working with victims in hospitals and the criminal justice system. However, as Patricia Yancey Martin points out in chapter 7, research findings are inconsistent with regard to the question of whether women are better than men in rape processing work. What Martin's interviews with rape processing officials reveal is that gender is an important cultural resource drawn on to justify particular policies and practices. Martin urges caution in advocating that only women should work with victims. She argues that such a notion rests on gender stereotypes that women are "naturally" better at emotion/relationship labor, while men are better suited for more technical work. Martin suggests that not all women treat female rape victims well, just as not all men treat them badly. Some women are uncomfortable doing "relationship work," and *any* rape case processor, man or woman, who is unmotivated and poorly trained will not be helpful to victims. In fact, Martin argues, this gendered division of labor reinforces gender stereotypes and dichotomous—mutually exclusive—notions of appropriate masculinity and femininity; lets men "off the hook" with regard to performing emotion/relationship work; forces women to do work they don't necessarily want to do; and ultimately can inhibit victims' ability to heal and achieve justice. Martin invites researchers to further examine the question of whether gender outweighs training, motivation, and skill in rape processing work by studying, from the victim's perspective, which factors are associated with greater benefits.

The response of the police to violence against women has been a particular concern of feminist activists and researchers. As Kathleen Ferraro states in chapter 8, the police are the "front line" of the official response to battering and other forms of violence against women. Ferraro notes that during the 1970s and 1980s, feminists loudly criticized the police for their frequent failure to arrest batterers. This failure to arrest amounted to more than just unresponsiveness since it could be construed as tacit support for abuse and thereby help keep women trapped in violent relationships, leading to their further victimization and sometimes even death at the hands of the abuser.

Following civil lawsuits in the 1970s as well as publication of Sherman and Berk's (1984) study lauding the effectiveness of mandatory arrest in reducing recidivism by batterers, many jurisdictions enacted mandatory or presumptive arrest policies that expanded police officers' power to arrest abusive intimate partners if they had probable cause, even if the victim did not want to press charges. Ferraro analyzes the implementation of one such policy in Phoenix, Arizona. She reports that despite the new policy, the police made arrests in only 18 percent of assaults involving intimate partners, and she identifies several extralegal factors that continued to influence police officers' decision making with regard to intimate partner assaults. These included notions about the ineffectiveness of arrest when offenders and victims are nonwhite, poor, homeless, gay, non-English speaking, drunk, high, or in some other way "deviant" in the eyes of the police; stereotypes about battered women; the judgment that battering is not a "serious" crime or dangerous, or that it is a "two-way street"; and the perception that mandatory arrest is an inconvenience to officers.

Ferraro's research demonstrates disparities between the written law and the law "in action." At the same time, it raises additional questions about the ability of mandatory arrest policies to keep battered women safe. Mandatory arrest along with similar policies such as no-drop prosecution are currently among the most controversial issues in the intimate partner violence literature. Critics point out that such policies remove decision making regarding safety and related concerns from battered women—the real "experts" on abuse—and place it in the hands of less knowledgeable (and often biased) others: the police. Moreover, an increasing number of women are being arrested for intimate partner violence because the police fail to determine—or claim they cannot determine—the primary aggressor (Ford, 2003; Miller, 2001). Ferraro's article was among the first to offer a "reality check" with regard to mandatory arrest, calling into question its ability to improve the police response to intimate partner violence and, more importantly, to increase women's safety.

The response of health care providers to women victims of sexual assault and battering has also drawn the attention of feminists. Battered women, for example, may seek help at a hospital emergency room instead of calling the police, although they may not identify their injuries as the results of intimate partner violence. Health care personnel, however, have been reluctant to systematically screen female patients for abuse (see, for example, Alpert and Sawires, 2002). In chapter 9, Demie Kurz addresses the resistance of health care personnel to assisting battered women. She did observational research in four hospital emergency departments. In three departments staff had received a single training about battering in the hope that they would begin to screen for it. Unfortunately, the majority of the health care workers in these hospitals did not see active screening and intervention with battered women as their job; they saw such tasks as interfering with their "appropriate" roles as medical providers. In fact, staff took a woman's battering seriously and considered it worthy of their time and attention in only 11 percent of the cases that Kurz observed in these hospitals. In nearly half of the cases, staff partially responded to battered women but did not pursue the case if they deemed the patient "unresponsive." Moreover, these health care workers often held negative stereotypes of battered women and expressed frustration over what they see as the woman's culpability in the abuse: e.g., she does not leave, she drinks or uses drugs, she provokes him. The women who received positive responses in these emergency departments were women the health care workers deemed to be "real" or "true" victims of intimate partner violence.

A bright spot in Kurz's analysis is the fourth hospital emergency department she observed where, largely through the efforts of a single committed physician assistant, battered women get more attention and better care. In contrast to the other three emergency departments, Kurz found that in 47 percent of the cases in this fourth department, battered women—even those who were considered evasive or were known to be alcohol or drug abusers—received positive responses from health care personnel. A major difference between this hospital and the other three is that the physician assistant, who regards helping battered women as "honorable work," has been able to persuade other staff to adopt her position. This physician assistant has managed to get protocols in place in her emergency department that get some staff more involved and help them to feel that they can make a difference in a battered woman's life. Still, even in this hospital, Kurz observed that 32 percent of cases received "no response" from health care personnel. As subsequent work has shown, convincing health care professionals that screening for and assisting battered women are legitimate and necessary aspects of providing good medical care remains a challenging task (Alpert and Sawires, 2002).

As we have noted, battered women are typically seen as helping perpetuate their own abuse by failing to leave their abusive partners. The question, "Why doesn't she just leave?" is so pervasive that, as Donileen Loseke and Spencer Cahill point out in chapter 10, it is raised not only by the general public, but also by individuals who claim specialized knowledge of battering and battered women. The authors are critical of the way many experts pathologize battered women because of their decision to maintain their relationship with abusive partners. As Loseke and Cahill phrase it, these experts practice "victimism"—i.e., the victim status of battered women takes precedence over all other statuses; the focal point is their victimization, while other aspects of their intimate relationships are ignored.

Loseke and Cahill suggest an alternative perspective for understanding women's decisions to stay with abusive partners. They cite research showing that women and men in nonviolent, but not necessarily happy or satisfying, intimate relationships have difficulty leaving their partners. Separation and divorce are not easy processes, emotionally or logistically. Thus, Loseke and Cahill reframe battered women's decisions to stay as normal rather than deviant behavior.

It is important to point out that while Loseke and Cahill are critical of experts who argue that battered women stay because they are economically dependent on their abusers or do not have supportive family and friends to which they can turn, there is a great deal of empirical research demonstrating the importance of financial stability as well as strong social support networks in motivating women to end abusive relationships (Baker, Cook, and Norris, 2003; Bell, 2003; Moe and Bell, 2004). The significance of this research is that it shows battered women not as passive victims with no options, but rather as active social agents engaged in careful decision making about whether staying or leaving is in their best interests and the best interests of their children. Moreover, leaving does not ensure a woman's safety (Davies, Lyon, and Monti-Catania,1998; DeKeseredy, 1997; Fleury, Sullivan, and Bybee, 2000). One of the most significant contributions of Loseke and Cahill's chapter, therefore, is to encourage both the public and experts to consider the multidimensional aspects of battered women's lives and to listen to what battered women themselves say they need and want (Nichols and Feltey, 2003). In doing this, we should not be surprised to hear many battered women say they do not want the relationship to end; they want the abuse to end.

The remaining two chapters in the book examine feminist grassroots activism on behalf of battered women. In chapter 11, Kathleen Tierney chronicles the first 10 years of the battered women's movement. Using social movements analysis, Tierney identifies factors that contributed to the success of the movement in raising public awareness of the problem of intimate partner violence. She shows how the battered women's movement, unlike many other social movements, did not gain momentum because the public demanded that the problem be addressed; the public was, at best, indifferent to the problem. Instead, the movement had a strong preexisting organizational base, movement members were flexible, and potential sponsors recognized benefits to themselves of providing the movement with resources.

Tierney concludes her chapter on what many would regard as a pessimistic note. She warns of what she sees as the inevitable cooptation of the battered women's movement: bowing to the pressures of funders—in particular, to be less radical and more mainstream, less political and more service-oriented. There is evidence that many agencies within the movement have "toned down" feminist rhetoric to make themselves more "appealing" to potential funders. And certainly some have compromised feminist principles through depoliticization and the adoption of increasingly bureaucratic—and, critics would add, exclusionary—policies and practices (Donnelly, Cook, and Wilson, 1999). Nevertheless, we find it heartening that, at the same time, so many have held fast to feminist values and feminist analyses of the problem. While agencies may try to avoid projecting a "militant image," most continue to actively lobby for meaningful social change, to openly challenge patriarchal inequality that privileges batterers over victims, and to remain open to innovation so as to more effectively meet the needs of battered women and their children.

In the final chapter, Patricia Gagné demonstrates the beneficial consequences of sustained feminist activism on behalf of battered women. Gagné analyzes feminist activism in the Ohio battered women's movement that ultimately contributed to the decision by former Governor Richard Celeste to grant clemency to 26 women who had been convicted of killing or assaulting abusive intimates. Gagné shows the creativity—and the flexibility that Tierney identified as a movement strength—that feminists brought to bear on the problem as they organized consciousness-raising groups within the prison and lobbied politicians. Rather than depoliticizing their strategies and goals, feminist activists organized the women inmates, provided them with support, and helped them carry on a campaign to educate authorities and the public about the injustice of their situation. Gagné's chapter is a blueprint for marginalized groups to understand how to enlist the aid of influential allies and to connect, rather than separate, the personal and the political. It is, in short, a story of empowerment and, we feel, a fitting way to conclude this book.

Taken together, the readings we offer here provide a barometer by which we can measure how the subfield of violence against women has developed over three decades. We get a sense of our roots and how much we have grown in a relatively short period of time. Although a celebration of success in many ways, these chapters also highlight controversies and debates with which we in the field continue to grapple. No doubt we will continue to turn to *Social Problems* to provide us with a lens through which we can analyze, question, and, most importantly, dialogue on these critical issues.

References

Abel, E. M.
1999 *Comparing women in batterer intervention programs with male batterers and female victims.* Paper presented at the Sixth International Family Violence Research Conference, Durham, NH. July.

Alpert, E. J., and P. Sawires (Eds.)
2002 Special issue: Health care and domestic violence. *Violence Against Women*, 8(6).

Archer, J.
2000 "Sex differences in aggression between heterosexual partners: A meta-analytic review." *Psychological Bulletin*, 126: 651–680.

Bachman, R.
2000 "A comparison of annual incidence rates and contextual characteristics of intimate partner violence against women from the National Crime Victimization Survey (NCVS) and the National Violence Against Women Survey (NVAWS)." *Violence Against Women*, 6:839–867.

Baker, C. K., S. L. Cook, and F. H. Norris
2003 "Domestic violence and housing problems: A contextual analysis of women's help-seeking, received informal support, and formal system responses." *Violence Against Women*, 9:754–783.

Barnett, O. W., C. Y. Lee, and R. Thelan
1997 "Gender differences in attributions of self-defense and control in interpartner aggression." *Violence Against Women*, 3:462–481.

Bell, H.
2003 "Cycles within cycles: Domestic violence, welfare, and low-wage work." *Violence Against Women*, 9:1245–1262.

Bergen, R. K.
1998 "Intimate violence: A brief introduction." In R. K. Bergen (Ed.), *Issues in Intimate Violence*, pp. ix–xi. Thousand Oaks, CA: Sage.

Bible, A., S. Das Dasgupta, and S. Osthoff (Eds.)
2002 Special issue: Women's use of violence in intimate relationships: Part 1. *Violence Against Women*, 8(11).

Campbell, R., and P. Y. Martin
2001 "Services for sexual assault survivors: The role of rape crisis centers." In C. M. Renzetti, J. L. Edleson, and R. K. Bergen (Eds.), *Sourcebook on Violence against Women*, pp. 227–242. Thousand Oaks, CA: Sage.

Crowell, N. A., and A. W. Burgess
1996 *Understanding Violence against Women*. Washington, DC: National Academy Press.

Das Dasgupta, S., A. Bible, and S. Osthoff (Eds.)
2003 Special issue: Women's use of violence in intimate relationships, Part 3. *Violence Against Women*, 9(1).

Davies, J., E. Lyon, and D. Monti-Catania
1998 *Safety Planning with Battered Women*. Thousand Oaks, CA: Sage.

DeKeseredy, W. S. (Ed.)
1997 Special issue: Post-separation woman abuse. *Violence Against Women*, 3(6).

Dobash, R. E., and R. Dobash
1979 *Violence against Wives: A Case against the Patriarchy*. New York: Free Press.

Dobash, R. P., R. E. Dobash, K. Cavanagh, and R. Lewis
1998 "Separate and intersecting realities: A comparison of men's and women's accounts of violence against women." *Violence Against Women*, 4:382–414.

Donnelly, D. A., K. J. Cook, and L. A. Wilson
1999 "Provision and exclusion: The dual face of services to battered women in three deep south states." *Violence Against Women*, 5:710–741.

Fiebert, M. S.
1997 "Annotated bibliography: References examining assaults by women on their spouses/partners." In B. M. Dank and R. Refinette (Eds.), *Sexual Harassment and Sexual Consent*. Vol. 1, pp. 273–276. New Brunswick, NJ: Transaction.

Fleury, R. E., C. M. Sullivan and D. I. Bybee
2000 "When ending the relationship does not end the violence: Women's experiences of violence by former partners." *Violence Against Women*, 6:1363–1383.

Ford, D. A.
2003 "Coercing victim participation in domestic violence prosecutions." *Journal of Interpersonal Violence*, 18:669–684.

Fox, J. A., and M. W. Zawitz,
2000 *Homicide Trends in the United States: 1998 Update*. Washington, DC: U.S. Department of Justice, National Institute of Justice.

Greenfeld, L. A.
1997 *Sex Offenders and Offenses*. Washington, DC: U.S. Department of Justice, Bureau of Justice Statistics.
1998 *Violence by Intimates*. Washington, DC: U.S. Department of Justice, Bureau of Justice Statistics.

Konradi, A.
1997 "Too little, too late: Prosecutors' pre-court preparations of rape survivors." *Law and Social Inquiry*, 22:1–54.

Madriz, E. I.
1997 "Images of criminals and victims: A study of women's fear and social control." *Gender & Society*, 11:342–356.

Miller
2001 "The paradox of women arrested for domestic violence: Criminal justice professionals and service providers respond." *Violence Against Women*, 7:1339–1376.

Mills, C. W.
1959 *The Sociological Imagination*. New York: Oxford University Press.

Moe, A. M., and M. P. Bell
2004 "Abject economics: The effects of battering and violence on women's work and employability." *Violence Against Women*, 10:29–55.

Nichols, L., and K. M. Feltey
2003 "'The woman is not always the bad guy': Dominant discourse and resistance in the lives of battered women." *Violence Against Women*, 9:784–806.

Osthoff, S., S. Das Dasgupta, and A. Bible (Eds.)
  2002 Special issue: Women's use of violence in intimate relationships: Part 2. *Violence Against Women*, 8(12).
Pleck, E.
  1987 *Domestic Tyranny: The Making of Social Policy against Family Violence from Colonial Times to the Present*. Oxford, UK: Oxford University Press.
Rennison, C. M.
  2001 *Intimate Partner Violence and Age of Victim: 1993–99*. Washington, DC: U.S. Department of Justice, Bureau of Justice Statistics.
Schechter, S.
  1982 *Women and Male Violence: The Visions and Struggles of the Battered Women's Movement*. Boston: South End Press.
Sherman, L. W., and R. A. Berk
  1984 "The specific deterrent effects of arrest for domestic assault." *American Sociological Review*, 49:261–272.
Stanko, E. A.
  1996 "Warnings to women: Police advice and women's safety in Britain." *Violence Against Women*, 2:5–24.
  2001 "Women, danger, and criminology." In C. M. Renzetti and L. Goodstein (Eds.), *Women, Crime and Criminal Justice*, pp. 13–26. Los Angeles: Roxbury.
Straus, M. A.
  1999 "The controversy over domestic violence by women: A methodological, theoretical, and sociology of science analysis." In X. B. Arriaga and S. Oskamp (Eds.), *Violence in Intimate Relationships*, pp. 17–44. Thousand Oaks, CA: Sage.
Tjaden, P., and N. Thoennes
  2000 "Prevalence and consequences of male-to-female and female-to-male intimate partner violence as measured by the National Violence Against Women Survey." *Violence Against Women*, 6:142–161.

Part I

FORMS OF VIOLENCE AGAINST WOMEN

CHAPTER 1

"Riding the Bull at Gilley's"
CONVICTED RAPISTS DESCRIBE THE REWARDS OF RAPE

Diana Scully and Joseph Marolla

Over the past several decades, rape has become a "medicalized" social problem. That is to say, the theories used to explain rape are predicated on psychopathological models. They have been generated from clinical experiences with small samples of rapists, often the therapists' own clients. Although these psychiatric explanations are most appropriately applied to the atypical rapist, they have been generalized to all men who rape and have come to inform the public's view on the topic.

Two assumptions are at the core of the psychopathological model; that rape is the result of idiosyncratic mental disease and that it often includes an uncontrollable sexual impulse (Scully and Marolla, 1985). For example, the presumption of psychopathology is evident in the often cited work of Nicholas Groth (1979). While Groth emphasizes the nonsexual nature of rape (power, anger, sadism), he also concludes, "Rape is always a symptom of some psychological dysfunction, either temporary and transient or chronic and repetitive" (Groth, 1979:5). Thus, in the psychopathological view, rapists lack the ability to control their behavior; they are "sick" individuals from the "lunatic fringe" of society.

In contradiction to this model, empirical research has repeatedly failed to find a consistent pattern of personality type or character disorder that reliably discriminates rapists from other groups of men (Fisher and Rivlin, 1971; Hammer and Jacks, 1955; Rada, 1978). Indeed, other research has found that fewer than 5 percent of men were psychotic when they raped (Abel et al., 1980).

Evidence indicates that rape is not a behavior confined to a few "sick" men but many men have the attitudes and beliefs necessary to commit a sexually aggressive act. In research conducted at a midwestern university, Koss and her coworkers reported that 85 percent of men defined as highly sexually aggressive had victimized women with whom they were romantically involved (Koss and Leonard, 1984). A recent survey quoted in *The Chronicle of Higher Education* estimates that more than 20 percent of college women are the victims of rape and attempted rape (Meyer, 1984). These findings mirror research published several decades earlier, which also concluded that sexual aggression was commonplace in dating relationships (Kanin, 1957, 1965, 1967, 1969; Kirkpatrick and Kanin, 1957).[1] In their study of 53 college males, Malamuth,

Haber, and Feshback (1980) found that 51 percent indicated a likelihood that they, themselves, would rape if assured of not being punished.

In addition, the frequency of rape in the United States makes it unlikely that responsibility rests solely with a small lunatic fringe of psychopathic men. Johnson (1980), calculating the lifetime risk of rape to girls and women aged 12 and over, makes a similar observation. Using Law Enforcement Assistance Administration and Bureau of Census Crime Victimization Studies, he calculated that, excluding sexual abuse in marriage and assuming equal risk to all women, 20 to 30 percent of girls now 12 years old will suffer a violent sexual attack during the remainder of their lives. Interestingly, the lack of empirical support for the psychopathological model has not resulted in the de-medicalization of rape, nor does it appear to have diminished the belief that rapists are "sick" aberrations in their own culture. This is significant because of the implications and consequences of the model.

A central assumption in the psychopathological model is that male sexual aggression is unusual or strange. This assumption removes rape from the realm of the everyday or "normal" world and places it in the category of "special" or "sick" behavior. As a consequence, men who rape are cast in the role of outsider and a connection with normative male behavior is avoided. Since, in this view, the source of the behavior is thought to be within the psychology of the individual, attention is diverted away from culture or social structure as contributing factors. Thus, the psychopathological model ignores evidence which links sexual aggression to environmental variables and which suggests that rape, like all behavior, is learned.

Cultural Factors in Rape

Culture is a factor in rape, but the precise nature of the relationship between culture and sexual violence remains a topic of discussion. Ethnographic data from pre-industrial societies show the existence of rape-free cultures (Broude and Greene, 1976; Sanday, 1979), though explanations for the phenomena differ.[2] Sanday (1979) relates sexual violence to contempt for female qualities and suggests that rape is part of a culture of violence and an expression of male dominance. In contrast, Blumberg (1979) argues than in pre-industrial societies women are more likely to lack important life options and to be physically and politically oppressed where they lack economic power relative to men. That is, in pre-industrial societies relative economic power enables women to win some immunity from men's use of force against them.

Among modern societies, the frequency of rape varies dramatically, and the United States is among the most rape-prone of all. In 1980, for example, the rate of reported rape and attempted rape for the United States was 18 times higher than the corresponding rate for England and Wales (West, 1983). Spurred by the Women's Movement, feminists have generated an impressive body of theory regarding the cultural etiology of rape in the United States. Representative of the feminist view, Griffin (1971) called rape "The All American Crime."

The feminist perspective views rape as an act of violence and social control which functions to "keep women in their place" (Brownmiller, 1975; Kasinsky, 1975; Russell, 1975). Feminists see rape as an extension of normative male behavior, the result of conformity or overconformity to the values and prerogatives which define the traditional male sex role. That is, traditional socialization encourages males to associate power, dominance, strength, virility, and superiority with masculinity, and submissiveness, passivity, weakness, and inferiority with femininity. Furthermore, males are taught to have expectations about their level of sexual needs and expectations for corresponding female accessibility, which function to justify forcing sexual access. The justification for forced sexual access is buttressed by legal, social, and religious definitions of women as male property and sex as an exchange of goods (Bart, 1979). Socialization prepares women to be "legitimate" victims and men to be potential offenders (Weis and Borges, 1973). Herman (1984) concludes that the United States is a rape culture because both genders are socialized to regard male aggression as a natural and normal part of sexual intercourse.

Feminists view pornography as an important element in a larger system of sexual violence; they see pornography as an expression of a rape-prone culture where women are seen as objects available for use by men (Morgan, 1980; Wheeler, 1985). Based on his content analysis of 428 "adults only" books, Smith (1976) makes a similar observation. He notes that, not only is rape presented as part of normal male/female sexual relations, but the woman, despite her terror, is always depicted as sexually aroused to the point of cooperation. In the end, she is ashamed but physically gratified. The message—women desire and enjoy rape—has more potential for damage than the image of the violence per se.[3]

The fusion of these themes—sex as an impersonal act, the victim's uncontrollable orgasm, and the violent infliction of pain—is commonplace in the actual accounts of rapists. Scully and Marolla (1984) demonstrated that many convicted rapists denied their crime and attempted to justify their rapes by arguing that their victim had enjoyed herself despite the use of a weapon and the infliction of serious injuries, or even death. In fact, many argued, they had been instrumental in making *her* fantasy come true.

The images projected in pornography contribute to a vocabulary of motive which trivializes and neutralizes rape and which might lessen the internal controls that otherwise would prevent sexually aggressive behavior. Men who rape use this culturally acquired vocabulary to justify their sexual violence.

Another consequence of the application of psychopathology to rape is it leads one to view sexual violence as a special type of crime in which the motivations are subconscious and uncontrollable rather than overt and deliberate as with other criminal behavior. Black (1983) offers an approach to the analysis of criminal and/or violent behavior which, when applied to rape, avoids this bias.

Black (1983) suggests that it is theoretically useful to ignore that crime is criminal in order to discover what such behavior has in common with other kinds of conduct. From his perspective, much of the crime in modern societies, as in pre-industrial societies, can be interpreted as a form of "self help" in which the actor is expressing a grievance through aggression and violence. From the actor's perspective, the victim is deviant and his own behavior is a form of social control in which the objective may be conflict management, punishment, or revenge. For example, in societies where women are considered the property of men, rape is sometimes used as a means of avenging the victim's husband or father (Black, 1983). In some cultures rape is used as a form of punishment. Such was the tradition among the puritanical, patriarchal Cheyenne where men were valued for their ability as warriors. It was Cheyenne custom that a wife suspected of being unfaithful could be "put on the prairie" by her husband. Military confreres then were invited to "feast" on the prairie (Hoebel, 1954; Llewellyn and Hoebel, 1941). The ensuing mass rape was a husband's method of punishing his wife.

Black's (1983) approach is helpful in understanding rape because it forces one to examine the goals that some men have learned to achieve through sexually violent means. Thus, one approach to understanding why some men rape is to shift attention from individual psychopathology to the important question of what rapists gain from sexual aggression and violence in a culture seemingly prone to rape.

In this chapter, we address this question using data from interviews conducted with 114 convicted, incarcerated rapists. Elsewhere, we discussed the vocabulary of motive, consisting of excuses and justifications, that these convicted rapists used to explain themselves and their crime (Scully and Marolla, 1984).[4] The use of these culturally derived excuses and justifications allowed them to view their behavior as either idiosyncratic or situationally appropriate and thus it reduced their sense of moral responsibility for their actions. Having disavowed deviance, these men revealed how they had used rape to achieve a number of objectives. We find that some men used rape for revenge or punishment while, for others, it was an "added bonus"—a last minute decision made while committing another crime. In still other cases, rape was used to gain sexual access to women who were unwilling or unavailable, and for some it was a source of power and sex without any personal feelings. Rape was also a form of recreation, a diversion or an adventure and, finally, it was something that made these men "feel good."

Methods

SAMPLE

During 1980 and 1981 we interviewed 114 convicted rapists.[5] All of the men had been convicted of the rape or attempted rape (n=8) of an adult woman and subsequently incarcerated in a Virginia prison. Men convicted of other types of sexual offense were omitted from the sample.

In addition to their convictions for rape, 39 percent of the men also had convictions for burglary or robbery, 29 percent for abduction, 25 percent for sodomy, and 11 percent for first or second degree murder, and 12 percent had been convicted of more than one rape. The majority of the men had previous criminal histories but only 23 percent had a record of past sex offenses and only 26 percent had a history of emotional problems. Their sentences for rape and accompanying crimes ranged from ten years to seven life sentences plus 380 years for one man. Twenty-two percent of the rapists were serving at least one life sentence. Forty-six percent of the rapists were white, 54 percent black. In age, they ranged from 18 to 60 years but the majority were between 18 and 35 years. Based on a statistical profile of felons in all Virginia prisons prepared by the Virginia Department of Corrections, it appears that this sample of rapists was disproportionately white and, at the time of the research, somewhat better educated and younger than the average inmate.

All participants in this research were volunteers. In constructing the sample, age, education, race, severity of current offense, and past criminal record were balanced within the limitations imposed by the characteristics of the volunteer pool. Obviously the sample was not random and thus may not be typical of all rapists, imprisoned or otherwise.

All interviews were hand recorded using an 89-page instrument which included a general background, psychological, criminal, and sexual history, attitude scales, and 30 pages of open-ended questions intended to explore rapists' own perceptions of their crime and themselves. Each author interviewed half of the sample in sessions that ranged from three to seven hours depending on the desire or willingness of the participant to talk.

VALIDITY

In all prison research, validity is a special methodological concern because of the reputation inmates have for "conning." Although one goal of this research was to understand rape from the perspective of men who have raped, it was also necessary to establish the extent to which rapists' perceptions deviated from other descriptions of their crime. The technique we used was the same others have used in prison research: comparing factual information obtained in the interviews, including details of the crime, with reports on file at the prison (Athens, 1977; Luckenbill, 1977; Queen's Bench Foundation, 1976). In general, we found that rapists' accounts of their crime had changed very little since their trials. However, there was a tendency to understate the amount of violence they had used and, especially among certain rapists, to place blame on their victims.

How Offenders View the Rewards of Rape

REVENGE AND PUNISHMENT

As noted earlier, Black's (1983) perspective suggests that a rapist might see his act as a legitimized form of revenge or punishment. Additionally, he asserts that the idea of "collective liability" accounts for much seemingly random violence. "Collective liability" suggests that all people in a particular category are held accountable for the conduct of each of their counterparts. Thus, the victim of a violent act may merely represent the category of individual being punished.

These factors—revenge, punishment, and the collective liability of women—can be used to explain a number of rapes in our research. Several cases will illustrate the ways in which these factors combined in various types of rape. Revenge-rapes were among the most brutal and often included beatings, serious injuries, and even murder.

Typically, revenge-rapes included the element of collective liability. That is, from the rapist's perspective, the victim was a substitute for the woman they wanted to avenge upon. As explained elsewhere (Scully and Marolla, 1984), an upsetting event, involving a woman, preceded a significant number of rapes. When they raped, these men were angry because of a perceived indiscretion, typically related to a rigid, moralistic standard of sexual conduct, which they required from "their woman" but, in most cases, did not abide by themselves. Over and over these rapists talked about using rape "to get even" with their wives or other significant woman.[6] Typical is a young man who, prior to the rape, had a violent argument with his wife over what eventually proved to be her misdiagnosed case of venereal disease. She assumed the disease had been contracted through him, an accusation that infuriated him. After fighting with his wife, he explained that he drove around "thinking about hurting someone." He encountered his victim, a stranger, on the road where her car had broken down. It appears she accepted his offered ride because her car was out of commission. When she realized that rape was pending, she called him "a son of a bitch," and attempted to resist. He reported flying into a rage and beating her, and he confided,

> I have never felt that much anger before. If she had resisted, I would have killed her. . . . The rape was for revenge. I didn't have an orgasm. She was there to get my hostile feelings off on.

Although not the most common form of revenge rape, sexual assault continues to be used in retaliation against the victim's male partner. In one such case, the offender, angry because the victim's husband owed him money, went to the victim's home to collect. He confided, "I was going to get it one way or another." Finding the victim alone, he explained, they started to argue about the money and,

> I grabbed her and started beating the hell out of her. Then I committed the act,[7] I knew what I was doing. I was mad. I could have stopped but I didn't. I did it to get even with her and her husband.

Griffin (1971:33) points out that when women are viewed as commodities, "In raping another man's woman, a man may aggrandize his own manhood and concurrently reduce that of another man."

Revenge-rapes often contained an element of punishment. In some cases, while the victim was not the initial object of the revenge, the intent was to punish her because of something that transpired after the decision to rape had been made or during the course of the rape itself. This was the case with a young man whose wife had recently left him. Although they were in the process of reconciliation, he remained angry and upset over the separation. The night of the rape, he met the victim and her friend in a bar where he had gone to watch a fight on TV. The two women apparently accepted a ride from him but, after taking her friend home, he drove the victim to his apartment. At his apartment, he found a note from his wife indicating she had stopped by to watch the fight with him. This increased his anger because he preferred his wife's company. Inside his apartment, the victim allegedly remarked that she was sexually interested in his dog, which, he reported, put him in a rage. In the ensuing attack, he raped and pistol-whipped the victim. Then he forced a vacuum cleaner hose, switched on suction, into her vagina and bit her breast, severing the nipple. He stated:

> I hated at the time, but I don't know if it was her [the victim]. (Who could it have been?) My wife? Even though we were getting back together, I still didn't trust her.

During his interview, it became clear that this offender, like many of the men, believed men have the right to discipline and punish women. In fact, he argued that most of the men he knew would also have beaten the victim because "that kind of thing (referring to the dog) is not acceptable among my friends."

Finally, in some rapes, both revenge and punishment were directed at victims because they represented women whom these offenders perceived as collectively responsible and liable for their problems. Rape was used "to put women in their place" and as a method of proving their "manhood" by displaying dominance over a female. For example, one multiple rapist believed his actions were related to the feeling that women thought they were better than he was.

> Rape was a feeling of total dominance. Before the rapes, I would always get a feeling of power and anger. I would degrade women so I could feel there was a person of less worth than me.

Another, especially brutal, case involved a young man from an upper middle class background, who spilled out his story in a seven-hour interview conducted in his solitary confinement cell. He described himself as tremendously angry, at the time, with his girlfriend whom he believed was involved with him in a "storybook romance," and from whom he expected complete fidelity. When she went away to college and became involved with another man, his revenge lasted 18 months and involved the rape and murder of five women, all strangers who lived in his community. Explaining his rape-murders, he stated:

> I wanted to take my anger and frustration out on a stranger, to be in control, to do what I wanted to do. I wanted to use and abuse someone as I felt used and abused. I was killing my girl friend. During the rapes and murders, I would think about my girl friend. I hated the victims because they probably messed men over. I hated women because they were deceitful and I was getting revenge for what happened to me.

AN ADDED BONUS

Burglary and robbery commonly accompany rape. Among our sample, 39 percent of rapists had also been convicted of one or the other of these crimes committed in connection with rape. In some cases, the original intent was rape and robbery was an afterthought. However, a number of the men indicated that the reverse was true in their situation. That is, the decision to rape was made subsequent to their original intent, which was burglary or robbery.

This was the case with a young offender who stated that he originally intended only to rob the store in which the victim happened to be working. He explained that when he found the victim alone,

> I decided to rape her to prove I had guts. She was just there. It could have been anybody.

Similarly, another offender indicated that he initially broke into his victim's home to burglarize it. When he discovered the victim asleep, he decided to seize the opportunity "to satisfy an urge to go to bed with a white woman, to see if it was different." Indeed, a number of men indicated that the decision to rape had been made after they realized they were in control of the situation. This was also true of an unemployed offender who confided that his practice was to steal whenever he needed money. On the day of the rape, he drove to a local supermarket and paced the parking lot, "staking out the situation." His pregnant victim was the first person to come along alone and "she was an easy target." Threatening her with a knife, he reported the victim as saying she would do anything if he didn't harm her. At that point, he decided to force her to drive to a deserted area where he raped her. He explained:

> I wasn't thinking about sex. But when she said she would do anything not to get hurt, probably because she was pregnant, I thought, "why not."

The attitude of these men toward rape was similar to their attitude toward burglary and robbery. Quite simply, if the situation is right, "why not." From the perspective of these rapists, rape was just another part of the crime—an added bonus.

SEXUAL ACCESS

In an effort to change public attitudes that are damaging to the victims of rape and to reform laws seemingly premised on the assumption that women both ask for and enjoy rape, many writers emphasize the violent and aggressive character of rape. Often such arguments appear to discount the part that sex plays in the crime. The data clearly indicate that from the rapists' point of view rape is in part sexually motivated. Indeed, it is the sexual aspect of rape that distinguishes it from other forms of assault.

Groth (1979) emphasizes the psychodynamic function of sex in rape, arguing that rapists' aggressive needs are expressed through sexuality. In other words, rape is a means to an end. We argue, however, that rapists view the act as an end in itself and that sexual access most obviously demonstrates the link between sex and rape. Rape as a means of sexual access also shows the deliberate nature of this crime. When a woman is unwilling or seems unavailable for sex, the rapist can seize what isn't volunteered. In discussing his decision to rape, one man made this clear.

> All the guys wanted to fuck her . . . a real fox, beautiful shape. She was a beautiful woman and I wanted to see what she had.

The attitude that sex is a male entitlement suggests that when a woman says "no," rape is a suitable method of conquering the "offending" object. If, for example, a woman is picked up at a party or in a bar or while hitchhiking (behavior which a number of the rapists saw as a signal of sexual availability), and the woman later resists sexual advances, rape is presumed to be justified. The same justification operates in what is popularly called "date rape." The belief that sex was their just compensation compelled a number of rapists to insist they had not raped. Such was the case of an offender who raped and seriously beat his victim when, on their second date, she refused his sexual advances.

> I think I was really pissed off at her because it didn't go as planned. I could have been with someone else. She led me on but wouldn't deliver. . . . I have a male ego that must be fed.

The purpose of such rapes was conquest, to seize what was not offered.

Despite the cultural belief that young women are the most sexually desirable, several rapes involved the deliberate choice of a victim relatively older than the assailant.[8] Since the rapists were themselves rather young (26 to 30 years of age on the average), they were expressing a preference for sexually experienced, rather than elderly, women. Men who chose victims older than themselves often said they did so because they believed that sexually experienced women were more desirable partners. They raped because they also believed that these women would not be sexually attracted to them.

Finally, sexual access emerged as a factor in the accounts of black men who consciously chose to rape white women.[9] The majority of rapes in the United States today are intraracial. However, for the past 20 years, according to national data based on reported rapes as well as victimization studies, which include unreported rapes, the rate of black on white (B/W) rape has significantly exceeded the rate of white on black (W/B) rape (LaFree, 1982).[10] Indeed, we may be experiencing a historical anomaly, since, as Brownmiller (1975) has documented, white men have freely raped women of color in the past. The current structure of interracial rape, however, reflects contemporary racism and race relations in several ways.

First, the status of black women in the United States today is relatively lower than the status of white women. Further, prejudice, segregation, and other factors continue to militate against interracial coupling. Thus, the desire for sexual access to higher status, unavailable women, an important function in B/W rape, does not motivate white men to rape black women. Equally important, demographic and geographic barriers interact to lower the incidence of W/B rape. Segregation as well as the poverty expected in black neighborhoods undoubtedly discourages many whites from choosing such areas as a target for house-breaking or robbery. Thus, the number of rapes that would occur in conjunction with these crimes is reduced.

Reflecting in part the standards of sexual desirability set by the dominant white society, a number of black rapists indicated they had been curious about white women. Blocked by racial barriers from legitimate sexual relations with white women, they raped to gain access to them. They described raping white women as "the ultimate experience" and "high status among my friends. It gave me a feeling of status, power, macho." For another man, raping a white woman had a special appeal because it violated a "known taboo," making it more dangerous and thus more exciting, to him than raping a black woman.

IMPERSONAL SEX AND POWER

The idea that rape is an impersonal rather than an intimate or mutual experience appealed to a number of rapists, some of whom suggested it was their preferred form of sex. The fact that rape allowed them to control rather than care encouraged some to act on this preference. For example, one man explained,

> Rape gave me the power to do what I wanted to do without feeling I had to please a partner or respond to a partner. I felt in control, dominant. Rape was the ability to have sex without caring about the woman's response. I was totally dominant.

Another rapist commented:

> Seeing them laying there helpless gave me the confidence that I could do it. . . . With rape, I felt totally in charge. I'm bashful, timid. When a woman wanted to give in normal sex, I was intimidated. In the rapes, I was totally in command, she totally submissive.

During his interview, another rapist confided that he had been fantasizing about rape for several weeks before committing his offense. His belief was that it would be "an exciting experience—a new high." Most appealing to him was the idea that he could make his victim "do it all for him" and that he would be in control. He fantasized that she "would submit totally and that I could have anything I wanted." Eventually, he decided to act because his older brother told him, "forced sex is great, I wouldn't get caught and, besides, women love it." Though now he admits to his crime, he continues to believe his victim "enjoyed it." Perhaps we should note here that the appeal of impersonal sex is not limited to convicted rapists. The amount of male sexual activity that occurs in homosexual meeting places as well as the widespread use of prostitutes suggests that avoidance of intimacy appeals to a large segment of the male population. Through rape men can experience power and avoid the emotions related to intimacy and tenderness. Further, the popularity of violent pornography suggests that a wide variety of men in this culture have learned to be aroused by sex fused with violence (Smith, 1976). Consistent with this observation, recent experimental research conducted by Malamuth et al. (1980) demonstrates that men are aroused by images that depict women as orgasmic under conditions of violence and pain. They found that for female students, arousal was high when the victim experienced an orgasm and *no* pain, whereas male students were highly aroused when the victim experienced an orgasm and pain. On the basis of their results, Malamuth et al. (1980) suggest that forcing a woman to climax despite her pain and abhorrence of the assailant makes the rapist feel powerful; he has gained control over the only source of power historically associated with women, their bodies. In the final analysis, dominance was the objective of most rapists.

RECREATION AND ADVENTURE

Among gang rapists, most of whom were in their late teens or early twenties when convicted, rape represented recreation and adventure, another form of delinquent activity. Part of rape's appeal was the sense of male camaraderie engendered by participating collectively in a dangerous activity. To prove one's self capable of "performing" under these circumstances was a substantial challenge and also a source of reward. One gang rapist articulated this feeling very clearly,

We felt powerful, we were in control. I wanted sex and there was peer pressure. She wasn't like a person, no personality, just domination on my part. Just to show I could do it—you know, macho.

Our research revealed several forms of gang rape. A common pattern was hitchhike-abduction rape. In these cases, the gang, cruising an area, "looking for girls," picked up a female hitchhiker for the purpose of having sex. Though the intent was rape, a number of men did not view it as such because they were convinced that women hitchhiked primarily to signal sexual availability and only secondarily as a form of transportation. In these cases, the unsuspecting victim was driven to a deserted area, raped, and in the majority of cases physically injured. Sometimes, the victim was not hitchhiking; she was abducted at knife or gun point from the street usually at night. Some of these men did not view this type of attack as rape either because they believed a woman walking alone at night to be a prostitute. In addition, they were often convinced "she enjoyed it."

"Gang date" rape was another popular variation. In this pattern, one member of the gang would make a date with the victim. Then, without her knowledge or consent, she would be driven to a predetermined location and forcibly raped by each member of the group. One young man revealed this practice was so much a part of his group's recreational routine, they had rented a house for the purpose. From his perspective, the rape was justified because "usually the girl had a bad reputation, or we knew it was what she liked."

During his interview, another offender confessed to participating in 20 or 30 such "gang date" rapes because his driver's license had been revoked making it difficult for him to "get girls." Sixty percent of the time, he claimed, "they were girls known to do this kind of thing," but "frequently, the girls didn't want to have sex with all of us." In such cases, he said, "It might start out as rape but, then, they (the women) would quiet down and none ever reported it to the police." He was convicted for a gang rape, which he described as "the ultimate thing I ever did," because unlike his other rapes, the victim, in this case, was a stranger whom the group abducted as she walked home from the library. He felt the group's past experience with "gang date" rape had prepared them for this crime in which the victim was blindfolded and driven to the mountains where, though it was winter, she was forced to remove her clothing. Lying on the snow, she was raped by each of the four men several times before being abandoned near a farm house. This young man continued to believe that if he had spent the night with her, rather than abandoning her, she would not have reported to the police.[11]

Solitary rapists also used terms like "exciting," "a challenge," "an adventure," to describe their feelings about rape. Like the gang rapists, these men found the element of danger made rape all the more exciting. Typifying this attitude was one man who described his rape as intentional. He reported:

> It was exciting to get away with it [rape], just being able to beat the system, not women. It was like doing something illegal and getting away with it.

Another rapist confided that for him "rape was just more exciting and compelling" than a normal sexual encounter because it involved forcing a stranger. A multiple rapist asserted, "it was the excitement and fear and the drama that made rape a big kick."

FEELING GOOD

At the time of their interviews, many of the rapists expressed regret for their crime and had empirically low self-esteem ratings. The experience of being convicted, sentenced, and incarcerated for rape undoubtedly produced many, if not most, of these feelings. What is clear is that, in contrast to the well-documented severity of the immediate impact, and in some cases, the long-term trauma experienced by the victims of sexual violence, the immediate emotional impact on the rapists is slight.

When the men were asked to recall their feelings immediately following the rape, only 8 percent indicated that guilt or feeling bad was part of their emotional response. The majority said they felt good, relieved, or simply nothing at all. Some indicated they had been afraid of being caught or felt sorry for themselves. Only two men out of 114 expressed any concern or feeling for the victim. Feeling good or nothing at all about raping women is not an aberration limited to men in prison. Smithyman (1978), in his study of "undetected rapists"—rapists outside of prison—found that raping women had no impact on their lives nor did it have a negative effect on their self-image.

Significantly, a number of men volunteered the information that raping had a positive impact on their feelings. For some the satisfaction was in revenge. For example, the man who had raped and murdered five women:

> It seems like so much bitterness and tension had built up and this released it. I felt like I had just climbed a mountain and now I could look back.

Another offender characterized rape as habit forming: "Rape is like smoking. You can't stop once you start." Finally one man expressed the sentiments of many rapists when he stated,

> After rape, I always felt like I had just conquered something, like I had just ridden the bull at Gilley's.

Conclusions

This chapter has explored rape from the perspective of a group of convicted, incarcerated rapists. The purpose was to discover how these men viewed sexual violence and what they gained from their behavior.

We found that rape was frequently a means of revenge and punishment. Implicit in revenge-rapes was the notion that women were collectively liable for the rapists' problems. In some cases, victims were substitutes for significant women on whom the men desired to take revenge. In other cases, victims were thought to represent all women, and rape was used to punish, humiliate, and "put them in their place." In both cases women were seen as a class, a category, not as individuals. For some men, rape was almost an afterthought, a bonus added to burglary or robbery. Other men gained access to sexually unavailable or unwilling women through rape. For this group of men, rape was a fantasy come true, a particularly exciting form of impersonal sex which enabled them to dominate and control women, by exercising a singularly male form of power. These rapists talked of the pleasures of raping—how for them it was a challenge, an adventure, a dangerous and "ultimate" experience. Rape made them feel good and, in some cases, even elevated their self-image.

The pleasure these men derived from raping reveals the extreme to which they objectified women. Women were seen as sexual commodities to be used or conquered rather than as human beings with rights and feelings. One young man expressed the extreme of the contemptful view of women when he confided to the female researcher.

> Rape is a man's right. If a woman doesn't want to give it, the man should take it. Women have no right to say no. Women are made to have sex. It's all they are good for. Some women would rather take a beating, but they always give in; it's what they are for.

This man murdered his victim because she wouldn't "give in."

Undoubtedly, some rapes, like some of all crimes, are idiopathic. However, it is not necessary to resort to pathological motives to account for all rape or other acts of sexual violence. Indeed, we find that men who rape have something to teach us about the cultural roots of sexual aggression. They force us to acknowledge that rape is more than an idiosyncratic act committed by a few "sick" men. Rather, rape can be viewed as the end point in a continuum of sexually aggressive behaviors that reward men and victimize women.[12] In the way that the motives for committing any criminal act can be rationally determined, reasons for rape can also be determined. Our data demonstrate that some men rape because they have learned that in this culture sexual violence is rewarding. Significantly, the overwhelming majority of these rapists indicated they never thought they would go to prison for what they did. Some did not fear imprisonment because they did not define their behavior as rape. Others knew that women frequently do not report rape and of those cases that are reported, conviction rates are low, and therefore they felt secure. These men perceived rape as a rewarding, low risk act. Understanding that otherwise normal men can and do rape is critical to the development of strategies for prevention.

We are left with the fact that all men do not rape. In view of the apparent rewards and cultural supports for rape, it is important to ask why some men do not rape. Hirschi (1969) makes a similar observation about delinquency. He argues that the key question is not "Why do they do it?" but rather "Why don't we do it?" (Hirschi, 1969:34). Likewise, we may be seeking an answer to the wrong question about sexual assault of women. Instead of asking men who rape "Why?", perhaps we should be asking men who don't "Why not?"

Notes

This research was supported by a grant (R01 MH33013) from the National Center for the Prevention and Control of Rape, National Institute of Mental Health. We are indebted to the Virginia Department of Corrections for their cooperation and assistance in this research.

1. Despite the fact that these data have been in circulation for some time, prevention strategies continue to reflect the "lunatic fringe" image of rape. For example, security on college campuses, such as bright lighting and escort service, is designed to protect women against stranger rape while little or no attention is paid to the more frequent crime—acquaintance or date rape.

2. Broude and Greene (1976) list a number of factors which limit the quantity and quality of cross-cultural data on rape. They point out that it was not customary in traditional ethnography to collect data on sexual attitudes and behavior. Further, where data do exist, they are often sketchy and vague. Despite this, the existence of rape-free societies has been established.

3. This factor distinguishes rape from other fictional depictions of violence. That is, in fictional murder, bombings, robberys, etc., victims are never portrayed as enjoying themselves. Such exhibits are reserved for pornographic displays of rape.

4. We also introduced a typology consisting of "admitters" (men who defined their behavior as rape) and "deniers" (men who admitted to sexual contact with the victim but did not define it as rape). In this chapter we drop the distinction between admitters and deniers because it is not relevant to most of the discussion.

5. For a full discussion of the research methodology, sample, and validity, see Scully and Marolla (1984).

6. It should be noted that significant women, like rape victims, were also sometimes the targets of abuse and violence and possibly rape as well, although spousal rape is not recognized in Virginia law. In fact, these men were abusers. Fifty-five percent of rapists acknowledged that they hit their significant woman "at least once," and 20 percent admitted to inflicting physical injury. Given the tendency of these men to under-report the amount of violence in their crime, it is probably accurate to say, they under-reported their abuse of their significant women as well.

7. This man, as well as a number of others, either would not or could not bring himself to say the word "rape." Similarly, we also attempted to avoid using the word, a technique which seemed to facilitate communication.

8. When asked towards whom their sexual interests were primarily directed, 43 percent of rapists indicated a preference for women "significantly older than themselves." When those who responded, "women of any age" are added, 65 percent of rapists expressed sexual interest in women older than themselves.

9. Feminists as well as sociologists have tended to avoid the topic of interracial rape. Contributing to the avoidance is an awareness of historical and contemporary social injustice. For example, Davis (1981) points out that fictional rape of white women was used in the South as a post-slavery justification to lynch black men. And LaFree (1980) has demonstrated that black men who assault white women continue to receive more serious sanctions within the criminal justice system when compared to other racial combinations of victim and assailant. While the silence has been defensible in light of historical racism, continued avoidance of the topic discriminates against victims by eliminating the opportunity to investigate the impact of social factors on rape.

10. In our sample, 66 percent of black rapists reported their victim(s) were white, compared to two white rapists who reported raping black women. It is important to emphasize that because of the biases inherent in rape reporting and processing, and because of the limitations of our sample, these figures do not accurately reflect the actual racial composition of rapes committed in Virginia or elsewhere. Furthermore, since black men who assault white women receive more serious sanctions within the criminal justice system when compared to other racial combinations of victim and assailant (LaFree, 1980), B/W rapists will be overrepresented within prison populations as well as overrepresented in any sample drawn from the population.

11. It is important to note that the gang rapes in this study were especially violent, resulting in physical injury, even death. One can only guess at the amount of hitchhike-abduction and "gang-date" rapes that are never reported or, if reported, are not processed because of the tendency to disbelieve the victims of such rapes unless extensive physical injury accompanies the crime.

12. It is interesting that men who verbally harass women on the street say they do so to alleviate boredom, to gain a sense of youthful camaraderie, and because it's fun (Benard and Schlaffer, 1984)—the same reason men who rape give for their behavior.

References

Abel, Gene, Judith Becker, and Linda Skinner
    1980 "Aggressive behavior and sex." *Psychiatric Clinics of North America* 3:133–51.
Athens, Lonnie
    1977 "Violent crime: A symbolic interactionist study." *Symbolic Interaction* 1:56–71.
Bart, Pauline
    1979 "Rape as a paradigm of sexism in society—victimization and its discontents." *Women's Studies International Quarterly* 2:347–57.
Benard, Cheryl, and Edith Schlaffer
    1984 "The man in the street: Why he harasses." Pp. 70–73 in Alson M. Jaggar and Paula S. Rothenberg (eds.), *Feminist Frameworks*. New York: McGraw-Hill.
Black, Donald
    1983 "Crime as social control." *American Sociological Review* 48:34–45.
Blumberg, Rae Lesser
    1979 "A paradigm for predicting the position of women: Policy implications and problems." Pp. 113–42 in Jean Lipman-Blumen and Jessie Bernard (eds.), *Sex Roles and Social Policy*. London: Sage Studies in International Sociology.
Broude, Gwen, and Sarah Greene
    1976 "Cross-cultural codes on twenty sexual attitudes and practices." *Ethnology* 15:409–28.
Brownmiller, Susan
    1975 *Against Our Will*. New York: Simon and Schuster.
Davis, Angela
    1981 *Women, Race and Class*. New York: Random House.
Fisher, Gary, and E. Rivlin
    1971 "Psychological needs of rapists." *British Journal of Criminology* 11:182–85.
Griffin, Susan
    1971 "Rape: The all American crime." *Ramparts*, September 10:26–35.
Groth, Nicholas
    1971 *Men Who Rape*. New York: Plenum Press.
    1979 *Men Who Rape: The Psychology of the Offender*. New York: Plenum Press.
Hammer, Emanuel, and Irving Jacks
    1955 "A study of Rorschack flexnor and extensor human movements." *Journal of Clinical Psychology* 11:63–67.
Herman, Dianne
    1984 "The rape culture." Pp. 20–39 in Jo Freeman (ed.), *Women: A Feminist Perspective*. Palo Alto: Mayfield.
Hirschi, Travis
    1969 *Causes of Delinquency*. Berkeley: University of California Press.
Hoebel, E. Adamson
    1954 *The Law of Primitive Man*. Boston: Harvard University Press.
Johnson, Allan Griswold
    1980 "On the prevalence of rape in the United States." *Signs* 6:136–46.
Kanin, Eugene
    1957 "Male aggression in dating-courtship relations." *American Journal of Sociology* 63:197–204.
    1965 "Male sex aggression and three psychiatric hypotheses." *Journal of Sex Research* 1:227–29.
    1967 "Reference groups and sex conduct norm violation." *Sociological Quarterly* 8:495–504.
    1969 "Selected dyadic aspects of male sex aggression." *Journal of Sex Research* 5:12–28.
Kasinsky, Renee
    1975 "Rape: A normal act?" *Canadian Forum*, September:18–22.
Kirkpatrick, Clifford, and Eugene Kanin
    1957 "Male sex aggression on a university campus." *American Sociological Review* 22:52–58.

Koss, Mary P., and Kenneth E. Leonard
 1984 "Sexually aggressive men: Empirical findings and theoretical implications." Pp. 213–32 in Neil M. Malamuth and Edward Donnerstein (eds.), *Pornography and Sexual Aggression*. New York: Academic Press.
LaFree, Gary
 1980 "The effect of sexual stratification by race on official reactions to rape." *American Sociological Review* 45:824–54.
 1982 "Male power and female victimization: Towards a theory of interracial rape." *American Journal of Sociology* 88:311–28.
Llewellyn, Karl N., and E. Adamson Hoebel
 1941 *The Cheyenne Way: Conflict and Case Law in Primitive Jurisprudence*. Norman: University of Oklahoma Press.
Luckenbill, David
 1977 "Criminal homicide as a situated transaction." *Social Problems* 25:176–87.
Malamuth, Neil, Scott Haber, and Seymour Feshback
 1980 "Testing hypotheses regarding rape: exposure to sexual violence, sex difference, and the 'normality' of rapists." *Journal of Research in Personality* 14:121–37.
Malamuth, Neil, Maggie Heim, and Seymour Feshback
 1980 "Sexual responsiveness of college students to rape depictions: Inhibitory and disinhibitory effects." *Social Psychology* 38:399–408.
Meyer, Thomas J.
 1984 "'Date rape': A serious problem that few talk about." *Chronicle of Higher Education*, December 5.
Morgan, Robin
 1980 "Theory and practice: Pornography and rape." Pp. 134–40 in Laura Lederer (ed.), *Take Back the Night: Women on Pornography*. New York: William Morrow.
Queen's Bench Foundation
 1976 *Rape: Prevention and Resistance*. San Francisco: Queen's Bench Foundation.
Rada, Richard
 1978 *Clinical Aspects of Rape*. New York: Grune and Stratton.
Russell, Diana
 1975 *The Politics of Rape*. New York: Stein and Day.
Sanday, Peggy Reeves
 1979 *The Socio-Cultural Context of Rape*. Washington, DC: United States Department of Commerce, National Technical Information Service.
Scully, Diana, and Joseph Marolla
 1984 "Convicted rapists' vocabulary of motive: Excuses and justifications." *Social Problems* 31:530–44.
 1985 "Rape and psychiatric vocabulary of motive: Alternative perspectives." Pp. 294–312 in Ann Wolbert Burgess (ed.), *Rape and Sexual Assault: A Research Handbook*. New York: Garland Publishing.
Smith, Don
 1976 "The social context of pornography." *Journal of Communications* 26:16–24.
Smithyman, Samuel
 1978 *The Undetected Rapist*. Unpublished Dissertation: Claremont Graduate School.
Weis, Kurt, and Sandra Borges
 1973 "Victimology and rape: The case of the legitimate victim." *Issues in Criminology* 8:71–115.
West, Donald J.
 1983 "Sex offenses and offending." Pp. 1–30 in Michael Tonry and Norval Morris (eds.), *Crime and Justice: An Annual Review of Research*. Chicago: University of Chicago Press.
Wheeler, Hollis
 1985 "Pornography and rape: A feminist perspective." Pp. 374–91 in Ann Wolbert Burgess (ed.), *Rape and Sexual Assault: A Research Handbook*. New York: Garland Publishing.

CHAPTER 2

The Myth of Sexual Symmetry in Marital Violence

Russell P. Dobash, R. Emerson Dobash, Margo Wilson, and Martin Daly

Long denied, legitimized, and made light of, wife-beating is at last the object of widespread public concern and condemnation. Extensive survey research and intensive interpretive investigations tell a common story. Violence against wives (by which term we encompass de facto as well as registered unions) is often persistent and severe, occurs in the context of continuous intimidation and coercion, and is inextricably linked to attempts to dominate and control women (e.g., Counts, Brown, and Campbell 1992; Dobash and Dobash 1979; Martin 1976; Pagelow 1984). Historical and contemporary investigations further reveal that this violence has been explicitly decriminalized, ignored, or treated in an ineffectual manner by criminal justice systems, by medical and social service institutions, and by communities (e.g., Bowker 1983; Dobash and Dobash 1977/1978, 1979, 1981a, 1992; Dobash, Dobash, and Cavanagh 1985; Gordon 1988; Pahl 1985; Pleck 1987, 1989; Smith 1989; Stark and Flitcraft 1983; Stark, Flitcraft, and Frazier 1979). Increased attention to these failures has inspired increased efforts to redress them, and in many places legislative amendments have mandated arrest and made assault a crime whether the offender is married to the victim or not.

A number of researchers and commentators have suggested that assaults upon men by their wives constitute a social problem comparable in nature and magnitude to that of wife-beating (Farrell 1986; McNeely and Mann 1990; McNeely and Robinson-Simpson 1987; Shupe, Stacey, and Hazelwood 1987; Steinmetz 1977/1978; Steinmetz and Lucca 1988; Straus and Gelles 1986, 1990a; Straus, Gelles, and Steinmetz 1980). Two main bodies of evidence have been offered in support of these authors' claims that husbands and wives are similarly victimized: (1) self-reports of violent acts perpetrated and suffered by survey respondents, especially those in two U.S. national probability samples (Straus and Gelles 1986); and (2) U.S. homicide data. Unlike the case of violence against wives, however, the victimization of husbands allegedly continues to be denied and trivialized. "Violence by wives has not been an object of public concern," note Straus and Gelles (1986:472). "There has been no publicity, and no funds have been invested in ameliorating this problem because it has not been defined as a problem."

We shall argue that claims of sexual symmetry in marital violence are exaggerated, and that wives' and husbands' uses of violence differ greatly, both quantitatively and qualitatively. We shall further argue that there is no reason to expect the sexes to be alike in this domain, and that efforts to avoid sexism by lumping male and female data and by the use of gender-neutral terms such as "spouse-beating" are misguided. If violence is gendered, as it assuredly is, explicit characterization of gender's relevance to violence is essential. The alleged similarity of women and men in their use of violence in intimate relationships stands in marked contrast to men's virtual monopoly on the use of violence in other social contexts, and we challenge the proponents of the sexual symmetry thesis to develop coherent theoretical models that would account for a sexual monomorphism of violence in one social context and not in others.

A final thesis of this chapter is that resolution of controversies about the "facts" of family violence requires critical examination of theories, methods, and data, with explicit attention to the development of coherent conceptual frameworks, valid and meaningful forms of measurement, and appropriate inferential procedures. Such problems are not peculiar to this research domain, but analysis of the claims regarding violence against husbands provides an excellent example of how a particular approach to construct formation and measurement has led to misrepresentation of the phenomena under investigation.

The Claim of Sexually Symmetrical Marital Violence

Authoritative claims about the prevalence and sexual symmetry of spousal violence in America began with a 1975 U.S. national survey in which 2,143 married or cohabiting persons were interviewed in person about their actions in the preceding year. Straus (1977/1978) announced that the survey results showed that the "marriage license is a hitting licence," and moreover that the rates of perpetrating spousal violence, including severe violence, were higher for wives than for husbands. He concluded:

> Violence between husband and wife is far from a one way street. The old cartoons of the wife chasing the husband with a rolling pin or throwing pots and pans are closer to reality than most (and especially those with feminist sympathies) realize. (Straus 1977/1978:447–448)

In 1985, the survey was repeated by telephone with a new national probability sample including 3,520 husband-wife households, and with similar results. In each survey, the researchers interviewed either the wife or the husband (but not both) in each contacted household about how the couple settled their differences when they had a disagreement. The individual who was interviewed was presented with a list of eighteen "acts" ranging from "discussed an issue calmly" and "cried" to "threw something at him/her/you" and "beat him/ her/you up," with the addition of "choked him/her/you" in 1985 (Straus 1990a:33). These acts constituted the Conflict Tactics Scales (CTS) and were intended to measure three constructs: "Reasoning," "Verbal Aggression," and "Physical Aggression" or "Violence," which was further subdivided into "Minor Violence" and "Severe Violence" according to a presumed potential for injury (Straus 1979; Straus and Gelles 1990a). Respondents were asked how frequently they had perpetrated each act in the course of "conflicts or disagreements" with their spouses (and with one randomly selected child) within the past year, and how frequently they had been on the receiving end. Each respondent's self-reports of victimization and perpetration contributed to estimates of rates of violence by both husbands and wives.

According to both surveys, rates of violence by husbands and wives were strikingly similar (Straus and Gelles 1986, 1990b; Straus et al. 1980). The authors estimated that in the year prior to the 1975 survey 11.6 percent of U.S. husbands were victims of physical violence perpetrated by their wives, while 12.1 percent of wives were victims of their husbands' violence. In 1985, these percentages had scarcely changed, but husbands seemed more vulnerable: 12.1 percent of husbands and 11.3 percent of wives were victims. In both surveys, husbands were more likely to be victims of acts of "severe violence": in 1975, 4.6 percent of husbands were such victims versus 3.8 percent of wives, and in 1985, 4.4 percent of husbands versus 3.0 percent of wives were victims. In reporting their results, the surveys' authors stressed the surprising assaultiveness of wives:

> The repeated finding that the rate of assault by women is similar to the rate by their male partners is an important and distressing aspect of violence in American families. It contrasts markedly to the behavior of women outside the family. It shows that within the family or in dating and cohabiting relationships, women are about as violent as men. (Straus and Gelles 1990:104)

Others have endorsed and publicized these conclusions. For example, a recent review of marital violence concludes, with heavy reliance on Straus and Gelles's survey results, that "(a) women are more prone than men to engage in severely violent acts; (b) each year more men than women are victimized by their intimates" (McNeely and Mann 1990:130). One of Straus and Gelles's collaborators in the 1975 survey, Steinmetz (1977/1978), used the same survey evidence to proclaim the existence of "battered husbands" and a "battered husband syndrome." She has remained one of the leading defenders of the claim that violence between men and women in the family is symmetrical (Steinmetz 1981, 1986; Steinmetz and Lucca 1988; Straus et al. 1980). Steinmetz and her collaborators maintain that the problem is not wife-beating perpetrated by violent men, but "violent couples" and "violent people" (see also Shupe et al. 1987). Men may be stronger on average, argues Steinmetz, but weaponry equalizes matters, as is allegedly shown by the nearly equivalent numbers of U.S. husbands and wives who are killed by their partners. The reason why battered husbands are inconspicuous and seemingly rare is supposedly that shame prevents them from seeking help.

Straus and his collaborators have sometimes qualified their claims that their surveys demonstrate sexual symmetry in marital violence, noting, for example, that men are usually larger and stronger than women and thus able to inflict more damage and that women are more likely to use violence in self-defense or retaliation (e.g., Stets and Straus 1990; Straus 1980, 1990b; Straus and Gelles 1986; Straus et al. 1980). However, the survey results indicate a symmetry not just in the perpetration of violence but in its initiation as well, and from this further symmetry, Stets and Straus (1990:154–155) conclude that the equal assaultiveness of husbands and wives cannot be attributed to the wives acting in self-defense, after all.

Other surveys using the CTS in the United States and in other countries have replicated the finding that wives are about as violent as husbands (Brinkerhoff and

Lupri 1988; Browning and Dutton 1986; Brutz and Ingoldsby 1984; Jouriles and O'Leary 1985; Kennedy and Dutton 1989; Mason and Blankenship 1987; Meredith, Abbott, and Adams 1986; Nisonoff and Bitman 1979; Rouse, Breen, and Howell 1988; Steinmetz 1981; Stets 1990; Szinovacz 1983). The CTS has also been used to study violence in dating relationships, with the same sexually symmetrical results (e.g., Arias and Johnson 1989; Arias, Samios, and O'Leary 1987; Cate et al. 1982; DeMaris 1987; Lane and Gwartney-Gibbs 1985; Laner and Thompson 1982; Makepeace 1986; Marshall and Rose 1990; Rouse et al. 1988; Sigelman, Berry, and Wiles 1984).

Some authors maintain not only that wives initiate violence at rates comparable to husbands, but that they rival them in the damage they inflict as well. McNeely and Robinson-Simpson (1987), for example, argue that research shows that the "truth about domestic violence" is that "women are as violent, if not more violent than men," in their inclinations, in their actions, and in the damage they inflict. The most dramatic evidence invoked in this context is again the fact that wives kill: spousal homicides—for which detection should be minimally or not at all biased because homicides are nearly always discovered and recorded—produce much more nearly equivalent numbers of male and female victims in the United States than do sublethal assault data, which are subject to sampling biases when obtained from police, shelters, and hospitals (McNeely and Robinson-Simpson 1987; Steinmetz 1977/1978; Steinmetz and Lucca 1988; Straus et al. 1980). According to McNeely and Mann (1990:130), "the average man's size and strength are neutralized by guns and knives, boiling water, bricks, fireplace pokers, and baseball bats."

A corollary of the notion that the sexes are alike in their use of violence is that satisfactory causal accounts of violence will be gender-blind. Discussion thus focuses, for example, on the role of one's prior experiences with violence as a child, social stresses, frustration, inability to control anger, impoverished social skills, and so forth, without reference to gender (e.g., Hotaling, Straus, and Lincoln 1990; Shupe et al. 1987; Steinmetz 1986; Straus et al. 1980). This presumption that the sexes are alike not merely in action but in the reasons for that action is occasionally explicit, such as when Shupe et al. (1987:56) write: "Everything we have found points to parallel processes that lead women and men to become violent. . . . Women may be more likely than men to use kitchen utensils or sewing scissors when they commit assault, but their frustrations, motives and lack of control over these feelings predictably resemble men's."

In sum, the existence of an invisible legion of assaulted husbands is an inference which strikes many family violence researchers as reasonable. Two lines of evidence—homicide data and the CTS survey results—suggest to those supporting the sexual-symmetry-of-violence thesis that large numbers of men are trapped in violent relationships. These men are allegedly being denied medical, social welfare, and criminal justice services because of an unwillingness to accept the evidence from homicide statistics and the CTS surveys (Gelles 1982; Steinmetz 1986).

Violence against Wives

Any argument that marital violence is sexually symmetrical must either dismiss or ignore a large body of contradictory evidence indicating that wives greatly outnumber husbands as victims. While CTS researchers were discovering and publicizing the mutual violence of wives and husbands, other researchers—using evidence from courts, police, and women's shelters—were finding that wives were much more likely than husbands to be victims (e.g., Byles 1978; Chester and Streather 1972; Dobash and Dobash 1977/1978, 1979; Levinger 1966; Lystad 1975; Martin 1976; O'Brien 1971; Stark et al. 1979; Vanfossen 1979). After an extensive review of extant research, Lystad (1975) expressed the consensus: "The occurrence of adult violence in the home usually involves males as aggressors towards females." This conclusion was subsequently supported by numerous further studies of divorce records, emergency room patients treated for non-accidental injuries, police assault records, and spouses seeking assistance and refuge (e.g., Fergusson et al. 1986; Goldberg and Tomlanovich 1984; Kincaid 1982; McLeer and Anwar 1989; Okun 1986; Warshaw 1989; Watkins 1982). Analyses of police and court records in North America and Europe have persistently indicated that women constitute 90 to 95 percent of the victims of those assaults in the home reported to the criminal justice system (Berk et al. 1983; Dobash and Dobash 1977/1978; Kincaid 1982; McLeod 1984; Quarm and Schwartz 1985; Vanfossen 1979; Watkins 1982).

Defenders of the sexual-symmetry-of-violence thesis do not deny these results, but they question their representativeness: these studies could be biased because samples of victims were self-selected. However, criminal victimization surveys using national probability samples similarly indicate that wives are much more often victimized than husbands. Such surveys in the United States, Canada, and Great Britain have been replicated in various years, with essentially the same results. Beginning in 1972 and using a panel survey method involving up to seven consecutive interviews at six-month intervals, the U.S. National Crime Survey has generated nearly a million interviews. Gaquin's (1977/1978) analysis of U.S. National Crime Survey data for 1973–1975 led her to conclude that men "have almost no risk of being assaulted by their wives" (634–635); only 3 percent of the violence reported from these surveys involved attacks on men by their female partners. Another analysis of the National Crime Survey data from 1973 to 1980 found that 6 percent of spousal assault incidents were directed at men (McLeod 1984).[1] Schwartz (1987) re-analyzed the same victimization surveys with the addition of the 1981 and 1982 data, and found 102 men who claimed to have been victims of assaults by their wives (4 percent of domestic assault incidents) in contrast to 1,641 women who said they were assaulted by husbands. The 1981 Canadian Urban Victimization Survey (Solicitor General of Canada 1985) and the 1987 General Social Survey (Sacco and Johnson 1990; Statistics Canada 1990) produced analogous findings, from which Johnson (1989) concluded that "women account for 80–90 percent of victims in assaults or sexual assaults between spouses or former spouses. In fact, the number of domestic assaults involving males was too low in both surveys to provide reliable estimates" (1–2). The 1982 and 1984 British Crime Surveys found that women accounted for all the victims of marital assaults (Worrall and Pease 1986). Self-reports of criminal victimization based on national probability surveys, while not without methodological weaknesses,[2] are not subject to the same reporting biases as divorce, police, and hospital records.

The national crime surveys also indicate that women are much more likely than men to suffer injury as a result of assaults in the home (Langan and Innes 1986;

Schwartz 1987; Solicitor General of Canada 1985; Worrall and Pease 1986). After analyzing the results of the U.S. National Crime Surveys, Schwartz (1987:67) concludes, "there are still more than 13 times as many women seeking medical care from a private physician for injuries received in a spousal assault." This result again replicates the typical findings of studies of police or hospital records. For example, women constituted 94 percent of the injury victims in an analysis of the spousal assault cases among 262 domestic disturbance calls to police in Santa Barbara County, California (Berk et al. 1983); moreover, the women's injuries were more serious than the men's. Berk et al. (1983:207) conclude that "when injuries are used as the outcome of interest, a marriage license is a hitting license *but for men only*." Brush (1990) reports that a U.S. national probability sample survey of over 13,000 respondents in 1987–1988 replicated the evident symmetry of marital violence when CTS-like questions about acts were posed, but also revealed that women were much more often injured than men (and that men downplayed women's injuries).

In response, defenders of the sexual-symmetry-of-violence thesis contend that data from police, courts, hospitals, and social service agencies are suspect because men are reluctant to report physical violence by their wives. For example, Steinmetz (1977/1978) asserts that husband-beating is a camouflaged social problem because men must overcome extraordinary stigma in order to report that their wives have beaten them. Similarly, Shupe et al. (1987) maintain that men are unwilling to report their wives because "it would be unmanly or unchivalrous to go to the police for protection from a woman" (52). However, the limited available evidence does not support these authors' presumption that men are less likely to report assaults by their spouses than are women. Schwartz's (1987) analysis of the 1973–1982 U.S. National Crime Survey data found that 67.2 percent of men and 56.8 percent of women called the police after being assaulted by their spouses. One may protest that these high percentages imply that only a tiny proportion of the most severe spousal assaults were acknowledged as assaults by respondents to these crime surveys, but the results are nonetheless contrary to the notion that assaulted men are especially reticent. Moreover, Rouse et al. (1988), using "act" definitions of assaults which inspired much higher proportions to acknowledge victimization, similarly report that men were likelier than women to call the police after assaults by intimate partners, both among married couples and among those dating. In addition, a sample of 337 cases of domestic violence drawn from family court cases in Ontario showed that men were more likely than women to press charges against their spouses: there were 17 times as many female victims as male victims, but only 22 percent of women laid charges in contrast to 40 percent of the men, and men were less likely to drop the charges, too (Kincaid 1982:91). What those who argue that men are reluctant or ashamed to report their wives' assaults overlook is that women have their own reasons to be reticent, fearing both the loss of a jailed or alienated husband's economic support and his vengeance. Whereas the claim that husbands underreport because of shame or chivalry is largely speculative, there is considerable evidence that women report very little of the violence perpetrated by their male partners (e.g., Dobash and Dobash 1979; Kantor and Straus 1990; Solicitor General of Canada 1985; Schwartz 1987).

The CTS survey data indicating equivalent violence by wives and husbands thus stand in contradiction to injury data, to police incident reports, to help-seeking statistics, and even to other, larger, national probability sample surveys of self-reported victimization. The CTS researchers insist that their results alone are accurate because husbands' victimizations are unlikely to be detected or reported by any other method. It is therefore important to consider in detail the CTS and the data it generates.

Do CTS Data Reflect the Reality of Marital Violence?

The CTS instrument has been much used and much criticized. Critics have complained that its exclusive focus on "acts" ignores the actors' interpretations, motivations, and intentions; that physical violence is arbitrarily delimited, excluding, for example, sexual assault and rape; that retrospective reports of the past year's events are unlikely to be accurate; that researchers' attributions of "violence" (with resultant claims about its statistical prevalence) are based on respondents' admitting to acts described in such an impoverished manner as to conflate severe assaults with trivial gestures; that the formulaic distinction between "minor" and "severe violence" (whereby, for example, "tried to hit with something" is definitionally "severe" and "slapped" is definitionally "minor") constitutes a poor operationalization of severity; that the responses of aggressors and victims have been given identical evidentiary status in deriving incidence estimates, while their inconsistencies have been ignored; that the CTS omits the contexts of violence, the events precipitating it, and the sequences of events by which it progresses; and that it fails to connect outcomes, especially injury, with the acts producing them (e.g., Berk et al. 1983; Breines and Gordon 1983; Browning and Dutton 1986; DeKeseredy 1991; Dobash and Dobash 1979, 1981b, 1990, 1992; Ferraro and Johnson 1983; Frieze and Browne 1989; Kurz 1989; Makepeace 1986; Okun 1986; Pagelow 1985; Pleck et al. 1977/1978; Russell 1982; Saunders 1986, 1988; Walker 1984).

Straus (1990b) has defended the CTS against its critics, maintaining that the CTS addresses context with its "verbal aggression" scale (although the assessment of "verbal aggression" is not incident-linked with the assessment of "violence"); that the minor-severe categorization "is roughly parallel to the legal distinction between 'simple assault' and 'aggravated assault'" (58); that other measurement instruments have problems, too; and that you cannot measure everything. Above all, the defense rests on the widespread use of the instrument, on its reliability, and on its validity. That the CTS is widely used cannot be gainsaid, but whether it is reliable or valid is questionable.

PROBLEMS WITH THE RELIABILITY AND VALIDITY OF CTS RESPONSES

Straus (1990b:64) claims that six studies have assessed "the internal consistency reliability" of the CTS. One of the six (Barling and Rosenbaum 1986) contains no such assessment, a second is unreferenced, and a third unpublished. However, a moderate degree of "internal consistency reliability" of the CTS can probably be conceded. For example, those who admit to having "beat up" their spouses are also likely to admit to having "hit" them.

The crucial matter of interobserver reliability is much more problematic. The degree of concordance in couples' responses is an assay of "interspousal reliability" (Jouriles and O'Leary 1985), and such reliability must be high if CTS scores are to be taken at face value. For example, incidence estimates of husband-to-wife and wife-to-husband violence have been generated from national surveys in which the CTS was administered to only one adult per family, with claims of victimization and perpetration by male and female respondents all granted equal evidentiary status and summated (Straus and Gelles 1990a). The validity of these widely cited incidence estimates is predicated upon interspousal reliability.

Straus (1990b:66) considers the assessment of spousal concordance to constitute an assay of "concurrent validity" rather than "interspousal reliability," in effect treating each partner's report as the violence criterion that validates the other. But spousal concordance is analogous to interobserver reliability: it is a necessary but by no means sufficient condition for concluding that the self-reports accurately reflect reality. If couples generally produce consistent reports—Mr. and Mrs. Jones both indicate that he struck her, while Mr. and Mrs. Smith both indicate that neither has struck the other—then it is possible though by no means certain that their CTS self-reports constitute valid (veridical) information about the blows actually struck. However, if couples routinely provide discrepant CTS responses, data derived from the CTS simply cannot be valid.

In this light, studies of husband/wife concordance in CTS responses should be devastating to those who imagine that the CTS provides a valid account of the respondents' acts. In what Straus correctly calls "the most detailed and thorough analysis of agreement between spouses in response to the CTS," Szinovacz (1983) found that 103 couples' accounts of the violence in their interactions matched to a degree little greater than chance. On several CTS items, mainly the most severe ones, agreement was actually below chance. On the item "beat up," concordance was nil, although there were respondents of both sexes who claimed to have administered beatings and respondents of both sexes who claimed to have been on the receiving end, there was not a single couple in which one party claimed to have administered and the other to have received such a beating. In a similar study, Jouriles and O'Leary (1985) administered the CTS to 65 couples attending a marital therapy clinic, and 37 control couples from the local community. For many of the acts, the frequency and percentage data reported are impossible to reconcile; for others, Jouriles and O'Leary reported a concordance statistic (Cohen's Kappa) as equalling zero when the correct values were negative.[3] Straus (1990b) cites this study as conferring validity on the CTS, but in fact, its results replicated Szinovacz's (1983): husband/wife agreement scarcely exceeded chance expectation and actually fell below chance on some items.

Straus (1990b) acknowledges that these and the other studies he reviews "found large discrepancies between the reports of violence given by husbands and by wives" (69). He concludes, however, that "validity measures of agreement between family members are within the range of validity coefficients typically reported" (71), and that "the weakest aspect of the CTS are [sic] the scales that have received the least criticism: Reasoning and Verbal aggression" (71), by which he implies that the assessment of violence is relatively strong.

Ultimately, Straus's defense of the CTS is that the proof of the pudding is in the eating: "The strongest evidence concerns the construct validity of the CTS. It has been used in a large number of studies producing findings that tend to be consistent with previous research (when available), consistent regardless of gender of respondent, and theoretically meaningful" (Straus 1990b:71). And indeed, with respect to marital violence, the CTS is capable of making certain gross discriminations. Various studies have found CTS responses to vary as a function of age, race, poverty, duration of relationship, and registered versus de facto marital unions (Brinkerhoff and Lupri 1988; Ellis 1989; Lockhart 1987; Okun 1986; Smith 1990; Stets 1990; Stets and Straus 1990; Straus and Gelles 1990b; Straus et al. 1980; Yllo and Straus 1981), and these effects have generally been directionally similar to those found with less problematic measures of violence such as homicides (Block 1991; Daly and Wilson 1988a, 1988b; Goetting 1989; Mercy and Saltzman 1989). However, the CTS has also failed to detect certain massive differences, and we do not refer only to sex differences.

Consider the case of child abuse by stepparents versus birth parents. In various countries, including the United States, a stepparent is more likely to fatally assault a small child than is a birth parent, by a factor on the order of 100-fold (Daly and Wilson 1988a, 1988b; Wilson, Daly and Weghorst 1980); sublethal violence also exhibits huge differences in the same direction (Creighton 1985; Daly and Wilson 1985; Fergusson, Fleming, and O'Neill 1972; Wilson and Daly 1987). Using the CTS, however, Gelles and Harrop (1991) were unable to detect any difference in self-reports of violence by step- versus birth parents. Users of the CTS have sometimes conceded that the results of their self-report surveys cannot provide an accurate picture of the prevalence of violence, but they have made this concession only to infer that the estimates must be gross underestimates of the true prevalence (Straus et al. 1980:35; Straus and Gelles 1990b:96). However, the CTS's failure to differentiate the behavior of step- versus birth parents indicates that CTS-based estimates are not just underestimates but may misrepresent between-group differences in systematically biased ways. One must be concerned, then, whether this sort of bias also arises in CTS-based comparisons between husbands and wives.

PROBLEMS WITH THE INTERPRETATION OF CTS RESPONSES

With the specific intention of circumventing imprecision and subjectivity in asking about such abstractions as "violence," the CTS is confined to questions about "acts": Respondents are asked whether they have "pushed" their partners, have "slapped" them, and so forth, rather than whether they have "assaulted" them or behaved "violently." This focus on "acts" is intended to reduce problems of self-serving and biased definitional criteria on the part of the respondents, However, any gain in objectivity has been undermined by the way that CTS survey data have then been analyzed and interpreted. Any respondent who acknowledges a single instance of having "pushed," "grabbed," "shoved," "slapped," or "hit or tried to hit" another person is deemed a perpetrator of "violence" by the researchers, regardless of the act's context, consequences, or meaning to the parties involved. Similarly, a single instance of having "kicked," "bit," "hit or tried to hit with an object," "beat up," "choked," "threatened with a knife or gun," or "used a knife or fired a gun" makes one a perpetrator of "severe violence."

Affirmation of any one of the "violence" items provides the basis for estimates such as Straus and Gelles's (1990b:97) claim that 6.8 million U.S. husbands and 6.25 million U.S. wives were spousal assault victims in 1985. Similarly, estimates of large numbers of "beaten" or "battered" wives and husbands have been based on affirmation of any one of the "severe violence" items. For example, Steinmetz (1986:734) and Straus and Gelles (1987:638) claim on this basis that 1.8 million U.S. women are "beaten" by their husbands annually. But note that any man who once threw an "object" at his wife, regardless of its nature and regardless of whether the throw missed, qualifies as having "beaten" her; some unknown proportion of the women and men who are alleged to have been "beaten," on the basis of their survey responses, never claimed to have been struck at all. Thus, the "objective" scoring of the CTS not only fails to explore the meanings and intentions associated with the acts but has in practice entailed interpretive transformations that guarantee exaggeration, misinterpretation, and ultimately trivialization of the genuine problems of violence.

Consider a "slap." The word encompasses anything from a slap on the hand chastizing a dinner companion for reaching for a bite of one's dessert to a tooth-loosening assault intended to punish, humiliate, and terrorize. These are not trivial distinctions; indeed, they constitute the essence of definitional issues concerning violence. Almost all definitions of violence and violent acts refer to intentions. Malevolent intent is crucial, for example, to legal definitions of "assault" (to which supporters of the CTS have often mistakenly claimed that their "acts" correspond; e.g., Straus 1990b:58). However, no one has systematically investigated how respondents vary in their subjective definitions of the "acts" listed on the CTS. If, for example, some respondents interpret phrases such as "tried to hit with an object" literally, then a good deal of relatively harmless behavior surely taints the estimates of "severe violence." Although this problem has not been investigated systematically, one author has shown that it is potentially serious. In a study of 103 couples, Margolin (1987) found that wives surpassed husbands in their use of "severe violence" according to the CTS, but unlike others who have obtained this result, Margolin troubled to check its meaningfulness with more intensive interviews. She concluded:

> While CTS items appear behaviorally specific, their meanings still are open to interpretation. In one couple who endorsed the item "kicking," for example, we discovered that the kicking took place in bed in a more kidding, than serious, fashion. Although this behavior meets the criterion for severe abuse on the CTS, neither spouse viewed it as aggressive, let alone violent. In another couple, the wife scored on severe physical aggression while the husband scored on low-level aggression only. The inquiry revealed that, after years of passively accepting the husband's repeated abuse, this wife finally decided, on one occasion, to retaliate by hitting him over the head with a wine decanter. (1987:82)

By the criteria of Steinmetz (1977/1978:501), this incident would qualify as a "battered husband" case. But however dangerous this retaliatory blow may have been and however reprehensible or justified one may consider it, it is not "battering," whose most basic definitional criterion is its repetitiveness. A failure to consider intentions, interpretations, and the history of the individuals' relationship is a significant shortcoming of CTS research. Only through a consideration of behaviors, intentions, and intersubjective understandings associated with specific violent events will we come to a fuller understanding of violence between men and women (Dobash and Dobash 1983, 1984; Eisikovits and Peled 1990). Studies employing more intensive interviews and detailed case reports addressing the contexts and motivations of marital violence help unravel the assertions of those who claim the widespread existence of beaten and battered husbands. Research focusing on specific violent events shows that women almost always employ violence in defense of self and children in response to cues of imminent assault in the past and in retaliation for previous physical abuse (e.g., Browne 1987; Campbell 1992; Dobash and Dobash 1979, 1984; Jones 1980; Pagelow 1984; Polk and Ranson 1991; Saunders 1986). Proponents of the sexual-symmetry-of-violence thesis have made much of the fact that CTS surveys indicate that women "initiate" the violence about as often as men, but a case in which a woman struck the first blow is unlikely to be the mirror image of one in which her husband "initiated." A noteworthy feature of the literature proclaiming the existence of battered husbands and battering wives (McNeely and Robinson-Simpson 1987; Shupe et al. 1987; Steinmetz 1977/1978; Steinmetz and Lucca 1988) is how little the meager case descriptions resemble those of battered wives and battering husbands (e.g., Browne 1987; Dobash and Dobash 1979; Dobash et al. 1977/1978; Pagelow 1984). Especially lacking in the alleged male victim cases is any indication of the sort of chronic intimidation characteristic of prototypical woman battering cases.

Any self-report method must constitute an imperfect reflection of behavior, and the CTS is no exception. That in itself is hardly a fatal flaw. But for such an instrument to retain utility for the investigation of a particular domain such as family violence, an essential point is that its inaccuracies and misrepresentations must not be systematically related to the distinctions under investigation. The CTS's inability to detect the immense differences in violence between stepparents and birth parents, as noted above, provides strong reason to suspect that the test's shortcomings produce not just noise but systematic bias. In the case of marital violence, the other sorts of evidence reviewed in this chapter indicate that there are massive differences in the use of confrontational violence against spouses by husbands versus wives, and yet the CTS has consistently failed to detect them. CTS users have taken this failure as evidence for the null hypothesis, apparently assuming that their questionnaire data have a validity that battered women's injuries and deaths lack.

Homicides

The second line of evidence that has been invoked in support of the claim that marital violence is more or less sexually symmetrical is the number of lethal outcomes:

> Data on homicide between spouses suggest that an almost equal number of wives kill their husbands as husbands kill their wives (Wolfgang 1958). Thus it appears that men and women might have equal potential for violent marital interaction; initiate similar acts of violence; and when differences of physical strength are equalized by weapons, commit similar amounts of spousal homicide. (Steinmetz and Lucca 1988:241)

McNeely and Robinson-Simpson (1987:485) elevated the latter hypothesis about the relevance of weapons to the status of a fact: "Steinmetz observed that when weapons neutralize differences in physical strength, about as many men as women are victims of homicide."

Steinmetz and Lucca's citation of Wolfgang refers to his finding that 53 Philadelphia men killed their wives between 1948 and 1952, while 47 women killed their husbands. This is a slender basis for such generalization, but fuller information does indeed bear Steinmetz out as regards the near equivalence of body counts in the United States: Maxfield (1989) reported that there were 10,529 wives and 7,888 husbands killed by their mates in the entire country between 1976 and 1985, a 1.3:1 ratio of female to male victims.

Husbands are indeed almost as often slain as are wives in the United States, then. However, there remain several problems with Steinmetz and Lucca's (as well as McNeely and Robinson-Simpson's) interpretation of this fact. Studies of actual cases (Campbell 1992; Daly and Wilson 1988b; Goetting 1989; Lundsgaarde 1977) lend no support to the facile claim that homicidal husbands and wives "initiate similar acts of violence." Men often kill wives after lengthy periods of prolonged physical violence accompanied by other forms of abuse and coercion; the roles in such cases are seldom if ever reversed. Men perpetrate familicidal massacres, killing spouse and children together; women do not. Men commonly hunt down and kill wives who have left them; women hardly ever behave similarly. Men kill wives as part of planned murder-suicides; analogous acts by women are almost unheard of. Men kill in response to revelations of wifely infidelity; women almost never respond similarly, though their mates are more often adulterous. The evidence is overwhelming that a large proportion of the spouse-killings perpetrated by wives, but almost none of those perpetrated by husbands, are acts of self-defense. Unlike men, women kill male partners after years of suffering physical violence, after they have exhausted all available sources of assistance, when they feel trapped, and because they fear for their own lives (e.g., Browne 1987; Campbell 1992; Daly and Wilson 1988b; Jones 1980; Polk and Ranson 1991; Wallace 1986; Wilbanks 1983).

A further problem with the invocation of spousal homicide data as evidence against sex differences in marital violence is that this numerical equivalence is peculiar to the United States. Whereas the ratio of wives to husbands as homicide victims in the United States was 1.3:1 (Maxfield 1989), corresponding ratios from other countries are much higher: 3.3:1 for a 10-year period in Canada, for example, 4.3:1 for Great Britain, and 6:1 for Denmark (Wilson and Daly 1992c). The reason why this is problematic is that U.S. homicide data and CTS data from several countries have been invoked as complementary pieces of evidence for women's and men's equivalent uses of violence (e.g., Steinmetz and Lucca 1988). One cannot have it both ways. If the lack of sex differences in CTS results is considered proof of sexually symmetrical violence, then homicide data must somehow be dismissed as irrelevant, since homicides generally fail to exhibit this supposedly more basic symmetry. Conversely, if U.S. homicide counts constitute relevant evidence, the large sex differences found elsewhere surely indicate that violence is peculiarly symmetrical only in the United States, and the fact that the CTS fails to detect sex differences in other countries must then be taken to mean that the CTS is insensitive to genuine differences.

A possible way out of this dilemma is hinted at in Steinmetz and Lucca's (1988) allusion to the effect of weapons: perhaps it is the availability of guns that has neutralized men's advantage in lethal marital conflict in the United States. Gun use is indeed relatively prevalent in the U.S., accounting for 51 percent of a sample of 1706 spousal homicides in Chicago, for example, as compared to 40 percent of 1060 Canadian cases, 42 percent of 395 Australian cases, and just 8 percent of 1204 cases in England and Wales (Wilson and Daly 1992c). Nevertheless, the plausible hypothesis that gun use can account for the different sex ratios among victims fails. When shootings and other spousal homicides are analyzed separately, national differences in the sex ratios of spousal homicide remain dramatic. For example, the ratio of wives to husbands as gunshot homicide victims in Chicago was 1.2:1, compared to 4:1 in Canada and 3.5:1 in Britain; the ratio of wives to husbands as victims of non-gun homicides was 0.8:1 in Chicago, compared to 2.9:1 in Canada and 4.5:1 in Britain (Wilson and Daly 1992c). Moreover, the near equivalence of husband and wife victims in the U.S. antedates the contemporary prevalence of gun killings. In Wolfgang's (1958) classic study, only 34 of the 100 spousal homicide victims were shot (15 husbands and 19 wives), while 30 husbands were stabbed and 31 wives were beaten or stabbed. Whatever may explain the exceptionally similar death rates of U.S. husbands and wives, it is not simply that guns "equalize."

Nor is the unusual U.S. pattern to be explained in terms of a peculiar convergence in the United States of the sexes in their violent inclinations or capabilities across all domains and relationships. Although U.S. data depart radically from other industrialized countries in the sex ratio of spousal homicide victimization, they do not depart similarly in the sex ratios of other sorts of homicides (Wilson and Daly 1992c). For example, in the United States as elsewhere men kill unrelated men about 40 times as often as women kill unrelated women (Daly and Wilson 1990).

Even among lethal acts, it is essential to discriminate among different victim-killer relationships, because motives, risk factors, and conflict typologies are relationship-specific (Daly and Wilson 1988b). Steinmetz (1977/1978; Steinmetz and Lucca 1988) has invoked the occurrence of maternally perpetrated infanticides as evidence of women's violence; imagining that the fact that some women commit infanticide somehow bolsters the claim that they batter their husbands, too. But maternal infanticides are more often motivated by desperation than by hostile aggression and are often effected by acts of neglect or abandonment rather than by assault (e.g., Daly and Wilson 1988b; Jones 1980). To conflate such acts with aggressive attacks is to misunderstand their utterly distinct motives, forms, and perpetrator profiles, and the distinct social and material circumstances in which they occur.

How to Gain a Valid Account of Marital Violence?

How ought researchers to conceive of "violence"? People differ in their views about whether a particular act was a violent one and about who was responsible. Assessments of intention and justifiability are no less relevant to the labelling of an event as "violent" than are more directly observable considerations like the force exerted or the damage inflicted. Presumably, it is this problem of subjectivity that has inspired efforts to objectify the study of family violence by the counting of "acts," as in the Conflict Tactics Scales.

Unfortunately, the presumed gain in objectivity achieved by asking research subjects to report only "acts," while refraining from elaborating upon their meanings and consequences, is illusory. As noted above, couples exhibit little agreement in reporting the occurrence of acts in which both were allegedly involved, and self-reported acts sometimes fail to differentiate the behavior of groups known to exhibit huge differences in the perpetration of violence. The implication must be that concerns about the validity of self-report data cannot be allayed merely by confining self-reports to a checklist of named acts. We have no more reason to suppose that people will consensually and objectively label events as instances of someone having "grabbed" or "hit or tried to hit" or "used a knife" (items from the CTS) than to suppose that people will consensually and objectively label events as instances of "violence."

If these "acts" were scored by trained observers examining the entire event, there might be grounds for such behavioristic austerity in measurement: whatever the virtues and limitations of behavioristic methodology, a case can at least be made that observational data are more objective than the actors' accounts. However, when researchers have access only to self-reports, the cognitions of the actors are neither more nor less accessible to research than their actions. Failures of candor and memory threaten the validity of both sorts of self-report data, and researchers' chances of detecting such failures can only be improved by the collection of richer detail about the violent event. The behavioristic rigor of observational research cannot be simulated by leaving data collection to the subjects, nor by active inattention to "subjective" matters like people's perceptions of their own and others' intentions, attributions of loss of control, perceived provocations and justifications, intimidatory consequences, and so forth. Moreover, even a purely behavioristic account could be enriched by attending to sequences of events and subsequent behavior rather than merely counting acts.

Enormous differences in meaning and consequence exist between a woman pummelling her laughing husband in an attempt to convey strong feelings and a man pummelling his weeping wife in an attempt to punish her for coming home late. It is not enough to acknowledge such contrasts (as CTS researchers have sometimes done), if such acknowledgments neither inform further research nor alter such conclusions as "within the family or in dating and cohabiting relationships, women are about as violent as men" (Straus and Gelles 1990b: 104). What is needed are forms of analysis that will lead to a comprehensive description of the violence itself as well as an explanation of it. In order to do this, it is, at the very least, necessary to analyze the violent event in a holistic manner, with attention to the entire sequences of distinct acts as well as associated motives, intentions, and consequences, all of which must in turn be situated within the wider context of the relationship.

The Need for Theory

If the arguments and evidence that we have presented are correct, then currently fashionable claims about the symmetry of marital violence are unfounded. How is it that so many experts have been persuaded of a notion that is at once counterintuitive and counterfactual? Part of the answer, we believe, is that researchers too often operate without sound (or indeed any) theoretical visions of marital relationships, of interpersonal conflicts, or of violence.

Straus (1990a:30), for example, introduces the task of investigating family violence by characterizing families as instances of "social groups" and by noting that conflicts of interest are endemic to groups of individuals, "each seeking to live out their lives in accordance with personal agendas that inevitably differ." This is a good start, but the analysis proceeds no further. The characteristic features of families as distinct from other groups are not explored, and the particular domains within which the "agendas" of wives and husbands conflict are not elucidated. Instead, Straus illustrates family conflicts with the hypothetical example of "Which TV show will be watched at eight?" and discusses negotiated and coerced resolutions in terms that would be equally applicable to a conflict among male acquaintances in a bar. Such analysis obscures all that is distinctive about violence against wives which occurs in a particular context of perceived entitlement and institutionalized power asymmetry. Moreover, marital violence occurs around recurring themes, especially male sexual jealousy and proprietariness, expectations of obedience and domestic service, and women's attempts to leave the marital relationship (Campbell 1992; Counts et al. 1992; Daly and Wilson 1988b; Daly, Wilson and Weghorst 1982; Dobash and Dobash 1979, 1984; Ellis 1989; Pagelow 1984; Polk and Ranson 1991; Smith 1990; Wilson 1989; Wilson and Daly 1992a, 1992b). In the self-consciously gender-blind literature on "violent couples," these themes are invisible.

Those who claim that wives and husbands are equally violent have offered no conceptual framework for understanding why women and men should think and act alike. Indeed, the claim that violence is gender-neutral cannot easily be reconciled with other coincident claims. For example, many family violence researchers who propose sexual symmetry in violence attribute the inculcation and legitimation of violence to socializing processes and cultural institutions (Baron and Straus 1988; Straus and Gelles 1990a), but then overlook the fact that these processes and institutions define and treat females and males differently. If sexually differentiated socialization and entitlements play a causal role in violence, how can we understand the alleged equivalence of women's and men's violent inclinations and actions?

Another theoretical problem confronting anyone who claims that violent inclinations are sexually monomorphic concerns the oft-noted fact that men are larger than women and likelier to inflict damage by similar acts. Human passions have their own "rationality" (deSousa 1987; Frank 1988), and it would be curious if women and men were identically motivated to initiate assaults in contexts where the expectable results were far more damaging for women. Insofar as both parties to a potentially violent transaction are aware of such differences, it is inappropriate to treat a slap (or other "act") by one party as equivalent to a slap by the other, not only because there is an asymmetry in the damage the two slaps might inflict, but because the parties differ in the responses available to them and hence in their control over the denouement. Women's motives may be expected to differ systematically from those of men wherever the predictable consequences of their actions differ systematically. Those who contend that women and men are equally inclined to violence need to articulate why this should be so, given the sex differences in physical traits, such as size and muscularity, affecting the probable consequences of violence.

In fact, there is a great deal of evidence that men's and women's psychologies are not at all alike in this domain. Men's violent reactions to challenges to their authority, honor, and self-esteem are well-known (e.g., Athens 1980; Luckenbill 1977; Toch 1969); comparable behavior by a woman is a curiosity. A variety of convergent evidence supports the conclusion that men (especially young men) are more specialized for and more motivated to engage in dangerous risk-taking, confrontational competition, and interpersonal violence than are women (Daly and Wilson 1990). When comparisons are confined to interactions with members of one's own sex so that size and power asymmetries are largely irrelevant, the differences between men and women in these behavioral domains are universally large (e.g., Daly and Wilson 1990; Goetting 1988; Wilson and Daly 1985, 1991).

We cannot hope to understand violence in marital, cohabiting, and dating relationships without explicit attention to the qualities that make them different from other relationships. It is a cross-culturally and historically ubiquitous aspect of human affairs that women and men form individualized unions, recognized by themselves and by others as conferring certain obligations and entitlements, such that the partners' productive and reproductive careers become intertwined. Family violence research might usefully begin by examining the consonant and discordant desires, expectations, grievances, perceived entitlements, and preoccupations of husbands and wives, and by investigating theoretically derived hypotheses about circumstantial, ecological, contextual, and demographic correlates of such conflict. Having described the conflicts of interest that characterize marital relationships with explicit reference to the distinct agendas of women and men, violence researchers must proceed to an analysis that acknowledges and accounts for those gender differences. It is crucial to establish differences in the patterns of male and female violence, to thoroughly describe and explain the overall process of violent events within their immediate and wider contexts, and to analyze the reasons why conflict results in differentially violent action by women and men.

Notes

The order of authorship was determined by a random process upon the completion of the manuscript. The authors wish to acknowledge the financial support of NATO, the Rockefeller Foundation, the Social Sciences and Humanities Research Council of Canada, the Natural Sciences and Engineering Research Council of Canada, and the Harry Frank Guggenheim Foundation; in addition, we thank several people for facilitating the development of the homicide datafiles, including K. Shaw of the British Home Office in London, F. Hird of the Scottish Home Office in Edinburgh, J. Turner and J. LaCroix of the Centre for Justice Statistics, Statistics Canada, as well as C.R. Block, R. Block, R.L. Drake, R. Gartner, and A. Wallace. This chapter was written while M. Wilson and M. Daly were Fellows of the Center for Advanced Study in the Behavioral Sciences with financial support from the John D. and Catherine T. MacArthur Foundation, the National Science Foundation #BNS87-008, the Harry Frank Guggenheim Foundation, and the Gordon P. Getty Trust, and while M. Daly was a Fellow of the John Simon Guggenheim Foundation.

1. McLeod (1984:191) claims that a higher proportion of the few assaulted husbands than of the numerous assaulted wives were seriously injured. Unfortunately, in much-cited conclusions, she mis-

described this result in terms implying absolute frequencies: "violence against men is much more destructive than is violence against women.... Male victims are injured more often and more seriously than are female victims." See Schwartz (1987) for correction and elaboration of this point.

2. Interviewees participating in a survey of criminal victimization may be unlikely to report incidents of domestic violence as criminal assaults, with resultant underestimation of the prevalence of such assaults. However, we know of no evidence that such underreporting is strongly biased by sex, as the sexual-symmetry-of-violence thesis demands. The limited available evidence suggests that husbands are no more reluctant to report spousal assaults than are wives (Schwartz 1987).

3. Impossible data in the Jouriles and O'Leary (1985) paper include such anomalies as no whole number constitutes 99 percent of a sample of 37 or 79 percent of a sample of 65, and no 2×2 array of husbands' and wives' responses could produce the summary statistics presented for certain items. As an example of Kappa miscalculations, 3 men in the "community sample" of 37 professed to have "thrown something at partner" in the last year, but the two women who professed to have been recipients of such acts were members of other couples (an "occurrence agreement" of 0 percent); Jouriles and O'Leary present a Kappa value of 0 for this case, but the correct value is $-.07$.

References

Arias, Ileana, and P. Johnson
   1989 "Evaluations of physical aggression among intimate dyads." *Journal of Interpersonal Violence* 4:298–307.
Arias, Ileana, Mary Samios, and K. Daniel O'Leary
   1987 "Prevalence and correlates of physical aggression during courtship." *Journal of Interpersonal Violence* 2:82–90.
Athens, Lonnie
   1980 *Violent Criminal Acts and Actors.* New York: Routledge.
Barling, Julian, and Alan Rosenbaum
   1986 "Work stressors and wife abuse." *Journal of Applied Psychology* 71:346–348.
Baron, Larry, and Murray A. Straus
   1988 "Cultural and economic sources of homicide in the United States." *Sociological Quarterly* 29:371–390.
Berk, Richard A., Sarah F. Berk, Donileen R. Loseke, and D. Rauma
   1983 "Mutual combat and other family violence myths." In *The Dark Side of Families*, ed. David Finkelhor, Richard J. Gelles, Gerald T. Hotaling, and Murray A. Straus, 197–212. Beverly Hills, Calif.: Sage.
Block, Carolyn R.
   1991 "Lethal violence in the Chicago Latino community." In *The Dynamics of the Victim-Offender Interaction*, ed. Anna V. Wilson. Cincinnati, Ohio: Anderson.
Bowker, Lee H.
   1983 *Beating Wife Beating.* Lexington, Mass.: Lexington Books.
Breines, Wini, and Linda Gordon
   1983 "Review essay: The new scholarship in family violence." *Signs: Journal of Women in Culture and Society* 8:490–531.
Brinkerhoff, Merlin B., and Eugene Lupri
   1988 "Interspousal violence." *Canadian Journal of Sociology* 13:407–434.
Browne, Angela
   1987 *When Battered Women Kill.* New York: Free Press.
Browning, James, and Donald Dutton
   1986 "Assessment of wife assault with the Conflict Tactics Scale: Using couple data to quantify the differential reporting effect." *Journal of Marriage and the Family* 48:375–379.

Brush, Lisa D.
  1990 "Violent acts and injurious outcomes in married couples: Methodological issues in the National Survey of Families and Households." *Gender and Society* 4:56–67.
Brutz, Judith L., and Bron B. Ingoldsby
  1984 "Conflict resolution in Quaker families." *Journal of Marriage and the Family* 46:21–84.
Byles, Jack A.
  1978 "Family violence: Some facts and gaps. A statistical overview." In *Domestic Violence: Issues and Dynamic*, ed. Vincent D'Oyley, 53–83. Toronto: The Ontario Institute for Studies in Education.
Campbell, Jacqueline C.
  1992 "If I can't have you, no one can: Issues of power and control in homicide of female partners." In *Femicide: The Politics of Woman Killing*, ed. Jill Radford and Diana E. H. Russell. New York: Twayne.
Cate, Rodney M., June M. Henton, James Koval, F. Scott Christopher, and Sally Lloyd
  1982 "Premarital abuse. A social psychological perspective." *Journal of Family Issues* 3:79–90.
Chester, Robert, and Jane Streather
  1972 "Cruelty in English divorce: Some empirical findings." *Journal of Marriage and the Family* 34:706–710.
Counts, Dorothy C., Judith Brown, and Jacqueline C. Campbell, eds.
  1992 *Sanctions and Sanctuary: Cultural Perspectives on the Beating of Wives*. Boulder, Colo.: Westview Press.
Creighton, Susan J.
  1985 "An epidemiological study of abused children and their families in the United Kingdom between 1977 and 1982." *Child Abuse and Neglect* 9:441–448.
Daly, Martin, and Margo Wilson
  1985 "Child abuse and other risks of not living with both parents." *Ethology and Sociobiology* 6:197–210.
  1988a "Evolutionary social psychology and family homicide." *Science* 242:519–524.
  1988b *Homicide*. Hawthorne, N.Y.: Aldine de Gruyter.
  1990 "Killing the competition: Female/female and male/male homicide." *Human Nature* 1:81–107.
Daly, Martin, Margo Wilson, and Suzanne J. Weghorst
  1982 "Male sexual jealousy." *Ethology and Sociobiology* 3:11–27.
DeKeseredy, Walter
  1991 "In defense of self-defense: Demystifying female violence against male intimates." In *Debates in Canadian Society*, ed. Ronald Hinch. Toronto: Nelson Canada.
DeMaris, Alfred
  1987 "The efficacy of a spouse abuse model in accounting for courtship violence." *Journal of Family Issues* 8:291–305.
deSousa, Ronald
  1987 *The Rationality of Emotions*. Cambridge, Mass.: Massachusetts Institute of Technology.
Dobash, R. Emerson, and Russell P. Dobash
  1977/1978 "Wives: The 'appropriate' victims of marital violence." *Victimology* 2:426–442.
  1979 *Violence against Wives: A Case against the Patriarchy*. New York: Free Press.
  1981b "Social science and social action: The case of wife beating." *Journal of Family Issues* 2:439–470.
  1984 "The nature and antecedents of violent events." *British Journal of Criminology* 24:269–288.
  1992 *Women, Violence and Social Change*. London: Routledge.
Dobash, Russell P., and R. Emerson Dobash
  1981a "Community response to violence against wives: Charivari, abstract justice and patriarchy." *Social Problems* 28:563–581.
  1983 "The context-specific approach." In *The Dark Side of Families*, ed. David Finkelhor, Richard J. Gelles, Gerald T. Hotaling, and Murray A. Straus, 261–276. Beverly Hills, Calif.: Sage.

1990 "How research makes a difference to policy and practice." In *Family Violence: Research and Public Policy Issues*, ed. Douglas J. Besharov, 185–204. Washington, D.C.: AEI Press.

Dobash, R. Emerson, Russell P. Dobash, and Katherine Cavanagh
  1985 "The contact between battered women and social and medical agencies." In *Private Violence and Public Policy*, ed. Jan Pahl, 142–165. London: Routledge.

Dobash, Rebecca, Russell P. Dobash, Cathy Cavanagh, and Monica Wilson
  1977/1978 "Wife beating: The victims speak." *Victimology* 2:608–622.

Eisikovits, Zvi, and Einat Peled
  1990 "Qualitative research on spouse abuse." In *Family Violence: Research and Public Policy Issues*, ed. Douglas J. Besharov, 1–12. Washington, D.C.: AEI Press.

Ellis, Desmond
  1989 "Male abuse of a married or cohabiting female partner: The application of sociological theory to research findings." *Violence and Victims* 4:235–255.

Farrell, Warren
  1986 *Why Men Are the Way They Are: The Male–Female Dynamic.* New York: McGraw-Hill.

Fergusson, David M., Joan Fleming, and David P. O'Neill
  1972 *Child Abuse in New Zealand.* Wellington: Government of New Zealand Printer.

Fergusson, David M., L. John Horwood, Kathryn L. Kershaw, and Frederick T. Shannon
  1986 "Factors associated with reports of wife assault in New Zealand." *Journal of Marriage and the Family* 48:407–412.

Ferraro, Kathleen J., and John M. Johnson
  1983 "How women experience battering: The process of victimization." *Social Problems* 30:325–338.

Frank, Robert J.
  1988 *Passions within Reason: The Strategic Role of the Emotions.* New York: Norton.

Frieze, Irene H., and Angela Browne
  1989 "Violence in marriage." In *Family Violence*, ed. Lloyd Ohlin and Michael Tonry, 163–218. Chicago: University of Chicago Press.

Gaquin, Deirdre A.
  1977/1978 "Spouse abuse: Data from the National Crime Survey." *Victimology* 2:632–643.

Gelles, Richard J.
  1982 "Domestic criminal violence." In *Criminal Violence*, ed. Marvin E. Wolfgang and Neil A. Weiner, 201–235. Beverly Hills, Calif.: Sage.

Gelles, Richard J., and John W. Harrop
  1991 "The risk of abusive violence among children with nongenetic caretakers." *Family Relations* 40:78–83.

Goetting, Ann
  1988 "When females kill one another." *Criminal Justice and Behavior* 15:179–189.
  1989 "Patterns of marital homicide: A comparison of husbands and wives." *Journal of Comparative Family Studies* 20:341–354.

Goldberg, Wendy G., and Michael C. Tomlanovich
  1984 "Domestic violence victims in the Emergency Department: New findings." *Journal of the American Medical Association* 251:3259–3264.

Gordon, Linda
  1988 *Heroes of Their Own Lives. The Politics and History of Family Violence. Boston 1880–1960.* New York: Viking.

Hotaling, Gerald T., Murray A. Straus, and Alan J. Lincoln
  1990 "Intrafamily violence and crime and violence outside the family." In *Physical Violence in American Families*, ed. Murray A. Straus and Richard J. Gelles, 431–470. New Brunswick, N.J.: Transaction Publishers.

Johnson, Holly
  1989 "Wife assault in Canada." Paper presented at the Annual Meeting of the American Society of Criminology, November, Reno, Nevada.

Jones, Ann
　1980　*Women Who Kill*. New York: Holt, Rinehart and Winston.
Jouriles, Ernest N., and K. Daniel O'Leary
　1985　"Interspousal reliability of reports of marital violence." *Journal of Consulting and Clinical Psychology* 53:419–421.
Kantor, Glenda K., and Murray A. Straus
　1990　"Response of victims and the police to assaults on wives." In *Physical Violence in American Families*, ed. Murray A. Straus and Richard J. Gelles, 473–487. New Brunswick N.J.: Transaction Publishers.
Kennedy, Leslie W., and Donald G. Dutton
　1989　"The incidence of wife assault in Alberta." *Canadian Journal of Behavioral Science* 21:40–54.
Kincaid, Pat J.
　1982　*The Omitted Reality: Husband-Wife Violence in Ontario and Policy Implications for Education*. Maple, Ontario: Learners Press.
Kurz, Demie
　1989　"Social science perspectives on wife abuse: Current debates and future directions." *Gender and Society* 3:489–505.
Lane, Katherine E., and Patricia A. Gwartney-Gibbs
　1985　"Violence in the context of dating and sex." *Journal of Family Issues* 6:45–59.
Laner, Mary R., and Jeanine Thompson
　1982　"Abuse and aggression in courting couples." *Deviant Behavior* 3:229–244.
Langan, Patrick A., and Christopher A. Innes
　1986　*Preventing Domestic Violence against Women*. Washington, D.C.: U.S. Department of Justice.
Levinger, George
　1966　"Sources of marital dissatisfaction among applicants for divorce." *American Journal of Orthopsychiatry* 36:803–806.
Lockhart, Lettie L.
　1987　"A reexamination of the effects of race and social class on the incidence of marital violence: A search for reliable differences." *Journal of Marriage and the Family* 49:603–610.
Luckenbill, David F.
　1977　"Criminal homicide as a situated transaction." *Social Problems* 25:176–186.
Lundsgaarde, Henry P.
　1977　*Murder in Space City*. New York: Oxford University Press.
Lystad, Mary H.
　1975　"Violence at home: A review of literature." *American Journal of Orthopsychiatry* 45:328–345.
Makepeace, James M.
　1986　"Gender differences in courtship violence victimization." *Family Relations* 35:383–388.
Margolin, Gayla
　1987　"The multiple forms of aggressiveness between marital partners: How do we identify them?" *Journal of Marital and Family Therapy* 13:77–84.
Marshall, Linda L., and Patricia Rose
　1990　"Premarital violence: The impact of family of origin violence, stress, and reciprocity." *Violence and Victims* 5:51–64.
Martin, Del
　1976　*Battered Wives*. San Francisco, Calif.: Glide Publications.
Mason, Avonne, and Virginia Blankenship
　1987　"Power and affiliation motivation, stress, and abuse in intimate relationships." *Personality and Social Psychology* 52:203–210.
Maxfield, Michael G.
　1989　"Circumstances in Supplementary Homicide Reports: Variety and validity." *Criminology* 27:671–695.

McLeer, Susan R., and R. Anwar
  1989 "A study of battered women presenting in an emergency department." *American Journal of Public Health* 79:65–66.
McLeod, Maureen
  1984 "Women against men: An examination of domestic violence based on an analysis of official data and national victimization data." *Justice Quarterly* 1:171–193.
McNeely, R. L., and CoraMae Richey Mann
  1990 "Domestic violence is a human issue." *Journal of Interpersonal Violence* 5:129–132.
McNeely, R. L., and Gloria Robinson-Simpson
  1987 "The truth about domestic violence: A falsely framed issue." *Social Work* 32:485–490.
Mercy, James A., and Linda E. Saltzman
  1989 "Fatal violence among spouses in the United States, 1976–1985." *American Journal of Public Health* 79:595–599.
Meredith, William H., Douglas A. Abbott, and Scot L. Adams
  1986 "Family violence: Its relation to marital and parental satisfaction and family strengths." *Journal of Family Violence* 1:299–305.
Nisonoff, Linda, and Irving Bitman
  1979 "Spouse abuse: Incidence and relationship to selected demographic variables." *Victimology* 4:131–140.
O'Brien, John E.
  1971 "Violence in divorce-prone families." *Journal of Marriage and the Family* 33:692–698.
Okun, Lewis
  1986 *Woman Abuse: Facts Replacing Myths*. Albany, N.Y.: SUNY Press.
Pagelow, Mildred D.
  1984 *Family Violence*. New York: Praeger.
  1985 "The 'battered husband syndrome': Social problem or much ado about little?" In *Marital Violence*. Sociological Review Monograph, Vol. 3, ed. Norman Johnson, 172–195. London: Routledge.
Pahl, Jan
  1985 *Private Violence and Public Policy: The Needs of Battered Women and the Response of the Public Services*. London: Routledge.
Pleck, Elizabeth
  1987 *Domestic Tyranny. The Making of Social Policy against Family Violence from Colonial Times to the Present*. New York: Oxford University Press.
  1989 "Criminal approaches to family violence, 1640–1980." In *Family Violence*, ed. Lloyd Ohlin and Michael Tonry, 19–57. Chicago: University of Chicago Press.
Pleck, Elizabeth, Joseph H. Pleck, Marlyn Grossman, and Pauline B. Bart
  1977/1978 "The battered data syndrome: A comment on Steinmetz' article." *Victimology* 2:680–683.
Polk, Kenneth, and David Ranson
  1991 "The role of gender in intimate violence." *Australia and New Zealand Journal of Criminology* 24:15–24.
Quarm, Daisy, and Martin D. Schwartz
  1985 "Domestic violence in criminal court." In *Criminal Justice Politics and Women: The Aftermath of Legally Mandated Change*, ed. C. Schweber and C. Feinman, 29–46. New York: Haworth.
Rouse, Linda P., Richard Breen, and Marilyn Howell
  1988 "Abuse in intimate relationships. A comparison of married and dating college students." *Journal of Interpersonal Violence* 3:414–429.
Russell, Diana E. H.
  1982 *Rape in Marriage*. New York: Macmillan.
Sacco, Vincent F., and Holly Johnson
  1990 *Patterns of Criminal Victimization in Canada*. Ottawa: Statistics Canada.

Saunders, Daniel G.
  1986 "When battered women use violence: Husband-abuse or self-defense?" *Violence and Victims* 1:47–60.
  1988 "Wife abuse, husband abuse, or mutual combat?" In *Feminist Perspectives on Wife Abuse*, ed. Kersti Yllo and Michele Bograd, 90–113. Newbury Park, Calif.: Sage.
Schwartz, Martin D.
  1987 "Gender and injury in spousal assault." *Sociological Focus* 20:61–75.
Shupe, Anson, William A. Stacey, and Lonnie R. Hazelwood
  1987 *Violent Men, Violent Couples: The Dynamics of Domestic Violence.* Lexington Mass.: Lexington Books.
Sigelman Carol K., Carol J. Berry, and Katharine A. Wiles
  1984 "Violence in college students' dating relationships." *Journal of Applied Social Psychology* 14:530–548.
Smith, Lorna J. F.
  1989 *Domestic Violence: An Overview of the Literature.* Home Office Research Study No. 107. London: HMSO.
Smith, Michael D.
  1990 "Sociodemographic risk factors in wife abuse: Results from a survey of Toronto women." *Canadian Journal of Sociology* 15:39–58.
Solicitor General of Canada
  1985 *Female Victims of Crime.* Canadian Urban Victimization Survey Bulletin No. 4. Ottawa: Programs Branch/Research and Statistics Group.
Stark, Evan, and Anne Flitcraft
  1983 "Social knowledge, social policy, and the abuse of women. The case against patriarchal benevolence." In *The Dark Side of Families*, ed. David Finkelhor, Richard J. Gelles, Gerald T. Hotaling, and Murray A. Straus, 330–348. Beverly Hills, Calif.: Sage.
Stark, Evan, Anne Flitcraft, and W. Frazier
  1979 "Medicine and patriarchal violence: The social construction of a 'private' event." *Internal Journal of Health Services* 9:461–493.
Statistics Canada
  1990 "Conjugal violence against women." *Juristat* 10 (7):1–7.
Steinmetz, Suzanne K.
  1977/1978 "The battered husband syndrome." *Victimology* 2:499–509.
  1981 "A cross-cultural comparison of marital abuse." *Journal of Sociology and Social Welfare* 8:404–414.
  1986 "Family violence. Past, present, and future." In *Handbook of Marriage and the Family*, ed. Marvin B. Sussman and Suzanne K. Steinmetz, 725–765. New York: Plenum.
Steinmetz, Suzanne K., and Joseph S. Lucca
  1988 "Husband battering." In *Handbook of Family Violence*, ed. Vincent B. Van Hasselt, R. L. Morrison, A. S. Bellack, and M. Hersen, 233–246. New York: Plenum Press.
Stets, Jan E.
  1990 "Verbal and physical aggression in marriage." *Journal of Marriage and the Family* 52:501–514.
Stets, Jan E., and Murray A. Straus
  1990 "Gender differences in reporting marital violence and its medical and psychological consequences." In *Physical Violence in American Families*, ed. Murray A. Straus and Richard J. Gelles, 151–165. New Brunswick, N.J.: Transaction Publishers.
Straus, Murray A.
  1977/1978 "Wife-beating: How common, and why?" *Victimology* 2:443–458.
  1979 "Measuring intrafamily conflict and violence: The Conflict Tactics (CT) Scales." *Journal of Marriage and the Family* 51:75–88.
  1980 "The marriage license as a hitting license: Evidence from popular culture, law, and social science." In *The Social Causes of Husband-Wife Violence*, ed. Murray A. Straus and Gerald T. Hotaling, 39–50. Minneapolis, Minn.: University of Minnesota Press.

1990a "Measuring intrafamily conflict and violence: The Conflict Tactics (CT) Scales." In *Physical Violence in American Families*, ed. Murray A. Straus and Richard J. Gelles, 29–47. New Brunswick, N.J.: Transaction Publishers.

1990b "The Conflict Tactics Scales and its critics: An evaluation and new data on validity and reliability." In *Physical Violence in American Families*, ed. Murray A. Straus and Richard J. Gelles, 49–73. New Brunswick, N.J.: Transaction Publishers.

Straus, Murray A., and Richard J. Gelles, eds.
1990a *Physical Violence in American Families*. New Brunswick, N.J.: Transaction Publishers.

Straus, Murray A., and Richard J. Gelles
1986 "Societal change and change in family violence from 1975 to 1985 as revealed by two national surveys." *Journal of Marriage and the Family* 48:465–480.
1987 "The costs of family violence." *Public Health Reports* 102:638–641.
1990b "How violent are American families? Estimates from the National Family Violence Resurvey and other studies." In *Physical Violence in American Families*, ed. Murray A. Straus and Richard J. Gelles, 95–112. New Brunswick, N.J.: Transaction Publishers.

Straus, Murray A., Richard J. Gelles, and Suzanne K. Steinmetz
1980 *Behind Closed Doors: Violence in the American Family*. New York: Doubleday/Anchor.

Szinovacz, Maximiliane E.
1983 "Using couple data as a methodological tool: The case of marital violence." *Journal of Marriage and the Family* 45:633–644.

Toch, Hans
1969 *Violent Men: An Inquiry into the Psychology of Violence*. Chicago: Aldine.

Vanfossen, B. E.
1979 "Intersexual violence in Monroe County, New York." *Victimology* 4:299–305.

Walker, Lenore E.
1984 *The Battered Woman Syndrome*. New York: Springer.

Wallace, Alison
1986 *Homicide: The Social Reality*. Sydney: New South Wales Bureau of Crime Statistics and Research.

Warshaw, Carole
1989 "Limitations of the medical model in the care of battered women." *Gender and Society* 3:506–517.

Watkins, Carol R.
1982 *Victims, Aggressors and the Family Secret: An Exploration into Family Violence*. St. Paul, Minn.: Minnesota Department of Public Welfare.

Wilbanks, William
1983 "The female homicide offender in Dade County, Florida." *Criminal Justice Review* 8:9–14.

Wilson, Margo
1989 "Marital conflict and homicide in evolutionary perspective." In *Sociobiology and the Social Sciences*, ed. Robert W. Bell and Nancy J. Bell, 45–62. Lubbock, Tex.: Texas Tech University Press.

Wilson, Margo, and Martin Daly
1985 "Competitiveness, risk taking, and violence: The young male syndrome." *Ethology and Sociobiology* 6:59–73.
1987 "Risk of maltreatment of children living with step-parents." In *Child Abuse and Neglect: Biosocial Dimensions*, ed. Richard J. Gelles and Jane B. Lancaster, 215–232. New York: Aldine de Gruyter.
1991 "Lethal confrontational violence among young men." In *Adolescent and Adult Risk-Taking*, ed. Nancy J. Bell and Robert W. Bell, 87–110. Lubbock, Tex.: Texas Tech University Press.
1992a "'Til death us do part." In *Femicide: The Politics of Woman Killing*, ed. Jill Radford and Diana E. H. Russell. New York: Twayne.
1992b "The man who mistook his wife for a chattel." In *The Adapted Mind: Evolutionary Psychology and the Generation of Culture*, ed. Jerome Barkow, Leda Cosmides, and John Tooby, 243–276. New York: Oxford University Press.

1992c "Who kills whom in spouse-killings? On the exceptional sex ratio of spousal homicides coming in the United States." *Criminology* 30:189–215.

Wilson, Margo, Martin Daly, and Suzanne J. Weghorst

1980 "Household composition and the risk of child abuse and neglect." *Journal of Biosocial Science* 12:333–340.

Wolfgang, Marvin E.

1958 *Patterns in Criminal Homicide*. Philadelphia: University of Pennsylvania Press.

Worrall, A., and Ken Pease

1986 "Personal crime against women: Evidence from the 1982 British Crime Survey." *The Howard Journal* 25:118–124.

Yllo, Kersti, and Murray A. Straus

1981 "Interpersonal violence among married and cohabiting couples." *Family Relations* 30:339–347.

CHAPTER 3

Safe Conduct

WOMEN, CRIME, AND SELF IN PUBLIC PLACES

Carol Brooks Gardner

> Being born a woman is my awful tragedy. . . . Yes, my consuming desire to mingle with road crews, sailors and soldiers, barroom regulars—to be part of a scene, anonymous, listening, recording—all is spoiled by the fact that I am a girl, a female always in danger of assault and battery. My consuming interest in men and their lives is often misconstructed as a desire to seduce them, or as an invitation to intimacy. Yes, God, I want to talk to everybody I can as deeply as I can. I want to be able to sleep in an open field, to travel west, to walk freely at night.
>
> Sylvia Plath, *The Journals of Sylvia Plath, 1950–1962*,
> written at the age of nineteen

Women have different experiences in public places than do men, particularly when they appear alone. Belying the U.S. middle-class ideal of an egalitarian etiquette for public places (Goffman 1963, 1971), analysis of actual conduct shows that public places are dotted with contacts that evince judgments of status and discrimination no less finely tuned and expressive than those evinced in private regions (Gardner 1980, 1983, 1988). Although many social categories receive treatment in public places demonstrably different from the expected norms of middle-class etiquette (people with disabilities, children, gay people, and ethnic minorities are among these), the situation of women in public is striking. Women may have made considerable progress in occupation, education, and home life; yet in public places they are regularly subject to inferior treatment by men in the form, for instance, of catcalls, evaluative "compliments," and verbal contacts that subtly go astray when gender, not the business at hand, becomes a topic (Gardner 1980, 1983, 1988, 1989).

Besides these routine ways that women can experience public places differently from men, there is the more dramatic case of crime in public. Researchers remark that, though men experience crime in higher numbers, women report greater fear of crime (Balkin 1979; Brown, Flanagan, and McLeod 1984; Clemente and Kleiman 1977; Dubow 1979; Riger and Gordon 1981). The place of gender-role expectations in this difference is crucial (Hindelang, Gottfredson, and Garofalo 1978; Janoff-Bulman and

Frieze 1987; Maxfield 1984). In public, fear of rape is a cardinal fear for women (Riger and Gordon 1981), since public places are the sites for most stranger rape (Ledray 1986). Women are never sure which of a man's activities are precursors to rape or other crime, and commonly class together any public harassment with public harassment preceding rape or other crimes (Grahame 1985; Kelly 1987). Popular advice and folk wisdom also can influence women's conduct in public, the way they are perceived, or the way they perceive themselves (Heath 1984; Brunvand 1981; Wachs 1988). Women's alleged responsibility for their own victimization has led them to define part of their task as "becoming streetwise," "taking necessary precautions," and "preventing crime" (S. Edwards 1987; Radford 1987).[1]

In this chapter, I discuss the character of advice to women with regard to crime prevention in public and the character of women's beliefs about crime-preventive behavior. My goal is conjecture about women's situation. In addition to my own experience, I use two types of empirical materials to illustrate this chapter: first, a review of the popular literature about crime prevention for women written in the last 20 years; and second, a set of 25 in-depth interviews with women about crime in public. I argue that the nature of both advice and experience is importantly related to possibilities for communication in public places in U.S. culture generally. For women, both advice and experience combine to affect the particular incarnation of the self appropriate to the situation of being in public places—a socially situated self, as Goffman defines it (1963:112).

This situated self appropriate to public places is supported, in addition to other elements, by various sets of strategies of presentation and impression management that may be thought of as rhetorics (Ball 1967). A rhetoric, sociologically speaking, is a "vocabulary of limited purpose," whose set of symbols communicates a particular set of meanings directed and arranged to present a specific impression. These vocabularies are visual and verbal, and they may appeal to other senses as well (Ball 1967:296). Such a rhetoric serves to legitimize and neutralize what otherwise might be seen as deviant (Ball 1967). In particular, women who wish to prevent crime in public are encouraged to take up a typical rhetoric that imputes limited competence. Correspondingly, the situated self they are encouraged to present is characterized by this rhetoric, which connotes ineptness rather than skill, apprehension rather than ability, a self debased rather than revered. My goal is not to judge the advice literature or my informants' activities as wise or unwise, but to contemplate the type of self that they can foster in women and suggest how the activities of that self can be played out given the general character of public places.

I begin by discussing the empirical materials I use here, then specify some pertinent general features of communication in public places, features I later suggest are at variance with the advice rhetoric aimed at helping prevent crime. Next, I discuss three elements of the rhetoric of limited competence offered to crime-conscious women in public. Finally, I describe how rhetorical strategies contribute to the situated selves women and men present in public and help to sustain the informal social control of public places.

Empirical Materials

The empirical materials I use to illustrate this chapter come from two sources: a survey of popular literature directed toward women about crime prevention, and interviews with 25 women residents of Santa Fe, New Mexico, in 1987.

I read all articles listed in *Reader's Guide to Periodical Literature* for the period 1970–1989 involving self-defense, crime prevention, women and crime, and women and rape and assault. Under similar headings and titles, I also read all books listed in *Books in Print* for the period 1965–1989, extending the period to gain more authors and perspectives.

This literature, perhaps partly the congealing of a folklore already in place, itself reveals gender stereotypes even in its broad dimensions. For example, there continue to be many books and articles directed to women in the name of street crime prevention. There is no complementary male-directed literature: when crime-prevention books for men are written, they are on self-defense skills. Some advice books for women are simply directed to the men who, it is assumed, will be their teachers (Tegner, 1965:201–16).

Though there is also a general, non-gender-specific literature on crime prevention and self-defense, the subset of literature directed at women stands apart in the extremity of measures advised. The asymmetry may be sound: perhaps any street harassment is more traumatic for women, who express more fear of crime in the first place; there is certainly no equal for men of women's generalized fear of rape.

Of course, I can claim no causal relationship here between these particular articles and the feelings and actions of informants with whom I spoke. Instead, I use the literature as a body of normative beliefs about women, crime, and conduct in public places. It represents what is available for, not necessarily what is taken up by, women in the culture. It is a remarkably consistent body of beliefs at that. It is also one that, in general, my informants said they knew.

The women I interviewed were from Santa Fe, New Mexico, a small but cosmopolitan city of some 52,000 residents. The interviewees were all middle-class. I interviewed these 25 women as part of a larger project studying gender behavior in public places that involved, ultimately, interviews with nearly 100 women. I approached these 25 informants in various public places in the city, often as a tag-end to a casual conversation, greeting, or service encounter, and asked them if they would be willing to be interviewed. No woman refused, but the resulting pool is, of course, a convenience sample rather than one systematically representative of the women of the city, much less of U.S. women as a whole. Had I used a sample of poor minority women living in high-crime areas, for example, I would probably have culled a more explicit shared set of folk wisdom in response to sure, not likely, crimes, and a more extreme set of responses in terms of weaponry. Certainly, too, such a sample would have had more direct experience as crime victims. They might also have expressed a set of strategies for dealing with crime similar to those of their male counterparts.

The interviews were free form and in depth, concentrating on public places as possible sites for crime. I asked informants about their perceptions of crime in public places in the city; their experience with crime, with near-crime, and with events they did not think of as crime but were nevertheless distasteful. I asked about their understandings of what to do in case of street crime and whether they ever had put these beliefs into practice. I also asked about their sources of information.

Interviews lasted from one to 3½ hours; the average interview was about two hours. Twenty of the 25 women had Anglo surnames, and five had Hispanic surnames. For the most part, these were young women: 16 were between 20 and 35, seven were between 36 and 45; only two were over 60. Twelve were married or living with a man. Six had had formal self-defense training, either in a women's self-defense class or through classes in martial arts; two others had attempted to train themselves in self-defense through books or videos; all but one identified themselves as purposive readers of literature on women and self-defense in, for example, newspapers and women's magazines. Three women identified themselves as victims of crime: one was a rape survivor; two others had experienced home robberies.

The Self and Communication in Public Places

As an arena for face-to-face interaction, communication between strangers in public places exhibits some general characteristics that are distinct from communication between acquaintances in public and from much communication in private places. This constellation of characteristics shapes possibilities for interaction that do and can occur, not only for women interested in preventing crime but for all other citizens as well.

In what follows, I briefly sketch the communication characteristics most relevant to the situation of the woman and crime prevention in public places. This communication influences what Goffman has spoken of as the situated self appropriate to public places. With *situated self*, Goffman implies a self as something constituted according to the social situation of the moment, rather than as any stable, trans-situational possession. A self is, in effect, loaned to its putative owner and defined in part by the social control requirements of particular situations (Goffman 1961:149–52). In problematic social situations, the relevant self develops strategies for coping that can be expressed as rhetorics. Yet these rhetorics will be modified by the nature of communication possible or thought proper to social situations. Thus, any rhetoric involving crime prevention will be modified by the character of communication possible and thought proper in a particular setting.

COMMUNICATION CHARACTERISTICS

Communicative acts between individuals in public are heavily *appearance dependent*. That is, they rely on appraisal of the physical look, manner, nonverbal communication, and dress of the other—what Goffman has referred to as an appreciation of "body idiom" (Goffman 1963:33–34): It is understood that, all other things being equal, the citizen will attempt to give the best possible appearance in public.[2] Public places function as front regions (Goffman 1973:107–23), where performances are expected to be cut and polished, where impressions of proper decorum are expressed by adhering to more formal standards of dress, permissible sound levels, and prescribed activities and attitudes. In this way, an etiquette manual will tell a woman that the way she looks in public signifies "the way she wants to be seen by the world" (Geng 1971:76–77), and all citizens will be advised to restrict conspicuous activities such as kissing and smoking (Vanderbilt 1972:246–47, 316–18).

With only appearance to rely on, however, inescapable stereotyping results, as, for example, when a Korean American in a black neighborhood is the object of catcalls that recapitulate stereotypes of Asian Americans (Navarro 1990), or a black who enters a Korean-American business experiences behavior reflecting stereotypes of blacks (Sims 1990). Or a citizen sometimes feels strangers fix reliably on blatant symbols of a status peripheral to the "real" self, as when a woman using an electric wheelchair says strangers bypass usual greetings to offer remarks on her chair (Gardner 1990).

Clearly, appearance dependence favors those whose appearance connotes statuses held in high regard; with regard to crime, it favors those taken stereotypically to be no easy victims or who can manipulate appearance to suggest strength or imperviousness to assault. Using traditional stereotypes, women will be seen by strangers as less capable of retaliation than men. As aspiring criminals will have to depend on judgments of appearance to select prospective victims, so those who seek to escape victimization must depend on assessment of strangers' appearance and manipulation of their own in order to avoid crime. One way to cope with crime in public therefore will be to develop an array of behavioral strategies that are also appearance dependent; alternatively, people will curtail others' visual access in order to prevent being judged a suitable target. The latter tack is taken in a small way by donning sunglasses that foil, among other things, a criminal judging one fearful and therefore an easy mark; similarly, a car may be used as a visual shell to both stymie appraisal of one's vulnerability and provide a physical baffle to intrusion.

Implicitly, then, in public the visual channel is preferred as an avenue of communication. A corollary of this appearance dependence is that silence is normative and speech between strangers is routinized and brief, and, aside from certain heavily scripted greetings or comments on the weather, is to be stimulated only by unusual circumstances. If talk is limited, routine, and warranted, then the citizen who fears crime will have no ordinary way to ascertain who is, and who is not, a potential foe—nor will seeming and actual foes have clear ways in which to make their identities less ambiguous.

Communication in public between strangers is also typically *transitory*; i.e., it is relatively fleeting compared to communication between acquaintances or communication in private places. It is also typically *episodic*: Face-to-face communication between strangers is interspersed with vacuum periods where contact is neither made nor attempted. Both these characteristics influence those fleeting contacts that are made, which therefore appear in relief and can become highly charged with meaning. Such brief, disjointed events will be all the person interested in preventing crime will have to judge the situation by; similarly they will be all the aspiring criminal will have to select a suitable target. Transitory and episodic communication can also favor purposeful strategies that cannot be sustained for long, as when a crime-fearing woman manages momentarily to adopt a no-nonsense expression.

Communication in public places also involves what Goffman (1963:20–21) refers to as *multiple social realities*. This phrase reflects the capacity of this one larger setting to host other, overlapping behavior settings—that is, a variety of individuals with highly differentiated motives, needs, wants, and agendas, as well as individuals from a great variety of social categories. Therefore, it is impossible to predict whether or not the given flow on a city street is likely to include someone with criminal intent. If one espouses a crime-preventive attitude or engages in crime-preventive strategies, it is hard to predict when this attitude or these strategies should be curtailed or suspended. At the same time, one's contact with even an innocuous-seeming stranger is necessarily history-less, so that suspicion can bleed onto even those one has no reason to fear.

BELIEFS ABOUT PUBLIC PLACES

Coupled with these characteristics of communication in public places are certain normative ideas about what everyday life in public places is or should be like. First, much face-to-face communication between strangers is felt to be *insignificant*. In general, public places are transitways to other regions, not loci of interest in themselves; laws against loitering, lolling, and vagrancy exist in part to insure that public places remain waystations, not goals. Our feeling that events in public places are insignificant coexists with an obligation to present an appearance typically more formal than can be presented in the "relaxed" settings of private places. Second, these communications are believed to be *egalitarian* in character, expressive of the effective ceasefire that exists between strangers even of varying classes, racial groups, and genders. Much of our etiquette of public places is based on this second notion. It argues that we suspend personal interests, tastes, and involvements in order to effect a courtesy and openness owed to all (Benton 1956:15, 96–114; Martin 1982:99–100, 250–52, 280–81; Post 1969:91–96).

Likewise, we feel that public places are not—nor, rightly, should they be—owned by any single group, and that, aside from certain strongly territorial neighborhoods, no one individual or group has rights of control over strangers; these feelings mean that we are all, in a sense, trespassers when in public. However, they also mean that the personal space of ill-meaning others will abut our own, and that we have as little apparent right to prepare a defense as they have to prepare an offense.[3] Because of these general yet seldom explicated beliefs, we may have vague dissatisfaction with canons of advice that involve extensive manipulation of events or appearances in public places— as crime prevention advice can seem to do.

We can also come to feel that individuals who attribute deep meaning to the small interchanges of face-to-face communication there make too much of what is, after all, trifling.[4] At the same time, these general features of communication in public places and our general feelings about the nature of public places importantly color the informal social control that is exerted there, making it necessarily random, brief, and directed to all—as impersonal, in fact, as public courtesy and goodwill are expected to be.

These same characteristics of and our feelings about communication in public places color the strategies that can be and are advised to those who would avoid crime. I will suggest that any crime-preventive rhetoric, however, will be somewhat at odds with other constituents of the general situated self we believe is appropriate to public places.

Safety, Public Places, and the Rhetoric of Limited Competence

Prescriptions to women in public places as to how to achieve safety are framed in terms of a rhetoric of limited competence, that is, a series of presentational strategies that project dependency and lack of skill. Further, this rhetoric of limited competence is by nature ambiguous (Zimmerman 1981:52): at the same time that it intends to communicate women's ability to deal with urban crime, it also communicates dependency and lack of skill.

The strategies that make up this rhetoric, part of the wisdom of the young urban woman in particular, about prudent behavior when on streets and even near home often ostensibly offer women ways to avoid harm. Yet they also advise women to adopt behavior that results in a profaned self, that is, a self that has unworthy qualities. This is much at odds with the understanding that one's public appearance should be one's best appearance. Thus, the situated self appropriate to public places when a woman believes she is "preventing crime" can come to seem to her ridiculous, and the presentation process can seem impractical as well.

THE APPARENT ESCORT

One key precaution for public behavior counsels the woman alone in public simply not to be alone or, at least, not to seem alone. There are several levels at and degrees to which this injunction can be observed, ranging from what is thought of as simple prudence (such as reluctance or refusal to go out at night unless accompanied), to common customs of deception (such as wearing a wedding ring when one is unmarried to ward off unwanted men), to more wide-ranging methods (such as pretending one has a roommate to confer safety when one does not). I discuss how first the advice literature, then my informants, explained these strategies.

The advice literature often recommends engineering an escort by, for instance, having "a male fellow employee escort you to your car and see you safely started—you might even drive him back to the office" (Barthol 1979:102), or even managing to be near a male by, for example, standing near the occupied ticket or toll booth in a subway station or near a police officer (Field 1980:112); walking close to a group of people walking, if they look safe and are not all males (Barthol 1979:99); never being embarrassed to ask a friend to accompany one home (Wegman 1978:57). Formal "ride switchboards" and "escort services" for women alone at night achieve the same goals (Rockwood and Thom 1979:82).

The women I interviewed often said they should effect a male escort, since attackers will presumably shy away from this strengthened front. This strategy is one that even non-crime conscious women say they choose for the ease it confers when in public. Women sometimes engineer accompaniment, even planning in advance. A lawyer in her fifties said she kept up a friendship with a neighbor woman of whom she was not too fond in order to have someone "to go to the movies with, to have a drink with, or just to keep me company when I take out the garbage." A grade school teacher in her thirties who lived alone with her two small children once had been followed home, robbed, and nearly raped. She had a well-worked-out network of female and male acquaintances—one who could be counted on to take in a play with her, another who walked her to the store, a third whose car was at her beck and call—that she reciprocally "paid back"—though not in kind—by pet-sitting or baking cakes or breads. A graduate student in her twenties who lived with a boyfriend, with a less well-organized network of escorts, commented that at some times she felt these were "unfortunately instrumental friendships," but appreciated also that she had little choice.

If a woman were to undertake some measures of impression management the advice literature recommends, she would appear to be self-plus-companion, or woman near a person who could be enlisted as companion if need be. The woman who stands near a convenient police officer seems to be protected, yet is not truly accompanied, of course; she mimics co-presence. In yet other cases, however, the crime-advice literature suggests a woman imply a companion, i.e., give the impression of being accompanied (and presumably protected) by displaying, not a man who is or seems a companion, but evidence of a man, for example, by telling a woman to place a man's hat or pipe on the seat of her parked car to indicate she "might be accompanied on her return" (Berman 1980:247).

A few women said they employed some of these strategies, though they also expressed some discomfort or awkwardness at discussing them. A married college professor in her thirties, whose three grown sons provide her with useful artifacts for these misleading signals of male co-presence or availability, referred to them laughingly as "male spoor." She added that she felt odd at using them. A homemaker in her fifties related that, having read such a recommendation, she borrowed her brother's spare hat and gloves; she was surprised to discover that they allayed her fears, and she found herself anxious when they were accidentally moved from her car during cleaning: she had converted the items of clothing into talismans of safety. She was now embarrassed at her emotional investment in them. Other informants used a variety of expressions—"weird," "odd," "funny," "dishonest," and the like—to describe discomfort with these practices.

Women sometimes effectively create a companion male by enacting the role themselves. These strategies, by the way, are not a part of the advice literature. Interestingly, these women spoke of the measures, not as uncomfortably unusual, but as practically utilitarian. Though it might formally express a less competent or independent self, then, the rhetoric that women use need not always be experienced as such. In effect, a woman who enacted the role of a protector becomes self and companion, emphasizing that, as her "real" female self, she is powerless when in public. In this spirit, some five informants said they wore slacks, especially dark slacks or jeans, flat shoes, and jacket or coat styles they felt were homologous with men's styles.

Women's primary rationale was not explicitly to "sham" male gender but to wear clothes that were "practical" for purposes of escaping notice, evading criminals, or practicing self-defense. One said that her purpose was not so much to seem male as not to seem female. A single mother in her thirties who often worked late as a hotel clerk said she always effected this style of dress, and cited its effect in public as a selling point: she "dressed like a man" and felt strangers were more likely to respect her if they felt it possible that she was a man. An art gallery owner in her thirties added that she tied her long hair at the nape of her neck in order to look less "feminine." A 24-year-old secretary who lived with her boyfriend and their toddler effectively withdrew signs of female gender rather than substituting male: she tried to leave no trace in her car "that it's a woman's car—no women's magazines, no clothes, none of my baby's toys or clothes." When using these strategies, informants did not express discomfort, perhaps because they were direct actions rather than deceptive use of symbols or attachment to them.

There are more traditional practices that indicate that a woman is protected by a man when she is in fact alone. Usually, these do not involve the woman in misrepresenting gender. She is not to suggest she is something she is not—i.e., a man—nor is she to destroy evidence that she is a woman. Instead, she should indicate, either truthfully or not, by use of verbal invocation or significant symbols that she has access to a man who could protect her if need be. The advice literature recommends practices such as suggesting a woman walk in the middle of the street at night and, if approached, "look up at one of the windows or down the block and yell, 'Hey, Tom, I thought we were going to meet on Elm Avenue,'" for a criminal will not be "sure if Tom is real or not" (Ingber 1987:140). Even when there is no special danger, companionship is not to be discarded lightly: a woman, when at the movies, is sometimes told to go with the companion who "decides to venture into the lobby to buy popcorn," since "It might turn out to be fun, and it's certainly safer" (Burg 1979:144). Speaking to or of an illusory male for effect is termed "the Invisible Man Routine" (Burg 1979:147–148). Some measures are to be played out with no audience at all, as when a woman is advised when in a hotel to leave the television playing softly while she is out and the do-not-disturb sign on the door (Burg 1979:147–48).

In this way, women informants said they sometimes purposefully mentioned a boyfriend or husband during a service encounter or public conversation with a male stranger, thereby also preventing pickups. Thus, a secretary in her twenties took care to mention her ex-husband, whom she could continue to invoke if she disliked or feared the man with whom she spoke, but of whom she would rapidly dispose verbally if she chose to encourage acquaintance. Women also perceived modest deceptions as allowable, such as wearing a wedding ring though unwed. One woman claimed the advantage of this method was its expressiveness to all men: it required no strategic insertion into a conversation otherwise about plumbing, the weather, or pizza delivery, only that she display her hand. A woman might claim both existence and availability, for example, by reporting, when talking on the phone, not only that she had a husband but that he was home.[5]

Informants said that such minor deceptions were suitable as routine precautions. In situations more directly menacing, a woman might take more active measures, as when the public realm threatened to encroach on the private. If she is home and a man claiming to be a repairperson knocks, a woman alone sometimes attempts to signal that a man is with her. She sometimes also attempts to signal that her home is occupied by a man while she is still on the street, involving tacks that occasionally make her feel "more than normally foolish," as reported a lawyer in her fifties who nevertheless says she does just such things. In the same way, a nurse in her thirties, who once believed a man was following her home, yelled up to her window, "Chet, honey, I'll get the door," and was chagrined to hear her dog Chet dutifully bark in response. An unmarried partner in a law firm, a woman in her forties, habitually yelled, "I'll get it, honey," when her bell rang; once she had to explain to her conservative parents at the door that there was no honey after all.

Two young women, a cosmetology student and a secretary both in their twenties, noted that when they answered the phone at home they often took care to modulate their voices to a lower pitch; a criminal caller trying to discover a woman was home alone would thereby be misled. After the first turn at talk assured them a familiar caller, they resumed normal pitch. These examples were recounted with some embarrassment, because it was possible that they would be noticed and mocked by friends or relatives—as both had been.

Accompanied, a woman can feel obliged as a student of safety precautions to make her accompaniment as obvious as possible as often as possible. Evidence of solitude can become uncomfortable for her, based in part on actual experience when accompaniment is ambiguous. A homemaker in her thirties noted that when she and her husband were standing some three feet apart in a theater lobby and not engaged in conversation, a strange man stepped up to her, took her arm familiarly, and attempted to walk her away: "What he was going to do I don't know. Then my husband grabbed him by the collar and [the strange man] grinned very charmingly and walked away."

If women believe that they cannot experience public places unaccompanied, then it is also true that some women come to count men less as individuals than as protectors, functioning either well or poorly, a conception congruent with traditional ideas of gentlemanly behavior (see Hanmer and Saunders 1983). When effective, men are sometimes thought of as saviors; when ineffective, as failed gallants. In this vein, an unmarried graduate student said humorously that she thinks of her escorts on dates more as St. Bernards than as human beings; male escorts, especially at night, are the price paid for a life in public, says a department store clerk in her twenties who does not enjoy dating but wants to get out of the house. A third woman, a gay nurse in her thirties, takes a gay male friend when she goes to bars in a certain part of town for the safety she will then have; an irony is that she is the superior defender by martial arts training. Thus, the situated self that women are constrained to present can come to affect their judgment of effectiveness of a companion's performance.

I have said that purposeful attempts to suggest a man exists where none does imply that the situated self of the woman in public is weak. Some women went beyond the door, so to speak, and said they fantasied protective accompaniment at home, sometimes somewhat elaborately. In this way, a woman who worked as a hotel clerk admitted ruefully her conversations with her nonexistent companion began outside the door of her house, but continued after she entered and while she systematically checked for unwanted criminal companions room by room, the conversation with the imaginary male interlocutor giving her heart. A single mother, she tried to mute them before her children, however, since she felt to act so was "a little odd." Another woman, a graduate student, said her initial words to her imaginary male roommate blended into talking to herself. A nurse reported that her briefly fabricated companion had had a name, habits in dress, and a preferred basketball team, all coincidentally her tastes also; her own actions reflected these tastes when, for instance, she picked out a tie of the sort that he would prefer and hung it deceptively on the bedroom door or left a Celtics game (not games involving other teams) blasting masculinely on the television when she had to go out at night.

Women sometimes say that, though they perform some of these measures, they feel they should apologize for them: they are "crazy" things to do, they make a woman feel "a little bizarre." This ritual accompaniment emphasizes to her that her "true" or "real" self provides insufficient protection for her own safety. She must create a tissue of a man, which can be suggested by the merest hints and evidences.

Caught up in these charades, however, other women report no discomfort. They speak humorously of their shadow mates, implying that they are not threats to a real self but strange rites required by the culture and not to be taken seriously. Perhaps a woman gains some sense of control over the situation of crime prevention if she can, in effect, design her own protector down to his tie. (On the beneficial and liberating aspects of imaginary others, see Caughey 1984.)

It is not enough to note that, if women feel they have to engineer or mimic the presence of a man or suggest that they themselves are men, this is a sad commentary on modern urban life. Also important is the character of the situated self of public places that—according to some informants—such strategies create. Alone in public, women occasionally report that they still think of how safe they would feel or how much easier things in general would be, were they accompanied or were they male. Thus, a woman's time in public can be altered in ways unfamiliar to male citizens, in fact with strategies unfamiliar to most males. It is difficult to think of a situation where a man shams female accompaniment or female gender to ensure his safety, or where others advise him to do so.[6]

PROFANING THE SELF IN THE NAME OF SAFETY

While behaving in a crime-conscious manner, women can come to feel constrained to present themselves in a way that belies their knowledge of proper female gender role behavior and proper public behavior in general, presenting an appearance whose worth they consciously denigrate rather than inflate. For the sake of preventing crime, women are advised to manipulate their dress and behavior in a number of ways that restrict apparel choices and emotional expressions, and require them to present something less than what otherwise would be considered their best possible appearance.

Minor strategies involve dress and manner; more major strategies are suggestions in the advice literature that, to deter crime, a woman should inform a man that she has some imperceptible—but loathsome—characteristic or disease or should enact a psychological or physically repulsive condition. Informants were aware of this range of crime-prevention wisdom, though by and large they put into practice only that involving appearance.

In general, the literature tells women in public to "dress with discretion so as not to stimulate interest" (*Good Housekeeping Magazine* 1972:193), or that "a woman is more likely to invite attack on the street if she is wearing tight, 'sexy' clothes. If you are heading for a party in a décolleté costume or an extra-brief skirt, it's best to ride up to the entrance rather than walk" (Hair and Baker 1970:94). Implicitly these cautions respond to the appearance dependence of communication in public. Whereas a woman wearing alluring clothing in a private context can use other communicative elements to assure others that she is not truly or only the sexually interested person she seems, the same woman in public lacks other communicative tools to mute the message clothing offers.[7]

Almost every woman I interviewed offered information about appearance, saying she tried to avoid "provocative" clothing that "invited" attacks from males, as well as an "inviting" manner. Most informants said they felt they should not behave in an over-friendly manner or in any way that suggests an over-friendly manner; that is, they should not employ a "sexy" walk or thrust their breasts out.

Some informants noted the drawbacks of dress and attitude manipulation: to succeed in making themselves unnoteworthy in public required an adjustment of appearance not worth the sacrifice. Certainly it violated expectations of other citizens in public as to appropriate female attire if a woman attempted to dress herself to look plain as a pie plate—all the more if she managed to be mistaken for a man. A grade school teacher, a warm and exuberant person, strongly felt that restrictions on one's manner were even more insidious: dressing differently was a surface measure, she thought, but damping her good humor undermined what was hers "naturally."

As well as manipulating dress and manner, women sometimes are told to avoid crime by making themselves too repulsive a target for approach. That the criminal will probably then turn to another woman as a target is apparently not to be a concern. In the literature, women are counseled to adopt "non-aggressive—but disgusting—behavior" (Wilson 1977:151); to claim "to be pregnant or epileptic or the carrier of a venereal disease" (Duckett 1982:68) or to have "herpes or even AIDS" (Kaye 1985:74); to "pretend to have an epileptic seizure, or fainting spell" (Berman 1980:247); to "faint or go limp; urinate, drool or even throw up" (Schraub 1979:153); to "quack like a duck" (Scribner 1988:69) or make sounds like a cow and flap her arms like an airplane (Pickering 1983:129). She is told not to be afraid to "make a scene [or] do anything to attract attention to yourself. That's exactly what you want" (Field 1980:120), though attracting attention to herself is not among the woman's desiderata in public places according to traditional norms (Benton 1956:8), nor is behaving "sexually aggressively" (Scribner 1988:69). She should "Act insane; eat grass, jump around, etc." (Krupp 1978:152); she should "Sing out loud. . . . Make a fool of yourself" (Kaye 1985:74). Some of this advice also is intended to disgust the potential criminal,[8] as when women are advised to tell rapists that they have venereal disease (Schraub 1979:153), even carrying an old penicillin bottle to bolster claims (Pickering 1983:121).

Informants reported knowing about, though very rarely putting into practice, this tack of purposefully inspiring disgust. Only one woman said she tried these more extreme tactics, a homemaker in her forties who effectively "gargled" and made noises at a man following her, but felt so foolish she was not sure her efforts were worthwhile. All such profanation requires a woman to present, not the more stringent definition of public comportment usually required of citizens, but a floridly flawed self. Here, the self is profaned because the actions are of such a nature as to make her seem out of role in public, silly because overcautious or simply unfathomable.

Thus, informants reported that they would feel ridiculous or humiliated if they were to practice crime prevention by stimulating disgust. For example, a lawyer in her thirties mused on the possibility of telling an assailant she had AIDS or venereal disease and then having to further convincingly hypothesize how she came by these "repulsive" diseases. Because of these feelings, she concluded she could never pull off this strategy.

But some women said they had contemplated being purposefully repulsive when they felt threatened. Thinking the matter over at the time, they knew themselves to be too poor deceivers to do so, whether because of inexperience or from overwhelming fear. Thus, a homemaker in her thirties, once confronted with a suspect man, decided to pretend to have an epileptic seizure, shortly thereafter remembering that she had no idea what such a seizure looked like. A nurse, who had been raped, offered that, "If anybody goes after me again, this [type of advice] won't help me. I'll be so scared I won't be able to spell AIDS, much less convince someone I've got it."

Such advice would indeed seem strange if offered to a man threatened with street violence. It is now a commonplace that an attractively dressed woman does not "cause" a man to rape her anymore than a well-dressed man causes a man to rob him. It is not so commonly noted that we do not advise men to fake insanity or to sham morally impugning disease with the alacrity that women are so advised. Of course, claims of sexually transmitted disease are aptly claimed when one fears sexual crimes like rape, not apt when one fears robbery.

The profanation of a woman's situated self in public places, then, results from beliefs she should either deliberately act ridiculous, inappropriately, or simply mute her personal attractions in hopes either of discomfiting her attacker or escaping his attention. At all levels, these strategies are at odds with the understandings that public places are regions where the individual presents a careful and "best" demeanor and look.

ANTICIPATED PERIL

A third type of distance from the normal citizens' situated self in public places is supplied by the advice to women and by their perception that they should take some measures of crime prevention in advance of actually appearing in public. Certain practices, in turn, bespeak an orientation to an action before that action is necessary. Evident precautions and planning contradict our general cultural feeling that events in public places are too trifling to warrant special thought and that an egalitarian civility prevails. Yet, tacitly appreciating the many social realities that public places contain and the impossibility of judging strangers with only transitory, episodic, and silent communications, women are also advised to extend their crime-consciousness back, before the actual moment of danger, in order to foil criminals. In effect, women are counseled to anticipate peril; some informants said they do just this, sometimes with awkward results.

The advice literature suggests there are some practices and some attitudes the woman should follow to prepare herself for the worst that might happen; moreover, she is to keep this advice in mind at all times: "Don't let down. Ever!" (Kaye 1985:74). Besides this general mental vigilance, there are preparations a woman can take to ward off or lessen the likelihood that she will become involved in danger, extending even to practices such as carrying a house key in her hand far in advance of when it will actually be needed (Schraub 1979:169), or positioning herself when she enters an elevator "near the control panel so you can hit the alarm button and as many floor buttons as possible if necessary" in case she is attacked (Krupp 1978:152).

Women are advised to take up many precautions in advance, sometimes far in advance, of trouble: a woman is told to carry her money in her bra (Barthol 1979:111), to hold her police whistle between her teeth as she walks home (Barthol 1979:111), to use her personal alarm "*before* a confrontation takes place, even if you're not sure you're in danger" (*Glamour Magazine* 1980:63). When a stranger enters an elevator she is on, she should pretend she has forgotten something and exit (*Today's Health Magazine* 1973); when on the street, she is told to scream or use her whistle "as soon as you think someone might be stalking you" (Berman 1980:247). Other citizens are certain to be puzzled, if not astounded, by such actions, as when a woman is told, if she thinks she is being followed, to run up and say "to a dependable soul: 'Hey Charlie, what's happening?'" (Krupp 1978:142).

Sometimes she must plan considerably ahead, as when she is told to choose her home with an eye to security (Wheeler 1982:69) or to get acquainted with her neighbors with a view toward enlisting them in case of danger (Bertram 1975:83). Such advice amounts to an honorable, not to say prudent, ulterior motive for making friends in the city.

Other long-range advice suggests that she make a list of dangerous public situations experienced by her and her friends and/or portrayed in local newspaper accounts for the last six months (Monkerud and Heiny 1980:14), that she mentally review crime-prevention techniques several times a day (Pickering 1983:7), that she make a calendar of self-defense practice times and a list of dangerous neighborhood features (Griffith 1978:165–69, 174–75). Preparations must continue inside her home, where she can practice "knowing how to scream," but into a pillow pressed over her face (Barthol 1979:25). Or a woman can practice screams driving with the windows rolled up: "anyone watching thinks you are singing!" (Barthol 1979:25).

Many manipulations of appearance involve consideration far beyond the immediate situation of danger, as when the advice literature tells a woman to choose her clothes with regard to their running and escape potential (Burg 1979:121) or for their noiselessness. She should not, for example, wear shoes with "tap-tap" heels that will alert "everyone within a couple of blocks that a female target approacheth!" (Barthol 1979:100–101).

With an eye to anticipating crime, informants reported following a number of strategies of both small and long duration. For example, a homemaker in her twenties said that, before she left the house, she always put her credit cards and large bills in her three-year-old's toy purse, reasoning that even if she were robbed her small daughter would not be; a nurse in her thirties transferred cash to a bra and a purse alarm to her pocket, judging the effect in the mirror to make sure there were no telling bulges. A lawyer in her thirties said she gave herself a "crime check" in a full-length mirror each time she left her house, noting dress and presentation that might "invite" crime and, for each outfit, any handbag both match the outfit but not be "snatchable."

Some preparations were long-term and came to infect other ordinary, pleasurable parts of informants' lives. A 20-year-old homemaker regretted that she could no longer grow long nails, since she needed to be ready to fight an attacker if need be. A graduate student in her twenties with the opposite beliefs about nails regretted a need to grow long nails to serve as weapons for self-defense, for they did not jibe with the professorial image to which she aspired. A cosmetology student felt that it took her "six times as long to find a house" because of her crime-preventive standards. A law partner in her forties enjoyed buying clothes when a teen but said the pleasure was now spoiled since she scrutinized potential purchases "with an eye to, 'will this provoke some depraved maniacal sadist to attack me?'"

Women sometimes took anticipatory walks through the street, mentally mapping common routes with an eye to potential help in case of danger. Compared to other citizens, they were overinvested in the act of public passage, commonly considered insignificant, warranting no practice runs, and as a result spontaneous. Evocatively, however, a married lawyer in her thirties described steps in thinking through a route or assessing an area and concluded, "I never go any place for the first time—I've been there already in my head." Plainly, there is the danger that erecting false events such as these will be inimical to the experiential integrity of the act itself, making it always a rehearsed one.

The woman who observes necessary strategies for anticipating peril when in public places is certain, sooner or later, to be vigilant when there is no cause. Given the extremity of the recommendations, this is likely to happen in some form or other many times daily. Sometimes, of course, she will not know circumspection is unneeded. Informants occasionally alluded to a low-grade guilt over their "paranoia" toward other citizens, who were seen in retrospect to have meant, or at least to have done, no harm to them. Sometimes they had been revealed to have had suspicions where none was warranted, as a secretary in her thirties was mocked by a man on the street for transparently carrying her keys "defensively," or the cosmetologist who stepped aside well in advance to avoid a man she feared, who then said to her, "You idiot."

When women anticipated peril from men they first took to be strangers, then turned out to know, they often reported feeling particularly "stupid." But one informant, a junior professor in her thirties, had a different attitude. After she nearly Mace'd her department chair, they both laughed, "then he started kidding me about what a paranoid I was, and that's where the laughter stopped. I apologize to no one for insuring that I stay alive."

In sum, measures advised by the rhetoric of limited competence sometimes respond to and sometimes contradict general features of communication in public places. Women informants reported taking pains to avoid crime when in public. Yet because they are fearful of crime and because the character of public places makes it impossible reliably to judge the many strangers one encounters, save by appearance, women need rely on what are necessarily quickly and clearly transmitted messages or on preparation that takes place outside of the region. Measures will likely be taken where unwarranted, so that a contingency of this rhetoric remains that either a stranger or an acquaintance can innocently rebuke the woman for strategies not immediately useful. The true culprit, of course, is not so much the advice she receives or the folk beliefs she bears, but the environing fear of crime.

Discussion

The significance of this rhetoric can be seen in terms of (1) its contribution to the situated self women present in public, including the possibility that crime consciousness will overwhelm the woman's other concerns in public places; (2) its relationship to an informal social control in public places; (3) its effect on the complementary situated self men must demonstrate in public.

In some ways, there is less discrepancy than might be suspected between the general situated self due public places and the rhetoric of crime prevention that is a part of it. In general, the situated self of public places subjects women to other imputations of limited competence and supplies them with a self regularly profaned, especially when they are youthful, by street remarks, by differential and commonly poorer treatment in shops and restaurants, by varying expectations of what items of information about the self a woman is obliged to disclose (Gardner 1980, 1983, 1988, 1989).

To some extent, the message of the rhetoric of limited competence is consistent with other experiences of the situated self of public places. Insofar as it is consistent, it emphasizes other negative experiences. At the same time, it makes more unlikely that women can achieve the egalitarian courtesy and trust that is, within limits, normative for public places in middle-class society. This carries an unpleasant connotation for women's place in society, suggesting that social control of women in public places both exists and is diffusely available for any man in public places. Indeed, it is exercised by men whether they intend it or not.

Part of women's status in public, then, is expressed by a heightened concern with crime, quite in contrast to the concerns reported by and advised for men. An examination of what I have called the rhetoric of limited competence shows how this is possible.

First, there is a great deal of anticipatory preparation, both mental and material, counseled for the woman who is going out. This vigilance, she often believes (and popular literature assures her), must typically be undertaken in a careful yet undetectable manner, conveying a masked strength that is appropriate also to her gender role. Added to the tasks of public presentation for all citizens, she faces another: remaining intently aware of the many possible dangers of public life. The logical extension of circumspection that is the fate of the over-alert game-player has been dealt with at length by Erving Goffman under the topic of "Where the Action Is" (see Goffman 1967:149–270).

Thus, women who attempt to be crime conscious, and simultaneously who are attempting to give the appearance of attractive and casual self-contained noninvolvement in public, understandably find it a strain simultaneously to prime themselves to run, scream, enter the nearest building, stand in a carefully considered "safe" spot, walk in the middle of the street with dignity, and refuse apparently innocent (and perhaps actually innocent) requests for aid, matches, and information. A woman can experience public places primarily as an exercise in self-defense, spoiling other possible gains.

Beyond admonishing women to take up a possibly burdensome menu of activities, the rhetoric of limited competence reinforces other negative informal social control women experience in public. As Radford (1987:43) suggests, a woman not seen to be controlled by one specific man in public can at will be controlled by any man. This informal control results in a wide scope of beliefs and actions by women, in response to the similarly wide band of behavior by men in public places that one writer has referred to as a "continuum of sexual violence" (Kelly 1987).

The experience of various types of negative control in public yields a situated self bounded in a neatly symbolic way by geography and site, as well as by circumstance and concern. Thus, beliefs about crime prevention could operate to keep women at home, where they are seen to be physically safer and less concerned with strategies of caution—and where, traditionally, they have belonged. And this social control exists outside public places, extending itself to poison major life decisions such as choosing a home as well as possibly occupying some part of her time in private with worry or with strategizing.

A further effect of crime-prevention beliefs is the portrait they paint of men. The felt obligation to behave in a crime-conscious manner can undermine, subtly or not so subtly, women's trust in the majority of quite innocent men whom women observe or with whom they come into contact in public places. Likewise, men conscious of women's fears in public will in part understand women's actions there according to how they find themselves reflected in women's behavior toward them.

In consequence, men sometimes may decide to go out of their way to appear innocent by, for example, conspicuously smiling and tipping a hat to a woman they pass in a run-down area or by ending any small piece of legitimate contact such as helping a woman open a door or manage a package with functional brevity and businesslike manner—all to communicate, in effect, that, though other males are suspected of harm they themselves are not and, furthermore, that they are sensitive enough to take the woman's point of view into consideration (Mehlman 1987). In this way, a man with no intention to fondle women in the subway reports placing his hands on a conspicuous subway pole to broadcast his innocence (Goffman 1971:38).

Other men who realize women's fears may exploit them short of the point of actual crime. Thus, most informants said they suspected any public approach by a man of having the nefarious as well as the innocent potential; all the more so do they suspect approaches, such as catcalls or pinches, that breach middle-class etiquette or enact conduct usually disapproved, such as following a woman for a block or two. It is important to appreciate that women's fear of crime in public places does not spoil public places for women alone, but that it also spoils, in some larger sense, men for women and women for men and public places for everyone.

Finally, although my analysis is one that treats all of these measures of crime prevention from the point of view of their possible effects on the situated self a woman presents in public places, my analysis is not meant to suggest, of course, that there are alternate strategies possible that would leave women in public places both safe and evidently self-possessed. Indeed, the concern of many of the women I interviewed—as well presumably as many of the women who read the popular literature on crime prevention—is to avoid the chance of rape or murder at the hands of unknown men who will assault them in public or follow them from public places to their homes. To analyze the character of the situated selves that these women believe and are told they must present in public in order to prevent crime is by no means to denigrate those beliefs and that advice: it is merely to note that along with those beliefs and advice comes what women themselves have sometimes noted to be sadly necessary measures.

Notes

Research for this chapter was supported by the President's Council of Indiana University, whom I thank. I also thank Wiliam Gronfein, the late Erving Goffman, and two anonymous reviewers for comments on previous versions of this chapter. Versions of the study were presented at the 1987 International Symposium on Victimology in San Francisco and at the 1987 annual Sociologists for Women in Society meetings. Finally, I thank all of my interviewees for their help.

1. Interestingly, there is also a contrary set of advice telling women in search of dates or husbands to turn casual contacts in public into grist for their mill, suggesting that they can recognize desirable men as well as men they need fear (Gallatin 1987; O'Connor and Silverman 1989; Sommerfield 1986).

2. This is true barring some general fear for theft of valuable goods. To hide one's assets becomes, then, a general rule of conduct whose prudence overwhelms the temptation toward conspicuous display.

3. Beliefs about insignificance and egalitarianism are fostered by some of the social scientific work on public places. Such work emphasizes the civility present there and treats breaches of civility as deviant. For example, Goffman emphasizes such quintessentially egalitarian rites as civil inattention, whereby individuals signal by means of a mutual glance, then a dropping of that glance, that due respect has been awarded and no harm is intended (1963:83–85). At the same time he relegates the flagrant disrespect some social categories receive in public to the deviant case of "exposed" positions (1963:125–28).

4. Of course, all I have said about the character of communication in public places with regard to women and crime may be as well said of the character of communication with regard to men in public places. An intriguing question for a future study, then, is the problem not of why women fear crime in public places but of why men do not.

5. Sometimes women understand the various threads of advice to be in conflict. Thus, an unmarried secretary in her thirties decided to wear a wedding ring in order to suggest an absent protector; on the other hand, she feared the ring was also a lure for thieves, and compromised by wearing it only during the daytime. She felt that theft was not likely in the daytime, but being followed home would be.

6. More familiar are admonishments to men to practice self-defense measures with an eye to attackers they might meet, a concern more elaborately advised for women, however. Women are also advised to invent another shadow presence, that of the imagined harasser or attacker; in this way, crime-preventive advice collaborates by exhorting a woman actively and extensively to role-play assaults with the criminal.

7. To be sure, all citizens will have reason to look out for crime, and all are cautioned, in some locales and circumstances, to conceal assets in the name of crime prevention—as are all citizens on vacation in unfamiliar parts (Gieseking 1980) and as, increasingly, city-dwelling children are (Hechinger 1984). But concealing monetary assets—appropriately understood as not integral to the self—is different from concealing physical assets, for bodily features are highly associated with the individual's "real" self.

8. Tacitly, the advice also assumes certain social categories and states—the epileptic, the mentally disabled, the pregnant, the menstruating—are worthy of disgust.

References

Balkin, Steven
   1979 "Victimization rate, safety, and fear of crime." *Social Problems* 26:343–58.
Ball, Donald
   1965 "Sarcasm as sociation: The rhetoric of interaction." *Canadian Review of Sociology and Anthropology* 2:190–98.
   1967 "An abortion clinic ethnography." *Social Problems* 14:293–301.
Barthol, Robert
   1979 *Protect Yourself.* Englewood Cliffs, N.J.: Prentice-Hall.
Benton, Frances
   1956 *Complete Etiquette.* New York: Random House.

Berman, Clifford
  1980 "Crime: How not to be a victim." *Good Housekeeping Magazine*, September, 247.
Bertram, Camille M.
  1975 "Protection: How, when, where, and what to do." *Harper's Bazaar Magazine*, March, 83, 131.
Brown, Edward J., Timothy Flanagan, and Maureen McLeod (eds.)
  1984 *Sourcebook of Criminal Justice Statistics—1983*. Washington, D.C.: U.S. Government Printing Office.
Brunvand, Jan Harold
  1981 *The Vanishing Hitchhiker: American Urban Legends and Their Meanings*. New York: Norton.
Burg, Kathleen Keefe
  1979 *The Womanly Art of Self-Defense*. New York: A & W Visual Library.
Caughey, John L.
  1984 *Imaginary Social Worlds*. Lincoln, Neb.: University of Nebraska Press.
Clemente, Frank, and Michael B. Kleiman
  1977 "Fear of crime in the United States: A multivariate analysis." *Social Forces* 56:519–31.
Dubow, Fred
  1979 *Reactions to Crime: A Critical Review of the Literature*. Washington, D.C.: U.S. Government Printing Office.
Duckett, Joy
  1982 "Rape prevention." *Essence Magazine*, September, 68.
Edmiston, Susan
  1973 "Up from cowardice." *Redbook Magazine*, August, 60–61, 162–63, 165.
Edwards, Audrey
  1982 "How three quick-thinking women escaped danger." *Essence Magazine*, September, 72.
Edwards, Susan
  1987 "'Provoking her own demise.'" In *Women, Violence and Social Control*, ed. Jalna Hanmer and Mary Maynard, 152–68. Atlantic Highlands, N.J.: Humanities.
Field, Jill Nevel
  1980 "Playing it safe: At home, on the street, in your car, on the bus or subway." *Mademoiselle Magazine*, September, 112, 120.
Gallatin, Dr. Martin
  1987 *How to Be Married One Year from Today: Lover Shopping for Men and Women*. New York: Shapoisky Publishers.
Gardner, Carol Brooks
  1980 "Passing by." *Sociological Inquiry* 50:328–56.
  1983 "Aspects of gender behavior in public places in a small southwestern city." Unpublished Ph.D. dissertation, University of Pennsylvania.
  1988 "Access information: Private lies and public peril." *Social Problems* 35:384–97.
  1989 "Analyzing gender in public places: Re-thinking Goffman's vision of everyday life." *American Sociologist* 20:42–56.
  1990 "Kinship claims and competence claims: People with disabilities in public places." Paper to be given at American Sociological Association annual meeting, Washington, D.C.
Geng, Veronica
  1971 "Scorn not the street compliment!" In *Cosmopolitan's New Etiquette Guide*, ed. Helen Gurley Brown, 75–79. North Hollywood, Calif.: Wilshire Book Company.
Gieseking, Hal
  1980 "Special report: Summer criminals." *Travel/Holiday Magazine*, June, 77–78.

Glamour Magazine
  1980 "Should you carry a personal alarm?" March, 63.
Goffman, Erving
  1961 *Asylums.* Chicago: Aldine.
  1963 *Behavior in Public Places.* Glencoe, Ill.: Free Press.
  1967 "Where the action is." In *Interaction Ritual,* 149–270. Garden City, N.Y.: Doubleday.
  1971 *Relations in Public.* New York: Basic Books.
  1973 *Presentation of Self in Everyday Life.* Woodstock, N.Y.: Overlook Press.
Good Housekeeping Magazine
  1972 "Street-safety precautions every woman should follow," October, 193.
Grahame, Kamini Maraj
  1985 "Sexual harassment." In *No Safe Place,* ed. Connie Guberman and Margie Wolfe, 111–30. Toronto: Women's Press.
Griffith, Liddon R.
  1978 *Mugging: You Can Protect Yourself.* Englewood Cliffs, N.J.: Prentice-Hall.
Hair, Robert A., and Samm Sinclair Baker
  1970 *How to Protect Yourself Today.* New York: Stein and Day.
Hanmer, Jalna, and Sheila Saunders
  1983 "Blowing the cover of the protective male: A community study of violence to women." In *The Public and the Private,* ed. Eva Gamarnikow, Meg Stacey, Linda Imray, Audrey Middleton, Jalna Hammer, Sheila Saunders, Patricia Allatt, Claire Ungerson, Ann Murcott, Marilyn Porter, Janet Finch, Peter Rushton, Hilary Graham, Laura McKee, and Margaret O'Brien. London: Heinemann.
Heath, Linda
  1984 "Impact of newspaper crime reports on fear of crime: Multimethodological investigation." *Journal of Personality and Social Psychology* 47:263–76.
Hechinger, Grace
  1984 *How to Raise a Street-Smart Child.* New York: Facts on File.
Hindelang, Michael J., Michael R. Gottfredson, and James Garofalo
  1978 *The Victims of Personal Crime.* Cambridge, Mass.: Ballinger.
Ingber, Dina
  1987 "Staying safe: The smart woman's guide to self-defense." *McCall's Magazine,* March, 138, 140, 142.
Janoff-Bulman, Ronnie, and Irene Hanson Frieze
  1987 "The role of gender in reactions to criminal victimization." In *Gender and Stress,* ed. Rosalind C. Barnett, Lois Biener, and Grace K. Baruch, 159–84. New York: Free Press.
Kaye, Elizabeth
  1985 "Preventing robbery and rape." *Harper's Bazaar Magazine,* April, 72, 74.
Kelly, Liz
  1987 "The continuum of sexual violence." In *Women, Violence, and Social Control,* ed. Jalna Hanmer and Mary Maynard, 46–60. Atlantic Highlands, N.J.: Humanities.
Krupp, Charla
  1978 "Solving your problem: 84 ways to feel safer." *Mademoiselle Magazine,* October, 142–43, 146, 152.
Ledray, Linda E.
  1986 *Recovering from Rape.* New York: Holt.
Martin, Judith
  1982 *Miss Manners' Guide to Excruciatingly Correct Behavior.* New York: Atheneum.
Maxfield, Michael G.
  1984 "The limits of vulnerability in explaining fear of crime: A comparative neighborhood analysis." *Research in Crime and Delinquency* 21:233–50.

Mehlman, Peter
　1987 "Male guilt." *Glamour*, April, 332.
Monkerud, Donald, and Mary Heiny
　1980 *Self-Defense for Women*. Dubuque, Iowa.: William C. Brown.
Navarro, Mireya
　1990 "For busy storeowner, nearby protests have raised fear of misunderstanding." *New York Times*, May 17.
O'Connor, Dr. Margaret, and Dr. Jane Silverman
　1989 *Finding Love: Creative Strategies for Finding Your Ideal Mate*. New York: Crown.
Pickering, Michael C. V.
　1983 *A Manual for Women's Self-Defense*. North Palm Beach, Fla.: The Athletic Institute.
Post, Elizabeth L.
　1969 *Emily Post's Etiquette*. New York: Funk & Wagnalls.
Radford, Jill
　1987 "Policing male violence—Policing women." In *Women, Violence, and Social Control*, ed. Jalna Hanmer and Mary Maynard, 30–45. Atlantic Highlands, N.J.: Humanities.
Riger, Stephanie, and Margaret T. Gordon
　1981 "The fear of rape: A study in social control." *Journal of Social Issues* 37:71–92.
Rockwood, Marcia, and Mary Thom
　1979 "Making your block, office, parking lot, community rape-proof." *Ms. Magazine*, March, 79–82.
Schraub, Susan
　1979 "Bazaar's anti-rape handbook." *Harper's Bazaar Magazine*, March, 152–53, 169.
Scribner, Marilyn
　1988 *Free to Fight Back*. Wheaton, Ill.: Harold Shaw.
Sims, Calvin
　1990 "Black shoppers call Korean merchants hostile and unfair." *New York Times*, May 17.
Sommerfield, Diana
　1986 *Single, Straight Men: 106 Guaranteed Places to Find Them*. New York: St. Martin's.
Tegner, Bruce
　1965 *Bruce Tegner's Complete Book of Self-Defense*. New York: Bantam.
Today's Health Magazine
　1973 "What a scream can do for you." June, 29–33, 64.
Vanderbilt, Amy
　1972 *Amy Vanderbilt's Etiquette*. Garden City, N.Y.: Doubleday.
Wachs, Eleanor
　1988 *Crime-Victim Stories*. Bloomington, Ind.: Indiana University Press.
Wegman, James
　1978 "How to be safe on the streets." *Glamour*, September, 57.
Wheeler, Elizabeth
　1982 "Protecting yourself." *Essence Magazine*, September, 69.
Wilson, Julie
　1977 "How to protect yourself." *Harper's Bazaar Magazine*, March, 93, 151.
Zimmerman, Mary K.
　1981 "The abortion clinic." In *Social Psychology through Symbolic Interaction*, ed. Gregory P. Stone and Harvey A. Farberman, 43–52. New York: Wiley.

CHAPTER 4

On Being Stalked

Robert M. Emerson, Kerry O. Ferris, and Carol Brooks Gardner

Stalking emerged as an identifiable social problem only in the last decade. During most of the 1980s, several national magazines called attention to "women being followed or harassed with letters, telephone calls, or unwanted gifts," but the term "stalking" was rarely if ever invoked; rather, these behaviors were interpreted as "sexual harassment," "obsession," or "psychological rape" (Lowney and Best 1995:37–39). But the 1989 murder of actress Rebecca Schaeffer generated great public and media attention for "celebrity-stalking," as repeated following, harassment, and threats came to be linked to incursions (some violent) on a number of high-profile entertainers, including David Letterman, Jodie Foster, and Theresa Saldana.

Public concern with such celebrity stalkings played a major role in the 1990 passage of California's antistalking law. Many other states quickly passed similar laws, and the National Institute of Justice offered a model antistalking code (NIJ 1993). The identification and criminalization of stalking went hand in hand with a shift in focus from celebrity victims pursued by strangers to a view of stalking "as a women's issue, a widespread precursor to serious violence, typically committed by men against former spouses or lovers" (Lowney and Best 1995:42; see also Dunn 1998:143–144). Thus, stalking became directly linked to domestic violence, primarily through the claims-making efforts of participants in the battered women's movement (Lowney and Best 1995). In this respect, stalking is no longer viewed solely as a status liability afflicting celebrities, sports figures, politicians, and the wealthy, but increasingly is seen as a more widespread, albeit gender-linked phenomenon that arises in ordinary couple and workplace relations.

This chapter will analyze the processes and experience of being stalked; it draws upon a variety of accounts by those who became objects of a range of relation-claiming actions by others. It suggests that many forms of what comes to be identified as stalking grow out of glitches and discontinuities in two very common and normal relationship processes—coming together and forming new relationships on the one hand, and dissolving and getting out of existing relationships on the other. In this way the processes and experience of being stalked are intricately linked to normal, everyday practices for establishing, advancing, and ending relationships.

In light of the recent formulation of stalking as a social problem, it is not surprising that empirical research on this topic remains scanty. Two primary lines of research have emerged: forensic and clinical studies of erotomania and obsession; and a more recent survey of stalking victims.

In the wake of the Saldana and Schaeffer attacks, a number of psychiatrically oriented studies appeared treating stalking behavior as an "obsessional" or "delusional" disorder known as "erotomania" (Harmon, Rosner, and Owens 1995; Leong 1994; Segal 1989, 1990; Wright et al. 1995). Zona et al. (1993), for example, rely on the concept of erotomania to distinguish among types of stalking cases brought to the Los Angeles Police Department's Threat Management Unit. They develop a typology of stalkers including "erotomanic stalkers," "love obsessional stalkers," and "simple obsessional stalkers." Erotomania involves "a delusional disorder in which the predominant theme of the delusion is that a person, usually of higher status, is in love with the subject." Love obsession adds to erotomania other severe psychiatric symptoms or diagnoses such as psychosis or schizophrenia. Simple obsession, representing the majority (70 to 80 percent) of official stalking cases, is distinguished by the fact that "there exists a prior relationship between the subject and the victim."

This line of research is of limited relevance to sociological analyses of stalking. The clinical and law enforcement samples are unrepresentative and overselective of the pathological and extreme. But more significantly, conceptualizing stalking as a result of mental imbalance obscures the relational bases of many stalkings, and makes the intricate social processes of stalking secondary to the stalkers' individual pathologies.[1] It also ignores pursued's and pursuer's differing perceptions of what is going on (differences that may be particularly marked at earlier stages before it becomes clear to all that "stalking" exists), privileging the former's version and discounting the latter's as pathology. Finally, preserving the distinction between stranger/celebrity and ex-partner stalkings not only ignores many processes common to both types, but is also static; it assumes the clear-cut, unproblematic existence of stalking as a phenomenon, and ignores the processes through which it comes to be recognized and defined.

The recently completed study of stalking victims by Tjaden and Thoennes (1998), conducted as part of the National Violence Against Women Survey, provides the most systematic and comprehensive view of stalking to date. The survey asked a large national sample of women and men whether they had ever experienced any of a number of acts associated with stalking, including being followed or spied on, receiving unsolicited phone calls, letters, or unwanted items, or noticing someone standing "outside your home, school, or workplace" (17). Respondents who answered yes to one or more of these items, who reported positively that someone had "done any of these things to them on more than one occasion," and who admitted to being "very frightened" or fearful of bodily harm (17) were counted as stalking victims.[2] Eight point two percent of the women in the sample and 2.2 percent of the men reported such experiences in their lifetime, with figures of 1 percent and 0.4 percent respectively being stalked within the last 12 months. While 78 percent of the stalking victims were women and 22 percent men, "94 percent of the stalkers identified by female victims and 60 percent of the stalkers identified by male victims were male" (5). Of women victims, a total of 48 percent reported being stalked by a spouse or ex-spouse, or cohabiting partner or ex-partner, 14 percent by dates or former dates, 19 percent by acquaintances, and 23 percent by strangers. Most men victims—a total of 70 percent—were stalked by acquaintances or strangers. Fifty-five percent of the cases involving women and 48 percent of those involving men were reported to the police, while 28 percent of the women and 10 percent of the men obtained a temporary restraining order (TRO).

While providing for the first time a clear overview of the demographic distribution of stalking, by its very design the Tjaden and Thoennes study cannot provide insight into the social processes that generate and give meaning to these distributions. Specifically, stalking is treated atemporally, as all of one piece, with little or no attention given to how it develops, comes to be recognized, and proceeds over time (this despite the fact that, on average, victims report the stalking incidents lasted 1.8 years: Tjaden and Thoennes 1998:12). Also neglected are the problematics of identifying stalking in the first place, changes over time in the stalker's attitudes toward or demands from the victim, and changes in the victim's responses to the problem over time.

In order to develop a fully sociological approach and to highlight how activities come to be identified as stalking, we must approach stalking in processual and interpretive terms. In this chapter we will describe the natural history of stalking as a way of highlighting the processual and interpretive character of this phenomenon. We reveal process by asking whether the kinds of activities associated with stalking occur in some kind of sequential pattern or stages, i.e., how do the components of stalking change and evolve over time? This focus on the social processes of stalking thus complements the findings of the Tjaden and Thoennes survey. We ask how people come to understand that they are being stalked, an interpretation that is often highly problematic because of the possible overlap between stalking and normal romantic or relational moves and actions.

In looking at stalking as social process, we assume that stalking does not suddenly just appear, but develops in identifiable stages and changes over time. We analyze these stages and developments from the view of the person who may ultimately come to identify (and/or be identified) as a victim of stalking. We examine the way in which victims assemble, over time, an interpretation that what is happening to them is indeed "stalking." Focusing on the experience of coming to see oneself as being stalked brings into focus a series of relational processes that existing studies of stalking have by and large ignored. These processes include following, learning about the details of another's life and routines, and proposing/claiming relationships of various degrees of closeness and intimacy. In approaching stalking in this way, we move away from defining actions and events as unproblematically pathological, and toward focusing on actions and events that are commonplace, familiar to us all as ordinary parts of the everyday pursuit of friendship or romance, or of the mundane rebuilding of failed relationships.

Taking a process approach also requires close attention to the earlier, more problematic stages of stalking—what might be termed "pre-stalking." In contrast, most existing studies of stalking rely heavily or even exclusively on data deriving from more serious or extreme cases, including those brought to the attention of the legal system (e.g., Zona et al. [1993]), or those resulting in newsworthy threats or violence. By focusing on more serious cases of stalking, these studies oversample cases where initial ambiguities about what was going on have been resolved. Hence, they neglect the earlier stages that precede clear recognition of "stalking," when most of the relevant activities were interpreted and treated as something other than stalking. These studies thus employ a form of "endpoint analysis" that retrospectively reinterprets "into more definitive form what at some earlier point had been hazy, ambiguous or downright confusing" (Emerson, Fretz, and Shaw 1995:61). To look at it another way, in everyday life, most instances of what later might be seen as "pre-stalking" are not seen as such by the participants. Retrospectively reframing earlier phenomena in the relations between pursuer and pursued in terms of an eventual threat and/or harm overdetermines and distorts the character of the earlier, emerging processes and meanings. In particular, this obscures what are often for the victim the most salient and disorienting quality of the experience—the gradual accretion of suspicions, awareness, and, finally, knowledge that she or he is being stalked.

A concern with social process necessarily leads to a concern with the interpretive procedures through which "stalking" comes to be defined and recognized. What actions and conditions coalesce into a stalking? How do victims/members define stalking as they experience it? In taking such an interpretive approach, we to a large extent avoid the use of legal, clinical, sociological, or other a priori definitions of stalking, and focus on the experiential definitions constructed by those who are stalked (or who eventually come to see themselves as having been stalked). Thus, we look at stalking as a problem of interpretation for the participants.

Matters of interpretation become critical because of the previously noted linkage of stalking and conventional relational processes. The core activities of "pre-stalking," activities such as writing, calling, following, visiting, and gathering information about the other, also mark familiar, everyday courtship and uncoupling practices. Those who become the focus of such attention may initially frame these activities as romantic pursuit or friendship-building, only later reinterpreting them as stalking. "Stalking" is therefore an interpretive outcome, not a necessary result of a particular bundle of facts.

Processes that characterize a variety of everyday, nonpathological relational ploys and practices appear at early points in many forms of stalking as well. Indeed, incipient or hoped-for relationships typically begin tentatively, with one or both parties unsure of the other, and uncertain about how to cultivate a deeper connection. Thus, many of the key processes involved in stalking appear in situations and relationships that never become identified as stalking, or even as problematic; in this sense, being followed, learning that another had acquired detailed access information about you, and receiving initial relationship proposals characterize ordinary interactions and relationship processes. Some of the actions employed by stalkers are extreme versions of actions that characterize ordinary intimacies: writing, calling, visiting, and gathering information appear in perverse, terrifying incarnations, but those behaviors derive from more familiar, everyday courtship and friendship actions. Similarly, the core dynamic in relational stalking—persistence in seeking a relationship in the face of continuing rejection—mirrors in extreme the dogged pursuit of "true love" idealized in the culture and media, as well as being a hyperbole of the manic love Lee (1973) noted in "normal" courtship.

This poses a deep and tricky problem for our analysis: we are interested in how people come to interpret events as stalkings, but in large part we rely on accounts of those who have definitely concluded that they have been stalked. Most of the phenomena we examine have already been framed as stalkings by victims; although they may have at some point also framed these phenomena as something else, most now see them as having been stalkings.

Data and Research Methods

In contrast to data collection methods that rely on clinical or law enforcement samples, or on random samples of the general population, we use multiple sources of data in an effort to maximize the range and diversity of "pre-stalking" and stalking cases. First, in order to avoid looking exclusively at serious cases that had advanced to some more or less clear-cut "stalking" outcome, we sought to locate informants who had experienced some of the behaviors associated with stalking but who had not necessarily come to interpret these experiences as stalking. To do so we conducted 41 personal interviews in 1996 to 1998 with people who had been followed, usually without having sought a restraining order or taken other legal action to remedy the problem. Thus the purpose of the interview was described to respondents in these terms:

> I'm interested in talking to people about some different experiences that they might have had in public places—but I'm especially interested in experiences people have had that concern being followed by another person either known or unknown to them. . . . The purpose of this study is to present the experience and opinion of all kinds of people about following.

Respondents were then asked about the details of any such following incidents, how they had been affected, and how they reacted. The interview also included one question about what they considered to be the difference between following and stalking.[3]

Clearly these following interviews were tilted toward collecting accounts of encounters between those who were initially unacquainted, cases that at least initially occurred in public place or workplace situations. The 41 subjects in this sample all currently lived in a midwestern city; 25 were women, 16 men; 25 were white, 12 were African American, and 4 were Asian American (1 of these is sub-Continental Indian); they had a range of occupations, from judge, psychiatrist, and professor, to business and civil-service workers, to students and homemakers, to those in lower-level white- and blue-collar jobs.

Second, we drew upon a study conducted in 1988 to 1989 of petitions for temporary restraining orders (TROs) brought under California's domestic violence and civil harassment statutes in Beach City Superior Court.[4] This research involved observation over almost a one-year period of the courthouse processes in which petitioners filled out and submitted the necessary court documents to request TROs, as well as shorter periods of observation of two legal aid clinics established to help petitioners complete these documents. A final part of this study involved lengthy, open-ended interviews conducted with ten persons whom we had earlier observed in court applying for a TRO. These interviews focused on the circumstances leading to the decision to seek a TRO, the petitioner's experience with the process, and developments after the initial TRO had been granted.

It is important to emphasize that most of the TRO cases observed involved incidents defined as domestic violence or spousal abuse between separated or separating couples, or as threats of violence or "harassment" between family members or neighbors. Some of these cases did involve accusations of following and other forms of behavior we will consider as components of the natural history of being stalked. But no petitioners or court staff used the term "stalking" to characterize even these latter set of incidents.[5] For example, even Brooke Perry,[6] who experienced what would appear to have been a classic instance of stalking (see below), did not once use this term during the lengthy interview where she described her complex relations with the persistent pursuer and harasser against whom she obtained a restraining order. Nonetheless, these cases give us a second collection of detailed accounts of following and harassment, but involving situations where the victim felt severely threatened and sought to pursue a difficult, time-consuming legal remedy.

Third, we collected accounts of having been followed and stalked more opportunistically, from students and acquaintances to whom we described our project. Where briefer incidents (usually following) were involved, we solicited written accounts from these informants. Where more complex, longer-term situations developed, we tape-recorded interviews focused on these events. We also included one instance where a student conducting research on the police observed a patrol officer deal with a citizen's complaint that she had been followed.

Finally, in addition to this diverse set of original data on following and stalking, we made use of an extensive collection of secondary materials. Here we relied on accounts published in newspapers, magazines, and books to collect extensive material on about a dozen noncelebrity stalkings and about 20 celebrity stalkings. Most of the former and many of the latter received media attention because they involved dramatic and/or violent outcomes.

In sum, we used a variety of methods to gather data, deliberately seeking to include more ambiguous "pre-stalking" instances of following, unwanted attention. As a result, our analysis is not limited to instances of mutually recognized or officially identified stalking, but includes instances where what occurred was never designated as "stalking."

We emphasize two additional implications of our methods of data collection for the analyses that follow. First, the bulk of our data derives from accounts provided by the victims rather than the perpetrators of following and stalking.[7] As a result, in what follows, we analyze the relevant meanings and processes explicitly from the victims' points of view (Holstein and Miller 1990). This restricted focus is necessary, we suggest, because the phenomenon of stalking is marked exactly by radical disjuncture between the perspectives and understandings of victims and pursuers. The core of our analytic task therefore is to delineate the victim's point of view, to specify the victim's growing recognition that the perpetrator holds and asserts a very different perspective and point of view. This disjuncture is reflected in the initially radical asymmetry in the use of the term "stalking": for much of the process only the victim sees and experiences "stalking"; from the other's point of view, what is occurring is something else again— for example, acts of devotion and affection intended to attract or establish a relation with a desired person.[8]

Second, despite our efforts to collect materials on the earlier stages of what may ultimately come to be recognized as stalking, we remain heavily dependent on retrospective accounts and the endpoints they incorporate. This is so because we rely not only on victims' accounts, but on accounts elicited some time after the events at issue and organized to highlightt some specific outcome to these events. Such accounts necessarily reflect a retrospectively created history and trajectory of following and stalking that tend to ignore the role that circumstantial contingencies and the victim's interpretive practices played in defining conduct as notable, as unusual, as "stalking," and so on. The personal stories that victims tell, for example, have a kind of logical connectedness and experiential coherence that was not present in the real-time, lived experience of what came to be seen as a stalking (see Gubrium, Holstein, and Buckholdt 1994). We self-consciously try to minimize the effects of endpoints in our analyses, wherever possible "writing against" (Abu-Lughod 1991) the determinism that pervades these accounts by continually posing the interpretive and behavioral contingencies that figure in the interactional mix from which "stalkings" come to be identified.[9]

The Concept of "Relational Stalking"

Looking at a variety of victim accounts of stalking, it becomes clear that these reports deeply implicate the nature and level of relationship between pursued and pursuer. Indeed, these reports suggest that much stalking is keyed to a variety of hitches and disjunctures surrounding relational coming together and splitting apart. A number of patterns are apparent here.

First, many reports of what ultimately came to be recognized as stalking identify the core dynamic as one-sided attempts to create a close, usually romantic relationship where the two parties were, at the start, either completely unacquainted, or only superficially acquainted. These cases include several variations: (a) The pursued can be a stranger initially encountered in some public or semi-public place, giving rise to what can be termed *unacquainted stalking*. (b) The victim can be a publicly identified figure—usually an official or celebrity—with whom the pursuer has come to feel he or she has a special understanding or emotional attachment; these involve celebrity or *pseudoacquainted stalking*. Finally, (c) eventual stalking can develop between those who had some contact in the past (e.g., former classmates), or who have some minimal present contact (e.g., coworkers in a large office or business); this can be termed *semi-acquainted stalking*.[10] While most of these various cases involve some hope or proposal of an intimate relation, some stalkings involve no explicit romantic claim; the former campaign worker who came to stalk Texas Senator Bob Krueger and his wife provides an example.

Second, other victim reports depict stalking as arising out of efforts to maintain or to recreate a close relationship that has been terminated or that one party sought to terminate. Here the parties involved are not only previously acquainted, but usually intimately linked. Many are "exes" (Ebaugh 1988) who lived together for some time and then begin to undergo formal processes of separation and divorce. In other instances, the attempted breakup of a more casual "dating" relationship generates stalking, as in this interview account from a study of strategies for breaking off intimate relationships:

> I was getting very upset, he was harassing me. I was seeing this car in my rearview mirror and I was getting very upset. . . . [I]t was a couple of weeks he followed me around. . . . Then a couple of days later he said he wanted to be friends, then he started calling me up and bothering me again. (Clark and LaBeff 1986:262)

Taken as a whole, the forms of stalking arising out of various glitches and troubles tied to coming together or splitting apart involve what we will term *relational stalking*. Relational stalking thus includes both people who were initially complete strangers, as well as those who have had a long-standing intimate relationship that one party has sought to end—and perhaps even has legally ended. All forms of relational stalking entail unilateral pursuit linked to some admiring or romantic interest in, or implied or specific assertions of rights to, a continuing, close, or intimate relationship with another. Furthermore, these relational claims (and in most cases, romantic expressions) are one-sided, frequently unreciprocated, and even explicitly contested by the person to whom they are addressed. Thus, at the core of relational stalking are reported efforts by one party to impose a relationship upon an uncooperative or even resistant other. In this sense, relational stalking involves a complex interpersonal trouble (Emerson and Messinger 1977) centered on continuing struggle over the very nature of the relationship that is to exist between two parties (as well as others who may become entangled).

Note that from very early on the pursued emphasizes that there is a radical asymmetry between their own and the pursuer's presumed understanding of what is taking place, of just what they are to one another: the pursued maintains that there is either no relationship, or a minimal or former relationship at best; the other's understanding is that there is, or will be, a close and intimate relationship. In brief, it is exactly the nature of the purported relationship between the two parties—what it is, what it was, and what it will be—that is fundamentally at issue. Relational stalking, then, involves *meta-relational troubles*, keyed to words and actions that define and comment upon whatever previous relationship the parties have had, and what the parties should be to and for one another in the future.

While accounts of radical differences in relational claims and assumptions are key to all cases of relational stalking, many eventual victims call attention to a clear-cut turning point where earlier professions of attraction or devotion devolved into jealous rages, threats, intimidation, or violent outbursts. In the various forms of unacquainted stalkings, this shift tends to occur with, and as part of, the recognized failure of the pursuer's efforts to establish the kind of relationship desired. In cases of stalkings involving exes, where the core dynamic is depicted as one-sided resistance to breakup, signs of devotion and insistence on prolonging the relationship are mixed with threats and acts of violence right from the initiation of breakup. In such cases the eventual stalker seeks almost simultaneously to reinstate the prior relationship and punish the ex for having shattered it.

Moreover, while some relational stalkings ultimately turn sour and come to be dominated by vituperation, threats, or violence, there is another class of stalkings that seem to have this character right from the start. Some stalkings appear never to have included any romantic or relational claims at all, but rather are almost from the start marked emotionally by anger, hostility, and perhaps threat, and behaviorally by following and a series of related activities explicitly focused on intimidating the victim and perhaps on extracting what the pursuer sees as payback or revenge. Such revenge stalking thus involves no expressions of admiration, romantic intent, or deep devotion, and no efforts to establish or claim an intimate relationship. Rather the stalker appears to view her- or himself as maltreated, and seems motivated by intimidation or revenge along with a willingness to act as an incarnate public advertisement of the error of the victim's ways. Judges, psychiatrists, and instructors—all in the business of communicating sometimes unpalatable truths or evaluations to a clientele—are the frequent objects of revenge stalking. Plastic surgeons also seem prone to this form of stalking from patients unhappy with the results of cosmetic surgery (Dull and West 1991). Here the dissatisfied patient may even come to think of her- or himself as avenging angel acting on behalf of a class of persons, as well as providing a walking billboard of surgical incompetence.

Again, relational stalking may ultimately come to involve, and may even be dominated by, the same sorts of threats, intimidation, and violence that characterize revenge stalking. But these threats and violence arise from and are linked to a distinctive interactional dynamic in which deeply contested claims about what kind of relationship exists between two parties—and hence what kind of obligations and responsibilities each has toward the other—are asserted and played out.

In sum, while relational stalkings center around accounts of actions directed toward imposing a relationship, revenge stalkings report only intimidation and threats where no active relational claim is being invoked. If the epitome of a relational stalking is an aborted or failed love relationship that the spurned party continues to pursue, the epitome of revenge stalking is a failed service relationship where the dissatisfied customer decides to press suit in public court in quasi-vigilante style. Further, where a relational stalker may initially advise a target that "I would never do anything to hurt you" despite behavior that may vitiate this stated sentiment, a revenge stalker's explicit spirit and aims are the opposite.

The Natural History of Relational Stalking

As described and recounted by those who have experienced it, relational stalking reveals a natural history; that is, the pursued talk about what they may ultimately come to term "stalking" as occurring in a series of stages, stages marked by a number of recurrent processes that eventually led to a situation where they came to confront another who unilaterally and asymmetrically claimed a relationship in the face of their own continued resistance.

While all forms of relational stalking reveal common processes, these processes are combined and accented differently in accounts of stalking involving initial strangers as opposed to the acquainted. For example, while the pursued usually rejected a stranger's relational proposal received *after* extensive following and acquisition of information, the rejection (or, perhaps more accurately, attempted rejection) of the acquainted begins the process in which the rejected seeks to update and keep information current, drawing on a core of extant knowledge of the pursued's identity, activities, and connections to do so.

In fact, the similarity and overlap between the activities and practices identified as constituting stalking and those of everyday relational and courtship pursuit posed a problem for informants, who routinely took special care both to point out these similarities and to highlight the differences. Our concern, again, lies in how those experiencing pursuit and following come to recognize and understand these activities, particularly in when and how they come to interpret these activities as "stalking." Thus, we do not seek to specify how the actions that comprise stalking differ from comparable ones of ordinary courtship; rather, we look at how those who come to identify themselves as inappropriately followed and/or "stalked" orient to and establish this distinction.

Of course, stalking may also involve actions that do not correspond so well to ordinary relational or courtship practices, or correspond only to the unpleasant realities of romantic relationships involving abuse. For example, a wife returns home to find that her ex-husband has painted filthy words all over the outside of her garage. To what, in "normal relationships," does that correspond? Similarly, a series of sweet love letters may become grotesque when their recipient pairs them with recurrent beatings from the same source. However, even here, it is the victim's task to show how such actions go beyond an exaggeration or realignment of some piece of normal, friendly communication.

In what follows, we construct the natural history of relational stalking in the sequence characteristic of unacquainted stalking. The core processes here include recognizing that one is being followed, learning that another is assembling detailed information about one's life and routines, fielding and putting off persistent relational proposals, countering continuing relational escalations, and handling threats and possible violence. We will also suggest sequential and substantive variations in these processes as recounted by those who have experienced acquaintance stalking.

Everyday Pursuits: Being Followed

Incipient or hoped-for relationships typically begin tentatively, with one or both parties unsure of the other, uncertain about how to cultivate a deeper connection. Even the most intense relationships have to grow from virtually nothing. Establishing and cultivating a relationship when the parties involved are initially unacquainted is especially problematic. Yet as Davis (1973:3) emphasizes, in contemporary urban, mass societies "the primal encounters between the previously unacquainted are a critical phase in personal relations." Of course, a significant number of a person's present intimates consist of "those who were at one time strangers to him and whom he can recall coming to know at a specific time and place" (Davis 1973:3).

Efforts to establish social relations with a stranger are often risky (Goffman 1963), and hence are pursued cautiously, relying on moves to promote casual encounters, to tie opening remarks to some small service (Davis 1973:5–6) or to a piece of public aid (Gardner 1988), to acquire information that might be useful for starting and building conversation, and so on. In light of the restrictions that ordinarily surround initiating engagements with strangers, it is not surprising that many delay making any overture, marking time in the hope of seeing a clear opening. Following another with whom one can envision a possible relationship, whether for shorter or longer periods, would appear to be particularly useful in this respect. Following allows one to look for natural opportunities to strike up a conversation, to acquire information about when and where one can expect to locate the other at another time and place, and to build up an initial store of information that might be used to stage a first engagement or to provide conversational material during that encounter.

Indeed, the relative frequency with which respondents reported that they had at some point followed or been followed by another suggests that following may be a relatively common event in many U.S. urban areas. While some followings involved disguised pursuit by an established romantic partner, many involved pursuit by strangers. Those involving strangers presumably began with some chance public encounter in which one party took note of another, then sought to keep the other in view.[11]

Our data provide at least glimpses into the fact that longer term intimate relationships may have initially involved public place following of someone who was a stranger. One respondent (California 1998), for example, reported that he met his former girlfriend while he was a college student and she a late-night shuttle bus driver, since "she had seen me in the library for the last two years and she had followed me around campus." Similarly, others reported that intimate relations developed out of public place service encounters. One woman said that her future fiancé "would come in where I was working over and over. It was positive. He was coming to see me and would always go through my checkout line at the grocery."

However, other followings do not turn out so positively, and do not lead to acknowledged or welcomed relationships. When following is made visibly apparent to the unacquainted, for example, even what turns out to be a one-time occurrence can become upsetting. Consider the account of a white male college student driving in gridlocked traffic after a professional basketball game, who noticed:

> a girl staring at me from another car, two lanes over. She was about my age and not bad looking, so I smiled at her, I guess, and she smiled back. . . . Then she began edging over into my lane, and she managed to get behind me in her car. . . . So I kind of kept an eye on her, sort of in my rearview mirrors, and there she was all the time, grinning and smiling at me.

Following sustained for days, weeks or even months, once detected by the pursued, can generate pervasive uneasiness, as in a young white woman's report:

> It was the summer of '95 when I started noticing that, whenever I went out to walk aerobics, I seemed to see the same maroon Chevy somewhere around me. Sometimes it would pass me; sometimes it kept pace with me for a little while—long enough for me to tell it wasn't anybody I knew. Sometimes I saw it parked ahead of me, with nobody in it but like it was waiting for me. . . . This lasted, on and off, maybe half the summer.

These feelings may be particularly intense when the pursued cannot identify the pursuer. One frequent consequence is to review one's past to try to infer who might be engaged in such an activity. This woman reported:

> It flickered through my mind, "Maybe it's one of my ex-boyfriends," who I have quite a lot of living in the general area. But I don't think I've parted from any of them with bad feelings. So I decided no, it wasn't that, and it wasn't any of their cars.

As in this case, even with pursuit persisting over an extended period, followed and follower may never make any direct visual or social contact. At times, lack of face-to-face engagement is a product of the follower's efforts to maintain distance and remain unidentifiable. The pursued's persistent efforts not visibly to acknowledge or ratify a pursuer's presence and interest may also prevent such contact, as indicated by the aerobic walker: "I never got a clear look at who it was. . . . I never would give him the satisfaction of looking over."

The followed often acknowledges such first overtures, initially responding to the other's presence, gesture, or greeting. But in many instances the pursued quickly decide against any further response. The young man in the basketball game gridlock described his subsequent reactions in these terms: "she was pretty and had a nice car, but I didn't smile back no more. I remember, for a while after this, after the gridlock broke, she followed me for a while, then I didn't see her." Likewise, a young black woman paralegal informant who was followed for several months to and from work by a white man in a pickup truck said: "he'd try to catch my eye and smile. The first time I saw him, I smiled back, but boy, never again."

Followings may also arise from more focused encounters, often brief and impersonal, linked to public places, such as everyday service encounters. And followings may arise among those who are distantly acquainted, as through occasional contact in a work setting. Computer technician Richard Farley and electrical engineer Laura Black, for example, were introduced by a coworker at their large Silicon Valley defense firm. While she thought nothing of their meeting and brief conversation, he reported, "I think I fell instantly in love with her. . . . It was just one of those things, I guess" (Gross 1992:191). Brooke Perry, who eventually sought a restraining order, was thrown into contact with her eventual stalker in two settings when "[he] joined the same religious organization as I belong to . . . [and] I got a job at the same office; I ended up working at the same business, at the same office as this individual. And . . . I saw him at the [religious] meetings as well as at work." And followings may develop from more prolonged workplace contacts, as in the case of a young white Midwestern man:

> I work at the big Denny's as night manager. One of the women I hired as a waitperson last summer used to follow me home—I found this out later. Honestly, I never really knew she liked me or anything and I hardly noticed her until my wife found her on our lawn one morning.

In these cases the pursued interpreted following as a bid to extend or deepen an existing if limited formal relationship (customer/server, co-workers) into a more intimate relationship.

As the above cases suggest, persons may not initially realize they are being followed, only at some later point coming to understand that this has been occurring. This realization may produce dramatic transformations of the awareness contexts (Glaser and Strauss 1965) between pursuer and pursued, the latter learning for the first time of the intense interest and sometimes quite extensive covert following. In some instances the trailing is even done quite openly and/or clumsily, in an effort to inform the pursued of the pursuit.

The famous are a special case with regard to following. Exposure to the famous through media creates a sense of "knowing" the other as a person (Horton and Wohl 1956), a pseudo-acquaintance. Also, if met in the flesh, the famous are "open" figures: strangers can approach them, address them by name, pose as critic of their oeuvre, and ask them for a small range of favors (autograph, handshake, photo op). Situational following is thus common and expected, if not always welcome, as when one young woman actor noted that, after an autograph, "women—and some guys, too—try to follow you into the john" (Pearlman 1997:182).

Persistent following that does not eventually lead to some sort of direct contact or overture can be particularly frightening and upsetting. The black woman repeatedly followed by a white man in a pickup truck over a period of months without any move toward personal contact, for example, came to interpret her pursuit as racially motivated intimidation and mockery:

> I think he just wanted to creep me out, and he definitely did that to the point where the thought of going to work or out in my car gave me stomach flips. After about two months it stopped, but still I thought about it. . . . In a way, I felt like he'd been teasing me—you know, it was like a parody of a person who's head-over-heels in love with you, romantically, and they follow you around all the time. [Why was it a parody?] Because black and white don't mix in this city, and because any black person who sees a peckerwood—excuse me—in a pickup anywhere near them is bound to be afraid. I was afraid.

In this respect learning that a follower wants to establish a relationship may provide a kind of ironic reassurance; his or her intentions are at least made visible and the process becomes a bit more comprehensible (if not necessarily more manageable).

In general, respondents reported that initial yet diffuse following could begin to generate a distinctive quality of stalking—the sense of menace. The eventual victim begins to experience the pursuer's persistent yet distanced attentions as "sinister" or "creepy," and begins to anticipate and dread the other's appearance jogging by their house, purchasing lunch in the restaurant where they regularly eat, or walking down the aisle of the supermarket they patronize. Even at initial junctures, victims can be aware that someone has noticed them in unusual ways, and may be alarmed by the pursuer's not attempting to advance the relationship in a "normal" fashion, as well as by trying for too much too soon. While this sense of menace may or may not be intended by the pursuer, it can seep into and color the pursued's daily life.

Here significant differences along gender lines appear in reactions to cross-gender following. When women followed and pursued men, the latter rarely expressed deep concern or upset, did not appear to be particularly threatened by the knowledge of their pursuit, and took few countermeasures in reaction. Consider this comment from a man:

> Didn't want to be mean to the girl who followed me. . . . I didn't really think she was psycho or anything. . . . Just felt weird and thought she was strange. No real threat—she couldn't rape me or anything. [A white man in his twenties who works in a white-collar job.]

Contrast this with the reactions of a woman who experienced persistent following:

> I could go to therapy with this [question] ! I thought this way [I'm about to tell you], but not anymore—well, I kind of am still cautious all the time.

> For instance, if I pull into the apartment complex and someone pulls in beside me, I won't park until they do. I look into my car before getting in. If it's empty, I jump in and hurry and lock the door. And then, I also make sure my feet are not close to the bottom of the car so no one can cut my Achilles. I used to be scared of being home alone. I'm not scared anymore with a baby. I am very cautious. Another thing, if home by myself, whatever room I'm in I close the door. For one, when the door is open someone could be watching. . . . And I am particularly cautious around men. They make me nervous. [A white woman homemaker in her twenties.]

In sum, following appears to be relatively common in everyday life, arising for a variety of purposes, usually short term and aimed at no one individual, and generally focused on and exploiting public places. There is thus considerable variation in whether someone who has come to recognize that they are being followed equates this with being stalked. The comments of a 27-year-old white woman student are typical in this regard: "[f]ollowing becomes stalking when the behavior is repeated. . . . It would seem the threat of harm would be greater. It could be (and often does) go on for many years. . . . In my mind, stalking seems more intentional, planned, premeditated than following." Thus, those who become aware that they have been followed tend to define this as stalking when the activity persists over a period of time, when no relational proposal is forthcoming, when the pursued begins to detect qualities of inappropriateness and threat, and when trailing is augmented by systematic efforts by the pursuer to increase knowledge about the life and routine of the pursued.

Access Information and Being Pursued

In order for any of the minimal encounters that commonly occur in our society—encounters between employees and customers, fellow pedestrians, coworkers, friends of friends, even fans and celebrities—to become more than a passing moment, one party must take steps to make it possible to make further contact with the other (Davis 1973). One way this may be done is to acquire some kind of access information (Gardner 1988) about the other; learning another's name, address, phone number, or workplace enables the unacquainted to attempt future contact on a more predictable basis. Providing access information about oneself and seeking such information about others is a normal, basic feature of many initial contacts between the unacquainted, especially those who envision possible future romantic contact (see, for example, Cloyd 1976). Indeed, many long-term romantic relationships spring from just such encounters that were extended in time and space by this kind of information.

While providing or acquiring access information is a constant, regular feature in everyday social life, people ordinarily seek to control and regulate who can legitimately accumulate such information about themselves. This tendency is particularly marked in public place encounters involving the unacquainted (Gardner 1988:384). There are strong gender differences in this regard: "women generally guarded their privacy, safety, and respectability by controlling the release of access information, whereas men often divulged the same information with little or no perception of personal risk" (Gardner 1988:384; see also Gardner 1995:131–148).

A key dynamic in the experience of those who are followed, whether briefly or persistently, involves just such efforts to restrict and control access information, even while regularly confronting evidence of the failure of these measures. As noted earlier, observable following often vividly conveys to the followed the detail or extent of the information another has acquired about oneself: a follower first noticed while walking near home who subsequently appears inside one's apartment building or at one's workplace provides a case in point. Or vice versa:

> One time this guy started talking to me at work. I didn't think nothing of it. He asked me what time I got off and I had told him. He had followed me all the way home. I was totally shocked when I seen him there.

Such instances dramatically remind the pursued how their most routine movements can be used by those who want to assemble access information.

On some occasions the followed learn that even a brief observation can be parlayed into detailed information. Consider the following complaint registered by a woman informant in her thirties who flagged down a police officer:

> The other day I was driving home from work—I work in Santa Barbara—and this man was following me. Anyway, he got my license plate number and gave that information to the DMV. He told them that he was a detective and he needed certain information about me. Now he knows where I live and stuff. What should I do?[12]

Those who learn they have been followed, then, may simultaneously learn that a stranger has been more or less systematically building up a wealth of working knowledge about their life and mundane activities. Thus, when a pursuer avers to the pursued, "I feel as if I've known you for a long time," the latter may hear this as an all too accurate statement.

Controlling the information from exes as opposed to the unacquainted reveals a somewhat different dynamic. The pursued knows that the ex already has detailed knowledge of their life circumstances, including telephone number, places of residence and business, the same information about a gallery of friends and family members, and customary hangouts and daily routines. The pursued, in turn, typically devote their efforts to blocking access—changing phone numbers, addresses, residences, locks, jobs, and even names, while enlisting the aid of friends, neighbors, and relatives to keep this new information from the other. Such efforts are often not successful, particularly if previous knowledge can be exploited to overcome efforts to restrict current access. For example, Danica Petersen reported that her ex-boyfriend knew she was a university student and lived near campus, and hence was able to locate her parked van: "[h]e spied around where he saw my van parked, prowling around . . . through the yards until he found where I lived by looking in the windows. . . . He hung around the student union area and began to try and figure out where my classes were and actually started following me to my classes."

Coworkers often are ideally placed to learn about one another's work and outside doings, so those concerned about being followed often have special concern about the availability and dissemination of information in the workplace. One professor, for example, eventually learned that the young white woman student who returned his wallet and briefcase lost from the poorly anchored trunk of his car had done so only after painstakingly recording all the information off his photo I.D.s and credit cards and photocopying his teaching schedule and student rosters. Similarly, Laura Black finally realized that, after she had declined to give Richard Farley information, he "asked a friend working in the ESL personnel office to look up Black's birthdate on the computer so he could surprise her. While the woman accessed Black's file on the computer, Farley leaned over her shoulder and memorized Black's home address as well" (Gross 1992:191).

Many of those who come to realize they have been persistently followed also learn of illicit steps pursuers have taken in order to learn about their lives. As a result, the pursued may become distrustful of normal appearances and claims. For example, a middle-aged man who was a driving student reported that a fellow, "angelic-looking" woman student told their driving instructor that the man had left his text behind (in fact, she had stolen his book from the rack under his desk) and volunteered to return it since "she was pretty sure we were neighbors—she just needed to look at the instructor's roster to get the exact address." The instructor obliged, also helpfully providing the phone number. As the informant noted: "that was step one into my private life. From then on, the fun never stopped."

The pursued may also discover that their pursuer will turn not only to public agencies and corporate sources, but also to their own families, friends, and intimates, drawing these parties into and implicating them unknowingly in the illicit acquisition of access information. One young black man acquired the phone number of a young black woman—she had introduced herself to him at a funeral—by calling every listing with her (rather common) last name in the phonebook. Although her number was unlisted, her father was listed. The man told her father how much her words at the funeral had meant to him and, deeply touched, her father gave the man his daughter's phone number. Then, apparently using the three-digit phone number prefix, the man "figured out about where I live and just went driving around till he saw me [on the street] one day." As notable as this pursuer's claims of noble emotions were his labor-intensive methods.[13]

Those being followed may discover that their pursuer is looking for means for gaining immediate access to their possessions, space, or person without their consent or cooperation. For example, the young black woman informant whose father gave out her phone number found her follower going through several large bags of her garbage; she assumed that he was looking for "maybe some schedule or page from my appointment book . . . or maybe he thought he'd luck out and find a dupe backdoor key, who knows." She reported the "distinct feeling [that] this man was after getting to me, getting in my house or maybe, oh boy, surprising me at work at a big meeting, or—I don't know what. But there was something different about that time."[14] Some victims even came to feel that the acquisition of detailed, intimate information had become an end in itself for the pursuer.

What is particularly disturbing to victims of persistent following is not simply discovering that the pursuer is seeking ways of gaining this direct access by all means possible, but also that the pursuer wants them to know that this is occurring. Some pursuers deliberately convey to their victims the amount and details of the intimate information they have acquired. For example, Richard Farley told Laura Black how he had painstakingly made a key for her house, and actually received a copy of the key from him in proof of his claim, accompanied by his promise that he would never use it. In the same way, other followers boasted to victims about their ability to circumvent any efforts the victims might take to curtail access to information or resources—or to victims' attempts to change information or resources. For example, when Brooke Perry got an unlisted phone number in an attempt to avoid harassing calls from her pursuer, she received this message on her answering machine: "'in case you're wondering how I got your number . . . I can get your number anytime, I've got a friend at GTE [the telephone company]. . . . I've had the number since the day you changed it."

These communications often create or heighten the pursuer's sense of being a victim of stalking, generating feelings of being threatened, menaced, or even shamed. The sense of being stalked thereby arises with feelings that another—an ex, a stranger—now knows more about one's life than many of one's intimates, and more than the victim wants known, that this information is ill gotten and illegitimate, and that the victim has lost control over what is known by whom. A black woman department store worker reflected on the man who followed her:

> He knew for sure where I lived, what my routine was, where I walked, where I shopped [for food] and took my dry cleaning. Just from that, he could have easily found out more about me, enough so he could insinuate his way more into my life. At the time, I was afraid he also would show up at [the large department store where she has a position working with the public] or inside my apartment.

These feelings are apt to become stronger as the pursued learns that the pursuer is continuing to collect and update information (and craftily to accumulate more access resources), even in the face of pervasive efforts to limit access to such information. In fact, the threats from having lost control over access information may persist as a sense of uncertainty even after overt following has stopped. The woman in the previous example continued: "and then, of course, when he stopped, I was never sure it was over. This was two years ago, and I'm still not sure."

It is here that we again find particularly significant gender differences. Tjaden and Thoennes (1998:3–5) report that both women and men may find themselves victims of stalking, and that both men and women can engage in stalking—although women are more often victims, and men stalkers. Beyond such frequencies, however, female victims of male pursuers and stalkers perceive risk, threat, and menace as much more pervasive and immediate than do male victims of female stalkers.

Initial Proposals and Initial Rejections

While relational stalking involves efforts to resist attempts to establish or maintain a relationship, neither following nor acquiring access information involve explicit relational proposals. But such proposals (for example, an overture by the pursuer to the pursued to begin or continue a relationship of a particular sort) are commonly made, and sometimes the pursued responds to them favorably: some offers to meet and some dating/relational proposals are accepted, and a number of short-term relations certainly develop briefly and then dissolve from such beginnings. Relationships between sports and rock stars and their "groupies" are notorious in this regard (see Chamberlain 1991; Des Barres 1987). And, indeed, some long-term relationships spring from such beginnings: one woman reported receiving a series of anonymous notes and gifts from the man who would eventually become her husband. Even fan/celebrity contacts may produce long-term relationships upon occasion: TV heartthrob Luke Perry, for example, married a woman whom he first met after she sent him a fan letter containing one of her undergarments. Similarly, a number of couples in the throes of breakups or long-term separations ultimately may reconcile, transforming what might have been a permanent end to the relationship into mere temporary separation. In all these instances, then, a proposal (or in the case of exes, a counterproposal) is accepted and a mutual relationship created or reestablished.

In the instances that came to be seen as stalking, however, those receiving proposals reported that they rejected them, but that rejection failed to end pursuit, and that implicit or explicit proposals continued. In this section we examine the sorts of initial proposals linked to episodes of following and the acquisition of knowledge, as well as the rejections of such proposals reported by respondents. But in many of the cases, relational claims and proposals did not end with such initial rejections, setting up the dynamic characteristic of stalking that we examine in the next section—experiencing persistent relational overtures despite continuing rejection.

Among the unacquainted, an overture may be offered during the very first meeting or verbal contact between the two parties; alternatively, it may arise much later after a substantial period of following and accumulating access information. In the first case, a pursuer who has made minimal contact with the pursued may simply rely on that contact to ask for a meeting or date, hence making a bid to begin a particular kind of relationship with the other. In the second, the pursuer may wait until accumulating a rich body of knowledge about the other, trying to select an opportune occasion and way to advance a proposal. Of course, relational proposals may continue to be offered, after the first rejection. Proposals vary, not only in timing, but in form and substance. The pursued may be asked directly for a phone number to call in the future for a meeting or date: Larry Stagner's first overt attempt to contact his former highschool classmate Kathleen Baty was to call her at her parents' home (but using a false name); Richard Farley approached Laura Black at work and asked her to attend a truck pull with him.

Others receive more indirect proposals in the form of anonymous phonecalls, letters, or gifts. Many of these actions make an announcement of relational interest rather than an explicit relational proposal. Thus, answering machines may become laden with flattering messages from an unidentified caller; anonymous notes of admiration may be left on a car, in a mailbox, or mailed to one's home; flowers may be left on the doorstep or sent to the workplace, perhaps with a card unsigned or minimally inscribed ("An Admirer," "Your Friend—I want to be," or "Your Adoring Audience," the last to a professor who thought it came from one of the roughly 500 students in a lecture class).[15]

As noted previously, while in some instances the pursued may have previously detected the interest of another in the intricacies of her or his daily rounds, in many cases the pursued becomes aware of this interest only upon receipt of a proposal. As a result, proposals may dramatically transform the awareness context between pursuer and pursued, the latter learning for the first time of the other's intense interest, prior covert following, and accumulation of information about her or his daily life. For some this process was extremely traumatic. For example, a white nurse in her thirties became extremely upset upon receiving a note that read, in part, "I am following you everywhere." Similarly, a white woman college student with one hand who had noticed for some time that a man in a red pickup truck was following her on her daily rounds recounted this experience:

> [While walking home], all of a sudden, I passed and saw an envelope with lettering on it. I thought it said, "Man with one hand"—*what*? I turned around and looked again and the letter was addressed, "For the woman with one hand." I picked it up and read it. It said I was an angel and he would build me anything. He was a carpenter. He said his whole life had changed after seeing me. I was shaking. . . . [I]n that letter he said he knew where I lived and had left a rose at my doorstep. I didn't get a rose, so I knew wherever he thought I lived was wrong. Nails and duct tape and string were with the letter, and I was supposed to leave a letter on how I felt.

In part, this relational proposal frightened its recipient because it revealed almost without warning that another had become fixated on her and sought to acquire close familiarity with her life (even if somewhat inaccurately to that point). Moreover, the recipient was frightened because she found something inappropriate and "off" about the proposal: it was excessive in its expressions of devotion, presumptuous in its projection of a future union, and peremptory in directing her reply.

A number of victims of future stalking noted this disturbingly inappropriate quality of initial proposals, which might be glossed as "something off," "it seemed funny somehow," "outré," or one of a dozen other phrases. But the more ordinary the proposal (asking for a date, for example), the more likely it was to be seen initially as unproblematic, the "off" quality becoming apparent only in retrospect. On the other hand, frequent hang-up phone calls, assumed names, or the use of devious means to make contact made many recipients uneasy or suspicious right from the start. In addition, recipients sometimes experienced elements of self-centeredness and inconsiderateness in such contacts and proposals. Thus, an Indian psychologist living in the Midwest was first contacted by a man who subsequently began to stalk her when he began to leave telephone messages at her office "expressing great interest in speaking more to me about the psychological implications of the Hindu pantheon," a topic in which she had absolutely no interest. Or, as a woman who had a dozen long-stemmed roses delivered to her office without a card pointed out, the person her office mates called her "Secret Admirer" also showed disregard for her: it "takes up forever to figure out what to do with all those flowers at work, which my boss doesn't appreciate. And, by the way: I hate roses."[16]

When the parties involved have a relationship or have had a prior relationship, relational proposals take on a different quality. In these situations the "proposal" is not to begin but to maintain a relationship that the other explicitly seeks to end, as rejection precedes rather than follows a consequential relational proposal. In this sense, an ex-to-be is actually *reacting* to the initiative of the other who desires to leave, offering a *counterproposal* to continue a relationship called into question (and see Vaughan 1986).

In some cases, relational proposals, whether to begin a new relationship or maintain an old one, are accepted, and a new relation may form, or an old one revive, at least temporarily. In other situations, the other may initially agree to a proposal, but subsequently decline any further meetings, hence rejecting any further relationship. But in the accounts provided by our respondents, the pursued rejected such initial proposals and the sustained or intimate relationships they sought to establish or maintain. In some situations involving the unacquainted, the pursued may reject immediately and consistently, declining any and all dates, meetings, or future contact. In doing so, however, they may use any of a number of standard accounts or excuses to deliver this rejection in ways that minimize damage to the proposer's ego. Consider the explanation offered by the woman followed home by a man customer:

> He asked me if I could give him my number and I told him no because I lived with my boyfriend. [In telling him this] I had lied. But that's the only way to get rid of him that I had at the time. It worked. As far as I knew, he never returned to work or at my home.

Or consider Laura Black's attempt at face-saving in rejecting Richard Farley's proposal to go out: "I tried to explain to him that I wasn't interested in being anything other than a work friend" (Gross 1992).

At first glance, these rejections might appear partial and somewhat equivocal. And, in point of fact, in many instances the proposer is not explicitly and forcefully told that his or her proposal would never be accepted under any imaginable conditions; most relational rejections are delivered in ways that offer the proposer at least some opportunity to save face. Thus, it may well be that persistence trades on ignoring the rejecting message being conveyed, or submerging the negative content of the communication in favor of its civil, face-saving form. Nonetheless, it should be apparent that such responses would be heard as clearly and firmly negative by many people. Moreover, the "clarity" of the rejecter's rejection is not the key issue here; in many situations, rejecters report experiences where the proposer ignored, denied, or rationalized even the most unambiguous rejections and continued to seek contact.[17] As a result, unmitigated rejections to proposals from the unacquainted and exes are more likely to be made to repeated rather than to initial proposals; it is at that point that it becomes clear to the recipient that the civility of refusals was being used to sustain morale.

Rejections vary in the pseudoacquainted stalking of fan/celebrity contacts, depending upon the nature of the contact. Since celebrities typically restrict direct access to their person, initial contacts are usually indirect—frequently letters or perhaps gifts sent to studios. Thus, initial rejections are delivered in an impersonal, automatic, often mass-produced fashion: either letters go unanswered and gifts unacknowledged, or form letters of thanks are sent out. Attempts at face-to-face confrontation with the celebrity can be met with the impersonal baffle of a security force or entourage—or direct request from the celebrity to cease and desist, which may be as invigorating for the fan as continued contact itself.

Similar processes can mark an ex's reactions to a counterproposal to continue the relationship the former has sought to downgrade or break off. Sometimes the counterproposal is rejected in unequivocal terms. But in other instances such a rejection is taken as encouraging simply because it involves face-to-face interaction, indirection, and a concern to minimize affront (on the strategic need for interactional subtlety, see Vaughan 1986:66). Even when conflict comes to a head and direct confrontation does occur, equivocation may nonetheless mark its resolution, for agreement on either may prove temporary, the abandoned only acquiescing long enough to placate the abandoner or vice versa. Consider the problems that can arise when one party demands that the other move out, often a key moment in uncoupling. One young white woman, for example, insisted to her boyfriend "that he had to make arrangements to leave immediately. No ifs, ands, or buts . . . 'I want you out of here. You have to go.' And he wouldn't leave." She was eventually able to get him to leave but then had to change the locks to keep him from simply returning when he wanted. In the face of concerted opposition, then, "breaking up" may come to involve continuing conflict marked by "rehashing" (Clark and LaBeff 1986:263) further proposals and rejections. Separations under these conditions take on an open-ended character, as reflected in the words of a former cohabiting partner and subsequent stalking victim: "I've been definitely breaking it off and it wasn't working too well."

Persistence and the Recognition of Stalking

Relational proposals and rejections are not limited to a single round, but occur again and again; the first rebuff of the pursuer's persistent advances and claims need not be the last. Moreover, persistence in the face of rejection sometimes pays off and may in fact produce a long-term relationship; some spouses recount having first met in this manner, including the woman quoted earlier who met her future fiancé as the result of his persistent use of her checkout line. However, when relational claims continue or even escalate in the face of rejection, the pursued not only explicitly depict themselves as victims of stalking, but also increasingly report the feelings of fear, frustration, and anguish characteristic of such victims. It is by highlighting the persistence in the face of multiple and consistent rejection that the other is identified as a stalker. As one respondent reflected, again in retrospect, actions become stalking "[w]hen the one incident becomes multiple incidents. When the follower is told that his/ her intentions are unwanted and still persists. When the person knows your schedule and shows up at your workplace, etcetera."

Critical in this regard is learning about the pursuer's increasingly labyrinthine efforts to accumulate personal information about one's life in the face of systematic resistance and strong discouragement. For example, denied entry by studio security when he tried to hand-deliver a stuffed animal, Robert Barrio used a private detective to find Rebecca Schaeffer at home. Similarly, turned down in his efforts to date Laura Black, Richard Farley convinced a security guard that Black's desk was his own in order to get an extra key that he then used to dig through her personal belongings. The pursued may experience these one-sided quests for personal information and recurrent intrusions into one's everyday routines in a variety of forms.

First, the pursued may receive increasingly frequent phone calls. Douglas Mann complained, "She is calling my job, I am this close to being fired from my job. . . .

[S]ometimes she'll call me, I'll hang up on her and she'll call me back twenty-five times. They're going to fire me for this if it continues." Others experienced persistent hang-up calls where no words were exchanged, but where it was clear to the respondents just who was calling. Brooke Perry recalled:

> I had received hang-up phone calls all the time . . . the first few weeks after I told him, you know, to bug off, uh, probably about five or six times a day. Anywhere from 5:30 in the morning until 1:30 at night. And, um, when I would confront him about the phone calls, he would simply deny it and tell me I'm crazy. . . . [T]his had been going on for about two years.

Second, the pursued may receive continued or ever-more-lavish gifts. Tina Teller reported: "[h]e would send me flowers so many times at work until I was embarrassed. I was like, 'I don't believe this.' They would call me, 'Tina, we don't believe you got some more flowers. Who is this guy?' And I was like, 'I wish he would stop.'" In general, persistent gift-giving becomes an imposition, with the recipient quickly coming to dislike and to decline these items. In turn the giver learns ways of leaving presents through which the presents need not be directly accepted. Danica Petersen recalled: "[he] started leaving gifts for me by the door, leaving gifts inside of the car, that he still had a key to." In this way the rejected pursuer becomes an uninvited part of the other's everyday life.

Third, the pursued may find that the pursuer begins to show up or regularly drop by home or work. Brooke Perry, for example, found that her pursuer had moved into her neighborhood and began jogging past her house every day. He then began to drop by her house at odd hours, and "at one point in time, he came over to my house like six o'clock in the morning, knocking on my door." Exes are particularly adept at "pop-up" appearances—Darlene Zygmunt, a 40-year-old white lawyer, said that her husband's pattern of "Jack-in-the-box appearances cumulatively told me that I could find him anyplace, from my living room to our old box at the Symphony to our daughter's playgroup, and anytime, from the middle of the night on the porch to walking past the glass walls of my office in the middle of the day."

Fourth, the pursued may find the pursuer intruding into his or her family and friendship networks, trying to elicit information and enlist allies. Particularly in the case of exes, family and friends can be besieged with calls from the pursuer. Suzanne Healy complained: "he called a girlfriend of mine named Sheila . . . and just lost it . . . and she just kept saying, 'Look, she doesn't want anything to do with you! Why don't you just leave her alone?'" Douglas Mann reported that his ex-girlfriend "just continues to call my mother at 3 o'clock in the morning . . . she just babbles on and on. My mother turns on the machine and just gets a 20-minute message."

As the result of these activities, the pursued experiences widening intrusion into the fabric of her or his daily life and, in response, may change her or his routines to try to make any contact at all more difficult, all the while denying that any sort of legitimate relationship exists. Phone numbers are changed, unlisted numbers obtained, a residence unknown to the stalker occupied temporarily, old haunts or areas where the stalker might be encountered avoided. Stalking victims devote considerable efforts to trying such "normal remedies" (Emerson 1981), generally involving avoidance and distancing, to prevent further contact (see also Tjaden and Thoennes's "self-protective measures undertaken by stalking victims," 1998:13).

Instead of finding the pursuer retreating in the face of explicit rejections and systematic avoidance, the pursued experiences continued and perhaps even escalating relational claims:

> [T]he door opened at 7 A.M. to reveal a letter that had been left on my porch sometime during the night or early morning. . . . Sometimes the letters were pleading: "I dreamt last night that you had a boyfriend and you were in bed with him. . . . I hope that wasn't true. Tell me it wasn't." [Or they] were simple and direct statements of how John felt: "I love you so much I can't wait until we see each other. It's been too long." (Horton 1992:16)

Moreover, as in this case, the pursued may begin to receive more sinister symbolic messages mingled with the expressions of devotion. On her birthday, Brooke Perry received a bottle of perfume, "Obsession," even though she did not wear it (and she was not the only stalked woman to receive an item from this product line).

With these developments, the pursued comes to realize that half-measures are not working, and turns from responses relying primarily on avoidance and distance to more exceptional, costly, disruptive remedies. Three such exceptional remedies stand out: first, the pursued might at this point seek out the pursuer to deliver an extreme denunciation and ultimatum. Laura Black eventually told Richard Farley, "I would not go out with you if you were the last man on earth." Similarly, Brooke Perry ultimately went directly to her pursuer to try to put an end to his relational overtures: "I said, 'I don't want anything to do with you, ever again. I don't want you coming over to my house. And I don't want you to call me. This is it. I don't want nothing to do with you.' You know, 'You're just too weird.'" Second, victims of persistent pursuit will sometimes turn to the legal system for help, calling the police, and/or seeking a restraining order against the pursuer. Finally, victims may make dramatic changes in their life circumstances with the intention of ending any further pursuit and contact. Danica Petersen, for example, tried a geographical cure, moving to Chicago, Minneapolis, and Texas in an effort to discourage Art Maldonado, but her unwanted suitor found and followed her each time.

This struggle can sometimes escalate to frightening levels of unreality. Brooke Perry's experience with her pursuer provides an extreme instance: "some people [at the church community center] approached me and congratulated me on my upcoming wedding. And I said, 'What are you talking about? To who?' 'Well, to Jason Wyatt.' So he was out, telling people that we were getting married. I mean, just totally berserk."

As the victim realizes that even the most unequivocal rebuffs and rejections do not deter the pursuer, the former's sense of menace deepens and takes on fatalistic, hopeless qualities. The victim repeatedly encounters the stalker's lack of response to what the victim considers the reality of the situation: the victim believes there is no relationship, but the stalker continues to evince belief that there is one. This is especially the point at which things that others might see as flattering or romantic—an overwhelming volume of flowers, little gifts on the doorstep every morning—become, to the victim, sinister, for they are presented in the face of outright rejection and become evidence, to the victim, of the stalker's intent to persist to the bitter end (whatever that might be).

It is precisely the experience of this type of persistence in the face of continuing rejection that can identify stalking for its victims. Victims not only see the other dismissing, brushing aside, and reinterpreting the most severe rejections in continuing to advance relational claims; they also directly encounter the now-stalker's refusal to address or acknowledge their contrary relational claim. As a result, the victim experiences a sense of radical non-alignment in the respective relational claims. Danica Petersen highlighted these processes:

> I tried to break off the relationship by telling him, you know, "It's over and I don't want to see you anymore." And I had several boyfriends in junior high school and high school and a couple during the first year of college, so it's not as if it was the first relationship. *But I had never experienced someone who when you told them that you didn't want to be with them anymore they didn't go away. Um, most people will say, "Oh, you know, sorry, uh, I'll get out of here now." And that's sort of the end of it. But this, this person, um, didn't accept the idea that I wanted to not be with him.* (Emphasis added.)

As a result the victim experiences stalking's distinctive relational dynamic: an explicitly rejected pursuer persists in seeking a relationship, elaborating new tactics for gathering access information and for making contact in the face of clear and sustained resistance, continuing rejections of overtures, and denials of willing contact. The consequence is a sense of unasked-for involvement in one's daily life imposed over and against deep resistance. As one stalking victim aptly stated: "[h]e just wanted to make it clear . . . that he was a part of my life whether I liked it or not" (Horton 1992:16).

The Turn toward Revenge: Hostility, Jealousy, Rage, and Violence

Full-blown stalking relationships are marked by deep changes in the pursuer's orientation and actions and in fact may become overwhelmingly, aggressively negative. Continuing rejection in the face of persistent relational claims and proposals often sours earlier expressions of devotion and affection, as the pursuer increasingly mixes expressions of hostility and jealousy and threats of reprisal with claims of love and relationship. The spurned pursuer may now become the prototypical stalker, following and seeking access to the other in order to intimidate, frighten, or injure. While threats of violence and the creation of a sense of menace may be as far as some stalkers ever go, other stalkings culminate in violence, often in ways that attract extensive media attention.

Some threats of violence are delivered indirectly. Holly Murphy, for example, recounted how her ex-husband called attention to his own "obsession": "[h]e still calls me . . . to tell me he loves and misses me—at one point he even called me and said that he's obsessed with me and he worships me. . . . And I said, 'You know, you sound like that guy who killed Rebecca Schaeffer.' He says, 'I can understand it. I can understand it.'" In declining to distance himself from the killer of Rebecca Schaeffer, this ex-husband intimates a chilling if unspecified outcome. Similarly, Texas senator Bob Krueger and his wife, stalked by a former campaign worker who just could not let go after Krueger lost the 1984 primary, began receiving obsessive overtures. Mrs. Krueger stated, "He'd tell us he loved us, that we meant the world to him." However, when the Kruegers spurned those overtures, his daily communiqués grew more sinister, until he finally made the specific threat that got him imprisoned: "I'm going to kill you. I'm going to kill you. I'm going to kill you. I've hired a killer to put a .22 caliber to your head while you lie sleeping next to your wife" (Ellis et al. 1993).

The indirect threats described above were embedded in verbal claims of love and admiration, serving to create an exasperating sense of mixed messages. Threats could also be more explicit and unencumbered by any expression of current love. Richard Farley's letter to Laura Black, written after she reported him to their company's personnel department, documents this transition from love to hate:

> Time to remove the kid gloves. I asked you to see me and you refused, that is your right. It's my option to make your life miserable, if that's what you really want. You asked me what I could do. Kill you? The answer to that was and still is no. If I killed you, you won't be able to regret what you did.

Even in cases such as these, stalking victims may have difficulty getting the legal system to take their complaints seriously, particularly if the stalker stops short of actual violence. Consider the account of a homemaker in her forties, who had been battered and stalked by her first husband:

> [When asked to rate kinds of stalking experiences, the] worst is being followed in the car. The man following me was my husband. We were separated. He would follow me home from work and try to run me off the road. The cops aren't much help, because in order to help me Phil would [actually] have to run me off the road. Phil would stare at me—a spooky, evil-eyed stare. He would stay in the parking lot and wait for me to get off of work. He wasn't allowed in the restaurant: the people [managers] of the restaurant knew Phil was dangerous to me, so they didn't allow him in the restaurant. My boss seen Phil hit me.

Here the victim obtained what protection she could informally from her employers, not the legal system. Yet a sense of menace, of continuing vulnerability to someone who appears willing to ignore the costs of formal punishment, pervades this account.

While stalkers who actually kill are relatively rare (with one exception, all our data on stalking deaths derive from media reports), these instances are extremely dramatic (Lardner 1995; *Newsweek* 1992).[18] Killing may serve as a way of linking the fates of the two parties, of creating a permanent relationship, if ex post facto, between stalker and victim. Larry Stagner seemed to take this approach when he kidnapped Kathleen Baty: "my life's over, please come with me this last time," he pleaded with her. This interpretation is supported by an additional theme that marks a number of killings: the stalker goes a step further, claiming not only that if the stalker could not have the pursued no one else could either, but also that "if I can't have you, I can't live." Often, in planning a violent outburst, the stalker mentioned his or her own intended death in the plan, whether he or she was ultimately successful or not. Thus, in a note to Laura Black, Richard Farley wrote: "[l]et's say you don't back down and I don't back down, and pretty soon, I crack under pressure and run amok, destroying everything in my path until the police catch and kill me." While he was not killed by the police, he wounded Black, killed seven others, and was ultimately sentenced to death for his killing rampage (Gross 1992). Leslie Vandenberg described her kidnapping by David Prince in these terms: "he drove me around and, uh, he was threatening me that he, they were going to find me dead in the morning or both of us dead in the morning. . . . [H]e threatened that he was going to choke me and he had a knife and he put the knife, like, to my chest, like he was going to stab me and then he went in the bathroom and said that he was just going to kill himself."

In some cases these suicidal intentions are realized: A number of stalker killings ended with the pursuer committing suicide, or trying to, after having slain the victim. Michael Cartier, who killed Kristin Lardner after stalking her for a month in the wake of the breakup, ran home and shot himself to death immediately after killing her (Lardner 1995), and Rick Varela stalked and eventually gunned down his ex-girlfriend Sarah Auerbach in her New York City dry cleaner's shop, then shot himself in the head in a nearby park (*Arizona Republic*, April 9, 1994). What is especially tragic about these outcomes is that they often provide the first situation in which all participants agree unequivocally that what is going on is indeed dangerous, and is indeed "stalking"—an agreement which may come too late to save the victims.

Conclusion

Stalking is an extremely complex phenomenon to address sociologically, since many aspects of what comes to be seen as "stalking" are routine features of budding or dissolving relationships. Following another who is seen as a possible romantic interest, collecting and accumulating information about that other's identity, life, and routines, making overtures and even explicit proposals to develop a relationship, and carrying on doggedly in pursuit of such a relationship even in the face of persistent (but from the pursuer's point of view, initial) rejections are regular, sometimes even commonplace activities in many ordinary relationships. Moreover, these activities appear in a range of normal relations: the initially unacquainted who may maneuver to create or avoid opportunities to meet, date, romance one another, the ex-spouse or former boy- or girlfriend who is trying to renew or maintain a relationship with an ex, the fan who seeks to cultivate some kind of special standing with a celebrity.

Consider, for example, the breakup of intimate relationships. Vaughan (1986) argues that the dynamics of "uncoupling" between exes-to-be are marked by the lack of synchronicity between the "initiator"—the person who initially becomes discontented with the relationship and "who first begins the social transition out of the relationship" (122)—and the other "partner," who for a long period of time remains unaware of the initiator's discontent and moves toward transition. Thus, the initiator often gives up on the relationship even while the partner may remain committed to it; only subsequently does the partner give up on the relationship and make his or her uncoupling transition, the initiator often continuing to "display discontent to convince the partner that the relationship is unsalvageable."[19] In this sense, uncoupling is a process of out-of-sync transitions from an initially shared social world; symmetry may finally be restored only when both partners come to accept the end of the relationship.

But until this sort of congruent alignment is established—an outcome that is hardly assured, and that in some instances may never occur—the parties involved may find themselves threatened by a kind of relational *havoc* (Goffman 1971). Havoc arises when each defines the relationship in ways that the other cannot or will not accept, when neither can get the other to change his or her definition and all that goes with it, and when exit does not occur. Presumably, in most uncouplings such havoc is either avoided or is of short duration: one or the other party eventually changes his or her definition of the relationship, or simply decides to move on without explicit resolution. Trouble arises when neither party changes their irreconcilable definitions of the relationship, yet some sort of contact continues. This is the breeding ground for stalking. Many instances of what may eventually come to be recognized as stalking grow out of these relational dynamics, dynamics involving deep yet persisting disjuncture and misalignment.

Instances that come to be interpreted as stalking thus make visible the problematics of ending a relationship, of producing exit: while leaving might appear to be an individual, unilateral act, in fact its accomplishment depends upon the other's acceptance or acquiescence. This quality is quite general: any relational outcome depends in some sense upon the actions and agreement of both parties. Thus, rejecting a proposal is not unilateral, but depends upon the other's reactions for its realization. If the other accepts the rejection and acts accordingly—that is, if the rejection is uncontested—all well and good. If not, statements of rejection, no matter how clear and forceful, do not assure that efforts to create or end a relationship will cease. Ironically, then, not having a relationship, or ending a relationship, requires the agreement, or at least the acquiescence, of both parties (Ferris 1990).

Those who report having been stalked frame this experience exactly as one marked by radical asymmetry: at the extreme, the victims of stalking describe efforts by someone with whom they "have" absolutely no relationship to impose a relationship on them. Victims' accounts, then, highlight this asymmetry, depicting both their own shortcircuitings and rejections of the relational proposals, and the other's claims and persistence in advancing and often escalating these proposals and claims. Victims thus describe stalking as a matter of relational misalignment and imposition as the pursuer increasingly inserts him- or herself in their life and routines, overcoming heightened avoidance and raised barriers to do so.

In these terms, stalking victims' accounts show one final, intriguing feature: they depict common alignment reemerging if and when their pursuer abandons efforts to claim intimate relations. Thus, when expressions of devotion give way to outbursts of rage and retaliation, when the pursuer now says "I used to love you but now I just want to make your life miserable," victim and pursuer come to share common definitional ground; both now acknowledge that what is taking place is "stalking" and that the latter is openly and appropriately termed a "stalker." The irony is that such interpretive symmetry is frequently a product of the very acts of exploitation, harassment, and violence that have come to epitomize stalking in the vernacular understanding.

Notes

Authors are listed in alphabetic order. The authors wish to express their gratitude for comments, data, and criticisms contributed by Melvin Pollner, Jack Katz, Stephanie Chiv, Robert Garot, Yvette Guerra, Byron Burkhalter, Maggie Kusenbach, Lakshmi Srinivas, Christine Morton, and Tamara Sniezek; they also acknowledge the interviewing and research assistance of Melissa Babione, Jill Bakehorn, Melissa Daigrepont, Johna Hawkins, Barry Stewart, and Jason A. Whitesel. And we are forever in debt to Jim Holstein, whose constructionist leanings are not quite as consistently reflected in the text as we or he would like.

1. In support of this critique, Tjaden and Thoennes (1998:8) report that only 7 percent of all stalking victims explained stalking as the result of mental illness or the abuse of drugs or alcohol.

2. Tjaden and Thoennes thus define stalking operationally as "'a course of conduct directed at a specific person that involves repeated visual or physical proximity, nonconsensual communication, or verbal, written, or implied threats, or a combination thereof, that would cause a reasonable person fear,' with repeated meaning on two or more occasions" (1998:2).

3. This question was worded as follows: "In your mind, at what point does *following* become *stalking?*" This question provided the only point in the interview guide where the term "stalking" was used.

4. This research was supported by National Science Foundation grant SES-8713255, "The Pro Se Litigant: Self-Representation in Consequential Civil Cases," Co-Principal Investigators Robert M. Emerson and Susan McCoin.

5. This tendency supports the constructionist argument of Lowney and Best (1995) that the term "stalking" gained currency only after 1992; the 1980s saw similar actions characterized as "harassment," "obsession," etc.

6. Throughout this chapter, we have altered names and in some cases other identifying details to protect the identities of those involved, except in those cases reported in the media. In the latter instances, individuals' names even when derived from the cited secondary source are a matter of public record.

7. We have collected four additional sorts of data that do not rely exclusively on victim accounts: First, in observing the processing of TRO petitions, we observed a number of instances in which the defendant appeared and challenged the accusations presented by the petitioner. Second, respondents in the following interviews were asked if they themselves (or a proxy) had ever followed another; fourteen of the 41 people interviewed reported that they had done so, although they invariably rated themselves on the low level of offense. Third, we conducted an additional seven interviews with individuals—four with men and three with women—who admitted to having followed or even "stalked" another. One of these men had killed his victim, an ex-girlfriend, and is presently incarcerated. Finally, we have collected a series of interviews and observations involving media fans, some of whom engage in activities that are or might be perceived as stalking. Given our focus on the perspectives of stalking victims, we draw upon these sources of data only occasionally, and then primarily when examining later stages where there is less equivocality among all parties that stalking is occurring.

8. For example, consider the following situation involving a fan's pursuit of a celebrity: Even after her favorite actor asked her to cease meeting him at the airport because of its connotations of stalking, Diane continued to wait each night outside the stagedoor when he performed in a local play, and on the night of the last performance, followed him and his after-theater companions to a Hollywood restaurant, where she dined at the next table with her friends. Diane

considered this following a very different matter than meeting unannounced airport arrivals, and certainly did not view herself as a stalker, although the celebrity gave every indication that this was just how he viewed her.

9. That is, while neither denying victims' stories nor discounting the incidents and experiences they report, we seek to provide a context for understanding how their observations and conclusions emerged from circumstances that were much more fluid, indeterminate, interpretively problematic, and open-ended than the endpoint accounts suggest.

10. Using the figures provided by Tjaden and Thoennes (1998:6), almost 40 percent of everyday stalkings involve acquaintances or strangers.

11. "Presumably" because in many instances the initial encounters that were so meaningful to one party went unnoticed by the other. Thus, victims' accounts of initial contacts are fundamentally retrospective in character, reconstructed after they become aware of a pursuer.

12. The Department of Motor Vehicles can allow conversion of publicly visible information (license plate numbers) into rich, specific access information, making these bureaus figure in stalking incidents; in the aftermath of the Rebecca Schaeffer killing, the power of the California DMV to divulge such information was severely restricted.

13. Some fans employ similar deceptions and ruses to acquire celebrity access information, perhaps with like rationalizations. One Los Angeles fan described how she and a friend learned the home addresses of some of their favorite television stars:

> My friend and I snuck into the [Studio] lot—he told the guard he was in some theater group. And we couldn't get onto the set, but I took a bunch of stuff, papers, from the bike messenger's basket when it was parked. I figure that's not stealing, they can just make more Xeroxes. Anyway, the addresses were on it. . . . [T]hey live in the hills, mostly, and I can go by their houses.

14. A number of eventual stalking victims came to learn that their pursuer had been accumulating *access resources*, that is, items that could provide immediate physical access to the person, space, or possessions of the pursued. Art Maldonado, for instance, kept a key which he used to gain access to Danica Petersen's car. Richard Farley lurked around Laura Black's home, doggedly (but unsuccessfully) seeking the code for her electronic garage door opener, and eventually obtaining a copy of her house key by taking a clay mold from her keyring while she was momentarily away from her desk, a tactic that many might heretofore have believed limited to spy novels.

15. Often these anonymous contacts seem intended as way-paving overtures to future face-to-face contact and proposal. As a young white woman who used a professor's voicemail for more than checking her assignments said: "I tried to leave a cheerful thought for him each day, so that when we finally did meet, he would, like subconsciously, have positive feelings about me because . . . he'd know my voice."

16. Despite the awkwardness and insensitivity of many of these overtures, many pursuers claim they try to be respectful and appreciative of the other—at least by their own lights. Thus, in making hang-up calls just to hear the other's voice, one caller said he "hung up with a respectful click, because I didn't want to scare her." Likewise, a young white man recalled placing such calls to his older Asian-American instructor on a regular basis "every evening at six, eight, and ten, because I wanted to make sure I didn't wake her up."

17. Clark and LaBeff (1986:262), for example, noted that the rejected sometimes refused to accept even the firmest announcements of termination, "the receiver of the news [making] extraordinary efforts, occasionally violent, to either hold on to the relationship, or make the life of the deliverer miserable."

18. These killings differ in some profound ways from the "hot-blooded" ones Katz (1988) has analyzed as "righteous slaughter," not only in their long-term, slow-burning character, but

also in their seeming lack of any claim to a higher good. Nonetheless, there may also be some parallels, especially in movement toward "transcendence."

19. Thus Vaughan insists that the initiator in uncoupling is not necessarily the party who ultimately comes to propose and push for separation. Uncoupling may eventually occur when "the partner responds to the initiator's display either by initiating a separation or by behaving so that the initiator has legitimate reason to do so" (1986:121).

References

Abu-Lughod, Lila
    1991 "Writing against culture." In *Recapturing Anthropology: Working in the Present*, ed. Richard G. Fox. Santa Fe, New Mexico: School of American Research Press.

Arizona Republic
    1994 "Murder-suicide of executives stuns upscale Wall Street." April 9.

Chamberlain, Wilt
    1991 *A View from Above*. New York: Penguin.

Clark, Robert E., and Emily E. LaBeff
    1986 "Ending intimate relationships: Strategies of breaking off." *Sociological Spectrum* 6:245–267.

Cloyd, Jerald W.
    1976 "The market-place bar: The interrelation between sex, situation, and strategies in the pairing ritual of *homo ludens*." *Urban Life* 5:293–312.

Davis, Murray S.
    1973 *Intimate Relations*. New York: The Free Press.

Des Barres, Pamela
    1987 *I'm With the Band: Confessions of a Groupie*. New York: Jove Books.

Dull, Diana, and Candace West
    1991 "Accounting for cosmetic surgery: The accomplishment of gender." *Social Problems* 38:54–70.

Dunn, Jennifer L.
    1998 "No place to hide: Violent pursuit in public and private." *Perspectives on Social Problems* 9:143–168.

Ebaugh, Helen Rose Fuchs
    1988 *Becoming an Ex: The Process of Role Exit*. Chicago: University of Chicago Press.

Ellis, David, J. Blackman, M. Sellinger, and C. Tamarkin
    1993 "Nowhere to hide." *People* (May 17): 63–72.

Emerson, Robert M.
    1981 "On last resorts." *American Journal of Sociology* 87:1–22.

Emerson, Robert M., and Sheldon L. Messinger
    1977 "The micro-politics of trouble." *Social Problems* 25:121–134.

Emerson, Robert M., Rachel I. Fretz, and Linda L. Shaw
    1995 *Writing Ethnographic Fieldnotes*. Chicago: University of Chicago Press.

Ferris, Kerry O.
    1990 "Breaking up is hard to do: Restraining orders and the process of ending relationships." Paper presented at the UCLA Center for the Study of Women, Graduate Student Conference (April).

Gardner, Carol Brooks
    1988 "Access information: Public lies and private peril." *Social Problems* 35:384–397.
    1995 *Passing By: Gender and Public Harassment*. Berkeley: University of California Press.

Glaser, Barney G., and Anselm L. Strauss
  1965 *Awareness of Dying*. Chicago: Aldine.
Goffman, Erving
  1963 *Behavior in Public Places*. New York: The Free Press.
  1971 "The insanity of place." Appendix to *Relations in Public*. New York: Basic Books, 335–390.
Gross, Linden
  1992 "Twisted love: A deadly obsession." *Cosmopolitan* (July):190–193.
Gubrium, Jaber F., James A. Holstein, and David R. Buckholdt
  1994 *Constructing the Life Course*. Dix Hills, New York: General Hall.
Harmon, Ronnie B., Richard Rosner, and Howard Owens
  1995 "Obsessional harassment and erotomania in a criminal court population." *Journal of Forensic Sciences* 40:188–196.
Holstein, James, and Gale E. Miller
  1990 "Rethinking victimization: An interactional approach to victimology." *Symbolic Interaction* 13:103–122.
Horton, Donald, and R. Richard Wohl
  1956 "Mass communication and para-social interaction: Observations of intimacy at a distance." *Psychiatry* 19:215–230.
Horton, Sue
  1992 "Secret admirer: Stalking as a hate crime." *LA Weekly* (September 18–24): 16–23.
Katz, Jack
  1988 *Seductions of Crime: Moral and Sensual Attractions in Doing Evil*. New York: Basic Books.
Lardner, George
  1995 *The Stalking of Kristin: A Father Investigates the Murder of His Daughter*. New York: Atlantic Monthly Press.
Lee, John A.
  1973 *The Color of Love*. Toronto, Canada: New Press.
Leong, Gregory B.
  1994 "De Clérambault syndrome (erotomania) in the criminal justice system: Another look at this recurring problem." *Journal of Forensic Sciences* 39:378–385.
Lowney, Kathleen S., and Joel Best
  1995 "Stalking strangers and lovers: Changing media typifications of a new crime problem." In *Images of Issues: Typifying Contemporary Social Problems* (2nd ed.), ed. Joel Best, 33–57. New York: Aldine de Gruyter.
National Institute of Justice
  1993 *Project to Develop a Model Anti-Stalking Code for States*. Washington, D.C.: U.S. Department of Justice.
Newsweek
  1992 "Murderous obsession." (July 13).
Pearlman, Cindy
  1997 "Stand by your fans: Janeane Garofalo." *Seventeen* (September):182.
Segal, Jonathan H.
  1989 "Erotomania revisited: From Kraepelin to DSM-III-R." *American Journal of Psychiatry* 146:1261–1266.
  1990 "Reply, 'letters to the editor.'" *American Journal of Psychiatry* 147:820–821.
Tjaden, Patricia, and Nancy Thoennes
  1998 *Stalking in America: Findings from the National Violence Against Women Survey*. Washington, D.C.: National Institute of Justice and Center for Disease Control and Prevention.

Vaughan, Diane
　1986 *Uncoupling: Turning Points in Intimate Relationships*. Oxford: Oxford University Press.
Wright, James A., Allen G. Burgess, Ann W. Burgess, Gregg O. McCrary, and John E. Douglas
　1995 "Investigating stalking crimes." *Journal of Psychosocial Nursing and Mental Health Services* 33:38–43.
Zona, Michael, Kaushal K. Sharma, and John Lane
　1993 "A comparative study of erotomania and obsessional subjects in a forensic sample." *Journal of Forensic Sciences* 38:894–903.

CHAPTER 5

The Locker Room and the Dorm Room

WORKPLACE NORMS AND THE BOUNDARIES OF SEXUAL HARASSMENT IN MAGAZINE EDITING

Kirsten Dellinger and Christine L. Williams

Sexual behavior is common in workplaces, but for the most part sociologists have not paid attention to it unless sexual harassment is involved. Sexual harassment researchers have found that a large proportion of women workers have experienced behaviors that might fit the legal definition of sexual harassment—between 40 and 50 percent (Welsh 1999). But that does not mean that the women surveyed actually considered themselves to have been harassed. Even those who reported an offensive act against them rarely answer "yes" to the survey question, "Have you ever been sexually harassed?" Why not?

    At least part of the answer lies in the fact that sexual harassment is a feature of many jobs. Many women are employed in jobs where they are routinely subjected to deliberate or repeated sexual behavior that is unwelcome, as well as other sex-related behaviors that they consider hostile, offensive, or degrading. Studies of restaurant servers (Giuffre and Williams 1994; Allison 1994), amusement park attendants (Adkins 1995), nursing home aides (Foner 1994), and maquiladora workers (Salzinger 2000) demonstrate that employees in a variety of fields encounter unwanted sexual behavior as a routine feature of their jobs. They rarely label their experiences sexual harassment, however, precisely because they are institutionalized as part of their jobs. Those who refuse to put up with such requirements end up quitting or being fired, or never taking the job in the first place.

    Yet not everyone who works in these jobs objects to their sexual aspects. Many people seek out and enjoy jobs that are highly sexualized. Meika Loe (1996), who studied the "Bazooms" restaurant chain, an establishment that requires waitresses to wear skimpy outfits and engage in sexual banter with customers, reported that 800 women applied for the job when she did. In a study of doctors and nurses in a teaching hospital, some high-ranking professional women claimed to enjoy the sexual elements of their jobs. A woman surgeon admitted that in the operating room, "[there's) teasing and joking and pinching and elbowing. It's fun. That's one reason people like being in that arena. That's part of the camaraderie" (Williams, Giuffre, and Dellinger 1999:86). Leslie Salzinger's (2000) study of a maquiladora plant found that women who initially resisted sexual objectification eventually became won over and gradually transformed themselves into sexual objects competing for the attentions of their male supervisors. But even in these cases, workers still draw boundary lines between sexual behaviors that they consider pleasurable, tolerable, and harassing.

In this chapter, we compare two highly sexualized workplaces in the same industry, magazine publishing, to better understand how workers define sexual harassment and distinguish it from other, acceptable, forms of sexual expression. One of the organizations we studied publishes a men's pornographic magazine, and the other a feminist magazine. We use pseudonyms for each of the organizations to protect the identities of the individuals interviewed: the men's pornographic magazine is referred to as *Gentleman's Sophisticate* and the feminist magazine as *Womyn*. The editorial departments of the two magazines are our focus.

We chose these two organizations for comparison because they are both highly sexualized but in very different ways. The magazines produced by these organizations represent distinctive ideals of sexuality: one committed to feminism, and the other to what Robert W. Connell (1995) has called "hegemonic masculinity," the structural and cultural privileging of white, heterosexual male power. In this chapter, we focus on the editorial departments at the two magazines because sexuality is an especially salient issue there. Editors are responsible for all of the written content published in their magazines (except for advertisements). Because members of these workplaces explicitly deal with sexuality as part of their jobs, we anticipated that editors at *Womyn* and *Gentleman's Sophisticate* would constantly have to draw boundary lines between acceptable and unacceptable expressions of sexuality.

The different values of feminism and hegemonic masculinity contained in the magazines are reflected in the organizational cultures of the two workplaces, but in complex ways. Organizational culture can be defined as the understandings, behaviors, and symbolic forms, including totems, rituals, taboos and myths, that are shared by members of a work organization (Reskin and Padavic 1994; Trice 1993). In these workplaces, the magazines themselves are among the most important symbols of the editors' shared organizational culture. Images from the magazines are posted throughout the workplaces, and copies of current and former issues are strewn about on desks. Although not all workers admire and identify with the magazines they edit—as we will see, this is especially the case at *Gentleman's Sophisticate*—the magazines, nevertheless, represent their collective effort and symbolize the values of the organization. Organizational culture also refers to the informal, emotional, and interpersonal dynamics of work, including the norms governing sexual interactions among workers (Gherardi 1995; Hearn and Parkin 1987). As we will show, editors consider these informal norms when drawing boundary lines between acceptable and unacceptable sexual behavior. While not all members of a workplace agree in every instance when a boundary has been crossed, we argue that understanding the process whereby workers make this determination requires taking organizational culture into account.

Although these two workplaces are in privately owned companies in the same industry, located in the same city, that employ people in the same occupations (editors, assistant editors, administrative assistants, secretaries, interns), there are several structural differences between them. Most importantly, all of the 18 members of the *Womyn* editorial staff are women, while six of the 12 editors at *Gentleman's Sophisticate*, including the top managers, are men. Overall, the occupation of editing is gender balanced

(*Employment and Earnings*, January 1998), but it is not unusual for organizations committed to feminism to employ only women. Some might find the comparison of an all-women work site and a gender-balanced work site to be problematic because the assumption of most research has been that sexual harassment is solely a cross-sex phenomenon. A discussion of homophobia as sexual harassment has been limited (Williams 1997). We believe the comparison between *Gentleman's Sophisticate* and *Womyn* is useful in pointing out that the nature of occupational segregation in the workplace often finds women dealing with "male cultures" or working with other women in sex-segregated settings. We rarely find men who must negotiate a "female culture." The asymmetrical nature of these cases in regard to gender composition actually allows us to examine the most common work experiences for women as they work in male dominated settings or as they work in women-only settings. If we are to understand women's experience with sexuality and sexual harassment at work, it is essential that we compare and contrast the workplace cultures that may develop in these different settings.

The ratio of men to women in a workplace is considered by some researchers to be an important predictor of the prevalence of sexual harassment (see Welsh 1999 for an overview of debates in this literature). Some researchers argue that the number of interactions between men and women at work is predictive of the likelihood of sexual harassment (Gruber 1998; Gutek, Cohen, and Konrad 1990). The findings from these studies would suggest that it is more likely that women editors would experience sexual harassment at *Gentleman's Sophisticate* than at *Womyn*, simply because there are more men employed at *Gentleman's Sophisticate*.

Other studies have endeavored to identify features of organizational culture that are conducive to sexual harassment. Pryor and his colleagues conducted a series of experiments that found that exposure to male supervisors and peers who sexually harass increases other men's likelihood of sexually harassing women (Hulin, Fitzgerald, and Drasgow 1996; Pryor, Giedd, and Williams 1995; Pryor, LaVite, and Stoller 1993). On the other side of the coin, Gruber (1998) found that workplaces with proactive methods of sexual harassment training were much more effective in reducing hostile environment harassment than workplaces that relied solely on less aggressive "get out the word" techniques.

These studies identify specific elements of organizational culture that are linked to the frequency and type of sexual harassment likely to occur in a workplace. But they do not address the meaning of sexual harassment, and how that meaning may be shaped by organizational context. In fact, these studies, like most quantitative studies of sexual harassment, assume that there is prior consensus regarding the meaning of sexual behaviors. As Welsh (1999:173) points out, "when using survey responses, it is common for researchers to define all unwanted sexual behaviors as sexual harassment, whether the respondent defines them as such (see Gruber 1998 for a notable exception)." Qualitative research is better suited to uncovering how the meaning of sexual behaviors varies in different organizational contexts. As Salzinger (2000) shows in her ethnography of a maquiladora, in certain workplace contexts, even egregious sexual behaviors on the part of management (ogling, demands for sexual access) may be accepted by workers as reasonable or inevitable conditions of their employment.

In addition to examining how organizational culture shapes workers' responses to sexual behavior, we explore the ambiguity that often surrounds sexuality for employees

(Williams 1997; Williams, Giuffre, and Dellinger 1999). Unlike most studies that focus on the presence or absence of sexual harassment, our goal is to document the process whereby individuals decide whether a certain behavior is harassing, tolerable, or pleasurable. Finally, by focusing on a sexually diverse group of workers, we consider both heterosexual and nonheterosexual interactions, an element missing from most studies of sexual harassment.

Methods

In 1996, the first author conducted 65 in-depth interviews and 10 weeks of fieldwork at *Womyn* and *Gentleman's Sophisticate* in New York City as part of a larger study on the ways in which organizations are gendered and sexualized. *Gentleman's Sophisticate* is owned by Publisher's, Inc., which employs approximately 270 people, and Bradwell, Inc. is the publisher of *Womyn* and it employs about 170 workers. (The names of the publishers and the magazines are pseudonyms.) Interviews were conducted with editors, accountants, and administrative assistants who worked at the two magazines, including both current and former employees. The larger sample includes 45 women and 20 men. Of all the respondents, 11 are African American, six are Latina/o, two are Asian American, and 46 are white. The full sample includes 54 heterosexual men and women, two gay men, three lesbian women, three bisexual women, and three individuals who declined to give their sexual orientation.

In this chapter, we draw on the interviews conducted with 28 members of the editorial departments at the two magazines. The editor-in-chief at each magazine was initially interviewed and asked for permission to interview and observe in the respective editorial departments. All of the members of the editorial staff at *Womyn* (18) and all but two of the editorial staff at *Gentleman's Sophisticate* (10) agreed to be interviewed. (The two refusals were on vacation during the summer research.) Interviews were conducted in a semi-structured format, and were tape-recorded and transcribed for analysis. Most lasted one hour, and were conducted in a variety of locations: in private offices and conference rooms during the workday and in cafes or parks during lunch breaks.

These interviews were augmented by 10 weeks of participant observation at the two organizations. During August and September 1996, the first author was employed as a temporary filing clerk in the accounting department of *Womyn*'s parent company, Bradwell Inc., where she worked for approximately 20 hours a week. The rest of the workday was spent conducting interviews or observing at both magazines. While filing, she observed the day-to-day workings of the accounting department at *Womyn*, and interacted frequently with members of the *Womyn* editorial staff, located in the same building down the hall. During this time, she received permission from the editor-in-chief to attend several editorial staff meetings. In November 1996, she was granted permission to observe full-time in the editorial offices for an additional two weeks. At *Gentleman's Sophisticate*, there are no regularly scheduled staff meetings, but the first author received permission from the editor-in-chief to observe the workings of the editorial department by "shadowing" the managing editor during two work days. She also attended formal and informal company gatherings including an evening art opening held at *Gentleman's Sophisticate* and two "happy hours" after work with members of the accounting department. Fieldnotes were recorded as soon as possible after observing and interviewing at each magazine.

The fieldwork portion of the study enables us to understand individuals' experiences, feelings, and expectations regarding sexual behavior in the context of the unstated, taken-for-granted rules of behavior that govern organizational life. The combination of in-depth interviews and participant observation at both workplaces provided valuable insights into the everyday work experiences of the editorial staffs.

Findings

GENTLEMAN'S SOPHISTICATE

The editorial department at *Gentleman's Sophisticate* employs six women and six men. A primary component of editors' jobs is to make decisions about the written content of the magazine. Their jobs include editing sexual advice columns, writing and copyediting captions for the euphemistically called "pictorials" or "artwork," and editing and screening sexually graphic reader mail for potential publication. To illustrate one facet of her job, one of the editors produced a letter signed, "A Big Fan in Michigan," who writes to the magazine each month describing his sexual practices in detail and grading the photos to determine the one he thinks deserves his monthly "Big Fan Masturbation Award." This editor decides whether or not to publish these letters.

When asked to describe her everyday work, Margaret, the managing editor, explained that among other tasks, she engages in detailed conversations about copy style:

> Many of the conversations that we have are on when things should be capitalized or not or . . . is blow job one word or two . . . is it hyphenated or is it not hyphenated? Those are serious conversations and it's a copy style decision that needs to be made . . . and sometimes I'll just stop and say, "I cannot believe this is a discussion that we have at work!" (laughing)

Everyone at *Gentleman's Sophisticate* has to confront the sexually explicit nature of the magazine and, consequently, of their jobs. When describing her responsibility for writing the captions beneath the sexually explicit pictorials, Tina, another woman editor, said that you just have to get used to the material and you have to have a sense of humor to deal with it:

> It used to be so hard. . . . It used to be like, torture. And now . . . you get used to what it's supposed to sound like. . . . You get used to it. So it's easier to write. . . . I mean they're funny—you really have to have a sense of humor, that's the one requirement to work here. You gotta be able to have anything go off your back. Because there's just so much, you know: You gotta have a really open mind.

When Tina started working at *Gentleman's Sophisticate*, the sexual aspect of her job felt to her like "torture." Since she was subjected to a working environment that she considered offensive and that made her uncomfortable, her experience could be interpreted as sexual harassment. But instead of labeling it sexual harassment, she eventually learned to define it as "funny"—something not to be taken seriously. The transformation of the material from "torturous" to "funny" can be understood as a form of emotional labor required of many workers at *Gentleman's Sophisticate* (Hochschild 1983). This process of identity management may be more visible in settings where workers must manage a "legitimate" identity while creating a stigmatized product (Goffman 1963), yet all workers probably engage in emotional labor to some extent (see Leidner 1993; Pierce 1995).

Emotional labor is shaped by workplace context. At least part of the reason for Tina's growing tolerance of her sexualized work environment might be attributed to the organizational policies at *Gentleman's Sophisticate*. Workers there are required to sign an acknowledgment that states that they are aware that they "will encounter and be called upon to work with pictures and written text that involve nudity and sexually explicit material." This measure was instituted, in part, to stave off the possibility of sexual harassment lawsuits. (Loe 1996 describes a similar policy in place at the "Bazooms" restaurant chain.) Margaret, the managing editor, explained the purpose of this requirement this way:

> I think that's more—not to eliminate the possibility that the company could be sued because a boss is harassing a single employee, but just in general, saying that you understand this is what you are going to work on when you are here. . . . So, that's something that we really do stress to people and we send them home with copies of the magazines and make them look at it and make sure that you feel comfortable with this.

It is interesting to note that in other contexts, workers have successfully brought "hostile environment" sexual harassment lawsuits against work organizations that permitted some employees to pin-up nude centerfolds in the workplace. In a 1991 landmark case, Lois Robinson went to court after officials at the Jacksonville Shipyard ignored complaints that pornographic pictures were prominently displayed in the workplace (Petrocelli and Repa 1998). Because their jobs require them to look at nude pin-ups, workers at *Gentleman's Sophisticate* do not define it this way.

Gentleman's Sophisticate will only hire employees who can tolerate exposure to sexual materials that might offend them. This practice may discriminate against women workers if women, in general, are less able to develop this tolerance. Boswell contends that some young interns leave after two days because they can't cope with the sexual materials:

> I've seen interns come in who are just very young. Especially women who are very young and they're here for about two days and they just like, scream and run out of the room because I don't know what they thought, but they obviously weren't thinking. "Oh, gee. I can't do this! Somebody said pussy." I mean, you know, "Oooh, there was a picture of a breast." You know, "My sister and her powerful group will not approve of me being here." I don't know what it is. But interns sometimes show up, do about two days and then just freak. But they're usually like eighteen to twenty-two and just don't have enough worldliness.

Only those who find ways to cope with the materials stay on; those who can't are quickly weeded out. Importantly, both men and women eventually learn this tolerance; the staff of the editorial department is gender balanced. However, few editors had actually sought out the opportunity to work in the pornography industry. Members of the editorial staff came from backgrounds in journalism, publishing, or business. None of the editors were involved in the sex industry prior to working at the magazine. Moreover, when individuals applied for a job at the parent company (which we have given the pseudonym Publisher's Inc.), some were unaware that they would be working for a men's pornographic magazine. The editors claimed that they accepted a job at *Gentleman's Sophisticate* not because it is pornography, but rather because it is an internationally known publication. Many of the editors talk about a period of adjustment in which they get used to working with the sexually explicit material on a daily basis, and most say that they learn to enjoy the work. This is similar to Salzinger's (2000) study of a maquiladora in Mexico, where she witnessed the process by which women adjusted to the sexual objectification expected of them. *Gentleman's Sophisticate* provides another case of how workers who decide to stay have to find some way to adjust to the norms of their workplace.

Workers at *Gentleman's Sophisticate* often reconcile the tension they experience with sexually explicit material using humor. Humor is one of the main strategies that people use to deal with unsettling or unwanted experiences (Fitzgerald, Swan, and Fischer 1995:120). One person referred to the culture of *Gentleman's Sophisticate* as a "locker room": a place filled with bawdy jokes and sexual bantering. Most of the sexual joking at *Gentleman's Sophisticate* is about the content of the magazine itself. People joke about breast implants, ads for penis enlargements, and the impossibility of certain sexual acts that are described in letters from readers. Editors also joke about the readers who buy the magazine and enjoy it. Boswell claims that most of the editors have contempt for the readers of the magazine, believing that they are all "in federal prisons and trailer camps." In fact, none of the editors claim that they enjoy reading the magazine and looking at the pictures; they consider the overarching view of sexuality portrayed in the magazine to be narrow and outdated.

Although joking is pervasive in the editorial department, it is almost never about personal matters. Tina says joking is "just business and never personal." When Bill is asked if he ever talks about sex at work, he doesn't think to mention sexual joking about the magazine. He says, "No, not at all. I just don't want to talk about sex . . . especially with women, because everything could be misconstrued, especially in these times when people are so sensitive." But when asked if he talks about sex in regard to the magazine, he clarifies that "that" kind of joking happens "all the time":

> Oh yeah, we laugh at a lot of stuff. Some of it is so ridiculous, you know, how many positions can you come up with and have it artful? We laugh at the pictorials. We laugh at the color. We laugh at the choice of girls. Yeah, we do that a lot. Sure. But to me, that's in the abstract. . . . If I met you outside of this environment and I brought a *Gentleman's Sophisticate* magazine with me . . . and started talking to you about it, that would be like approaching you, hitting on you. For us, it's like an "in" thing. It's like we work here.

Working with the magazine and joking about it is an "in" thing at *Gentleman's Sophisticate* "as long as it is not personal." Talking about sex is fine if it is about the magazine, or if it is "abstract." If it is concrete talk about an individual's sexual behavior or desires, then it is "sensitive" and likely to be "misconstrued." Bill acknowledges that while this "abstract" sexual talk and joking is considered part of the job here, in other contexts, it might be interpreted as an inappropriate "come on" or even as sexual harassment.

On several occasions, the editors shared jokes that were "going around the office that day." During an interview with a male editor, he said, "You'll get good and raunchy jokes and you pass those around. And the popular joke last week was . . . oh yeah, 'Why do women fake their orgasms? [Why?] Because they think we care.'"

Although the editor said that this was a very popular joke with both men and women, the joke only makes sense if told from a male point of view. The joke is "on" women for thinking that men care about their sexual pleasure. Messner (1992) has noted that male locker room jokes are almost always about degrading women. However, at *Gentleman's Sophisticate*, both men and women participate in this type of humor. When the first author arrived for an interview, a woman employee who escorted her to her appointment told her a blow job joke in the hallway, and then "offered" her to a man in the elevator as "his own personal girl." Thus, even though the editorial department at *Gentleman's Sophisticate* is not an all-male domain, the description of the culture in the editorial department as a male locker room is apt given the emphasis on the bawdy depiction and discussion of sex from a male heterosexual point of view, with most of the jokes at women's expense.

But just because the work culture is sexualized does not mean that absolutely anything goes. Boundary lines are still drawn at the organization. Margaret, the managing editor, said:

> I watched in the production room one day and one of the men who works there held open an issue of [a competing pornographic magazine] which happened to have a Black centerfold and said, "Can you imagine what our relationship would be like if you looked like this?" Comments like that are totally inappropriate. It doesn't matter that I work here. It's inappropriate and that's an inappropriate discussion to have. So I think people think they're not crossing the line just because you work here and in reality they really are. That line is still there and should still be there.

Margaret's boundary line between acceptable and harassing sexual behavior is personal sexual innuendo. In this sense, working at *Gentleman's Sophisticate* may really be like the men's locker rooms where there may be lots of fantasy talk and sexual joking, but little actual emotional and personal intimacy (Curry 1991; Lyman 1987).

The racist stereotype embedded in the man's remark is also important in understanding why Margaret used this example to illustrate her boundary line. Both Margaret and the man in the production room are white. His comment insinuates that if she were Black, she would be more sexually available to him, reflecting a popular "controlling image" of Black women (Collins 2000). It is also significant that *Gentleman's Sophisticate* does not regularly publish images of women of color. From a production standpoint (one that is surely influenced by racist assumptions about sexuality in the larger culture) (West 1993), Black sexuality is defined as unacceptable. In this context, the fact that the centerfold was Black may have marked this "joke" as different from and more offensive than the regular joking about sex that occurs on a daily basis.

According to Lyman (1987) and Curry (1991), joking in all-male settings (sports locker rooms and fraternities) is a form of male bonding. The success of the male bond relies on several things: avoiding talk of personal relationships and other intimate matters, being able to put someone down (often by degrading and objectifying women and gays and lesbians), and being able to "take" a joke without losing one's cool. All-male arenas that are highly sexualized (like locker rooms or fraternities) may foster even more humorous and joking relationships than other contexts because joking is a way of releasing sexual tension, and maybe even denying its existence.

Sexual joking is enjoyed by most editors, unless it crosses the line into the personal. When this happens, editors claim that their organization responds speedily and decisively to protect those who feel victimized. Brian provided one example of this organizational commitment to protecting workers. Part of his job is fielding calls from prospective writers and models. Brian received a phone call from "Ginger Petty" who said she had been doing research on S&M and wanted to submit her work to *Gentleman's Sophisticate*. Over the course of the conversation, Ginger began telling Brian about her own sexual fantasies, and how she would like to be "disciplined" by Brian. Brian thought the incident was "hilarious" and went to tell Margaret, his boss, about it:

> I went over to tell Margaret about the call, laughingly. Just saying, "This really takes the cake!" And she laughed, too, but she said, "You know, in truth, if it were Nicole [the other woman that was working there at the time], who'd gotten this call, I don't think I'd be laughing right now." She said, "I think I'd be concerned. It would be more than a joke, but 'assault' is the wrong word. Like a harassment type of call." But she asked me. "Do you at all feel offended or whatever?" And I said, "Please! Honestly! I mean, not even close!" But I thought it was very nice that she extended that kind of sensitivity because I could have been.

Margaret is sensitive to the possibility that Ginger Petty's call could be harassment because it seems to cross personal boundaries. It is interesting; that this workplace norm allows Margaret to consider the possibility that a man may be harassed by a woman, but Brian does not share Margaret's definition of this particular situation as sexual harassment, although he appreciates his boss's reasoning and her sensitivity.

Margaret attributes Brian's lack of concern over the incident to the fact that he is a man. Brian is also gay, and this may help to explain his decision not to label this incident as sexual harassment. He describes the environment at *Gentleman's Sophisticate* as "liberating" in many ways. He says that he enjoys the freedom of self-expression one is allowed in regards to sexuality. On the one hand, Brian reports that he is out at work and that he enjoys joking with women colleagues and "playing around a little with ideas of gender roles . . . within certain parameters." He also explains that he has learned to slip into what he calls "hyper-hetero extreme" talk around his straight friends to make them uncomfortable. He sees himself at the forefront of sexual joking and uses this talk as a way to make his straight friends "squirm." He explains,

> I feel like it's a parody. I feel like I'm really making fun of them and the way they talk and they may not get it that way, but I get a kick out of teasing them and seeing that they really don't feel comfortable with it. . . . Actually, in truth, there's got to be some element of hostility in it too, for me. You know, for the years that I had to listen to this shit. For all the years that I had to swallow and maybe even make believe that it was who I was. Now, I can do it better than you can! I can teach you! And doesn't it make you squirm?

Giuffre and Williams (1994) report a similar incident in their study of sexual harassment in restaurants when a gay waiter explained that the open sexual environment allowed him to make straight co-workers uncomfortable with his sexual banter. He, too, saw this joking as a kind of payback for all the times he and other gay people had been oppressed and excluded by the norms of compulsory heterosexuality. Granted his penchant for engaging in "hyper-hetero-extreme" talk, it is understandable why Brian did not see the Ginger Petty incident as sexual harassment.

Women in other departments said they felt protected from sexual harassment owing to a powerful woman lawyer employed by the firm who they perceived as vigorously pursuing all complaints of harassment. This is consistent with Gruber's (1998) finding that sexual harassment complaints may be less frequent in workplaces with proactive sexual harassment procedures. Women employees at *Gentleman's Sophisticate* said they felt empowered to complain about any individual who crossed the line from "business sex" to "personal sex." This sense of the individual's right to personal autonomy, and protection from individual harassers, is consistent with the overarching values of free choice and individual rights which characterized the organization culture as a whole. Thus, while the norms and values of the locker room might seem to foster sexual harassment, employees in general felt that their workplace was free of sexual harassment, and that anyone who dared cross the line would be quickly reprimanded.

Some editors acknowledged that sexual harassment did sometimes occur at *Gentleman's Sophisticate*. These instances were perceived as the result of a few "Neanderthals" outside the editorial department who didn't understand the difference between joking and harassment. According to Boswell,

> There's very little sexual harassment that does go on. Probably less than in other companies because again, it's not really an issue. I mean, that's not to say, I don't observe like "Troglodytes speaking coarsely with their women." But the strange thing is that other men will speak up and say, "Hey, knock it off!" or "Gentlemen, stop this!" I mean, for the most part, people cool it. . . . There's a couple of guys that roam around the office that are real sort of pigs, and classic male chauvinists, but because the company is so upwardly mobile, it's just sort of like, "Ahh, he's just a retrograde." There are a couple of people in the organization that are just sort of hardwired into their Italian-Stallion souls and they can be good about it for about a week, but sooner or later, the genetics reassert themselves and you have to slap them again. But in a company of hundreds of people, who cares?

Boswell describes the men who sexually harass women employees as throwbacks to the 1970s, a time when the magazine was at the height of its popularity. They are men who have failed to evolve with the times. Interestingly, the editors often described the readers of *Gentleman's Sophisticate* in a similar way. They, too, are considered Neanderthals stuck in another era's vision of sexuality. In both instances, the editors attempt to separate themselves from what they perceive as a lower class, unsophisticated view of sexuality and masculinity. This tension between the editors' sexual tastes and preferences, and the expressions of sexual desire represented in the magazine, reflects what Connell (1995) has characterized as a key feature of masculinity. Different forms of masculinity constantly compete for dominance; the hegemonic form of masculinity is always defined in terms of its difference from, and superiority over, alternative forms of masculinity, and all versions of femininity. Thus, the "Neanderthal" readers of *Gentleman's Sophisticate*, and the "Neanderthal" men at the organization who sexually harass women, function as foils for the men editors to define themselves as superior to other men.

By separating business sex from personal sex, the culture of the editorial department supports the idea that sexual harassment is an individual problem and not an organizational issue. Although the editors are subjected to a sexualized work environment, they rarely complain about it or label it sexual harassment. Men and women editors seem to enjoy joking in the locker room environment. Only when sexual bantering crosses over into the personal do some editors feel like they are being sexually harassed. Perhaps for this reason, editors distance themselves from the content of the magazine. Because anyone who enjoys the magazine is a retrograde, lower class "Neanderthal," an employee who took the magazine too seriously and admitted to finding it personally stimulating would likely be looked upon with suspicion by others, perhaps as the sort of "Neanderthal" likely to sexually harass women.

WOMYN

The editorial department at *Womyn* employs a staff of 18 women. Included in this number are four unpaid interns. Unlike *Gentleman's Sophisticate*, the editors at *Womyn* are not offered training in sexual harassment policy, nor are they asked to sign any acknowledgment about the sexual content of their magazine. When asked whether the company had a formal sexual harassment policy, the editor-in-chief replied, "We don't have any formal policy here at *Womyn* except we clearly, as feminists, know where we stand on the issue."

Many other members of the editorial staff seemed surprised when asked if they had a formal policy regarding sexual harassment. Most said they weren't sure and then explained that *anybody* who would choose to work at *Womyn* would simply understand that sexually harassing behavior is not tolerated. In other words, the editors saw the feminist norms and values within their workplace culture as protection against sexual harassment.

Working at *Womyn* means knowing where one stands on all sorts of important feminist issues. This feminist sensibility creates an environment where editors believe they are doing more than "just a job." Brett, a senior editor at *Womyn*, said,

> I think it's hard to work at *Womyn* and look at it as a job in journalism. It's more of a calling. I feel like I live it everyday . . . I don't think my work is just a piece of journalism. I think it's a piece of activism.

The motto, "the personal is political" is very much alive at *Womyn*. People's personal identities are intricately tied to their work identities. This encourages the formation of intimate ties among co-workers. Natasha, a copy editor who was new to the department when she was interviewed, described the sense that when she was being welcomed to the job she was also being welcomed to a "sisterhood":

> I felt this whole school marmish excitement about the way we were speaking to one another. You know, I felt it was like, girls' novels, you know, like eighth grade girls' novels. . . . The image is patent leather shoes and girls who are pledging undying friendship. You know what I mean?

Being an editor at *Womyn* requires a certain amount of personal disclosure, often about sexual matters. Editors at *Womyn* reflect on and share their opinions about topics ranging from date rape to sexual harassment to the nature of sexual pleasure and desire. While it is necessary to consider these topics from an editorial standpoint, sexuality permeates the more informal conversations as well. People talk about their own sex lives and what they do and don't like to do in bed, as well as having serious conversations about their sexual identities and their relationships. Many women at the magazine explain that this sharing creates very close bonds among the workers that extend beyond the walls of the editorial department. This environment of trust leads to an openness about sexuality that some editors described as "dorm room" culture. Stacey describes some aspects of this dorm room:

> It's just like all of us hanging around all the time. We're so touchy. And we're always having parties just together without our partners. And so we're always dancing together and having sleep overs and stuff.

When at work, employees frequently give each other pats on the back, hugs, and the occasional back rub. There is also a great deal of joking about sex. Almost every editor repeated a joke around the office that there are three main topics of conversation: Food, Hair, and Sex. It is quite common for workers to bring snacks and treats to share that are placed for collective consumption at the so-called trough. Offering food is an effective means of achieving integration into predominately female work groups, as the first author discovered after she donated homemade brownies to the trough (see also Reskin and Padavic 1994).

When asked for examples of how people joke about sex at *Womyn*, Brett explains that things can get pretty explicit:

> There's always discussion of—literally—what kind of sex people do and what they like. It's very graphic sometimes. It's very technical. . . . And I do think, very much, that that has to do with an all-women staff. I think it's totally comfortable. Both straight and lesbians. It doesn't matter. Everybody talks about everything.

Another member of the staff, Samantha, reinforces the idea that *Womyn* is a very sexualized, but safe environment:

> I think this is a very sexual place in a lot of ways. And there's a lot of sexual energy in here, but it's very positive. And maybe, if it was a place where you

> felt threatened in some way, that the energy could be a form of harassment, you know what I mean? But it's so non-threatening.

When asked what makes it non-threatening, she replied, "For me, it's probably just the all-women environment."

According to Brett and Samantha, if the same conversations involved men, they would probably consider them sexual harassment. Once again, this indicates how social context matters in the definition of sexual harassment. It also helps to explain why the male/female ratio is an important predictor of the likelihood of experiencing sexual harassment (Gruber 1998). A feminist all-women dorm room culture that encourages personal disclosure about sex shapes the definition of sexual harassment very differently from the male-dominated locker room culture that promotes impersonal, heterosexual, and often degrading sex talk. While talk of "the personal" is taboo and possibly constitutes harassment in the locker room, it is normative and expected in the dorm room.

Some women may seek out a sex-segregated work environment in hopes of finding this pleasurable, non-threatening atmosphere. In fact, most of the editors described the dorm room environment as very liberating. Vera, a former editor, explained, "For the most part, conversations about our emotional and sexual lives are wonderful and liberating and one of the best parts of being at *Womyn*. It is special."

But even in this all-women environment, boundary lines were drawn between acceptable and unacceptable behavior. Here we focus on two examples where power dynamics between workers, especially between editors and interns, led to uncomfortable situations that the editors thought could be defined as sexual harassment.

(1) At *Womyn*, all staff members, including interns, attend and participate in editorial meetings. While internship programs are common in the magazine publishing industry, the high level of participation interns enjoy at *Womyn* seems to be quite unusual. During a staff meeting to generate ideas for a special issue on sexuality, the editor-in-chief asked the interns for their input. She wanted to draw on their experiences going off to college for the first time, dealing with boyfriends and girlfriends, perhaps even handling date rape. When asked whether anyone was ever uncomfortable about the way people talked about sex at work, the assistant to the editor-in-chief said that after the staff meeting about the sex issue, an intern approached her and said:

> "God, can I answer this?" You know, "I feel so embarrassed" or "I wanted to say something, but I was so embarrassed that everybody's sitting around. You know, can I talk about it?"

The intern did not want to be forced to self-disclose. The request for information in a public forum felt impersonal to her and exploitative, like she was being used, not comforted and supported by her friends.

The interns did not describe these experiences as sexual harassment, however. At *Womyn*, workers give each other the benefit of the doubt that they know what sexual harassment is and they are opposed to it in all its manifestations. Sexual harassment is implicitly defined as something that "other" people do—not feminists. For this reason, some workers at *Womyn* may not feel empowered to complain about a coworker's or supervisor's behavior, despite its potentially negative impact.

(2) A second incident where people expressed discomfort with sexuality at *Womyn* was linked to the ambiguous hierarchy in the editorial department. The emphasis on sisterhood in the dorm room culture can lead to confusing relationships between members of the organization who hold differing amounts of power. Kara contends that things can get a "bit odd" when people talk or joke about sex at work. When asked for an example of when things "get odd," she said:

> The last batch of interns that we had, one of my interns hit on me—quite strongly. And that was a very uncomfortable situation. But, I think it would have been something that would not have happened at any other office. I had just come to *Womyn* and I wasn't as aware of the demarcation lines. It was horrifying.

Kara explained that after a party at a co-worker's house, a few interns and other *Womyn* staff decided to go dancing. At the end of the night she and one intern were the only ones left and they decided to go to a strip show at a lesbian bar. Kara identifies herself as heterosexual and assumed that the intern she was with was heterosexual as well. Sometime that night the intern made a pass at Kara which she characterized as extremely aggressive and similar to some sexual interactions she had experienced in college "when people were half-drunk." As Kara reflected back on this night, she was clearly upset at herself for taking the intern to a bar. She felt this was completely inappropriate behavior on her part:

> I would have never done that in another workplace. NEVER!! After it happened, I was like, "How could you not see that this was completely inappropriate behavior? You do not take your intern to [a lesbian bar with a strip show]. That is ridiculous!"

There are many important issues that may explain why, at *Womyn*, the lines of demarcation between acceptable and unacceptable sexual expression were unclear to Kara, but one major issue seems to have impacted her definition of this situation as "horrifying": the de-emphasis on hierarchy. She says, "Here you have a very strange thing where there is a hierarchy but we are not supposed to talk about it. We are not supposed to acknowledge it and we are all supposed to be friends."

Oerton (1996) points out that U.S. feminists have been in the forefront of creating flatter, non-hierarchical organizations as part of their effort to transform social inequality. The assumption is that when organizations lack formal hierarchies there will be an absence of gendered and sexualized inequalities. In the case of *Womyn*, a definite hierarchy exists, but its existence is informally denied. Kara implies that the invisible hierarchy at *Womyn* may have encouraged her to think it was acceptable to go out to a bar and socialize with an intern, and for the intern to believe it was acceptable to express sexual interest in Kara. But Kara believes that in a hierarchical situation, sexual relationships should not be permitted because in situations of unequal power, subordinates are vulnerable to abuses of power, including sexual harassment.

In both of these examples, the respondents identified unequal power as the defining feature of sexual harassment. Unpaid interns are seen as especially vulnerable: they fear that the dorm room disclosure of personal sexual information may be exploitative when hierarchical positions come into play, particularly in editorial meetings; or that interns may be easily taken advantage of by those who are more powerful. From the viewpoint of these editors, the key feature of sexual harassment is not that it is sexual, or even personal, but rather, that it involves the exploitation of someone in a less powerful position by someone with organizational power over them.

The dorm room culture at *Womyn* encourages open and frank discussion of sexuality. Editors are expected to discuss their sexual needs and desires. Most staff members say they enjoy intimacy between coworkers involved in sharing and joking about personal aspects of their lives. Editors at *Womyn* did not consider sexual harassment to be a problem at their organization because there were no men in the department, and perhaps more importantly, because they shared a feminist analysis of sexual harassment as an abuse of power. In this regard, it is interesting that both of the examples of sexual harassment we described were described *not* by the person who was the target of the possible harassment, but by the person occupying the more powerful position who was concerned about the vulnerabilities of those less powerful values. The editors at *Womyn* felt safe from sexual harassment because the norms and values of the dorm room culture supported constant vigilance against it, even by those who are in charge.

Discussion

The organizational cultures of the editorial departments at *Gentleman's Sophisticate* and *Womyn* are quite distinct. Imagine that it is your first day of work as an editor at *Gentleman's Sophisticate*. Pictures of naked women are hanging on the walls, and copies of the pornographic magazine lay scattered on coffee tables and on the desks of your colleagues. Your new colleagues stop you in the hallway to tell a dirty joke. Getting "one up" on people by telling especially crude or "politically incorrect" jokes will enhance your status and put you in the "in" crowd. You are told to sign an agreement that says that you understand that exposure to sexually explicit materials will not "count" as sexual harassment in this workplace. If you are shocked or offended by this sexualized atmosphere, you have to let it "roll off your back," or else you'll probably quit or be fired. If you agree to stay on the job, you might begin to define yourself as someone who doesn't let those things bother them. But everyone—including your boss and the legal department—agrees that there is a "line" beyond which the sexual bantering becomes sexual harassment. That line is the personal, and anyone who violates it is likely to be reprimanded.

Now imagine your first day of work at *Womyn*. You learn that "Food, Sex, and Hair" are the popular topics of conversation. Office sex talk requires personal disclosure and soul-searching discussions of the political implications of your intimate sexual relationships. If you don't fully participate in this personal disclosure, you will be marginalized to some degree. You notice that your coworkers share backrubs, go out dancing together, and hold slumber parties. The topic of sexual harassment in this workplace will probably not come up, since everyone here is a feminist who presumably knows where everyone else stands on the issue. The consensus is that sexual harassment is an abuse of organizational power, meaning that the least powerful members of the organization, the interns, are the most vulnerable.

Both workplaces are sexualized, although very differently. Editors at *Womyn* would surely object to normative behaviors at *Gentleman's Sophisticate*, and vice versa. To characterize this difference we have suggested the analogy of the "locker room v. the dorm room." Because locker rooms are implicitly assumed to be male, dorm rooms, female, these gendered metaphors capture both the cultural values of the two workplaces as well as the skewed numerical proportions of men and women who work in high-level management positions in them. We have argued that these different organizational cultures help explain why workers at *Gentleman's Sophisticate* and *Womyn* define sexual harassment differently. While not all individuals at each workplace share the same interpretation of specific interactions, they do seem to share similar understandings of the meaning of sexual harassment and the difference between acceptable and unacceptable sexual behavior.

This finding has important implications for the study of sexual harassment. It challenges the validity of research that uses seemingly objective lists of unwanted sexual behaviors to gauge the prevalence of harassment (Williams 1997). The meaning of sexual harassment varies depending on organizational context. The boundary between acceptable and unacceptable sexual behavior is the result of a complex interplay between the characteristics of individual workers, the structural features of an organization, and the cultural norms in any given workplace. Researchers should consider this context when measuring the prevalence of harassment. This perspective draws on a long tradition of sociologists beginning with Emile Durkheim and later Goffman who suggest that the rituals or performances we engage in on a daily basis are complicated interactions "which hold society together, but in a stratified way" (Collins 1994:219). Perhaps the definition of sexual harassment as an illegal act has led us to assume that sexual harassment is the exception in the workplace instead of the norm. We suggest that taking a closer look at the workplace norms regarding sexuality that shape interactions and rituals at work will be a more fruitful avenue than focusing on individual behaviors or definitions of sexual harassment taken out of context.

Our research also has important insights for policy makers working to find remedies for sexual harassment. According to legal scholar Vicki Schultz (1998a, 1998b), many sexual harassment policies promote the misguided belief that all forms of sexual expression are harmful to women. In some cases, concern over sexual harassment litigation has led companies to forbid men and women from travelling together on business; in others a "five second rule" has been imposed prohibiting men from looking at women for more than five seconds at a time. These draconian measures, ostensibly imposed to "protect" women, can actually harm them by denying them equal opportunities and respect. Schultz insists that not all sexual behavior is harmful to women. She writes, "sexuality is part of the human experience, and so long as organizations still employ people rather than robots, it will continue to flourish in one form or another. And sexuality is not simply a tool of gender domination; it is also a potential source of empowerment and even pleasure for women on the job" (1998b:14). She urges courts to conduct in-depth investigations of the meaning of sexual expression in a given workplace before determining whether something is sexual harassment.

Our research supports the view that sexual behavior itself is not necessarily harmful to women. Sometimes an offensive nude pin-up is sexual harassment; sometimes it isn't. Sometimes demands for personal disclosure about sexual behavior are sexual harassment; sometimes they aren't. Individuals who experience unwanted sexual behavior take culture into consideration when deciding whether they have experienced sexual harassment; researchers and policy makers should do likewise.

Our research did not uncover rampant sexual harassment at *Womyn* or *Gentleman's Sophisticate*, but it did reveal the type of behaviors that the editors would consider harassment. According to Schultz, this information would be valuable to the courts if one of the editors were to file a complaint of sexual harassment against their employer. She argues that sexually explicit behavior must be examined in the "larger workplace context" to determine if it, along with any objectionable "nonsexual behavior . . . created a discriminatory work environment" (1998a:1795). She would insist that the fact that the workplaces are sexual does not in itself constitute proof that the women employed there were sexually harassed. Schultz writes, "Sex should be treated just like anything else in the workplace: Where it furthers sex discrimination, it should go. Where it doesn't, it's not the business of our civil rights laws" (1998b:15). For a finding of sexual harassment, the complainant would have to link their experience to blocked opportunities or some other form of gender discrimination.

We need more case studies of organizational sexuality in a variety of workplace settings to broaden our understanding of how organizational culture influences workplace definitions of acceptable and unacceptable sexual joking and behavior. In this study, we examined two extreme cases chosen to highlight how culture matters. But what about editors who work for other magazines which are not strongly associated with gender and sexual ideology, such as *Businessweek* and *Time*? And how do workers in other industries, like retail or computing, draw boundary lines? By examining organizational sexuality in a number of work contexts, we can begin to understand sexual harassment as part of the larger phenomenon of sexuality at work without falling into the trap of equating all sex at work with harassment. A research agenda attuned to the complex ways that organizational sexuality is put to use in the service of pleasure *and* discrimination will move us closer to the goal of eliminating blocked opportunities for women (and men) without reducing them to helpless victims in need of protection from sex.

Note

We would like to thank David Smith, Valerie Jenness, and the anonymous reviewers for their help and advice in improving this chapter. Our special thanks goes to Patti Giuffre, Jeff Jackson, Laurie Cozad, Sue Grayzel, Nancy Bercaw, and Elizabeth Boyd for reading and commenting on earlier versions of this chapter, and to Max Williams for providing the financial support necessary to complete the final revisions. We would also like to express our sincere appreciation for the participants in this study who were willing to talk openly about their work lives. Research on which this chapter is based was supported by the American Sociological Association's Fund for the Advancement of the Discipline.

References

Adkins, Lisa
  1995 *Gendered Work: Sexuality, Family, and the Labour Market*. Buckingham, UK: Open University Press.
Allison, Anne
  1994 *Nightwork: Sexuality, Pleasure, and Corporate Masculinity in a Tokyo Hostess Club*. Chicago: The University of Chicago Press.
Collins, Patricia Hill
  2000 *Black Feminist Thought: Knowledge, Consciousness, and the Politics of Black Empowerment*. New York: Routledge.
Collins, Randall
  1994 *Four Sociological Traditions*. New York: Oxford University Press.
Connell, Robert W.
  1995 *Masculinities*. Berkeley: University of California Press.
Curry, Timothy Jon
  1991 "Fraternal bonding in the locker room: A profeminist analysis of talk about competition and women." *Sociology of Sport Journal* 8:119–135.
Fitzgerald, Louise F., Suzanne Swan, and Karla Fischer
  1995 "Why didn't she just report him?: The psychological and legal implications of women's responses to sexual harassment." *Journal of Social Issues* 51, 1:117–138.
Foner, Nancy
  1994 *The Caregiving Dilemma: Work in an American Nursing Home*. Berkeley: University of California Press.
Gherardi, Sylvia
  1995 *Gender, Symbolism and Organizational Cultures*. London: Sage.
Giuffre, Patti A., and Christine L. Williams
  1994 "Boundary lines: Labeling sexual harassment in restaurants." *Gender and Society* 8, 3:378–401.
Goffman, Erving
  1963 *Stigma: Notes on the Management of a Spoiled Identity*. Englewood Cliffs, N.J: Prentice Hall.
Gruber, James E.
  1998 "The impact of male work environments and organizational policies on women's experiences of sexual harassment." *Gender and Society* 12, 3:301–320.
Gutek, Barbara A., Aaron Gruff Cohen, and Alison M. Konrad
  1990 "Predicting social-sexual behavior at work: A contact hypothesis." *Academy of Management Journal* 33:560–577.
Hearn, Jeff, and Wendy Parkin
  1987 *Sex at Work: The Power and Paradox of Organization Sexuality*. New York: St. Martin's Press.
Hochschild, Arlie Russell
  1983 *The Managed Heart: Commercialization of Human Feeling*. Berkeley: University of California Press.
Hulin, Charles L., Louise F. Fitzgerald, and Fritz Drasgow
  1996 "Organizational influences on sexual harassment." In *Sexual Harassment in the Workplace: Perspectives, Frontiers, and Response Strategies*, Margaret S. Stockdale, ed., 127–150. Thousand Oaks, Calif.: Sage.
Leidner, Robin
  1993 *Fast Food, Fast Talk: Service Work and the Routinization of Everyday Life*. Berkeley: University of California Press.
Loe, Meika
  1996 "Working for men—at the intersection of power, gender, and sexuality." *Sociological Inquiry* 66:399–421.

Lyman, Peter
   1987 "The fraternal bond as a joking relationship: A case study of the role of sexist jokes in male group bonding." In *Changing Men: New Directions in Research on Men and Masculinity*, Michael Kimmel, ed. Newbury Park, Calif.: Sage.

Messner, Michael A.
   1992 *Power at Play: Sports and the Problem of Masculinity*. Boston: Beacon Press.

Oerton, Sarah
   1996 *Beyond Hierarchy: Gender, Sexuality, and the Social Economy*. London: Taylor and Francis.

Petrocelli, William, and Barbara Kate Repa
   1998 *Sexual Harassrnent on the Job: What It Is and How to Stop It*, third edition. Berkeley, Calif.: Nolo Press.

Pierce, Jennifer L.
   1995 *Gender Trials: Emotional Lives in Contemporary Law Firms*. Berkeley: University of California Press.

Pryor, John B., Janet L. Giedd, and Karen B. Williams
   1995 "A social psychological model for predicting sexual harassment." *Journal of Social Issues* 51, 1:69–84.

Pryor, John B., Christine M. LaVite, and Lynnette M. Stoller
   1993 "A social psychological analysis of sexual harassment: The person/situation interaction. *Journal of Vocational Behavior* 42:68–83.

Reskin, Barbara, and Irene Padavic
   1994 *Women and Men at Work*. Thousand Oaks, Calif.: Pine Forge.

Salzinger, Leslie
   2000 "Manufacturing sexual subjects: 'Harassment,' desire and discipline on a Maquiladora shopfloor." *Ethnography* 1:67–92.

Schultz, Vicki
   1998a "Reconceptualizing sexual harassment." *Yale Law Journal* 107 (April), 6:1683–1805.
   1998b "Sex is the least of it: Let's focus harassment law on work, not sex." *The Nation* (May 25) 266:11–15.

Trice, Harrison M.
   1993 *Occupational Subcultures in the Workplace*. Ithaca, N.Y.: ILR Press.

Welsh, Sandy
   1999 "Gender and sexual harassment." *Annual Review of Sociology* 25:169–190.

West, Cornell
   1993 *Race Matters*. New York: Vintage Books.

Williams, Christine L.
   1997 "Sexual harassment in organizations: A critique of current research and policy." *Sexuality and Culture* 1:19–43.

Williams, Christine L., Patti Giuffre, and Kirsten Dellinger
   1999 "Sexuality in the workplace: Organizational control, sexual harassment, and the pursuit of pleasure." *Annual Review of Sociology* 25:73–93.

Part II

INSTITUTIONAL RESPONSES TO VIOLENCE AGAINST WOMEN

CHAPTER 6

Prosecutorial Justifications for Sexual Assault Case Rejection
GUARDING THE "GATEWAY TO JUSTICE"

Cassia Spohn, Dawn Beichner, and Erika Davis-Frenzel

All of the decision makers in the American criminal justice system have a significant amount of unchecked discretionary power, but the one who stands apart from the rest is the prosecutor. The prosecutor decides who will be charged, what charge will be filed, who will be offered a plea bargain, and the type of bargain that will be offered. The prosecutor also may recommend the sentence the offender should receive. As Supreme Court Justice Jackson noted in 1940, "the prosecutor has more control over life, liberty, and reputation than any other person in America" (Davis 1969:190).

None of the discretionary decisions made by the prosecutor is more critical than the initial decision to prosecute or not, which has been characterized as "the gateway to justice" (Kerstetter 1990:182). Prosecutors have wide discretion at this stage in the process; there are no legislative or judicial guidelines on charging and a decision not to file charges ordinarily is immune from review. As the Supreme Court noted in Bordenkircher v. Hayes [(434 U.S. 357, 364 (1978)], "So long as the prosecutor has probable cause to believe that the accused committed an offense defined by statute, the decision whether or not to prosecute, and what charge to file or bring before a grand jury, generally rests entirely in his discretion."

This chapter examines prosecutorial discretion at charging. In an attempt to understand the factors that influence the decision to charge or not, we examine the official reasons given by prosecutors to explain case rejections in sexual assault cases. As explained in more detail below, we use data on cases closed by arrest in Miami during 1997 to test Frohmann's (1991) contentions regarding prosecutorial justifications for case rejection. We create a typology of reasons for case rejection and we highlight the victim, suspect, and case characteristics associated with each type of case. We also examine the degree to which victim characteristics affect prosecutors' charging decisions.

Prior Research

PROSECUTOR'S CHARGING DECISIONS

Studies of the charging process demonstrate that prosecutors exercise their discretion and reject a significant percentage of cases at screening (Frazier and Haney 1996; Spears and Spohn 1997). This research also indicates that case rejections are motivated primarily by prosecutors' attempts to "avoid uncertainty" (Albonetti 1987) by filing charges in cases where the odds of conviction are good and rejecting charges in cases where conviction is unlikely. These studies suggest that prosecutors' assessments of convictability are based primarily—although not exclusively—upon legal factors such as the seriousness of the offense (Albonetti 1987; Jacoby et al. 1982; Mather 1979; Miller 1969; Myers 1982; Neubauer 1974; Rauma 1984; Schmidt and Steury 1989), the strength of evidence in the case (Albonetti 1987; Jacoby et al. 1982; Miller 1969; Nagel and Hagan 1983), and the culpability of the defendant (Albonetti 1987; Mather 1979; Miller 1969; Neubauer 1974; Schmidt and Steury 1989; Swiggert and Farrell 1976).

Several studies conclude that prosecutors' assessments of convictability, and thus their charging decisions, also reflect the influence of suspect and victim characteristics. In deciding whether to go forward with a case, in other words, prosecutors attempt to predict how the background, behavior, and motivation of the suspect and victim will be interpreted and evaluated by other decision makers, and especially by potential jurors. As Frohmann (1997:535) notes, "Concern with convictability creates a 'downstream orientation' in prosecutorial decision making—that is, an anticipation and consideration of how others (i.e., jury and defense) will interpret and respond to a case." With respect to suspect characteristics, research demonstrates charging is more likely if the defendant is nonwhite (Spohn et al. 1987) or the defendant is black and the victim is white (LaFree 1980; Paternoster 1984; Spohn and Spears 1996; but see Kingsnorth et al. 1998). Other research reveals that prosecutors are more likely to file charges against men (Nagel and Hagan 1983; Spohn et al. 1987) and those who are unemployed (Schmidt and Steury 1989).

There is compelling evidence that victim characteristics also play a role in the charging process. According to many prosecutors, a "stand-up" victim is an essential element of a strong case. Stanko (1988) defines this as a person whom a judge or jury would consider credible and undeserving of victimization. In assessing victim credibility, prosecutors rely on stereotypes about appropriate behavior; they attribute credibility to victims "who fit society's stereotypes of who is credible: older, white, male, employed victims" (Stanko 1988:172). Victims who do not fit this image or who engage in "precipatory behavior" (Amir 1971) are deemed less credible. Another important factor is the relationship between the victim and the suspect. Several studies conclude that prosecutors are less likely to file charges if the victim knew the offender (Albonetti 1987; Simon 1996; Stanko 1988). These studies suggest that a prior relationship with the offender may raise questions about the truthfulness of the victim's story and may lead the victim to refuse to cooperate as the case moves forward (Myers and Hagan 1979; Vera Institute of Justice 1981).

The findings of these studies suggest that prosecutors' charging decisions, like judges' sentencing decisions, are guided by a set of "focal concerns" (Steffensmeier et al. 1998). According to the focal concerns perspective, judges' sentencing decisions reflect their assessment of the blameworthiness or culpability of the offender, their desire to protect the community by incapacitating dangerous offenders or deterring potential offenders, and their concerns about the practical consequences, or social costs, of sentencing decisions. Because judges rarely have enough information to accurately determine an offender's culpability or dangerousness, they develop a "perceptual shorthand" (Hawkins 1981:280; Steffensmeier et al. 1998:767) based on stereotypes and attributions that are themselves linked to offender characteristics such as race, gender, and age. Thus, "race, age, and gender will interact to influence sentencing because of images or attributions relating these statuses to membership in social groups thought to be dangerous and crime prone" (Steffensmeier et al. 1998:768).

The focal concerns that guide prosecutors' charging decisions are similar, but not identical. Like judges, prosecutors take into consideration the seriousness of the offense, the degree of harm to the victim, and the culpability of the suspect; they are more likely to file charges when the offense is serious, when it is clear that the victim has suffered real harm, and when the evidence against the suspect is strong. Prosecutors, like judges, also are motivated by what Steffensmeier and his colleagues (1998:767) refer to as the "practical constraints and consequences" of decisions, but the nature of their concerns is somewhat different. Although both sets of officials are concerned about maintaining relationships with other members of the courtroom workgroup, prosecutors' concerns about the practical consequences of charging decisions focus on the likelihood of conviction rather than the social costs of punishment. Their "downstream orientation" (Frohmann 1997), in other words, forces them to predict how the victim, the suspect, and the incident will be viewed and evaluated by the judge and jurors. Because these predictions are inherently uncertain, prosecutors develop a "perceptual shorthand" that incorporates stereotypes of real crimes and credible victims. As a result, prosecutors consider, not only the legally relevant indicators of case seriousness and offender culpability, but also the background, character, and behavior of the victim, the relationship between the suspect and the victim, and the willingness of the victim to cooperate as the case moves forward.

SEXUAL ASSAULT CASE PROCESSING DECISIONS

Our study focuses explicitly on prosecutors' charging decisions in sexual assault cases. Estrich (1987) and others argue that the factors that influence decision making in sexual assault cases differ somewhat from the factors that affect decision making in other types of cases. More to the point, they suggest that case outcomes are affected by stereotypes about rape and rape victims, and that only "real rapes" will be taken seriously. Estrich (1987:28), for example, suggests that criminal justice officials differentiate between the "aggravated, jump-from-the-bushes stranger rapes and the simple cases of unarmed rape by friends, neighbors, and acquaintances."

Studies of sexual assault case processing decisions, including the decision to charge or not, support these assertions. These studies reveal that sexual assault case outcomes are affected by the victim's age, occupation, and education (McCahill et al. 1979; Spears and Spohn 1997), by "risk-taking" behavior such as hitchhiking, drinking, or using drugs (Kalven and Zeisel 1966; LaFree 1981; McCahill et al. 1979; Spears and Spohn 1997), and by the reputation or moral character of the victim (Kalven and Zeisel 1966; McCahill et al. 1979; Reskin and Visher 1986; Spears and Spohn 1997).[1] Sexual assault case outcomes also are affected by the relationship between the victim and the suspect. Stranger rapes are investigated more thoroughly (McCahill et al. 1979) and are less likely to be unfounded by the police (Kerstetter 1990) or rejected by the prosecutor (Battelle Memorial Institute 1977; but see Spohn and Holleran 2001). A prior relationship similarly affects the decision to dismiss the charges rather than prosecute fully (Vera Institute of Justice 1981), the likelihood that the defendant will be convicted (Battelle Memorial Institute 1977), the odds of incarceration (McCahill et al. 1979), and the length of the sentence (Kingsnorth et al. 1999).

Evidence such as this has led to conclusions that the response of the criminal justice system to the crime of rape is predicated on stereotypes about rape and rape victims. LaFree (1989), for example, asserts that nontraditional women, or women who engage in some type of "risk-taking" behavior, are less likely to be viewed as victims who are deserving of protection under the law. Frohmann (1991) similarly maintains that the victim's allegations will be discredited if they conflict with decision makers' "repertoire of knowledge" about the characteristics of sexual assault incidents and the behavior of sexual assault victims. The authors of a recent comprehensive review of research on the treatment of acquaintance rape in the criminal justice system (Bryden and Lengnick 1997:1326) reach a similar conclusion, noting that "the prosecution's heavy burden of proof has played an important role in the justice system's treatment of acquaintance rape cases, but so have public biases against *certain classes* of alleged rape victims" (emphasis added).

PROSECUTORIAL ACCOUNTS OF CASE REJECTIONS

The notion that decisions in rape cases are affected by the "typifications of rape held by processing agents" (LaFree 1989:241) plays a central role in the research conducted by Frohmann (1991, 1997) . In contrast to the studies discussed above, most of which are statistical analyses of the factors associated with sexual assault case-processing decisions, Frohmann's qualitative research used data gathered during observations of the case screening process and interviews with prosecutors to analyze prosecutorial explanations of and justifications for case rejection. According to Frohmann (1991:214), "Examining the justifications for decisions provides an understanding of how these decisions appear rational, necessary, and appropriate to decision-makers as they do the work of case screening."

Frohmann (1991) suggests that prosecutors' concerns about convictability lead them to question the credibility of the rape victim and the veracity of her story. She suggests that "prosecutors are actively looking for 'holes' or problems that will make the victim's version of 'what happened' unbelievable or not convincing beyond a reasonable doubt" (Frohmann 1991:214). This focus on victim credibility reflects prosecutors' orientation toward potential jurors. Thus, "the ability to construct a credible narrative for the jury and the jurors' ability to understand what happened from the victim's viewpoint are pivotal in prosecutors' assessment of case convictability" (Frohmann 1997:536).

Frohmann's observations and interviews led her to conclude that prosecutors use a variety of techniques to discredit victims' accounts of sexual assault and, thus, to justify case rejections. One technique, which Frohmann (1991) labels "discrepant accounts," involves using inconsistencies in the victim's story or incongruities between the victim's account and prosecutors' beliefs about "typical" rapes to justify case rejection. The victim's credibility, in other words, will be called into question if her story changes with each re-telling or is contradicted by the version told by the suspect or other witnesses. Her account also may be discredited if it conflicts with prosecutors' "repertoire of knowledge" about the characteristics of sexual assault incidents and the behavior of sexual assault victims. These beliefs, which Frohmann (1991:217) refers to as "typifications of rape-relevant behavior," are further subdivided into the following categories:

(1) Typifications of rape scenarios: the victim's version of what happened is inconsistent with the prosecutor's beliefs about what typically happens in this type of sexual assault (e.g., the typical kidnapping-rape involves a variety of sexual acts and the victim states that the assault included only forced intercourse) or her behavior at the time of the assault raises questions about her character (e.g., the fact that she was walking alone late at night suggests that she is a prostitute);
(2) Typifications of post-incident interaction: the behavior of the victim of an acquaintance rape is incongruent with the behavior of the typical victim (e.g., she has consensual sexual intercourse with the suspect following the alleged incident);
(3) Typifications of rape reporting: the victim failed to make a prompt report and her reasons for late reporting are inconsistent with officially acknowledged and legitimate reasons (e.g., the victim did not report the crime for several days and there is no evidence that her failure to report was motivated by physical injury or psychological trauma);
(4) Typifications of victim's demeanor: the victim's facial expressions, mannerisms, and body language are inconsistent with those of a typical rape victim and/or suggest that the victim is not telling the truth.

As Frohmann (1991) notes, incongruities between the victim's version of the alleged assault and these official typifications can be used to discredit the victim's account and to justify case rejection.

A second technique used by prosecutors to discredit victims' allegations of sexual assault, according to Frohmann (1991), is to impute ulterior motives to the victim. Prosecutors use their knowledge about the victim's current circumstances, relationship with the suspect, and behavior at the time of the incident to question her assertion that the sexual activity was non-consensual and/or to suggest that she had a reason to file a false complaint. Evidence that the victim was attempting to cover up non-marital sexual activity or illegal behavior or to explain away a pregnancy or sexually transmitted disease, in other words, can be used to justify case rejection or to bolster the argument for rejection based on "discrepant accounts."

In a later study, Frohmann (1997) identified an additional method—the "construction of discordant locales"—used by prosecutors to account for sexual assault case rejection. Frohmann argued that legal agents, including prosecutors, tend to ascribe the stereotypical features of a neighborhood to the victims, suspects, and jurors who live or pass through there. Because victims and suspects typically reside in racially mixed, lower-class neighborhoods that differ significantly from the white middle- and upper-class neighborhoods inhabited by potential jurors, the likelihood of conviction rests to some extent on potential jurors' ability to understand, interpret, and make sense of the behavior of the victim and suspect. Cultural differences in the places where victims and jurors live, in other words, "lead to misinterpretation by jurors of victims that would result in 'not guilty' verdicts if the cases were forwarded."

Although Frohmann's research on prosecutorial accounts of case rejections is widely cited, to our knowledge it has not been replicated. There are no other studies that focus explicitly on the reasons given by prosecutors to justify rejection of charges in sexual assault cases. In addition, Frohmann provides no information on the frequency with which prosecutors used discrepant accounts, ulterior motives, or discordant locales to justify case rejection. She notes that the various explanations often were used in conjunction with one another, but again provides no estimates of the frequency with which this occurred.

The purpose of this chapter is to replicate and extend Frohmann's important work. Using data on cases cleared by arrest in Miami, we examine prosecutorial accounts of case rejection. We apply a modified version of Frohmann's typology to categorize cases based on the reason(s) given. We also describe and compare the characteristics of cases that fall into each category.

RESEARCH DESIGN

We obtained data on all sexual battery[2] cases (N=140) involving victims over the age of 12 that were cleared by arrest in 1997[3] from the Sexual Crimes Bureau of the Miami-Dade (Miami, Florida) Police Department.[4] Officials in the Sexual Crimes Bureau provided us with photocopies of the incident report, arrest affidavit, and closeout memorandum for each case. The incident report, which is the document prepared by the police officer who took the complaint, includes a description of the crime, statements made by victims and witnesses at the time the initial complaint was made, and a narrative description of the investigation conducted by the officer from the Sexual Crimes Bureau who was assigned to the case. The narrative of the investigation includes statements made by the victim, by witnesses, and by the suspect during the course of the investigation. The arrest affidavit contains information about the background characteristics of the defendant and the charges filed at arrest. The closeout memorandum, which was prepared by the state's attorney to whom the case was assigned, summarizes the disposition in the case. For cases in which charges were not filed by the state's attorney, the closeout memo also includes a statement of the reasons for case rejection.

We use the information included in the closeout memorandums to examine and categorize prosecutorial justifications for charge rejection. Although Frohmann (1997) argues that the official reason given to explain case rejection may not always be the "real" reason, the closeout memorandums in these cases generally included a detailed rationale for case rejection. There were very few cases, in other words, where the state's attorney indicated that the case was "no actioned" and then simply provided a cryptic reason, such as "victim refused to cooperate" or "insufficient evidence to prove allegations beyond a reasonable doubt." We contend that the detailed descriptions of the reasons for case rejection, coupled with the written case narratives, some of which were more than 100 pages long, provide sufficient information on which to base conclusions regarding the prevalence of various types of prosecutorial justifications for case rejection.

We supplement the information obtained from the case narratives and the closeout memorandums with information about the charging process obtained from interviews with prosecutors in the Dade County State's Attorney's Office. The principal investigator interviewed seven of the prosecutors whose names appeared on the closeout memos for the 1997 cases. Prosecutors were not asked about specific cases. Rather, the interviews, which were anonymous and confidential, focused on such things as the factors that generally influence decision-making in sexual assault cases, how attorneys evaluate victim credibility and the strength of evidence in the case, the types of cases that are most (and least) likely to be prosecuted successfully, and the reasons why victims would report a sexual assault and then decide not to cooperate. We use the attorneys' answers to these questions to illustrate and elaborate upon our findings regarding the justifications for charge rejection.

THE CONTEXT OF CASE SCREENING IN DADE COUNTY

Sexual battery cases are screened by one of three units in the Dade County State's Attorney's Office. The most serious cases (i.e., sexual batteries classified as 1st degree felonies) are handled by the Felony Division. This division, which is responsible for prosecution of all cases assigned to the Dade County Circuit Court, screens all 1st degree felonies. If charges are filed, the case is prosecuted vertically. The Sexual Battery Unit, technically, is responsible for screening and (vertical) prosecution of less serious (i.e., those classified as 2nd and 3rd degree felonies) sexual batteries. However, according to the Chief of the Felony Division of the Dade County State's Attorney's Office,[5] the unit primarily handles cases involving children, which tend to be more difficult to prosecute and, thus, more time consuming. Therefore, most arrests for sexual battery are screened by the Felony Screening Unit (FSU), which reviews and makes charging decisions for all 2nd and 3rd degree felonies. The FSU includes 22 assistant state attorneys, some of whom are assigned permanently and some of whom rotate through the unit. If charges are filed, the case is forwarded to the Felony Division for assignment to one of the circuit judges. The case is then prosecuted by one of the three attorneys assigned to that courtroom.

The prosecutor has a number of options at screening. She can reduce the charge to a misdemeanor, file different (i.e., more serious, less serious, or additional) charges than what is indicated on the arrest affidavit, or file charges identical to those on the arrest affidavit. She also can reject the charges, which in Dade County is reflected in a decision to "no action" the case. Finally, she can send the case back to the police department for further investigation; officially, the case is "no actioned," but it can be refiled if additional evidence is obtained.

The standard used in screening cases in Dade County is a modified reasonable doubt standard. According to the Chief of the Felony Trial Division, "we will not file charges unless we believe in good faith that we can get a conviction." She also indicated that the office policy is "to file the highest (most serious) charge that we can in good faith file and to file all of the charges that we can legitimately file." She explained that this policy reflects a belief that it is better to start the plea bargaining process "from a position of strength rather than a position of weakness" and that filing less serious charges in the beginning leaves little room for bargaining at a later stage in the process. As a result, "we do a certain amount of charge bargaining to effectuate guilty pleas."

Findings

Consistent with previous research, Dade County prosecutors rejected charges in more than one third of the sexual battery cases that resulted in an arrest during 1997. As shown in table 6.1, which displays the final disposition for each case in the data file, 58 of the 140 cases (41.4%) were rejected by the prosecutor at the initial screenings. Charges were filed and then later dismissed by the prosecutor in an additional 16 (11.4%) cases. The remaining 66 cases (47.1%) were fully prosecuted; of these, all but two resulted in a conviction, either by plea or at trial.

PROSECUTORIAL JUSTIFICATIONS FOR CHARGE REJECTIONS

We used the following procedures to categorize the justifications for charge rejection. Each of the three researchers independently read and categorized the written reasons

Table 6.1. Disposition of Sexual Battery Cases in Miami, 1997

	Percent	N
Case Disposition		
Charges Rejected by Prosecutor	41.4	58
Charges Filed But Later Dismissed	11.4	16
Defendant Convicted by Plea or Trial	45.7	64
Defendant Not Convicted	1.4	2
Most Serious Charge at Arrest		
Armed Sexual Battery	12.1	17
Sexual Battery	52.1	73
Sexual Battery on a Minor	10.7	15
Other Sex Offense	24.3	34
Non-sex Offense	0.7	1
Most Serious Charge Filed by Prosecutor		
Armed Sexual Battery	6.4	9
Sexual Battery	18.6	26
Sexual Battery on a Minor	6.5	9
Other Sex Offense	19.3	27
Non-sex Offense	7.9	11
Not Charged	41.4	58

for case rejection provided in the closeout memorandums. In classifying the justifications, we used Frohmann's (1991) categories of "discrepant accounts" and "ulterior motives," plus three additional categories—the victim failed to appear for the pre-file interview or could not be located, the victim refused to cooperate in the investigation or asked that the case be dropped, and the victim recanted her testimony. Although our initial classifications were remarkably similar, there were several cases where we disagreed. We discussed these cases, re-read relevant portions of the case narratives, and resolved the discrepancies.

The types of reasons used to justify case rejection in these sexual battery cases are presented in table 6.2. Although we attempted to put each case into a single category, there were a number of cases in which prosecutors gave more than one type of reason. In one case, for example, the closeout memo stated in part:

> there are lots of reasonable doubts arising from the victim's story to R.T.C. (the rape treatment center), to the detective, and to me. Furthermore, there appears to be a motive for the victim to fabricate. . . . Victim clearly indicated that she has always disliked suspect, who was mother's live-in boyfriend.

Because the closeout memorandum mentioned both inconsistencies in the victim's story to the rape treatment center, the detective, and the state's attorney, and the fact that the victim had a motive to fabricate the allegations, this case was included under discrepant accounts and ulterior motives. A few additional cases were similarly "double-categorized."

As shown in table 6.2, most of the justifications for charge rejection did not involve either discrepant accounts or ulterior motives. Rather, 30 of these cases' charges were rejected because the victim failed to appear for the pre-file interview or could not be located, because the victim was unwilling to cooperate and/or asked that charges be

Table 6.2. Prosecutorial Justifications of Case Rejection

Type of Justification	Number of Cases[a]
Discrepant Accounts	
• Inconsistencies in victim's accounts or between victim's and suspect's accounts.[a]	13
• Using typifications of rape relevant behavior	
• Typifications of rape scenarios	4
• Typifications of rape scenarios and inferences about the victim based on this	5
• Typifications of rape reporting	2
Ulterior Motives	7
Other Reasons	
• Victim failed to appear or could not be located	15
• Victim would not cooperate or asked that case be dropped	10
• Victim recanted	5
Unable to Classify	4

[a] Although 58 of the 140 cases were rejected at screening, the number of cases does not add up to 58 because some of the cases were placed in more than one category.

dropped, or because the victim recanted her testimony. Prosecutors used discrepant accounts to justify charge rejection in 24 cases; most of these involved inconsistencies in the victim's and suspect's accounts of the incident. In seven cases, the decision to reject the case was based on the victim's motive to lie or bias against the suspect. There also was one case (not included here) where the charges were dismissed because the suspect pled guilty in another case.[6]

In the sections that follow, we describe the justifications included in each category in more detail. Using information provided in the case narratives, as well as the close-out memos, we also discuss the types of cases that fall into each category.

CASE REJECTION BASED ON DISCREPANT ACCOUNTS

As previously mentioned, a common justification for rejection of a sexual assault case is the detection of inconsistencies, either in the victim's recounting of events or between her statements and statements made by the suspect or witnesses. In one discrepant account case, the victim reported that the suspect, who was her former boyfriend, came to her residence in an attempt to reconcile their relationship. The victim stated that the suspect pushed his way into her apartment and refused to leave or to allow her to leave. He bound her arms behind her back with duct tape and sexually assaulted her. Following the assault, the suspect released the victim and apologized for his actions. He then began banging his head against the wall and later attempted to jump from an exterior stairwell. The victim stopped him from jumping, but during the struggle, the suspect fell down a flight of stairs. At this point, the victim telephoned police. The suspect was arrested and taken into police custody. Following review of the case, the ASA decided not to charge, using the following justification:

> The victim made *inconsistent statements* as to whether or not the defendant penetrated her. She told fire rescue that he didn't penetrate her and she told the uniformed officer that he did penetrate her. *Additionally, the allegation is that the defendant bound the victim prior to the rape. The victim indicated during her pre-file conference that she has permitted the defendant to bind her and have sexual intercourse with her in the past.* She indicated that the defendant has a video of this. *The defendant told the officers that this was consensual sex.* The duct tape used to bind the victim was kept in her home (in her bedroom closet). *Additionally, after the act, the victim calls 911 and doesn't report the rape.* She reports that the defendant might have injured himself because she saw him lying in the stairwell. Also *the victim declined to go to the rape treatment center on the day of rape so there is no DNA evidence.* The victim also said that *a couple of days before the assault, she and the defendant had consensual sex although they had broken up.* For the foregoing reason, it is the undersigned belief, along with the chief of the domestic crimes unit, that there is insufficient evidence to file the case.

In this justification, the prosecutor states that the victim gave different accounts of the assault to the fire rescue team, who responded to the 911 call regarding the suspect's injuries, and to the investigating police officer. Additionally, the prosecutor discredits the victim's allegation of rape based on her prior relationship with the suspect and based on the similarities between the alleged assault and prior consensual sexual relations between the victim and the suspect. Thus, the victim's consensual relationship with the suspect in the recent past and the suspect's claim that the act was consensual, coupled with the victim's late reporting and inconsistent statements, provides adequate justification for the prosecutor to refuse to file charges in the case.

CASE REJECTION BASED ON TYPIFICATIONS OF RAPE-RELEVANT BEHAVIOR

The next two cases illustrate prosecutorial case rejection based on incongruities between the victim's version of events and the prosecutor's knowledge of typical behavior in rape cases like this. As Frohmann (1991:217) notes, "In the routine handling of sexual assault cases, prosecutors develop a repertoire of knowledge about the features of these crimes." If the victim's account contradicts this "repertoire of knowledge," the prosecutor may conclude that the victim is not credible, and the case, as a result, not convictable.

The victim in the first case is a white, 17-year-old female, who made allegations of "date rape" against a black male teacher's aide at her high school. According to the victim's report to police, she went to the suspect's house to watch a movie. She stated that she and the suspect watched the movie while lying on his bed, during which time they engaged in consensual foreplay. Subsequently, the suspect tried to convince her to engage in sexual intercourse; when she refused, he attempted to force intercourse on her. The victim then demanded that the suspect take her home and he complied. The victim reported the incident nearly two weeks later by submitting an anonymous letter to the school principal. The prosecutorial rejection read:

> This case was no actioned because it is this ASA's opinion that the charge of sexual battery by physical force cannot be proven beyond a reasonable doubt because there were several facts that would prevent the state from *showing the defendant was on notice that his actions were against the victim's consent.* See note in file regarding these actions by the victim. *At no time during the alleged incident did the defendant threaten physical harm or prevent the victim from leaving the apartment.*

The note alluded to in the closeout memo lists a number of things the victim did that are inconsistent with the ASA's beliefs about a typical sexual assault:

- The victim *admits to flirting* with the defendant and finding him attractive.
- *The victim allowed the defendant to remain in the room wearing nothing other than boxer shorts.*
- *The victim laid on the defendant's bed.*
- Prior to the start of the movie, *the victim asked the defendant for a hug.*
- *The victim allowed the defendant to touch her* throughout the beginning of the movie. While she kept her hand on top of his to guide his hand, *at no time did she remove his hand so that it wouldn't be touching her.*
- *The defendant was allowed to kiss the victim*; the victim left to go to the bathroom, but then came back, *sat on top of the defendant and continued to kiss him.*
- In response to the defendant's questions about the color of her underwear, *the victim showed him the top of her underwear.*

- In response to his requests to remove her pants, *the victim [said] that she "put up a little struggle, but it was very little."*
- *The victim allowed the defendant to kiss her breast.*
- *After the defendant first kissed the victim's vagina, the victim remained in the room, on the bed, partially undressed.*
- *Even after the defendant's first attempt at penetration, the victim remained in the room partially undressed and complied with his request to stand by the chair and his request to walk back again to the bed.*
- *The victim allowed the defendant to drive her home.*
- *The victim did not immediately call the police and instead waited for a full disclosure until she was upset that the defendant had not been fired from the school.*

According to the extensive written justification presented above, the prosecutor believed that the sexual acts between the victim and the defendant were consensual; she notes that the victim allowed the suspect to engage in certain types of activities and made no attempt to flee when he demanded more. The language used by the prosecutor—the victim *asked for* a hug," "the victim *allowed* the defendant to touch her . . . [and] kiss her," "the victim *remained* in the room . . . and *complied with* his request"—implies that the victim subtly encouraged, or at the very least did not object to, the defendant's behavior. The prosecutor's written justification also suggests that the victim's general behavior during and after the incident was inconsistent with the behavior of a typical rape victim. The prosecutor notes, for example, that the victim allowed the defendant to drive her home after the incident. All of these facts, considered together, lead the prosecutor to conclude that she would not be able to prove that the sexual contact was non-consensual.

A second case that was rejected because it conflicted with the prosecutor's "repertoire of knowledge" about typical sexual assaults involved a 19-year-old black female who claimed that her ex-boyfriend, a 20-year-old black male, attempted to force her to engage in oral sex. The victim stated that she allowed the suspect to perform oral sex on her, but when he demanded fellatio in return, she refused. The suspect then choked the victim and attempted to put his penis inside her mouth. The suspect's attempts were interrupted by his mother, who heard the victim screaming. The written justification for case rejection indicated:

> In this case *the victim and defendant have a long history of breaking up and returning to an intimate relationship.* The victim reports that in this case, *she went to the defendant's home in the early morning hours* in response to his telephone call. . . . *She reports that he performed oral sex on her which she told detectives was consensual.* The victim said that the defendant then demanded something in return and attempted to force her to perform oral sex on him. . . . The defendant and his mother refused to give the detective a statement. *The victim was not seen at RTC and there was no sign of injury (nor was any reported) to the victim.* Without any corroborative evidence either in the form of witnesses or medical evidence, there is insufficient evidence to prove this case beyond a reasonable doubt.

The justification for the preceding case emphasizes the prior volatile relationship between the victim and the suspect. It also highlights two aspects of the victim's behavior that appear to be inconsistent with those of a typical victim in a non-consensual rape: [1] the victim went to the suspect's house early in the morning; and [2] the victim consented to some sexual acts, but refused to engage in others. Coupled with the lack of evidence that the victim suffered any type of injury, these facts apparently led the prosecutor to conclude that the victim's allegations were unfounded.

CASE REJECTION BASED ON TYPIFICATIONS OF RAPE SCENARIOS AND INFERENCES ABOUT THE VICTIM

The following case further illustrates the use of prosecutorial typifications of rape scenarios by incorporating inferences based on the victim's character and behavior at the time of the incident. In this case, the victim, a 31-year-old white female, stated that she went out drinking with her boyfriend, the suspect (her half-brother), and several other people. When the victim got home, she was extremely intoxicated and went directly to bed. A short time later, the suspect entered her bedroom, removed her clothing, and began engaging in sexual intercourse with her. The victim woke up and demanded that the suspect stop. The suspect then attempted to force the victim to engage in fellatio; when she resisted, he resumed having sexual intercourse with her. Due to her intoxication, the victim passed out during the incident. When she awoke, she reported the incident to the police. The prosecutor provided the following written justification:

> This case is being no actioned for the following reasons: 1) *the victim was very intoxicated on the night of the incident. She had consumed 2 beers, 2 long island iced teas, 2 glasses of wine, a large glass of vodka and coke, and medication for AIDS.* 2) She told me under oath that she has *no recollection of the events that took place in her bedroom* that evening. There is no way to prove an essential element of the crime, which is the victim's lack of consent. She told me *she's not sure whether she consented or not*. It is the undersigned's belief that this case cannot be proved beyond a reasonable doubt.

The reasons for not charging in this case clearly are related to the victim's behavior on the night of the alleged assault. The prosecutor notes not only that the victim had engaged in risky behavior by drinking to intoxication, but also that she was taking medication for a sexually transmitted disease. By referring to "medication for AIDS," which is irrelevant to the victim's intoxication, the prosecutor implies that the victim is sexually promiscuous. These inferences about the victim's character and behavior at the time of the incident, coupled with the fact that the victim cannot recall what happened and doesn't know whether she consented or not, provide sufficient justification to reject the case.

CASE REJECTION BASED ON TYPIFICATIONS OF RAPE REPORTING

Included in prosecutors' "repertoire of knowledge" about rape case scenarios are beliefs about rape reporting. Prosecutors expect victims to report the incident to the police soon after it occurs. If the victim does not report the crime promptly, "her motives for reporting and the sincerity of her allegations are questioned if they fall outside the typification of officially recognizable/explainable reasons for late reporting" (Frohmann 1991:219). A late report, in other words, will lead the prosecutor to question the victim's credibility and the veracity of her story unless she can provide a legitimate explanation: she was emotionally traumatized by the incident; she was embarrassed or worried about the reaction of family and friends; or she was afraid of retaliation by the suspect.

Delay in reporting was a key factor in the rejection of a spousal sexual battery case. In this case, the victim, a white 38-year-old female, stated that her husband forced her to engage in vaginal intercourse against her will. The victim stated that after the assault, she remained in their bed and fell asleep. The victim stated that she did not attempt to make any noise or summon help because she did not want her guests to know what was happening. The victim did not contact the police immediately following the incident; in fact, she left the country and did not report the incident until she returned. The victim also stated that she had consensual sex with the suspect after the rape. The prosecutor provided the following justification for case rejection:

> *The victim reported the crime approximately six weeks after it occurred.* The victim did not respond to the rape treatment center or call the police the night of the crime. The victim left the country and called the police upon her return. There is no physical or corroborating evidence. *Given the lack of evidence and the time between the date of the incident and the date of the report the state has no choice but to no action this case.*

In this case, the victim's failure to make a prompt report raised questions in the mind of the prosecutor. Because the victim offered no explanation for the late report and because there are other elements of the case that appear to conflict with prosecutors' typifications of rape (the victim and suspect are married, the victim did not cry out or summon help at the time of the incident, and the victim and suspect engaged in consensual sexual relations following the incident), the prosecutor reports that she "has no choice" but to reject the case.

CASE REJECTION BASED ON ULTERIOR MOTIVES

The final justification for case rejection discussed by Frohmann (1991) involves ulterior motives on the part of the victim. As Frohmann (1991:221) notes, "Ulterior motives rest on the assumption that a woman consented to sexual activity and for some reason needed to deny it afterwards." The prosecutors interviewed by Frohmann described a number of motives for filing a false complaint, including the victim's need to cover up illegal (i.e., drug abuse or prostitution) or otherwise deviant behaviors (i.e., premarital or extramarital sex). Frohmann suggested that prosecutors used their knowledge of the victim's current situation, as well as information regarding the relationship between the victim and suspect, to construct these notions of victim motive.

One of the ulterior motive cases included in our study involved a 13-year-old black female, who reported that her stepfather fondled her, digitally assaulted her as often as five times per week, and attempted to rape her. Although the felony review unit initially filed charges in this case, facts that came to light as the case moved toward trial caused the state's attorney to whom it was assigned to file a motion to dismiss the charges. The ASA filed the following justification for dismissing the charges prior to trial:

> The victim is the stepdaughter of the defendant. The victim disclosed to her school counselor that the defendant had sexually molested her starting in Kansas when she was eleven and continuing up until approximately one week before she disclosed to him. *The victim, when initially interviewed by this ASA, was very credible as there was physical evidence of penetration. While preparing for trial, however, motives for the victim to fabricate became apparent. In addition, the victim repeatedly [said] that she had never been involved with anyone else and had never had a boyfriend. Sunday night before the trial was to begin, this ASA was contacted by defense counsel that he was adding two witnesses to the defense list. The first was [a 16-year-old male], who would testify that while visiting the defendant during the summer of 1997, he and the victim had consensual sex. The second was the victim's cousin by marriage, who would testify that she had overheard the victim threaten the defendant "that she would do to him what she had done to her grandfather."* On Monday morning, the victim was confronted by this ASA with these allegations. The victim admitted that she and the stepbrother had made out, petted, and that she had "hunched" with him, but had not had sex. The victim then became hysterical in the ASA's office and stated that she did not wish to go forward with the trial.

In this case, the prosecutorial justification for dismissal of charges was twofold: first, the willingness of the victim's cousin to testify that the victim had threatened that she would do to her stepfather "what she had done to her grandfather"; and second, the availability of a witness who could contradict the victim's statements about her sexual inexperience. Although the victim ultimately decided not to pursue the case, in the presence of this motive for the victim to fabricate, it is unlikely that the prosecutor would have proceeded with a trial.

The second case illustrates a different type of ulterior motive. The victim in this case was a white 46-year-old female who had been living with the suspect, a white 45-year-old male, for seven years. According to the victim's statements to police, the suspect held her in her apartment for three days, during which time he forced her to submit to sexual intercourse four times. In addition to the sexual assaults over the three-day period, the victim filed a second report. In the second case, the victim advised that while she and the suspect were arguing, he became extremely angry, grabbed a knife, and threatened to kill her. At this point, she called the police and the suspect was arrested. The victim later helped the suspect make bond and let him back into the house. The prosecutor included the following facts in the closeout memo:

> Under oath, the victim recanted the events as she had reported them in both cases. *She says that she lied to the police because she was jealous and wanted [the suspect] to leave and didn't know any other way to get him out. The victim insisted that all of the sexual contact during the second incident was consensual and that she was always free to leave.* [A friend of the victim told me] that the

victim said that she was going to say nothing happened and the friend told her that if she lied she could go to jail and she would not bond her out. The victim denies this conversation and insists . . . that her jealousy is the reason why she told the lies. *The victim and defendant have been living together for seven years with no children in common.* The victim is illiterate and depends on the defendant for financial support.

According to the prosecutor who reviewed this case, the victim stated that she fabricated the sexual assault because she was jealous and wanted the suspect to leave the house, but "didn't know any other way to get him out." Additional information presented in the written justification suggests that the prosecutor may have believed that the victim actually had ulterior motives for *recanting* her original testimony. The prosecutor notes that the victim's statement that she fabricated the sexual assault is inconsistent with the statements made by a witness in the case and also implies that she recanted her original statements to protect her relationship with and financial support by the suspect. In this case, in other words, the prosecutor suggests that the victim's statement that she fabricated the complaint because of ulterior motives was itself based on ulterior motives.

A CASE INCORPORATING MULTIPLE JUSTIFICATIONS

A number of the closeout memos examined for this study provided multiple justifications for case rejection. One case, for example, involved the alleged sexual assault of a Hispanic woman by a Hispanic man with whom she was acquainted. The victim's report indicated that the suspect drove her to the local correctional center to visit her husband. Following the prison visit, the victim and suspect ate dinner at a restaurant, stopped and bought a bottle of rum from a liquor store, and went to the beach together. After spending several hours at the beach, the suspect drove the victim home. According to the victim, it was at this time that the defendant forced her to have sexual intercourse with him. The justification in this case read:

> This case was no actioned because it is the opinion of this ASA that the case cannot be proven beyond a reasonable doubt due to insufficient corroborating evidence. *The victim and defendant were with each other several hours prior to the offense. Despite saying that she did not drink much alcohol beyond a couple of sips, the victim is unable to account for several hours prior to the incident from her leaving the beach after 8:00 P.M. and returning around midnight (shortly before the alleged incident).* The victim also *gave the police a false name.* It was several days later when the victim finally admitted that she gave a false name because she was worried about confidentiality and the victim later admitted that her bigger concern for giving a false name was that she may have had a misdemeanor arrest warrant against her in her true name. *Furthermore, there is an inadequate explanation for the delayed reporting* and the victim's husband is in ICDC for a misdemeanor battery against victim. According to the husband's and the landlord's statements, the husband had been calling all night and learned that the victim was out with the defendant. When the husband's telephone call woke the victim up, *the victim did not immediately report the alleged incident to the husband. The victim did not*

report the incident to the police until several hours after the alleged offense and a couple of hours after the husband's telephone call.

The written justification provided by the prosecutor in this case highlights several reasons for case rejection: (1) the inconsistent statements made by the victim (she gave the police a false name and then lied about her reasons for doing so); (2) delay in reporting (she did not report the crime until two hours after she talked with her husband on the telephone); (3) ulterior motives (the husband was told that the victim was out with the suspect until midnight and the victim did not report the rape until after she talked with her husband); and (4) inferences about the victim (she spent most of the day with the suspect (a man to whom she is not married), cannot explain where she was or what she was doing from 8 P.M. to midnight, and is married to a man who is in jail for physically assaulting her). Reading between the lines, it appears that the prosecutor believed that the victim and the suspect engaged in consensual sexual intercourse and that the victim fabricated the sexual assault to cover this up and to account for her failure to answer her husband's phone calls until after midnight. In conjunction with the inconsistencies in the victim's statements and the lack of corroborating evidence, these assumptions led the prosecutor to reject the case.

CASE REJECTION BASED ON LACK OF VICTIM COOPERATION

The prosecutorial justifications for case rejection discussed thus far are consistent with Frohmann's (1991:224) assertion regarding the "centrality of victim discredibility." They confirm that prosecutors use a variety of techniques to discredit the victim's allegations and justify rejecting the case. However, as shown in table 6.2, a substantial number of the written justifications in these cases focused on the *victim's lack of cooperation* and not on the *prosecutor's concerns* about the victim's character, reputation, or behavior at the time of the incident. There were 15 cases in which the victim failed to appear for the pre-file interview or could not be located to arrange an interview, 10 cases in which the victim would not cooperate or asked that the case be dropped, and five cases in which the victim formally recanted her testimony.

The written justifications in the 15 cases in which the victim failed to appear or could not be located describe repeated unsuccessful attempts to contact the victim. One case, for example, involved the alleged kidnaping and sexual assault of a 16-year-old black female by an 18-year-old black male. The victim claimed that the suspect, who was the boyfriend of one of her friends, offered to drive her to the grocery store. Instead, he drove her from Ft. Lauderdale to Miami; when she insisted that he take her home, he stopped the car, fondled and digitally penetrated her, and attempted to rape her. The prosecutor assigned to this case attempted to contact the victim and her girlfriend, both of whom resided in Broward County, a number of times; she also subpoenaed the victim and other witnesses to appear for a pre-file interview. The prosecutor's justification for rejecting the case stated:

> All witnesses *subpoenaed repeatedly*. All *failed to appear*. Victim in Broward [County]. Did locate, had investigations personally serve victim. *Victim still failed to appear.*

Another "failure to appear" case involved a 30-year-old Hispanic female who was an admitted crack addict. She reported that she smoked crack on the night of the alleged assault and stated that about 5:00 A.M. she approached the suspect, whom she knew from the neighborhood, and asked if she could borrow enough money for transportation home. She stated that she accompanied the suspect to the 1979 Chevrolet van where he was living and that he sexually assaulted her there. The suspect denied that the victim had been in his van that evening and stated that he did not sexually assault her. The prosecutor's closeout memo stated,

> Victim *failed to appear for pre-file conference twice*. Detectives *did not think she intended to pursue this case*. Personal service attempted. Subpoena served on her brother who said he does not know of victim's whereabouts, but if he sees her, he would deliver the subpoena.

The justifications provided in the "could not locate" cases were somewhat different. In several of these cases, the prosecutor attributed his/her difficulty in locating the victim either to the fact that the victim did not have a phone (or the phone had been disconnected) or was "a street person," "homeless," a "prostitute," or a "runaway." Typical of these justifications for case rejection are the following:

> *Victim is a runaway* with substance abuse and psychological problems. . . . *With no way to find victim*, state could not proceed with case.

> Victim and witness are *homeless prostitutes*. Unable to locate.

> Victim *can't be located*. Victim is a *street person*. She *failed to appear* for deposition twice. Detective *cannot locate* her. The witness who had permitted her to be on his property also *tried to locate her without any success*.

As these written justifications document, prosecutors often made aggressive attempts to locate the victims and witnesses in these cases. It is certainly possible that, had these victims been found, their allegations eventually would have been discredited by the prosecutor's use of one of the techniques Frohmann (1991) describes. However, the fact that they could not be located limited the prosecutor's options. Without a victim/witness, the prosecutor had no choice but to reject the case.

Prosecutors' options also were limited in those cases in which the victim would not cooperate, asked that the case be dropped, or recanted. Although prosecutors are not legally precluded from pursuing a case with a reluctant victim, their goal of "avoiding uncertainty" (Albonetti 1987) makes this unlikely. The closeout memos filed in several of these cases suggested that the prosecutor assigned to the case believed that the victim *had been* sexually assaulted. One case, for example, involved a woman who claimed that she had been sexually assaulted by her ex-boyfriend, who broke into her house in the middle of the night The prosecutor, apparently convinced that the victim was telling the truth, made numerous attempts to secure her cooperation and even had the victim arrested and held in jail for four days for failure to cooperate. Eventually, however, the victim recanted her testimony. The prosecutor explained that the case was rejected because *the victim refused to assist in the prosecution* of this case. She *failed to appear* in my office after personal service on August 5, 1997 and August 12, 1997. . . . Thereafter, I had the court issue a writ of bodily attachment against her. She was arrested on 9/19/97 and held for 4 days. On 9/23/97, I took a sworn statement from her where *she recanted entirely*. Therefore, it is impossible to prosecute this case without her cooperation.

In several of the cases rejected because of the victim's lack of cooperation, the prosecutor's written justification implied that the assault may have been fabricated or that the sexual contact was consensual. In one case, for example, a 27-year-old woman claimed that she was sexually assaulted by her 21-year-old boyfriend at his parents' house (where they were living). She reported that they were "having problems in their relationship," and that on the night in question, she found him in his room with another woman. She stated that they got into an argument when he returned from driving the other woman home and that he grabbed her when she attempted to leave the bedroom. She also stated that during the course of the assault, he tore her underwear, pulled her hair, punched her, and bit her on the breast. The suspect admitted that he and the victim engaged in sexual intercourse, but insisted that it was consensual; he also stated that they had engaged in "rough sex" in the past. The incident report indicated that the police officer investigating the crime repeatedly asked the victim to obtain the ripped underwear so that they could be examined for physical evidence, and attempted to contact the victim and the witnesses in the case without success. Three weeks later, the case was rejected by the prosecutor, who noted that the victim "*recanted, without explanation, her statements made orally and in writing* to the detective at the time the defendant was arrested." The prosecutor also stated that the victim acknowledged that the defendant "*could have believed that all of the acts he did during this incident were done with her consent.*"

Other cases in the "victim would not cooperate/asked that charges be dropped" category involved teenage girls who admitted under questioning that the sexual contact was consensual. In some of these cases, the complaint was filed, not by the alleged victim, but by the victim's parents. The written justifications filed in these cases included the following:

> Victim is fourteen years old; defendant is nineteen years old. Both parties *engage in consensual sex*. Victim *does not want to prosecute*. Initially, victim's mother wants to prosecute, but acknowledges later on that she just *wanted to teach her daughter a lesson*.

> No actioned. 1) The victim was 15 years old having consensual sexual intercourse with the defendant who was 27 years old. 2) *She does not want the State to prosecute* this case. 3) She indicated that she loves the defendant.

As the closeout memos in these cases indicate, the victim's decision not to cooperate may be based on a number of different considerations. Regardless of the motivation, her lack of cooperation obviously makes it difficult, if not impossible, for the prosecutor to proceed with the case.

CASE REJECTION BASED ON DISCORDANT LOCALES

We noted earlier that Frohmann (1997) identified an additional technique—the "construction of discordant locales"—that prosecutors use to account for sexual assault case rejection. According to Frohmann (1997:533), "When jurors, victims, and defendants are from discordant locales, prosecutors anticipate that jurors will misunderstand the victim's actions and misinterpret case facts and thus lower the probability of guilty verdicts at trial." Like Frohmann, who stated that evidence of prosecutors' use of discordant locales was provided in oral, rather than written, accounts, we found no direct evidence of this justification in the written closeout memos. Although there were a number of references to victims who were "crack addicts," "homeless prostitutes," or "living on the streets," none of the attorneys explicitly stated that he/she believed that jurors would be unable to understand the victim's lifestyle or behavior at the time of the incident.

Prosecutors interviewed for this study indirectly referred to this issue in discussing the ways in which they evaluate victim credibility. Several attorneys; for example, stated that they asked themselves whether the victim's story "made sense." One attorney commented that he asked himself, "Can she explain to me—and later to the jury—why she behaved the way she did?" This attorney also noted that he was trying a case involving a woman from Finland who claimed that she was raped by a cab driver. He stated that

> there are a number of things about this case that jurors aren't going to like. She's white, but she goes to a bar with a cab driver (who is Haitian) to look for her boyfriend (who is black). She goes to a bar where everyone but her is black, she sits in the front seat of the cab, and she has a boyfriend who might be curious about where she was and what she was doing.

Although the attorney acknowledged that this would not be an "easy" case to try, he stated that he believed the victim and that his job would be "to convince the jury that she's telling the truth." In this case, in other words, the prosecutor used discordant locales not to justify case rejection, but to structure his case strategy.

Case Outcomes and Case Characteristics

The findings discussed thus far indicate that prosecutors use a variety of techniques to justify charge rejection. They also provide clues to the characteristics of the cases found in each category. However, the cases used to illustrate the various types of justifications were not randomly selected from all rejected cases; as a result, the characteristics of *these cases* may not accurately represent the types of cases in each category. To explore this issue, we used the quantitative data collected for this study to compare the victim, suspect, and case characteristics[7] of sexual battery cases that were rejected or dismissed (all types of justifications) with the characteristics of cases that were fully prosecuted. We also compare the characteristics of cases that were rejected because of discrepant accounts or ulterior motives on the part of the victim with those that were rejected because the victim could not be located, refused to cooperate, or recanted.

The victim, suspect, and incident characteristics of rejected/dismissed and fully prosecuted cases are presented in table 6.3. Although most of these variables are self-explanatory, several require elaboration. Our victim/suspect relationship variable includes four relationship types. We classified cases in which the suspect and victim were complete strangers or in which the victim had not met, and could not identify, the suspect as cases involving "strangers." We categorized cases in which the suspect and victim were relatives as cases involving "relatives." We classified cases in which the suspect and victim were friends or acquaintances, or the suspect was either an authority figure or the boyfriend of the victim's mother or another relative as cases involving "acquaintances." The final category—"intimate partners"—includes cases in which the victim and the suspect were (or had been) dating, were currently living together, or were (or had been) married to each other. We labeled this category "intimate partners," rather than "partners," because most of the relationships involved prior consensual sexual intercourse; 43 of the 49 (87.8%) victims indicated that they had had a prior sexual relationship with the suspect.

Our measures of risk-taking behavior by the victim and the victim's moral character are summary measures that incorporate several types of risky behavior and moral character issues. Both of these items are intended to capture what LaFree (1989:50) refers to as "nontraditional" behavior or behavior that deviates from gender norms; they are behaviors that might be *perceived* (by jurors and thus, by prosecutors) as risky or nontraditional. The risk-taking variable is coded 1 if the police file indicated that at the time of the assault, the victim was walking alone late at night, was hitchhiking, was in a bar alone, was using alcohol or drugs, willingly accompanied the suspect to his residence, or invited the suspect to her residence. The moral character variable is coded 1 if the police file contained information about the victim's prior sexual activity with someone other than the suspect, out of wedlock pregnancy or birth, pattern of alcohol and/or drug abuse, prior criminal record, work as a prostitute, work as an exotic dancer or in a massage parlor, or history of running away from home. Measures of offense seriousness include whether the offender used a gun or knife during the assault (yes = 1; no = 0) and whether the victim suffered collateral injuries such as bruises, cuts, burns, or internal injuries (yes = 1; no = 0). The strength of evidence in the case is measured by the existence of a witness to the assault (yes = 1; no 0) and the presence of physical evidence, such as semen, blood, clothing, bedding, or hair, that can corroborate the victim's testimony (yes = 1; no = 0).

Comparison of rejected and prosecuted cases. As shown in table 6.3, there are important differences between cases that were rejected/dismissed and those that were fully prosecuted. Prosecutors rejected charges more often if the victim was a racial minority or if the suspect was black; they rejected charges less often if the victim was between 13 and 16 years old. Charge rejection also was more likely if the victim engaged in any risk-taking behavior at the time of the incident, or if the victim's moral character was called into question by evidence in the file. Somewhat surprisingly, cases involving strangers were substantially more likely than those involving other types of victim/suspect relationships to be rejected or dismissed.

The data presented in table 6.3 also indicate that prosecutors were less likely to reject or dismiss the charges if the suspect used a gun or knife to commit the crime, if the victim was injured, if there was a witness who could corroborate the victim's testimony,

Table 6.3. Case Outcomes and Case Characteristics for Sexual Battery Cases: Cases Rejected/Dismissed and Cases Prosecuted

	\multicolumn{6}{c}{Charges Rejected or Dismissed}		
	All Rejections & Dismissals		Rejected— Victim Credibility or Motives[a]		Rejected—Lack of Cooperation or Recanted[b]		Case Fully Prosecuted	
	%	N	%	N	%	N	%	N
Victim Characteristics								
Race								
Black	58.1	43	43.5	10	61.3	19	47.0	31
White	31.1	23	43.5	10	25.8	8	45.5	30
Hispanic/Other	10.9	8	12.9	3	12.9	4	7.6	5
Age (mean)	22.4		25.6		23.3		21.1	
13 to 16 years old	37.0	27	27.3	6	25.8	8	43.9	29
Evidence of risk-taking behavior[c] (% yes)	33.8	25	39.1	9	32.3	10	21.2	14
Questions about moral character[d] (% yes)	50.0	37	43.5	10	51.6	16	30.3	20
Relationship to the suspect								
Stranger	20.5	15	0.0	0	25.8	8	4.5	3
Acquaintance	32.9	24	43.5	10	32.3	10	30.3	20
Relative	13.7	10	21.7	5	12.9	4	27.3	18
Intimate Partner	32.9	24	34.8	8	29.0	9	37.9	25
Prior sexual relationship w/suspect (% yes)	31.1	23	34.8	8	29.0	9	33.3	22
Suspect Characteristics								
Race								
Black	64.9	48	56.5	13	64.5	20	48.5	32
White	18.9	14	30.4	7	19.4	6	25.8	17
Hispanic/Other	16.2	12	13.0	3	16.1	5	25.8	17

	27.7		30.2		27.9		30.8	
Age (mean)								
Case & Incident Characteristics								
Most serious chg. at arrest = sexual battery	77.0	57	78.3	18	87.1	27	72.7	48
Offender used a gun or knife (% yes)	12.2	9	4.3	1	16.1	5	16.7	11
Victim injured (% yes)	24.3	18	26.1	6	25.8	8	34.8	23
Physical evidence available (% yes)	60.8	45	52.2	12	67.7	21	51.5	34
Witness to incident (% yes)	27.4	20	26.1	6	19.4	6	38.1	24
Incident reported within one hour (% yes)	25.0	18	26.1	6	22.6	7	27.7	18
Victim physically resisted suspect (% yes)	58.1	43	56.5	13	51.6	16	57.6	38
Suspect claims victim consented (% yes)	32.4	24	26.1	6	41.9	13	31.8	21
Suspect claims incident fabricated (% yes)	24.3	18	21.7	5	16.1	5	24.2	16
Location where assault occurred								
Victim's residence	51.4	38	69.6	16	51.6	16	45.5	30
Suspect's residence	17.6	13	13.0	3	19.4	6	18.2	12
Somewhere else	31.0	19	17.4	4	29.0	9	36.4	24
At least one aggravating circumstance[e]	35.1	26	34.8	8	38.7	12	43.9	29

[a] In these cases the justification for rejecting or dismissing the charges was based on discrepant accounts or ulterior motives (see table 6.2).

[b] In these cases the justification for rejecting or dismissing the charges was either that the victim failed to appear or could not be located, the victim asked that the case be dropped, or the victim recanted (see table 6.2).

[c] This variable was coded 1 if the police report contained any reference to the following types of risk-taking behavior by the complainant: walking alone late at night; hitch-hiking; accompanying the offender to his residence; inviting the offender to complainant's residence; being in a bar alone; being in an area where drugs are known to be sold; alcohol use at the time of the incident; or drug use at the time of the incident.

[d] This variable was coded 1 if the police report included any information about the complainant's prior sexual activities with someone other than the offender; pattern of alcohol use; pattern of drug use; work history in a disreputable situation (e.g., go-go dancer, massage parlor); criminal record; out of wedlock pregnancy or birth; or work as a prostitute.

[e] One of the following aggravating circumstances was present: the victim and suspect were strangers, there were multiple offenders, the suspect used a gun or knife, or the victim suffered some type of collateral injury.

or if the assault took place somewhere other than the victim's or the suspect's home or apartment. In contrast, prosecutors rejected charges *more often* if there was physical evidence to connect the suspect to the crime. Moreover, the odds of charge rejection or dismissal did not vary depending upon the promptness of the victim's report, whether the victim physically resisted the suspect, or whether the suspect claimed that the victim consented or fabricated the incident.

We used logistic regression to further explore the effect of victim, suspect, and case characteristics on the decision to prosecute. The results of this analysis, shown in table 6.4, generally are consistent with the results of the bivariate analysis.[8] Prosecutors were more likely to prosecute if the suspect used a gun or knife, if the victim suffered some type of collateral injury, if the victim was younger, and if the victim and suspect were acquaintances/relatives or intimate partners rather than strangers. Prosecutors were less likely to file charges if there were questions about the victim's moral character or behavior at the time of the incident. To test the possibility that charging was more likely if the victim was a young teenager, we re-ran the analysis with a dichotomous variable measuring the victim's age (age 13 to 16 = 1; age 17 and over = 0). We found that prosecutors were nearly four times more likely to file charges if the victim was between 13 and 16 years old than if the victim was older than 16 ($B = 1.31$; $SE = .57$; odds ratio = 3.71). To test for differences in the likelihood of charging between the two categories of non-strangers, we re-ran the analysis with intimate partners as the reference group; we found that there were no differences in the odds of charging in cases involving intimate partners and acquaintances/relatives ($B = .30$; $SE = .61$). Consistent with prior research then, charging decisions in these jurisdictions were based on a combination of case characteristics and victim characteristics.

Comparison of cases rejected for different reasons. As noted above, we also compared the characteristics of cases that were rejected because of discrepant accounts or ulterior motives on the part of the victim with those that were rejected because the victim could not be located, refused to cooperate, or recanted. Although the results of these comparisons must be interpreted with caution because of the relatively small number of cases in each category, there are some intriguing differences. We found, for example, that cases rejected because the victim could not be located or refused to cooperate were more likely than those rejected because of victim credibility or motive problems to involve questions about the victim's moral character. There was evidence of an out of wedlock pregnancy or birth in six of these cases, evidence that the victim had a prior sexual relationship with someone other than the suspect in four, evidence of a history of drug abuse in two, evidence suggesting that the victim was a prostitute in two, and evidence that the victim had repeatedly run away from home in two. Cases rejected because of discrepant accounts or ulterior motives on the part of the victim involved evidence of prior sexual relations with someone other than the suspect (3 cases), evidence of a history of drug or alcohol abuse (3 cases), evidence suggesting that the victim was a prostitute (3 cases), and evidence of an out of wedlock pregnancy or birth (2 cases). Evidence that the victim had engaged in risk-taking behavior was somewhat more common in cases rejected because of discrepant accounts or ulterior motives, but the types of risky behavior found in the two categories were very similar; either the victim invited the suspect to her home or apartment, accompanied him to his home or apartment, or used drugs and/or alcohol at the time of the incident.

Table 6.4. The Effect of Victim, Suspect, and Case Characteristics on the Decision to Prosecute: Miami, 1997

	B	SE	exp(B)
Victim Characteristics			
Race = White	.30	.55	1.34
Age	−.11*	.04	0.90
Risk-taking behavior	−1.22*	.57	0.30
Questions about moral character	−1.17*	.48	0.31
Relationship to Suspect			
Stranger (reference)			
Acquaintance/Relative	2.28*	1.02	9.80
Intimate Partner	1.98*	.96	7.28
Suspect Characteristics			
Race = White	.76	.68	2.14
Age	.05	.03	1.05
Case & Incident Characteristics			
Suspect used a gun or knife	1.69*	.82	5.40
Victim injured	1.89*	.70	6.62
Physical evidence available	.00	.48	1.00
Witness to incident	.78	.50	2.19
Incident reported within one hour	.61	.56	1.83
Victim physically resisted suspect	−.22	.47	0.80
Constant	−1.61	1.33	
Nagelkerke R^2		.40	
N of Cases		127	

* $P \leq .05$

There also were differences in the types of victim/suspect relationships found in the two categories of case rejection. Eight of the cases rejected because the victim failed to appear or refused to cooperate, but none of the cases rejected because of discrepant accounts or ulterior motives, involved a victim and suspect who were complete strangers.[9] With only two exceptions, on the other hand, the case and incident characteristics of the two types of cases did not vary. The suspect was more likely to claim that the victim consented in cases rejected for lack of cooperation (41.9%) than in cases rejected because of discrepant accounts or ulterior motives (26.1%). The other exception is that a larger percentage of the cases rejected for a lack of cooperation involved an assault that took place in the victim's home or apartment (69.6% versus 51.6%).

Discussion

The purpose of this study was to replicate and extend Frohmann's (1991) research on prosecutorial accounts of case rejection. Using data on all sexual assaults cleared by arrest in Miami in 1997, we examined the decision to charge or not, focusing on the prosecutor's written justification for charge rejection. Consistent with previous research, we found that more than half of the sexual battery cases were rejected at screening, or filed and then later dismissed.

This finding confirms the importance of the decision to charge or not and suggests that the prosecutor does "control the doors to the courthouse" (Neubauer 1988:200).

However, our findings regarding prosecutors' reasons for rejecting charges suggest that the explanation for the high rate of charge rejection is complex. Frohmann (1991, 1997) argues that the decision to reject charges in sexual assault cases is inextricably linked to prosecutors' "downstream concern with convictability," which is itself linked to stereotypes concerning real rapes, credible victims, and rape-relevant behavior. Although the findings of our study are consistent with her assertion that charging decisions primarily reflect the prosecutor's assessment of the likelihood of conviction, they also suggest that this assessment is based on factors other than typifications of rape and rape victims. In a substantial number of the cases examined for this study, the decision to reject charges could be traced to the victim's failure to appear for a pre-file interview, the victim's refusal to cooperate in the prosecution of the case, or the victim's admission that the charges were fabricated. In these types of cases, in other words, the odds of conviction were low (or nonexistent), not because the prosecutor believed that the facts in the case contradicted potential jurors' assumptions about rape and rape victims, but because the unavailability of a victim who was willing to testify made it impossible to proceed with the case.

When we compared the characteristics of cases that were rejected/dismissed to those of cases that were fully prosecuted, we found that the decision to prosecute reflected both legally relevant case characteristics (use of a weapon and injury to the victim) and characteristics of the victim. Prosecution was more likely if the victim and the suspect were non-strangers or if the victim was a young teenager; it was less likely if there were questions about the victim's moral character or behavior at the time of the incident. (This pattern of results was confirmed by a logistic regression analysis of the decision to charge or not.) Further analysis comparing the characteristics of cases rejected for different reasons revealed that evidence of risk-taking was somewhat more common in cases rejected because they didn't fit with prosecutors' typifications of rape cases and rape-relevant behavior or because it appeared that the victim had ulterior motives, while questions about the victim's moral character surfaced more often in cases rejected because the victim could not be located or refused to cooperate. We also found that cases rejected for lack of cooperation were more likely than those rejected for discrepant accounts or ulterior motives to involve a victim and suspect who were complete strangers, a suspect who claimed that the victim consented, and an assault that took place in the victim's residence.

A number of these findings merit comment. The results of our multivariate analysis of the decision to charge or not are consistent with previous research demonstrating that prosecutors attempt to avoid uncertainty by filing charges in cases where the likelihood of conviction is good and by rejecting charges when conviction seems unlikely. This is confirmed by the fact that all but two of the cases that were prosecuted resulted in a conviction. It also is confirmed by our findings regarding the predictors of charging decisions. As noted above, the odds of charging were greater in the more serious cases in which the victim was young, the suspect used a gun or knife, or the victim was injured. Our results also reveal, however, that there are "extralegal sources of uncertainty" (Albonetti 1987:311) and that one of the primary focal concerns of prosecutors in sexual battery cases is the credibility of the victim. In these cases, most of which involved victims and offenders who were non-strangers, prosecutors' anticipation of a consent defense and downstream orientation toward judges and juries apparently led them to scrutinize more carefully the character and behavior of the victim. Evidence that challenged the victim's credibility or fostered a belief that she was not entirely blameless increased uncertainty about the outcome of the case and thus reduced the odds of prosecution.

The comments of the state's attorneys interviewed for this study are consistent with these conclusions. When we asked prosecutors to identify the factors that influenced their decision to file charges in a sexual battery case, all of them mentioned the strength of evidence in the case and the credibility of the victim. A prosecutor who had been prosecuting rape cases in Dade County for more than eight years, in fact, stated that "the *key factor* is the credibility of the victim." As he noted,

> As long as I have sufficient belief in the victim's credibility, I can overcome almost everything else. The bottom line is whether the jury will believe the victim. Rape cases rarely involve witnesses and don't always involve physical evidence, so it all comes down to the victim and her credibility.

When asked to explain how they evaluated victim credibility, all of the respondents noted that inconsistencies between the victim's and suspect's account of the incident and inconsistent or contradictory statements by the victim would lead them to question her credibility. One prosecutor noted, for example, that she asked herself, "Is what the victim telling me plausible and consistent with everything else I know about this case? Is her story consistent with the evidence we have and with the statements of other witnesses?" Other respondents emphasized the victim's demeanor during the interview, as well as inconsistencies in the victim's and the suspect's version of the incident. One respondent explained that,

> You have to look at the victim, her demeanor and her behavior. You have to look closely at the allegations that have been made. If there is other evidence or testimony that conflicts with what she's saying—if, for example, the suspect has an entirely different account of the encounter and there are witnesses who corroborate his story—then you have to determine what set of circumstances you accept and what you don't find credible.

These comments suggest that Dade County state's attorneys, like the prosecutors in Frohmann's study (1991:214), "are actively looking for 'holes' or problems that will make the victim's version of 'what happened' unbelievable or not convincing beyond a reasonable doubt."

When asked what the typical juror is looking for in a sexual battery case, each of the respondents acknowledged that jurors come into the courtroom with preconceived ideas about rape. According to one prosecutor, "jurors tend to be suspicious of cases involving people who know each other or victims who don't fit the stereotype of a rape victim." Another respondent explained that,

> People come into the jury box with the perceptions they get from TV. They expect the victim to be dragged off the street by a stranger and brutally assaulted. Then they get these convoluted stories that involve people who generally know each other and that don't jibe at all with their perceptions of rape. The process has to start with jury selection. You have to emphasize that

crimes committed by family members, friends, and lovers are serious. If you can't get them to admit that, you have to try to get them off the jury.

A third prosecutor, who asserted that "the cases the jurors wrestle with . . . are the date-rape type of cases," noted that in these types of cases "jurors typically have questions about her behavior at the time of the incident—why did she agree to go back to his room after the date, why did she agree to watch pornographic movies with him, and so on." These statements confirm Frohmann's (1991) assertion that it is the prosecutors' orientation toward potential jurors that motivates them to scrutinize the victim's background and behavior and look for holes in her story.

Our findings concerning the effect of the victim/suspect relationship are somewhat surprising. Not only were there very few cases involving strangers in the data file, which included all cases of sexual battery that resulted in an arrest in 1997, but cases involving strangers were *less likely* than those involving acquaintances, relatives, or intimate partners to be prosecuted. This clearly contradicts general assertions that crimes involving strangers are regarded as more serious than crimes involving non-strangers (Black 1976; Gottfredson and Gottfredson 1988), as well as more specific assertions that sexual assaults involving acquaintances are not regarded as "real rapes" (Estrich 1987) and that women victimized by these crimes are not regarded as "genuine victims." At least in this jurisdiction, prosecutors are not reluctant to proceed with cases involving friends, relatives, and intimate partners.

This conclusion is somewhat at odds with the comments made by the prosecutors we interviewed. When asked whether the relationship between the victim and suspect influenced the decision to charge or not, most respondents indicated that it did play a role. One prosecutor noted that "family relationships and interpersonal dynamics complicate a sexual battery case." He added that it doesn't necessarily change the way you look at the evidence, but it probably will change the way the jury looks at the evidence. Other respondents explained that acquaintance cases are complicated by the possibility that the victim might have a motive to lie or to fabricate. As one attorney noted,

> We have to recognize that there are situations in which people make false allegations—a woman may be angry at her husband, who is having an affair, and may see this as a way to get back at him. Or, a woman may falsely claim that she was raped in order to cover up a premarital or extramarital sexual relationship or to explain away a sexually transmitted disease or pregnancy. In these situations, you have to determine whether the victim is being truthful. You have to see if there are circumstances that allow you to conclude that the allegation is real.

The fact that a fairly substantial number of the stranger cases were rejected because the victim could not be located or refused to cooperate also is puzzling. Because it seemed unlikely that a woman attacked by a complete stranger would disappear or fail to show up for a pre-file interview or would refuse to cooperate or ask that the charges be dropped, we examined the characteristics of each of these eight cases in more detail. Four of these cases did not involve a suspect who used a weapon or collateral injury to the victim; in two of these cases, the victim did not make a prompt report, willingly went to the suspect's residence, and had a history of prior consensual sex with someone other than the suspect. In the other two cases, the victim reported the crime within one hour, but there was either evidence of risk-taking behavior or questions about her moral character. In the remaining four cases, the suspect did use a weapon or injure the victim. In one of these more aggravated cases, the victim made a prompt report and there was no moral character evidence or evidence that she had engaged in risky behavior; in this case, the victim indicated that she did not want to pursue the case and asked that the charges be dropped. In the other three cases, the victim either was walking alone late at night or was a prostitute. Although this suggests that all of these stranger cases, with one exception, had some type of evidentiary problem, the problems found in most of the cases do not appear to be so damaging that they would motivate the victim to disappear, request that the charges be dropped, or recant.

The comments of the prosecutors interviewed for this study provide some clues to victim motivation in these types of cases. According to one state's attorney, "When a woman has just been raped, she wants everyone's help. But once she knows what it is going to mean to proceed with the case through the criminal justice system, she may decide it's not worth it." Another attorney voiced a similar opinion, stating,

> Although we do our best to process cases in a timely fashion, I think that sometimes victims just get worn down by all of the delays. The victim is asked to tell her story over and over—to the police, to the prosecutor, at the deposition—and if the case drags on too long, she loses interest or decides that it simply isn't worth it. I also think that we have to acknowledge that sometimes women get subtle or not-so-subtle messages from police and prosecutors that their veracity is being questioned or that the case is unlikely to lead to a conviction.

A third prosecutor focused more on the victim's fear of public exposure. He stated that

> A sexual battery charge deals with probably the most intimate relationship between a man and a woman. I do believe that quite a number of people are petrified about having to describe the gory details of the violation to strangers. We're asking someone who has been violated and probably feels very humiliated to describe the attack in great detail to jurors who are complete strangers. I don't find it all that surprising that some women don't want to put themselves through that. In addition, there are situations involving prostitutes or drug addicts or homeless women who are reluctant to proceed with the case because they know that their lifestyle is a strike against them and they suspect that the jury won't believe them.

These comments suggest that the victim's reluctance to proceed with a case against a stranger who sexually assaulted her may be motivated both by her disillusionment with the criminal justice system and by her reluctance to have her private life made public.

Although the explanations presented above also could apply to cases in which the victim and suspect were non-strangers, the closeout memos and the comments of prosecutors suggested additional reasons why the victim in non-stranger cases might refuse to cooperate or recant. In a number of these cases, it was clear that the prosecutor believed the victim had been sexually assaulted and was reluctant to drop the charges; there were a number of cases where the victim was subpoenaed to testify at the pre-file interview and one where the victim was arrested and held in jail for four days in an attempt to induce her to cooperate. The fact that the victims in these cases either failed to appear or refused to cooperate suggests that the victim believed prosecution was not in her best interest. This was confirmed by the prosecutors we interviewed. One noted for example, that "there are cases where the victim actually forgives the offender or is reconciled with the offender." She added that in cases in which the offender is a close relative or an intimate partner, "as time goes by she may come to believe that it wasn't that big a deal. There are a lot of the dynamics of domestic violence cases working in sexual assault cases involving intimates." Another stated that some of these cases involve

> women who are attacked by men they know, perhaps even by men with whom they have an intimate relationship, and who reconcile with the offender and decide that they no longer want to prosecute. In those situations, there is not much to be gained by filing charges, since she won't show up and won't agree to testify if the case goes forward.

Several respondents emphasized that in these types of cases, they "take what the victim wants into account." One noted, however, that "society has an interest in the outcome of this case as well" and that "you can't always let the victim dictate what will happen." As he explained,

> When I have a victim who comes in and tells me that she wants to leave his punishment up to God, which happens more than you would think, I'll say to her, "Fine, God can deal with him when he gets there, but we have to decide what to do about this now." I ask the victim what would satisfy her—what would make her think that justice had been done.

Considered together, the results of our analysis and the comments of the state's attorneys we interviewed suggest that the reluctance of victims to proceed with the case can be attributed to a combination of factors: a belief that prosecution of the suspect is not in her own interest; a belief that prosecution of the suspect is not worth either the time and effort required or the humiliation of testifying about her victimization; and a belief, either arrived at independently or communicated by police and prosecutors, that her character and behavior at the time of the incident make conviction unlikely. The victims in these cases, in other words, may have made a rational decision that pursuing the case would be too traumatic and/or would be a waste of time given the low odds of conviction.

Although we can only speculate, the acquaintance and intimate partner cases in which the victim disappeared, asked that the charges be dropped, or recanted also may reflect the fact that these victims were using "prosecution as a power resource" (Ford 1991:320). Like battered women, in other words, these victims of sexual violence may have brought charges in order to send a message that further violence will not be tolerated and to achieve, at least in the short-run, a satisfactory solution to their interpersonal problems. As Ford (1991:326) notes, "victims who are otherwise powerless in the face of violence seek to use prosecution for leverage in managing conjugal conflict or arranging favorable settlements." Because victims' names were redacted from the case materials we received, we were not able to question them about their reasons for recanting or asking that charges be dropped. Given what we know about the motivations of battered women, this would be an interesting avenue for future research.

Conclusion

Our study confirms that prosecutors guarding the "gateway to justice" often use "assumptions about relationships, gender, and sexuality" (Frohmann 1991:224) in making the decision to accept or reject charges in sexual assault cases. Consistent with Frohmann's (1991) work, we found that Dade County State's Attorneys used a variety of techniques to discredit the victim's allegations and thereby justify charge rejection. We also found, however, that not all charge rejections reflected prosecutorial concerns about the victim's character, reputation, and behavior at the time of the incident. A substantial number of cases were rejected because the victim failed to appear for a pre-file interview, asked that the charges be dropped, or recanted her testimony. In these cases, in other words, prosecution was terminated, not because of the prosecutor's concerns about convictability, but because of the victim's unwillingness to go forward. Although it is possible that the victim's decision was motivated by signals from police and prosecutors that the odds of conviction were low, her decision also might have been based on either a rational calculation of the costs and benefits of pursuing the case or a belief that the problems that led her to seek charges had been resolved. Future research should examine this issue more closely and should attempt to determine why sexual assault victims decide not to pursue prosecution.

The results of our study also confirm that prosecutors' charging decisions, like judges' sentencing decisions, are guided by a set of "focal concerns" (Steffensmeier, et al. 1998). Because prosecutors are concerned about reducing uncertainty and securing convictions, they are more likely to file charges when the crime is serious, when it is clear that the victim has suffered real harm, and when the evidence against the suspect is strong. Our findings also suggest, however, that the focal concerns that structure prosecutors' charging decisions in sexual assault cases are somewhat different than those found in other types of cases. Because victim credibility plays a particularly important role in sexual assault cases, the perceptual shorthand that prosecutors develop to reduce uncertainty and assess convictability rests explicitly on stereotypes about rape, rape victims, and rape-relevant behavior. As Estrich (1987) and LaFree (1989) have noted, criminal justice officials, including prosecutors, use a set of victim characteristics to create an image, not of a *typical* rape victim, but of a *genuine* rape victim. Complainants whose backgrounds and behavior conform to this image will be taken more seriously and their allegations treated more seriously than complainants whose backgrounds and behavior are at odds with this image. The results of our study, which highlight the pivotal role of victim credibility and demonstrate that cases involving questions about the victim's moral character and behavior at the time of the incident are more likely to be rejected, indicate that prosecutors' focal concerns in sexual assault cases incorporate these stereotypes.

A final comment concerns the prosecution of sexual assault cases in the post-rape reform era. Beginning in the mid-1970s, most states, including Florida,[10] adopted reforms designed to shift the focus in a rape case from the character and behavior of the victim to the behavior of the offender; the overall goal of these reforms was to encourage reporting and reduce case attrition (see Estrich 1987; Spohn and Horney 1992). The most common reforms included changes in the definition of rape, elimination of resistance and corroboration requirements, and enactment of rape shield laws designed to preclude the use of testimony concerning the victim's sexual history. As Spohn and Horney (1992) note, these reforms were designed primarily to increase the odds of successful prosecution in cases in which the victim and the suspect were acquainted and the suspect claimed that the victim consented. Although research evaluating the impact of the rape law reforms generally concludes that the statutory changes did not produce the widespread instrumental changes that reformers anticipated, there is evidence that the reforms did encourage arrest and prosecution in "borderline cases" in which the victim and the offender were non-strangers and the suspect did not use a weapon or seriously injure the victim. Our findings are consistent with this. Most of the cases included in this study were cases in which the victim and the offender were non-strangers. Moreover, cases involving acquaintances/relatives and intimate partners were more likely than those involving strangers to be prosecuted and there were no differences in the likelihood of charging between the two types of non-stranger cases.

Although these results are encouraging, the fact that over half of the sexual battery cases were not prosecuted, coupled with the fact that prosecutors questioned the victim's credibility in a substantial number of the cases that were rejected, suggests that the prosecution of sexual assault cases remains problematic. The rape law reforms notwithstanding, prosecutors continue to use a decision making calculus that incorporates stereotypes of real rape and legitimate victims.

Notes

This chapter is based on work supported by the National Institute of Justice under Grant 98-WT-VX-0003. Points of view are those of the authors and do not necessarily reflect the position of the National Institute of Justice. An earlier version of this chapter was presented at the annual meeting of the Academy of Criminal Justice Sciences in New Orleans, Louisiana, in March 2000. We would like to thank the anonymous reviewers and the editorial staff for their helpful comments.

1. A recent study of sexual, assault case processing decisions in Sacramento County, California (Kingsnorth et al. 1999), on the other hand, found that victim characteristics did not affect the decision to prosecute fully, the decision to go to trial rather than plead guilty, or the likelihood of incarceration. The presence of "negative" victim characteristics did affect the length of the sentence.

2. Sexual battery is defined as "oral, anal, or-vaginal penetration by, or union with, the sexual organ of another or the anal or vaginal penetration of another by any other object" Florida Statutes 794.011 (1)(h). Depending upon the presence of aggravating circumstances, sexual battery is either a capital felony, a life felony, a first degree felony, or a second degree felony (794.011(2 thru 5). If the offender is 18 or older and the victim is less than 12 and the offender injures the victim's sexual organs, the crime is a capital felony; if the offender in this situation is less than 18, the crime is a life felony. Non-consensual sexual battery involving a victim 12 years of age or older and an offender who either uses or threatens to use a deadly weapon or uses physical force likely to cause serious personal

injury is a life felony. Non-consensual sexual battery on a person 12 years of age or older is a first degree felony under the following circumstances: the victim is physically helpless to resist; the offender threatens to use force or violence likely to cause serious personal injury or threatens to retaliate against the victim or any other person and the victim believes that the offender has the ability to carry out the threat; the offender administers any narcotic, anesthetic, or other intoxicating substance which mentally or physically incapacitates the victim; the victim is mentally defective and the offender has reasons to believe this or has actual knowledge of this fact; the victim is physically incapacitated; or the offender is in a position of control or authority as an agent or employee of government. A person who commits non-consensual sexual battery upon a person 12 years of age or older and, in the process, does not use physical force and violence likely to cause serious personal injury commits a felony of the second degree.

3. In 1997, 1,237 sexual batteries were reported to the Sexual Crimes Bureau of the Miami-Dade Police Department. Of these, 243 were cleared by arrest. (Personal communication, Karin Montejo, Major, Sexual Crimes Bureau, Miami-Dade Police Department.)

4. The Miami-Dade Police Department serves unincorporated Miami-Dade County. It does not provide law enforcement services to the city of Miami, the city of Miami Beach, or 28 other municipalities in Dade County, each of which has its own law enforcement agency.

5. Information obtained during personal interview.

6. One of the anonymous reviewers suggested that some of the cases that were rejected or dismissed by the prosecutor actually might have processed as a violation of probation. We reviewed all of the closeout memorandums and found only one that mentioned this possibility. This case was a familial sexual battery that was not reported for more than one year; the ASA noted in the closeout memorandum that she "found out the defendant was on probation for a similar offense out of Texas." She stated that she attempted to plead the case with a concurrent offer for the Texas case, but the defendant turned down the offer. She then dismissed the charges. Because the probation violation was a Texas case, we do not know if the defendant's probation was revoked.

7. Previous researchers examining case processing decisions, including the decision to charge or not, typically differentiated between legal and extralegal predictors of decision-making. We abandon this dichotomy and instead examine victim characteristics, suspect characteristics, and case characteristics. Our decision is motivated by two concerns. First, although the concepts of legal and extralegal factors have been used extensively by researchers analyzing and predicting the outcomes of criminal cases, they have been neither precisely nor consistently defined. There is disagreement as to the proper categorization of factors even among researchers examining the effect of these factors on the outcomes of sexual assault cases. Some researchers, for example, categorize a prompt report to the police as an extralegal variable, while others contend that its relationship to the preservation of evidence makes it legally relevant (Bryden and Lengnick 1997; Kerstetter 1990). Second, while many of the extralegal factors traditionally examined by researchers are characteristics of the defendant (for example, race, gender, and social class), in this project we are particularly interested in examining the effect of victim characteristics. (For a more extensive discussion of the problems with the legal/extralegal dichotomy in sexual assault cases, see Matoesian [1995:693–696]).

8. Because there were only 140 cases in the analysis and because we were concerned about testing a model with a small number of cases and a relatively large number of independent variables, we did not control for all of the independent variables included in table 6.3. We excluded evidence of a prior sexual relationship between the victim and the suspect, the most serious charge at arrest (which was sexual battery for over three-fourths of the cases in each category), the type of defense mounted by the suspect (which was missing for over 25 percent of the cases, generally because the suspect did not make a statement to the police), and the location of the assault.

9. We could not determine the reason for case rejection in seven of the 15 cases involving strangers. In these cases, the closeout memorandum either was missing or simply indicated that the cases were rejected because there was insufficient evidence to prosecute.

10. See Florida Statutes §794.011 (Sexual Battery) and §794.022 (Rules of Evidence).

References

Albonetti, Celesta
 1987 "Prosecutorial discretion: The effects of uncertainty." *Law and Society Review* 21:291–313.
Amir, Menachem
 1971 *Patterns in Forcible Rape*. Chicago: University of Chicago Press.
Battelle Memorial Institute Law and Justice Study Center
 1977 *Forcible Rape: A National Survey of the Response by Prosecutors*. National Institute on Law Enforcement and Criminal Justice. Washington, DC: U.S. Government Printing Office.
Black, Donald
 1976 *The Behavior of Law*. New York: Academic Press.
Bryden, David P., and Sonja Lengnick
 1997 "Rape in the criminal justice system." *Journal of Criminal Law and Criminology* 87:1194–1384.
Davis, Kenneth Culp
 1969 *Discretionary Justice: A Preliminary Inquiry*. Baton Rouge, LA: Louisiana State University Press.
Estrich, Susan
 1987 *Real Rape*. Cambridge, MA: Harvard University Press.
Ford, David A.
 1991 "Prosecution as a victim power resource: A note on empowering women in violent conjugal relationships." *Law and Society Review* 25:313–334.
Frazier, Patricia A., and Beth Haney
 1996 "Sexual assault cases in the legal system: Police, prosecutor, and victim perspectives." *Law and Human Behavior* 20:607–628.
Frohmann, Lisa
 1991 "Discrediting victims' allegations of sexual assault: Prosecutorial accounts of case rejections." *Social Problems* 38:213–226.
 1997 "Convictability and discordant locales: Reproducing race, class, and gender ideologies in prosecutorial decision-making." *Law and Society Review* 31:531–55.
Gottfredson, Michael R., and Don M. Gottfredson
 1988 *Decision-Making in Criminal Justice: Toward the Rational Exercise of Discretion*. 2nd Edition. New York: Plenum.
Hawkins, Darnell
 1981 "Causal attribution and punishment for crime." *Deviant Behavior* 1:207–230.
Jacoby, Joan, L. Mellon, E. Ratledge, and Susan Turner
 1982 *Prosecutorial Decision-Making: A National Study*. Washington, DC: U.S. Department of Justice, National Institute of Justice.
Kalven, Harry, and Hans Zeisel
 1966 *The American Jury*. Boston: Little, Brown and Company.
Kerstetter, Wayne
 1990 "Gateway to justice: Police and prosecutorial response to sexual assaults against women." *Criminology* 81:267–313.
Kingsnorth, Rodney, John Lopez, Jennifer Wentworth, and Debra Cummings
 1998 "Adult sexual assault: The role of racial/ethnic composition in prosecution and sentencing." *Journal of Criminal Justice* 26:359–371.
Kingsnorth, Rodney, Randall C. MacIntosh, and Jennifer Wentworth
 1999 "Sexual assault: The role of prior relationship and victim characteristics in case processing." *Justice Quarterly* 16:275–302.
LaFree, Gary D.
 1980 "The effect of sexual stratification by race on official reactions to rape." *American Sociological Review* 45:842–854.

1981 "Official reactions to social problems: Police decisions in sexual assault cases." *Social Problems* 28:582–594.

1989 *Rape and Criminal Justice: The Social Construction of Sexual Assault.* Belmont, CA: Wadsworth.

Mather, Lynn
1979 *Plea Bargaining or Trial?* Lexington, MA: Heath.

Matoesian, Gregory M.
1995 "Language, law, and society: Policy implications of the Kennedy Smith rape trial." *Law and Society Review* 29:669–701.

McCahill, Thomas W., Linda C. Meyer, and Arthur M. Fischman
1979 *The Aftermath of Rape.* Lexington, MA: Lexington Books.

Miller, Frank
1969 *Prosecution: The Decision to Charge a Suspect with a Crime.* Boston: Little, Brown and Company.

Myers, Martha
1982 "Common law in action: The prosecution of felonies and misdemeanors." *Sociological Inquiry* 52:1–15.

Myers, Martha, and John Hagan
1979 "Private and public trouble: Prosecutors and the allocation of court resources." *Social Problems* 26:439–451.

Nagel, Ilene, and John Hagan
1983 "Gender and crime: Offense patterns and criminal court sanctions." In *Crime and Justice: An Annual Review of Research*, Vol. 4, Michael Tonry and Norval Morris, eds. Chicago: University of Chicago Press.

Neubauer, David
1974 "After the arrest: The charging decision in Prairie City." *Law and Society Review* 8:475–517.
1988 *America's Courts and the Criminal Justice System.* Pacific Grove, CA: Brooks/Cole.

Paternoster, Raymond
1984 "Prosecutorial discretion in requesting the death penalty: A case of victim-based racial discrimination." *Law and Society Review* 18:437–478.

Rauma, David
1984 "Going for the gold: Prosecutorial decision-making in cases of wife assault." *Social Science Research* 13:321–351.

Reskin, Barbara, and Christy Visher
1986 "The impacts of evidence and extralegal factors in jurors' decisions." *Law and Society Review* 20:423–438.

Schmidt, Janell, and Ellen Hochstedler Steury
1989 "Prosecutorial discretion in filing charges in domestic violence cases." *Criminology* 27:487–510.

Simon, Lenore M.
1996 "Legal treatment of the victim-offender relationship in crimes of violence." *Journal of Interpersonal Violence* 11:94–106.

Spears, Jeffrey, and Cassia Spohn
1997 "Prosecutors' charging decisions in sexual assault cases." *Justice Quarterly* 14:501–524.

Spohn, Cassia, John Gruhl, and Susan Welch
1987 "The impact of the ethnicity and gender of defendants on the decision to reject or dismiss felony charges." *Criminology* 25:175–191.

Spohn, Cassia, and David Holleran
2001 "Prosecuting sexual assault: A comparison of charging decisions in sexual assault cases involving strangers, acquaintances, and intimate partners." *Justice Quarterly* 18(3):651–688.

Spohn, Cassia, and Julie Horney
1992 *Rape Law Reform: A Grassroots Revolution and Its Impact.* New York: Plenum Press.

Spohn, Cassia, and Jeffrey Spears
1996 "The effect of offender and victim characteristics on sexual assault case processing decisions." *Justice Quarterly* 13:649–679.

Stanko, Elizabeth
    1988 "The impact of victim assessment on prosecutor's screening decisions: The case of the New York County District Attorney's Office." In *Criminal Justice: Law and Politics*, George Cole, ed. Pacific Grove, CA: Brooks/Cole Publishing Company.
Steffensmeier, Darrell, Jeffery Ulmer, and John Kramer
    1998 "The interaction of race, gender, and age in criminal sentencing: The punishment cost of being young, black, and male." *Criminology* 36:763—798.
Swiggert, Victoria Lynn, and Ronald A. Farrell
    1976 *Murder, Inequality, and the Law*. Lexington, MA: D.C. Heath.
Vera Institute of Justice
    1981 *Felony Arrests: Their Prosecution and Disposition in New York City's Courts*. New York: Longman.

CHAPTER 7

Gender, Accounts, and Rape Processing Work

Patricia Yancey Martin

Understandings of rape are fused with cultural representations of sexuality and gender. For example, the connections between rape and consent/coercion in sexual relations and power/domination in non-sexual gender relations are contested issues (MacKinnon 1987). Most rapists are men (or boys) and most victims are women (or girls), a condition that makes gender an issue in the perpetration and prevention of rape, as well as in research and theorizing about it. Given the gendered character of rape crimes, one might expect officials who process them to have a "theory" about gender and rape. Yet officials who work with rape victims in law enforcement, hospital, prosecution, and court contexts often talk about rape in non-gendered ways. They refer to "perpetrators," "assailants," "targets," and "victims," not men and women, and characterize rape as a "crime of opportunity" involving "unfortunate victims" whose bad luck placed them in the wrong place at the wrong time. All the while, processing work with victims and rapists is pervasively gender-organized (McCahill, Meyer, and Fischman 1979; Martin and Powell 1994). For example, most police chiefs, sheriffs, and uniformed law officers are men; most hospital emergency room (ER) physicians are men, most ER nurses are women; rape crisis centers (RCCs) are all or mostly women organizations; most prosecutors, particularly chief prosecutors, are men, most victim-witness-advocates (VWAs) are women; and most judges who preside over rape proceedings are men. These conditions hold in Florida, from which data for this study are taken, and across the United States (Martin and Powell 1994; Stepnick and Orcutt 1996). Despite the pervasiveness of these gendered work arrangements, we know little about how officials use gender to account for or perform work with rape victims, e.g., whether they address it in processing protocols. Do processors say women (or men) work better with victims and, if so, for what reason? Do they say gender is irrelevant? This study addresses these questions.

This study focuses on officials' talk about gender and processing work (defined below) in the form of *justificational accounts* about work with rape victims (Scott and Lyman 1968; Frohmann 1991; Chase 1995). Similar to Thorne's (1993) research on teachers and "kids" in elementary school, I explore how processing officials talk about and enact gender in work with rape victims. My findings show that officials talk about and use gender in varying ways, from one organization and community to another.

They also confirm the generalization that, in processing officials' hands, gender is a malleable cultural resource (cf. Stacey and Thorne 1985; Gerson and Peiss 1985; Holstein 1987).

Rape processing refers to "work done by organizations to move rape cases through the law enforcement, judicial, therapeutic, and advocacy networks of a local community" (Martin and Powell 1994:861; LaFree 1989; Chandler and Torney 1981). Rape victims' odds of recovery are affected by how processing officials treat them (Holmstrom and Burgess 1978; Williams and Holmes 1981; Sales, Baum, and Shore 1984; Koss 1993). Cluss et al. (1983) found that victims who prosecuted recovered more slowly and had more problems six months after a rape than those who did not prosecute; they suggest that the adversarial nature of the U.S. legal system may explain this result (Konradi 1997). Additional harm results when officials refuse to be trained in rape processing, to treat victims responsively in face-to-face encounters, or to cooperate with officials in other organizations (Martin and Powell 1994).

Due to its embeddedness in local communities, processing work has a *political dimension* (Martin 1997a). Florida sheriffs, prosecutors, judges, and public defenders are elected officials, concerned with the public's perceptions and approval. Even when they have minimal concern with victims' well-being, they try to avoid being seen as incompetent or uncaring. They are wary of rape crisis centers (RCCs), often forcing RCCs to struggle for access to victims, resources, and the right to participate in processing networks (Byington et al. 1991; Martin, DiNitto, Byington, and Maxwell 1992; Matthews 1994; Fried 1994). These conditions suggest that rape victims are affected by community political forces as well as organizational conditions, a point to which I return in the discussion (Martin 1997a).

This study assumes that processing organizations are embedded in society's *gender institution* (see Lorber 1994; Connell 1987, 1995), meaning, among other things, that they are stratified in men's favor, that work is divided based on gender, and that cultural beliefs and practices about gender permeate them (Reskin 1988; Ely 1995; Pierce 1995). I try to make explicit and visible the gender aspects of rape processing work and organizations that are usually implicit and invisible (Scott 1997). Those who study organizations can learn from this effort about how gender is socially constructed at work (West and Zimmerman 1987), including where and how it is implicated in officials' justificational accounts.

Background: Gender and Rape Processing Work

Many feminists and some social scientists say the gender of rape processors is important and that women are better with victims. For example, Holmes says rape victims receive better treatment from police when the department has "female personnel to work solely on rape cases" (1980:129) and Caringella-MacDonald (1985:219) suggests that an increase in women officers improves the treatment rape victims receive (cf. Hageman and Hastings, 1978:322, on prosecutors). Jensen and Karpos (1993) conjecture that women police officers "found," or accept as valid, rape cases that men officers reject.

Such claims appear to rest on untested assumptions about gender, however. Do women share a common vulnerability to being raped or a common sympathy for all women who are raped? Research on women's supposed greater sympathy and support for victims is inconclusive (see Chancer 1987). Weir and Wrightsman (1990:916) agree that women *generally* are more sympathetic but they found that some women have little sympathy for victims, and "women who are unable to empathize with rape victims are especially harsh when confronted with rape cases." Walsh's study of probation officers (1984:343) found that, compared to women, men were more sympathetic toward victims and made harsher recommendations for offenders' sentences.

Casting doubt on gender's significance, victims in one study rated physicians, all of whom were men, more favorably than they rated nurses, all of whom were women (Holmes 1980) These victims also rated the police, mostly men, *high* while they rated prosecutors, mostly men, *low*. McCahill et al. (1979) found that, while more victims preferred a woman processor, nearly an equal number said either a man or woman was acceptable. In other studies, women and men medical students viewed rape victims' culpability similarly (Gilmartin-Zena 1983; cf. Alexander 1980 on nurses), although women physicians and nurses sympathized with women beaten by their husbands more than men physicians or nurses did (Rose and Saunders 1986). Warshaw's (1989) analysis of ER medical records showed no differences in nurses' and physicians' treatment of battered women, however, casting doubt on the presumption that more sympathetic attitudes produce more responsive behavior. A study of men and women rape crisis therapists found "no evidence of different attitudes or treatment of female victims by male and female therapists" (Bassuk and Assler 1983:307).

With some exceptions, research on gender and juries concerns attitudes rather than behavior, or is based on "mock" rather than actual jurors. These studies typically report either no differences between women and men (Feild 1978a, b) or find women more sympathetic (Feldman-Summers and Lindner 1976; Dietz et al. 1982). However, two studies of actual juries yielded null or counter-intuitive results. Nelligan (1988) found no association of gender composition and jury verdicts in 86 rape trials, and Visher (1982) found that juries with a higher proportion of women were more likely to *acquit*. Individual women were no less likely than individual men to favor conviction, but the collective decision of juries with five to eight women was to convict less often (cf. Sealy 1981; LaFree, Reskin, and Visher 1985). In regard to police work, LaFree (1981) found that officers' gender did not predict rape processing outcomes, although prosecution rates were higher in special units with more women attorneys. McCahill, Meyer, and Fischman (1979) found that police outcomes were more favorable when a police*woman* attended a rape victim's sworn statement interview, even if she said and did nothing. (One implication of this finding is that *women's presence* in rape processing work may affect *men's behavior* toward victims.) Research on the gender of defense attorneys or judges is limited and the little that exists is inconclusive (Villemur and Hyde 1983).

Gendered Organizations, Frames, and Accounts

GENDER

Gender is a cultural resource that organizations use in varying ways. By cultural resource, I mean an available repertoire of claims, including their rationales, that organizational members use to establish or justify practices, policies, or arrangements (see Scott and Lyman 1968:47–51). Consistent with Thorne (1993) and others, I view gender at the level of the group as a shifting, fluid, contextually dependent phenomenon that members sometimes make salient, sometimes ignore, and yet routinely (although not inevitably) use for varied ends (Holstein 1987; Pierce 1995; West and Fenstermaker 1993; Fenstermaker, West, and Zimmerman 1991). Leidner (1991, 1993) found, for example, that gender served as a cultural resource for employers when McDonald's Corporation framed *women as better able than men to handle the hostile public*, and Combined Insurance framed *men as better able than women to handle the hostile public*. Such findings show gender's "plasticity" in the hands of employers (and employees), who use it to organize and accomplish, as well as account for, preferred arrangements. This study explores whether gender is used in similarly plastic ways by those who process rape victims.

Gendered organization theory refers to feminist critiques of organizations that make problematic and visible the gender relations and dynamics of organizations that classical management and organization theories ignore (see Calas and Smircich 1996 for a review). Foremost among these theorists is Joan Acker (1990, 1992), who argues that organizations presume a division of labor that valorizes men's bodies and lives and produces systematic advantages for men over women. Acker views the "gender-free" worker who is sought to fill jobs conceptualized as "empty slots" available to the best qualified person as a myth (1990). Employers create many jobs with women or men in mind, e.g., secretarial jobs for women, managerial jobs for men. Women are expected to "be like men" in terms of being free to dedicate time and energy to paid work. If workers *should* be free of gestation, breast-feeding, home/childcare responsibilities, and constraints on travel, long hours, overtime, and night shifts, those who are free of them—most men—enjoy advantages over those who less readily are, that is, women.

The division of labor and hierarchies in organizations that process rape victims are extensively gendered (Martin and Powell 1994: Table 1) and raced (S. Martin 1980, 1994). Members bring ideas about gender to the organization, do their work in gender-organized structures, and socially construct gender in work relations and activities. Well-intentioned people routinely "do gender," even as they claim and believe they act in gender-free ways (Hall 1993a, 1993b; Collinson and Hearn 1996; Martin 1996). In line with these premises, this study explores how gender is used, ignored, or transcended in accounts of rape processing work.

ORGANIZATIONAL FRAMES

Contemporary frame analysis, adapted from Goffman (1974), defines frames as interpretive schema that people use in social situations to answer questions such as, "What is going on here?" or "What is appropriate for me to do here?" (March and Olsen 1989; Snow et al. 1986). In a recent paper on rape processing work, Marlene Powell and I explored how the frames of processing organizations influence members to view and treat victims unresponsively. Organizations develop their own distinctive frames or "cognitive schemata through which [members] interpret and give meaning to concrete events" (Martin and Powell 1994:859, following Goffman 1974). Such frames help members make sense of their work with victims, rapists, and groups in the community, defining the behavioral responses that are appropriate in given situations, and specifying actions for particular positions and jobs.

Organizational frames specify "rules and routines" for members to follow. Even those who disagree usually comply because conformity is normative in work contexts (Scott and Lyman 1968). For example, when a police dispatcher instructs an officer to meet a rape victim, the officer normally obeys. A typical frame orients the officer to go to the victim, assure her safety (e. g., if injured, call an ambulance), secure the crime scene and protect physical evidence, and ascertain whether "probable cause" exists that a rape occurred (Martin and Powell 1994). If the frame says a *woman officer* should meet the victim, the dispatcher contacts a woman, who goes. If the frame is silent on gender, the closest appropriate officer is dispatched. An organization can thus specify gender in its processing protocols or not.

JUSTIFICATIONAL ACCOUNTS

When I asked about gender, processing officials offered a range of accounts to justify including or excluding gender in their organizational policies, arrangements, and practices. In the absence of organizational accounts, many offered their own. "An account is a linguistic device employed whenever an action is subjected to evaluative inquiry. Such devices . . . prevent conflicts from arising by verbally bridging the gap between action and expectation" (Scott and Lyman 1968:46; Conley and O'Barr 1990; Chase 1995). One type of account is *justifications*: "socially approved vocabularies . . . [that] assert . . . positive value" of the claim being made (Scott and Lyman 1968:51). As part of their frame, bureaucratic organizations provide employees with standardized accounts to use in talk with outsiders (e.g., rape victims or the general public), to assert the value of what they do (54–56). Many members of the public believe rape processing organizations treat rape victims in "untoward" ways, thus accounts that justify their practices help these organizations maintain public support. For example, the giving of lie detector tests to victims, aggressively challenging their stories, and plucking live pubic hairs are viewed by outsiders as reprehensible acts that officials justify by noting their "positive value" for the victim, the organization, or both (see Martin et al. 1985; DiNitto et al. 1986; and Martin and DiNitto 1987 on rape exams).

Anti-rape activists associated with second wave feminism (the movement that began in the late 1960s/early 1970s) accused legal-justice officials of deplorable behavior toward rape victims. Many accusations concerned gender; for example, they complained about *men* police officers who observe *women* victims during post-rape exams; *men* detectives who challenge women's accounts of being raped; *men* prosecutors who failed to file charges when women reported a rape (Holmstrom and Burgess 1978). Criminal justice organizations have improved their treatment of victims over two decades but suspicions of them persist (Frohmann and Mertz 1994). Given this history, officials can reasonably be expected to justify their stance on gender by offering reasons for ignoring or incorporating it in their work.

I use processors' justificational accounts to explore gendered organization theory's claim that work organizations are extensively gendered versus bureaucratic theory's claim that work organizations are gender-free (Acker 1990). Gender can be incorporated in formal structures and practices, but it can also be incorporated informally, when members view women or men as better at some tasks or when they remove themselves from particular situations. Through inductive analysis, I identify *five gender frames* that processors use in justifying gender's relevance or irrelevance.

Methods, Sample, and Data

The data were collected between 1984 and 1996. Colleagues and I conducted a 1984 statewide needs assessment study in Florida that involved structured interviews with 200 members of 130 organizations in 28 metropolitan areas, including 43 law enforcement agencies, 20 hospitals, 20 prosecution offices, and 25 RCCs (cf. Martin et al. 1985; Martin and Powell 1994; Martin 1997a). Although gender was not the focus of the original study, we encountered many comments about gender in the field. Qualitative interview data from 15 of the 1984 respondents who spontaneously brought up the issue of gender were supplemented by data from interviews explicitly about gender with judges (four men), defense attorneys (three men, one woman), and prosecutors (three men, one woman) in 1988–1989; police officers (three men) in 1993; victim-witness advocates (two in police departments, one in a prosecution office, all women) in 1995–1996; and RCC counselor/advocates (three women) in 1996. I observed two rape trials, one in 1989 and one in 1993, and took notes on gender. Additional interview data were collected by Tara Wall (1993), Marlene Powell (1993), and Colleen Paeplow (1995). Because my data from judges, defense attorneys, and rape trials are not as rich as those from other contexts, I focus on law enforcement, hospitals, prosecutors, and rape crisis centers.

Respondents served as informants about their organizations' policies, practices, and arrangements. I said my goal was to understand their work with rape victims, rapists, and the community. In response to a question about "problems," some informants mentioned gender. If not, I asked: "Is gender an issue in the work you do . . . with victims, rapists, or the community?" and followed up with requests for rationales and examples. I analyzed the data using grounded theory (Glaser and Strauss 1967; Martin and Turner 1986) and theory extending methods (Burawoy 1991) with a goal of identifying how officials socially construct gender. I did not have an a priori list of ways gender is or is not relevant to the work, nor did I document the prevalence of claims or practices. Although many men are also raped, I use the pronoun *she* for rape victims because about 95 percent of Floridians over 14 years of age who come to the attention of law enforcement are girls or women. I use the term *victim* to underscore that someone was criminally violated (Abarbanel and Klein 1988; but see Konradi 1996, 1997).

Gender Accounts in Rape Processing Work

Table 7.1 lists the justificational accounts induced from the data organized in five gender frames: (a) women are better than men, (b) men are better than women, (c) some women and some men are worse, (d) "it depends . . ." and (e) gender is irrelevant. The accounts in table 7.1 are not mutually exclusive nor are they exhaustive of all possible accounts of rape processing work and gender. Many informants gave multiple accounts that overlapped in content and, often, contradicted each other as well (see Conley and O'Barr 1990). Some reflect individual's claims, lacking correspondence to organizational policy or practice; I include them, however because they have meaning to the individual and may therefore affect victims. Other accounts reflect organizational policy. A police department that requires women to conduct rape victims' "sworn statement" or official interviews (Kerstetter 1990) normally offers an account that justifies the policy by describing its benefit for victims, the department, or both, whereas a department that ignores gender usually offers an account that asserts its irrelevance.

Table 7.1. Justificational Accounts: Gender and Rape Processing Work

Frame

I. Women are better because
  a) women comfort victims more
  b) women believe, understand, and sympathize with victims more
  c) women "care" more about rape and helping victims
  d) women are better at relating to victims

II. Men are better because
  a) men help victims feel safer by protecting and avenging them
  b) jurors believe men prosecutors more
  c) men have more credibility when talking about rape with boys, men, and the public
  d) men are better at comforting men and boys who are raped and also men associates of women victims

III. Some women and some men are worse because
  a) women are threatened by (women) rape victims
  b) women fail to believe rape victims
  c) women are "soft on crime" and resist prosecution
  d) men believe rape victims "asked for it"
  e) men believe "folklore" that says rape cases cannot be won
  f) men are discomfitted by rape
  g) men resist involvement in rape processing work
  h) men refuse to develop relationships with or explain decisions to victims
  i) men are unskilled, untrained, and inexperienced in rape processing work
  j) men refuse to let victims be emotional with them
  k) men judge rape victims instead of empathizing with them

IV. It depends . . .
  a) if the victim cares about gender, we let her/him choose
  b) rape victims do best when processed by someone of their own gender

V. Gender is irrelevant because
  a) men and women are equally effective if equally trained and skilled
  b) other priorities (promptness, quality of evidence) are more important
  c) rape victims do not care about their processors' gender
  d) burdening one gender with all rape cases is unfair
  e) men and women are equally inept at dealing with rape victims

FRAME ONE: WOMEN ARE BETTER

Accounts that depict women as better (table 7.1, Frame One) focus on interpersonal dynamics of victim processing work. Women are better because they have more relationship skills, e.g., comforting, believing, caring about, or helping victims. These accounts assume that victims need and deserve to be comforted, believed, and responsively treated during processing (Martin and Powell 1994).

A rape crisis counselor offered one such account when she said a victim is more comfortable talking to a woman about the "horrible things" the rapist did to her. "It's less embarrassing [to tell a woman] and she doesn't have to be so careful about what she says." A police officer said victims are more comfortable around women because, "Women officers are more supportive [of victims]" and another said, "A woman officer helps a victim's peace of mind and sense of safety." An RCC counselor/advocate implied that any woman, but only a particular sort of man—a *kind* man—can comfort victims:

> I am sure some women would be [comfortable] with a nice, warm man. A *kind* man who is different from the person that hurt her might be real helpful. But we just feel like it is important to have the comfort level of having a female counselor in there. [white woman, age 30]

A police officer said victims are more comfortable with women because some victims fear men after a rape: "Victims want to be around women . . . many [rape] victims are afraid of men [after a rape]" (white man, age 52, detective).

Law enforcement organizations have heavy workloads, round-the-clock schedules, and few women officers, thus a policy requiring women poses problems. Yet some agencies have one. For example, one department dispatches a *civilian woman* to meet and transport every (woman) rape victim to the examination site. This woman stays with the victim until a detective, usually a man, arrives to conduct the victim's interview. Another department requires women to conduct the interview; the proximally closest officer, woman or man, meets the victim and takes her to the hospital or the police station where a woman detective meets and interviews her. However, departments with policies routinely violate them because they have so few women officers; "[C]ompliance is a problem," one officer said. One department that formerly had a policy requiring a woman to meet rape victims abandoned it for this reason. I underscore these points to emphasize that accounts about gender may contradict the practices that are followed.

Some accounts allege that comfortable victims provide better evidence and make better witnesses in court, framing the victim's comfort as an organizational utility (cf. Table 2 in Martin and Powell 1994). This justification was offered by a rural sheriff who planned to hire a woman officer:

> I hope to recruit a female officer because a female will help us make victims feel comfortable. And we get much better information from her [sic] then. Without good evidence, you don't win [the case]. (white man, 42 years old)

Another account says women believe, understand, and sympathize with victims more due to a common fear of rape that all women share and that men neither have nor understand:

> I think there is an extremely special bond between women in that as women we share certain fears, certain issues, and probably certain coping responses that men truly can't understand fully . . . simply because they have nothing to relate it to. Men are raised to be protectors, providers, and take care of themselves. They aren't raised that you need to be afraid when you are walking alone at night. You need to watch out when strange men approach you. You need to be careful when you are alone in parking lots. You know all those messages we get as women that men don't get. [white woman, age 28] (cf. Gordon and Riger 1991)

Still another account says women care about rape and helping victims more than men do. An RCC advocate [white woman, age 28] said women will prosecute rape cases that men will "not touch." A woman prosecutor in her city is: "aggressive on rape . . . going to the extreme of prosecuting date rapes" and she "sometimes *wins* [date rape case convictions]" (emphasis hers). Men prosecutors, in contrast, dislike rape cases because they are "messy" and hard to win and they will do anything to avoid them: They "won't touch these cases with a ten foot pole."

A final account depicts women as more skilled at developing relationships. Konradi (1996, 1997) argues that prosecutors must "establish a relationship" with victims to be effective, for example, through becoming acquainted, listening to her story, building trust, informing her about the legal-justice process, answering questions, introducing her to courtroom procedures, and helping her feel comfortable. Relationship work is time-consuming and uncertain and women, more than men, take the time and trouble to do it. Failing to develop a relationship with a victim can lower the odds of conviction, according to this account. (I present data under Frame Three on men's "relationship" deficits in contrast to women's alleged strengths [cf. Pierce 1995 on women and men litigators' and paralegals' "relationship" work; and women's "relational practice" in Fletcher 1997]).

FRAME TWO: MEN ARE BETTER

Frame Two accounts depict men as better at performing stereotypical or normative masculine practices like protecting, avenging, persuading, and speaking in public.

A deputy sheriff said men can better protect rape victims and help them feel safe. As a supervisor of a "crimes against persons" unit, he discussed rape victims' feelings of vulnerability and questioned whether they can feel safe with *another woman* who is, as a woman, also susceptible to being raped. His comments depict himself [and other men, in data not quoted] as victims' protectors, rescuers, and avengers:

> I always put myself lower than her . . . I put her "back in control" [of the situation]. I'm a big man so it's important I don't tower over her. If she stands up, I sit down. If she sits on a chair, I sit on the floor. Often, I'll hold her hand. This one girl, she wouldn't let go [of] my hand. Her mother rode [with her] to the station and they sat in the back seat; I had to hold her [the victim's] hand over my shoulder all the way. I tell a victim, "We'll get the bastard." I tell her she's safe with me. Some people say rape victims are afraid of

men . . . but if you're big and strong and on her side, she feels safe. She feels like you'll "go get him" for her. She feels safer with a man than a woman; after all, she's a woman and she was raped. [white male detective, age 43]

Another Frame Two account depicts men as better because rape trial jurors *like* men more and, as a result, are more likely to convict. Part of a three-attorney special sex crimes unit, an assistant prosecutor said jurors dislike seeing two women, victim and prosecutor, on one side because it looks like the women have "gang[ed] up on a man. [It] . . . looks like prejudice or a woman-man thing. To see a male against male [male prosecutor vs. male rapist] . . . makes the case more credible, particularly for male jurors" [assistant prosecutor, white man, age 35]. His claim that men have more legitimacy with jurors was endorsed by other prosecutors, including a woman whose boss offered her the lead prosecutor job in a high profile rape case that she declined. Men are more effective prosecutors, and women are more effective defense attorneys, in her view:

> I told them you need an older man and a younger man [as prosecutor] to stand before that jury and be outraged. And the defense, if they were smart, would have a woman defense attorney, about 35 years old, who would put her hand on the defendant's shoulder and say, "This is a fine young man. How can you think he is dangerous? I am not afraid of him."[white woman, age 33]

Some accounts depict men as better at communicating with men, boys, and the public about rape. Criminal justice officials tend to view rape as a woman's problem and target women for public education work. When asked about this, a sheriff said he tries to reach women: "Well, we do [give educational talks] when we can get a group of women together. The senior citizens . . . are pretty good about coming out [to attend a presentation]." He did not target boys or men for this work. Some RCC activists say men are best at reaching men and boys with rape prevention messages and that rape can be eliminated only if men tell other men (and boys) to stop:

> We've got to have men talk to boys and men about this [rape]. They have to impress on them [men on boys] that such behavior will not be tolerated. Only men can stop this [rape]. But if they would do this, rape could be eliminated. Rape is something men let other men get away with and blame it on us [women]. [RCC director of battered women's shelter/rape crisis center, white woman, age 35]

Another woman RCC director hired a man as deputy to speak for the RCC because he enhanced the center's "credibility": "Credibility is higher when a man represents us in the community. It gives us credibility when they see a man speaking on behalf of our issues." Few Florida RCCs serve boy or men rape victims but this one does because, again, this practice enhances the center's community reputation.

A fourth account that justifies men's superiority depicts men as better in work with boy or men victims and with male significant others of women/girl victims. (I discuss the issue of a "gender match"—men with men, women with women—under Frame Four.)

FRAME THREE: SOME WOMEN AND SOME MEN ARE WORSE

Frame Three accounts catalog various deficiencies of women or men in processing work. Some are the flip side of the virtues named in Frames One and Two. They generally refer to some women's mistreatment of rape victims and many men's refusal or inability to relate effectively to victims.

One Frame Three account says that some women are threatened by rape and as a result treat victims harshly. Women who are threatened protect themselves by denying that rape can happen unless a victim precipitated it, according to one RCC director. She said victims expect a woman to believe them and be supportive, and they become upset if she does not. Victims do not expect men to be supportive, however, and are "impressed" when men act this way. Women in law enforcement and hospital ERs who see many victims are threatened and thus skeptical:

> Female law enforcement officers and also ER nurses are often very brusque with clients [her term for victims], with the attitude . . . "prove to me you were really raped" or "prove you caused it somehow." Because if the client did not cause her own rape, this makes the officer [or nurse] very threatened . . . or some of them. They realize they're vulnerable too and they don't want to think this. They want to think [that] only those who somehow "ask for it" get it. So, we usually get better results with male officers than females. The victim expects the female officer to be real supportive and when she isn't, this is really offensive and upsetting. . . . [T]he client does not expect sensitivity and support from male officers and when they receive it, they are so grateful. They [victims] often get really impressed with their officer, especially if he treats them real well. [RCC director, urban area, white woman aged 37]

In telling about a woman's failure to believe a rape victim, a man police officer says some women are less skilled than men (including himself) at processing work:

> From my experience, I've found that if you approach [a victim] low key, [are] sensitive, and allow [her] space, I think a man can do as good a job with a rape victim although there may be some initial resistance [from the victim] but normally he can do as good. I recall one case specifically. I came in and a female uniformed officer was the initial officer [and] she grabbed me before I went in to talk to the rape victim [and said], "I think she's lying." "Yeah, OK," [I said]. So I went in and I knew within a minute and a half of speaking to the woman, this woman was traumatized; something serious had happened to her. It never occurred to me that she was lying. And she [the victim] said "keep her [the woman officer] away from me," was her attitude. "I don't want to deal with this female officer." . . . I think it is how you approach the problem more so than the gender that determines who can handle a rape case or an assault on a woman. [training officer for 50-person police department, white man, age 40]

This man acknowledged the cultural belief that women are better in work with victims: "If I were a woman I would probably feel more comfortable initially thinking that I was going to be dealing with a woman." But not all women believe victims, he said.

Another account depicts women as "soft on crime." One police officer said "feminist do-gooders" fail to appreciate the value of prosecution. He complained that "all you social workers" focus on victims' well-being ahead of prosecution, which is a mistake. Women will sacrifice prosecution to protect victims from the stresses of prosecution, which is wrong-headed. Women should realize that rape can be stopped *only* if "society put[s] 'em in jail and show[s] the bad guys out there [that] it [rape] doesn't pay" (white man, age 40).

Men's shortcomings are even more richly accounted for than women's. An assistant prosecutor said most men are sexists who think rape victims asked for it; they also believe "prosecution folklore" that says rape cases cannot be won so they "settle cheap" instead of prosecuting vigorously:

> Most men are still sexists. They think back on their own lives and figure most women probably asked for it. So . . . they don't want the [rape] case and they settle cheap. Too, the general [typical] assistant prosecutor has had no training in the sensitivity of these cases or [they have] no experience. They are uncomfortable with the topic . . . the details. So you get avoidance behavior. They're convinced through years of prosecution folklore that rape cases can't be won . . . so they plead 'em and settle cheap. [assistant prosecutor in Sex Crimes Unit, white man, age 35]

Some accounts say men resist encounters with rape victims due to resentment or discomfort. A nurse said the physicians in her ER: "hate rape exams" and one will "see a child with a cold before [he will see] a rape victim." This behavior hurts victims and wastes the time of nurses and police officers, she said. A prosecutor said her men colleagues expect rape victims to simply accept their decisions and be grateful; they will not "establish a relationship" or explain themselves:

> It takes a lot of work to establish a relationship with the victims and lots of male prosecutors won't take the trouble or time to do that. They see the victim only just before trial and the victim doesn't act right and so they lose [the case]. You can't do it that way. [Men] . . . just expect victims to accept their decisions. . . . Males [prosecutors] have reasons for what they do but they don't explain this to the victim. They expect the victim to just be grateful and accept whatever they think is best. [white woman, age 35, assistant prosecutor]

Another account says men lack skill in rape case prosecution due to a lack of training and experience. Men's discomfort with rape prompts them to avoid these cases, which are then assigned to women by default. The VWA quoted below does not say women are more skilled even though they "handle" most of the rape cases:

> We have two women in the office who handle most of them . . . not all but most. [Are they assigned these cases?] Yes. The feeling is that they will relate better to the children, especially. [And they prosecute adult cases too?] Yes, not all of them but a good number. [And why is that?] The men are

GENDER, ACCOUNTS, AND RAPE PROCESSING WORK 179

> just not comfortable with these cases. We get them [men attorneys] and they go first into misdemeanor offenses court. Then, after awhile, they move up to civil [cases]. And finally, if they stay that long, they move to felony crimes. And they don't get anything about these things [how to prosecute rape cases, treat victims, etc.] in law school. So they don't know what is happening and they don't understand. [VWA supervisor prosecutor's office, white woman, age 44]

Men are depicted as deficient emotionally; they dislike victims' emotionality and are unwilling to "deal with it." The VWA supervisor quoted above said she never has hired a man VWA for these reasons:

> Well, they [men] want to do case management . . . just call up [the victim] and say, "You have to be in court on blah blah." When the victim gets emotional, they hand me the phone. They don't want to handle her emotions and if one starts to cry or get angry, they don't want to deal with it. . . . They don't want to deal with the emotional aspects of the job and that's what our job is! It's our job to support the victim, keep her involved and informed, and help them with their reactions and frustrations. . . . I try to keep my mind open and I'm not saying I wouldn't hire a man. But so far, I haven't found one I would hire.

A police department VWA similarly explained that victims "hold back" with men due to a lack of trust on their part:

> [M]y point is that from a victim's standpoint, it is the victim's reluctance to trust the male to fall apart on [release their emotions on]. It is not necessarily that a male advocate wouldn't be capable of handling that [the victim's falling apart]. It is just the victim's lack of trust in that particular role. [white woman, age 30]

Rape victims worry that men judge them after a rape, according to a sheriff's department VWA, thus victims are better off being processed by women who are better able to relate:

> Back to whether male or females can be better at this job . . . I think that females . . . females that are battered or raped or victims of *males* [emphasis mine] normally don't want to deal with males: They want a female that's compassionate with them, can empathize with them, rather than another male sitting down, maybe judging them. Whether he's [actually] judging them or not, of course he's not, it's the feeling of "I can talk to her, she's a woman, she can relate to this." [white woman, age 45]

FRAME FOUR: IT DEPENDS . . .

Frame Four is a mixed category, alleging that gender is pertinent under some conditions. One account represents gender as relevant if victims care about it. This was expressed by a police officer whose department lets victims choose whether a woman or man will conduct their official interview. This practice "sets the victim on a course of recovery" by helping her regain "control of her life":

> We try to accommodate her preference. Getting the first available officer to the scene assures a prompt response and the protection of evidence. Letting the victim decide if she wants a woman, or man benefits her healing. . . . It helps a victim gain control of her life. . . . Rape victims are real vulnerable. The slightest criticism can make things worse. So, we tell our officers: "Your first job is to help her on her way to recovery." We are concerned about the case but the victim comes first. The reason we let her choose if she wants a male or female for the [official/sworn statement] interview is to assist [in] her recovery. [police lieutenant, white man, age 40]

A second account says a "gender match" helps victims. RCC and law enforcement staff, especially, emphasize victims' need and right to avoid embarrassment by having someone of their own gender process them. Having a woman process a woman (or girl) victim and a man process a man (or boy) victim minimizes unnecessary humiliation. The practice is given lip service more than enacted in many organizations, however. As a police officer quoted below said (see Frame Five), a gender match may be desirable but it is impractical.

FRAME FIVE: GENDER IS IRRELEVANT

Frame Five accounts assert gender's irrelevance. One says training, skill, and competence matter more than gender. Men and women who are equally informed and skilled process victims equally well; neither is superior for any reason related to gender. Staff are assigned to rape cases based on availability, expertise, and skill—not gender. In explaining such an account, a police officer stressed the need to treat victims in a sensitive way, irrespective of the processor's gender:

> The police are better trained now. They are more sensitive and understanding. . . . Part of their training is to sensitize and personalize the issue which is important because one of the most difficult things victims used to face was the initial contact with the police which involved a lot of victim blaming. The police academy has specific training for a whole range of areas. A component of it deals with the technical stuff like evidence collection but they [officers in training] also get a very strong component now that deals with the issues of interviewing and interpersonal techniques and sensitivity. They . . . get in touch with what it might be like to be a rape survivor. That is a far cry from what used to happen when everything was ignored except for the evidence collection piece. As more women have become police officers it adds an option for the survivor to have a female investigating officer. That doesn't necessarily mean that a woman is going to be any more sensitive, however. [police officer, white man, age 35]

Another account says organizational issues like promptness and quality of physical evidence matter more than gender. One police department does not give victims a choice about gender because promptness is more important. "If you ask, you ask for trouble. A gender fit [a woman officer with a woman victim] may help a victim but promptness matters more" (white man, age 50). Protecting physical evidence is the top priority at another department and "who does the work doesn't matter."

Another account says victims are unconcerned about their processors' gender. A police officer makes this point and claims that women are no more skilled at rape processing work than men are:

> We have found it doesn't matter who starts the initial investigation. . . . I have seen female officers do a lot worse job of interviewing a rape victim than males. Female victims don't care if they have a male investigator or officer. . . . I have had several [rape victims] where they have told me that when a female officer had responded to the call, "I just wasn't comfortable with that person" . . . not because they were female but because they just didn't feel like they [women officers] were listening to them. [police detective, white man, age 50]

One prosecutor, in the name of fairness, rotates rape cases through his staff, irrespective of gender. It would be wrong to assign cases to only men or only women because rape cases are too burdensome:

> These cases are really hard on us [the prosecutors]. They [the cases] will burn out an attorney in no time at all. We rotate them [through the assistant prosecutors] so no one will be too burdened. You have to do that or it kills the people who get stuck with them. I wouldn't think of giving them just to women . . . or men. [assistant prosecutor, white man, age 45]

A final account says gender is irrelevant because women and men are equally inept with rape victims. An RCC advocate says neither gender knows how to respond to victims:

> In general people have no idea of how to deal with rape victims. And when I say people, I mean the professionals that have to deal with them—law enforcement officers, sheriffs, deputies. They have no idea what they are up against and they are freaked out by it and they don't want to do it, whether or not they feel sorry for her. They may feel sorry for her but they just don't want to be involved in this messy, messy stuff. Men or women don't know how. Women are facing up to the fact that this could be them when they are dealing with it so it's just as much for them. [white woman, age 28]

Discussion

In accord with gendered organization theory, my results show that gender is fused (or conflated; Martin 1996, 1997b) with work in rape processing organizations. A police department that requires women to interview victims constructs the societal gender order as well as processing work. By incorporating gender into talk, policies, and work relations, organizations socially construct women and men, not only disembodied labor.

Dorothy Smith (1987) describes a young girl who, in buying a candy bar, unwittingly contributes to the worldwide system of capitalism. Without her and similar actions by millions of others, capitalism could not exist as a system of global profit-making. Similarly, processing organizations that use primarily men or only women for "gender appropriate" tasks contribute (unwittingly?) to a societal-wide system of gender relations. In this practice, gender has the imprimatur of bureaucratic authority, and the "doings of work" and "doings of gender" mutually reproduce each other (Acker 1990; Collinson and Hearn 1996; Martin 1997b).

My results show gender as a rich cultural resource for processing organizations. Officials' accounts about gender reveal it as a constituent part of organization culture and practice, disconfirming bureaucratic theory's claim that gender is irrelevant to the organization of work. While some organizations formally specify gender in their protocols, many do not. Yet these same organizations routinely process victims within a gendered division of labor and use gender in both formal and informal ways. For example, an ER nurse said the two men nurses in her department: "voluntarily remove themselves from the [rape examination] rotations" although the ER had no policy requiring them to (Paeplow 1995). When asked why, she "guess[ed]" it was because they were "uncomfortable." A woman VWA told a similar story: "The one or two [rape victims] that I know that he [the man VWA in her department] has handled . . . he has been real anxious to get a female involved. And I don't know if that is his apprehension or the victim's apprehension" (Paeplow 1995). When men nurses and VWAs "voluntarily remove themselves" from work with victims, they enact the cultural stereotype that only women should do this work (cf. Williams 1995). In tolerating the men's behavior, furthermore, their colleagues affirm this stance. If the organization framed men as appropriate (and trained them), they would likely perform the work, thereby undermining rather than reproducing stereotyped gender relations.

Several accounts associated with Frames One, Two, and Three depict women's virtues and men's failings in stereotypical ways (cf. Paeplow 1995). While unsurprising, typifications of women as good and men as flawed at "relationship work" with victims can cause problems for organizations that unreflexively accept them. Many organizations have few women members; thus, policies requiring a woman processor may be impossible to follow. Also, some accounts suggest that not all women treat victims well, and that some men do. Furthermore, practices premised in gender stereotypes let men off the hook and force women to perform work they may find threatening. Ironically, requiring men to perform relationship work with rape victims could be a benefit. Men who are well-trained and motivated can use their gender privilege—and organization rank privilege—to help victims heal and achieve justice (Schmitt and Martin 1997). Comments from some of my informants suggest that some men, and their organizations, do exactly that. Equally important, requiring men and women to perform work that contradicts gender stereotypes can help undermine, rather than reproduce, cultural beliefs that women and men are binarily, and oppositionally, gendered beings (Lorber 1996).

Only one of the five frames depicted gender as irrelevant. At a minimum, these results confirm gender's susceptibility to contradictory uses by organizations (Holstein 1987). My results suggest that a particular gender composition or division of labor cannot anticipate officials' justificational accounts. For example, police departments everywhere employ many more men than women, yet some departments incorporate gender in their processing protocols while others do not. This finding urges caution in concluding that gender composition "causes" particular dynamics. Official policy and employees' informal practices (and interorganizational politics in the community; see Martin 1997a) can override gender composition and division of labor effects (cf. Zimmer 1988).

Although conflicts over men's place developed later on, the earliest RCCs were women-only organizations (Rose 1977; Gornick, Burt, and Pittman 1985; Hyde 1997). Florida RCCs in the 1990s took varied stands on gender. Some were all-women organizations that used no men as employees or volunteers, but most used men in multiple roles. Relations with RCCs are affected by mainstream officials' beliefs that RCCs are havens for "feminists," "man-haters," "lesbians," and/or "crazies" (Oerton 1996). Relations among processing organizations are shaped by *gender politics in the community* and victims' well-being is affected by how these politics play out. Research is needed on the influence of gender politics on interorganizational relations in the community (Martin 1997a).

Due to limitations of my data, I cannot say whether particular frames are more or less characteristic of RCCs, police departments, prosecution offices, or hospitals. I see patterns, however, that call for more research. For example, RCCs have formal policies about gender more often than other organizations, although the content of their policies varies. Police organizations are second most likely to have a gender policy, or to have considered one, again with varied content. Few prosecutors and hospitals have formal policies, although they perform processing work within a highly gendered division of labor, suggesting that talk and practice diverge and that research on gender at work must pay attention to both.

My impression is that processors talked about and used gender in the mid-1990s similar to the mid-1980s. Recent interviews failed to suggest that they are clearer about gender's significance or impact than they were a decade earlier. One change over the decade is the growth in VWAs in prosecutors' and law enforcement organizations. Some offices had them in the 1980s but nearly all do so today. These jobs are held mostly by women, and a division of labor where women do "emotional-relational" work and men do "technical-legal" work appears to have emerged. Research on this occupation and its place in processing contexts would be useful.

I cannot say whether some accounts, or associated practices, are better for victims. Organizations that frame gender as irrelevant because training and skill are more relevant may have a point. In declaring gender's irrelevance, they can hold everyone to a common and, one hopes, high standard of behavior in work with victims. Additionally, such a stance could challenge assumptions that women or men are "naturally" better at certain kinds of work. Rape processing work has many faces—from (a) comforting and sympathizing with victims, to (b) informing and advocating for victims, to (c) charging and prosecuting rapists, to (d) cooperating with staff in other organizations, to (e) educating the public about rape. Rape processing organizations are fertile sites for studying how these activities and gender are intertwined, culturally and in practice, in acknowledged and unacknowledged ways. A useful next step might systematically compare gender accounts, arrangements, and practices across organizations, jobs, and genders and assess their significance for victims and organizations alike.

Note

I thank Diana DiNitto, Diane Byington, Sharon Maxwell, Meena Harris, Christine Mowery, Michelle Fondell, and Annette Schwabe for help with collecting data and/or library research. Taro Wall, Colleen Paeplow, and Marlene Powell graciously let me use some of their data in my analysis. Judith Lorber, Jill Quadagno, Elaine Hall, Susan Chase, David Collinson, Margaret Collinson, Christine Williams, Dana Britton, and, especially, Mary Rogers offered valuable advice on earlier drafts. The Department of Sociology and Criminal Justice at the University of Delaware and the Department of Sociology at The Ohio State University supported me in 1993 and 1994 while I worked on the chapter. A version of the chapter was presented at the 1995 American Sociological Association meeting in Washington, D.C. The research was funded by the State of Florida Department of Health and Rehabilitative Services (Grant #LC118) and the Florida State University Faculty Research and Creativity Support program (COFRS).

References

Abarbanel, Gail, and Aileen Klein
 1988 *Sexual Assault on Campus: What Colleges Can Do*. Santa Monica, CA: Rape Treatment Center.
Acker, Joan
 1990 "Hierarchies, bodies, and jobs: A theory of gendered organizations." *Gender and Society* 4:139–158.
 1992 "Gendering organizational analysis." In *Gendering Organizational Analysis*, eds. A. J. Mills and P. Tancred, 248–260. Newbury Park, CA, and London: Sage.
Alexander, Cheryl
 1980 "The responsible victim: Nurses' perceptions of victims of rape." *Journal of Health and Social Behavior* 21:22–33.
Bassuk, Ellen, and Robert Assler
 1983 "Are there sex biases in rape counseling?" *American Journal of Psychiatry* 140:305–308.
Burawoy, Michael
 1991 *Ethnography Unbound: Power and Resistance in the Modern Metropolis*. Berkeley: University of California Press.
Byington, Diane, Patricia Y. Martin, Diana DiNitto, and Sharon Maxwell
 1991 "Organizational effectiveness and affiliation of rape crisis centers." *Administration in Social Work* 15:83–103.
Calas, Marta B., and Linda Smircich
 1996 "From 'the woman's' point of view: Feminist approaches to organization studies." In *Handbook of Organization Studies*, eds. Steward R. Clegg, Cynthia Hardy, and Walter R. Nord, 218–257. London and Newbury Park, CA: Sage.
Caringella-MacDonald, Susan
 1985 "The comparability in sexual and nonsexual assault case treatment: Did statute change meet the objective?" *Crime and Delinquency* 31:206–222.
Chancer, Lynn
 1987 "New Bedford, Massachusetts, March 6, 1983–March 22, 1984: The before and after of a gang rape."*Gender and Society* 1:239–260.
Chandler, Susan Meyers, and Martha Torney
 1981 "The decisions and processing of rape victims through the criminal justice system." *California Sociologist* 4:155–169.

Chase, Susan
    1995 *Ambiguous Empowerment: The Work Narratives of Women School Superintendents.* Amherst: University of Massachusetts Press.

Cluss, Patricia A., Janie Boughton, Ellen Frank, Barbara Duffy Steward, and Deborah West
    1983 "The rape victim: Psychological correlates of participation in the legal process." *Criminal Justice and Behavior* 10:342–357.

Collinson, David, and Jeff Hearn
    1996 "Breaking the silence: On men, masculinities, and managements." In *Men as Managers, Managers as Men: Critical Perspectives on Men, Masculinities, and Managements*, eds. David Collinson and Jeff Hearn, 1–24. Newbury Park, CA: Sage.

Conley, John M., and William M. O'Barr
    1990 *Rules versus Relationships: The Ethnography of Legal Discourse.* Chicago: University of Chicago Press.

Connell, Robert
    1987 *Gender and Power.* Stanford: Stanford University Press.
    1995 *Masculinities.* Berkeley: University of California Press.

Dietz, Sheila R., Karen Tiemann Blackwell, Paul C. Daley, and Brenda J. Bentley
    1982 "Measurement of empathy toward rape victims and rapists." *Journal of Personality and Social Psychology* 43:372–384.

DiNitto, Diana, Patricia Y. Martin, Diane B. Norton, and M. Sharon Maxwell
    1986 "Who should examine rape survivors?" *American Journal of Nursing* 86:538–540.

Ely, Robin
    1995 "The power in demography: Women's social construction of gender identity at work." *Academy of Management Journal* 38:589–634.

Feild, Hubert S.
    1978a "Juror background characteristics and attitudes towards rape." *Law and Human Behavior* 2:73–93.
    1978b "Attitudes toward rape: A comparative analysis of police, rapists, crisis counselors, and citizens." *Journal of Personality and Social Psychology* 36:156–179.

Feldman-Summers, Shirley, and Karen Lindner
    1976 "Perceptions of victims and defendants in criminal assault cases." *Criminal Justice and Behavior* 3:135–150.

Fenstermaker, Sarah, Candace West, and Don Zimmerman
    1991 "Gender inequality: New conceptual terrain." In *Gender, Family, and Economy: The Triple Overlap*, ed. Rae Lesser Blumherg, 298–307. Newbury Park, CA: Sage.

Fletcher, Joyce
    1997 "The disappearance of women's 'relational practice' at work." Unpublished manuscript. Northeastern University.

Fried, Amy
    1994 "'It's hard to change what we want to change.' Rape crisis centers as organizations." *Gender and Society* 8:562–583.

Frohmann, Lisa
    1991 "Discrediting victims' allegations of sexual assault: Prosecutorial accounts of case rejections." *Social Problems* 38:213–226.

Frohmann, Lisa, and Elizabeth Mertz
    1994 "Legal reform and social construction: Violence, gender, and the law." *Law and Social Inquiry* 19:829–851.

Gerson, Judith M., and Kathy Peiss
    1985 "Boundaries, negotiations, consciousness: Reconceptualizing gender relations." *Social Problems* 32:317–331.

Gilmartin-Zena, Patricia
    1983 "Attribution theory and rape victim responsibility." *Deviant Behavior* 4:357–374.

Glaser, Barney G., and Anselm Strauss
  1967 *The Discovery of Grounded Theory: Strategies for Qualitative Research*. Chicago: Aldine.
Goffman, Erving
  1974 *An Essay on the Organization of Experience: Frame Analysis*. Boston: Northeastern University Press.
Gordon, Margaret T., and Stephanie Riger
  1991 *The Female Fear: The Social Construction of Rape*. Champaign-Urbana: University of Illinois Press.
Gornick, Janet, Martha Burt, and Karen Pittman
  1985 "Structure and activities of rape crisis centers in the early 1980s." *Crime and Delinquency* 31:247–268.
Hageman, Mary J. C., and Charles Hastings
  1978 "Patterns in forcible rape in Wichita, Kansas: A case of the 'open system theory.'" *Journal of Police Science and Administration* 6:318–323.
Hall, Elaine
  1993a "Waitering/waitressing: Engendering the work of table services." *Gender and Society* 7:329–346.
  1993b "Smiling, deferring, and flirting: Doing gender by giving 'good service.'" *Work and Occupations* 20:452–471.
Holmes, Karen
  1980 "Justice for whom? Rape victims assess the legal-judicial system." *Free Inquiry in Creative Sociology* 8:126–130.
Holmstrom, Lynda Lyttle, and Anne Wolbert Burgess
  1978 *The Rape Victim: Institutional Responses*. New York: Wiley and Sons.
Holstein, James A.
  1987 "Producing gender effects on involuntary mental hospitalization." *Social Problems* 34:141–155.
Hyde, Cheryl
  1997 "Gender (in)visibility: Men, women, and rape crisis center work." Unpublished manuscript. School of Social Work, University of San Francisco.
Jensen, Gary, and Mayaltani Karpos
  1993 "Managing rape: Exploratory research on the behavior of rape statistics." *Criminology* 31:363–385.
Kerstetter, Wayne A.
  1990 "Gateway to justice: Police and prosecutorial response to sexual assault against women." *Journal of Criminal Law and Criminology* 81:267–313.
Konradi, Amanda
  1996 "Preparing to testify: Rape survivors negotiating the criminal justice process." *Gender and Society* 10:404–432.
  1997 "Too little, too late: Prosecutors' pre-court preparation of rape survivors." *Law and Social Inquiry* 22:1–54.
Koss, Mary
  1993 "Rape: Scope, impact, interventions, and public policy responses." *American Psychologist* 1062–1068.
LaFree, Gary D.
  1981 "Official reactions to social problems: Police decisions in sexual assault cases." *Social Problems* 28:582–594.
  1989 *Rape and Criminal Justice: The Social Construction of Sexual Assault*. Belmont, CA: Wadsworth.
LaFree, Gary D., Barbara Reskin, and Christy Visher
  1985 "Jurors' responses to rape victims' behavior and legal issues in sexual assault trials." *Social Problems* 32:389–407.

Leidner, Robin
    1991 "Serving hamburgers and selling insurance: Gender, work, and identity in interactive service jobs." *Gender and Society* 5:154–177.
    1993 *Fast Food, Fast Talk*. Berkeley: University of California Press.

Lorber, Judith
    1994 *Paradoxes of Gender*. New Haven, CT: Yale University Press.
    1996 "Beyond the binaries: Depolarizing the categories of sex, sexuality, and gender." *Sociological Inquiry* 66:143–159.

MacKinnon, Catherine
    1987 *Feminism Unmodified: Discourses on Life and Law*. Cambridge: Harvard University Press.

March, James G., and Johan P Olsen
    1989 *Rediscovering Institutions: The Organizational Basis of Politics*. New York: Free Press.

Martin, Patricia Yancey
    1996 "Gendering and evaluating dynamics: Men, masculinities, and managements." In *Men as Managers, Managers as Men*, eds. David Collinson and Jeff Hearn, 186–209. London: Sage.
    1997a "The politics of rape: Processing work in organization and community context." Unpublished manuscript. Department of Sociology, Florida State University.
    1997b "Men, masculinities, and work: From (some) women's standpoints." Unpublished manuscript. Department of Sociology, Florida State University, Tallahassee.

Martin, Patricia Yancey, and Diana DiNitto
    1987 "The rape exam: Beyond the hospital emergency room." *Women and Health* 12:5–28.

Martin, Patricia Yancey, Diana DiNitto, Diane Byington, and Sharon Maxwell
    1992 "Organizational and community transformation: A case study of a rape crisis center." *Administration in Social Work* 16:123–145.

Martin, Patricia Yancey, Diana DiNitto, Diane Harrison, and M. Sharon Maxwell
    1985 "Controversies surrounding the rape kit exam in the 1980s." *Crime and Delinquency* 31:223–246.

Martin, Patricia Yancey, and Marlene Powell
    1994 "Accounting for the 'second assault': Legal organizations and rape victims." *Law and Social Inquiry* 19:853–890.

Martin, Patricia Yancey, and Barry A. Turner
    1986 "Grounded theory and organizational research." *Journal of Applied Behavioral Science* 22:141–157.

Martin, Susan Ehrlich
    1980 *Breaking and Entering: Policewomen on Patrol*. Berkeley: University of California Press.
    1994 "Outsider within the station house: The impact of race and gender on black women police." *Social Problems* 41:383–400.

Matthews, Nancy
    1994 *Confronting Rape: The Feminist Anti-rape Movement and the State*. London and New York: Routledge.

McCahill, Thomas W., Linda C. Meyer, and Arthur M. Fischman
    1979 *The Aftermath of Rape*. Lexington, MA: D. C. Heath.

Nelligan, Peter J.
    1988 "The effects of the gender of jurors on sexual assault verdicts." *Sociology and Social Research* 72:249–251.

Oerton, Sarah
    1996 "Sexualizing the organization, lesbianizing the women: Gender, sexuality, and 'flat' organizations." *Gender, Work, and Organization* 3:26–37.

Paeplow, Colleen
    1995 "The unwritten rule: The gendered processing of rape victims." Unpublished master's thesis, Department of Sociology, Florida State University, Tallahassee Florida.

Pierce, Jennifer
　1995 *Gender Trials: Emotional Lives in Contemporary Law Firms.* Berkeley: University of California Press.
Powell, Marlene
　1994 "Organizational frameworks and rape victims: Explaining the second assault." Unpublished manuscript, Department of Sociology, Florida State University, Tallahassee.
Reskin, Barbara
　1988 "Bringing the men back in: Sex differentiation and devaluation of women's work." *Gender and Society* 2:58–81.
Rose, Karla, and Daniel G. Saunders
　1986 "Nurses' and physicians' attitudes about women abuse: The effects of gender and professional role." *Health Care for Women International* 7:427–438.
Rose, Vicki M.
　1977 "Rape as a social problem: A by-product of the feminist movement." *Social Problems* 25:75–89.
Sales, Esther, Martha Baum, and Barbara Shore
　1984 "Victim readjustment following assault." *Journal of Social Issues* 40:117–136.
Schmitt, Fredrika, and Patricia Yancey Martin
　1997 "'Unobtrusive mobilization' by an institutionalized rape crisis center: 'It comes from the victims.'" Unpublished manuscript. Department of Sociology, Colgate University and Florida State University.
Scott, Joan
　1997 "Comment on Hawkesworth's 'confounding gender.'" *Signs: Journal of Women in Culture and Society* 22:697–702.
Scott, Marvin B., and Stanford M. Lyman
　1968 "Accounts." *American Sociological Review* 33:46–62.
Sealy, A. Philip
　1981 "Another look at social psychological aspects of juror bias." *Law and Human Behavior* 5:187–200.
Smith, Dorothy
　1987 *The Everyday World as Problematic: A Feminist Sociology.* Boston: Northeastern University Press.
Snow, David A., E. Burke Rochford, Steven I. Worden, and Robert D. Benford
　1986 "Frame alignment processes, micromobilization, and movement participation." *American Sociological Review* 51:464–481.
Stacey, Judith, and Barrio Thorne
　1985 "The missing feminist revolution in sociology." *Social Problems* 32:301–316.
Stepnick, Andrea, and James D. Orcutt
　1996 "Conflicting testimony: Judges' and attorneys' perceptions of gender bias in legal settings." *Sex Roles* 34:567–579.
Thorne, Barrie
　1993 *Gender Play: Girls and Boys in School.* New Brunswick: Rutgers University Press.
Villemur, Nora K., and Janet Shibley Hyde
　1983 "Effects of defense attorney, sex of juror, and age and attractiveness of victim on mock juror decision making in a rape case." *Sex Roles* 9:879–889.
Visher, Christy Ann
　1982 "Jurors' decisions in criminal trials: Individual and group influences." Unpublished doctoral dissertation, Department of Sociology, Indiana University, Bloomington.
Wall, Tara
　1993 "Rape processing by police: How societal and job constraints have prevented significant progress in altering police treatment of rape victims." Unpublished paper. Department of Sociology, University of Delaware, Newark.

Walsh, Anthony
    1984 "Gender-based differences: A study of probation officers' attitudes about, and recommendations for, felony sexual assault cases." *Criminology* 22:371–387.

Warshaw, Carole
    1989 "Limitations of the medical model in the care of battered women." *Gender and Society* 3:506–517.

Weir, Julie A., and Lawrence S. Wrightsman
    1990 "The determinants of mock jurors' verdicts in a rape case." *Journal of Applied Social Psychology* 20:901–919.

West, Candace
    1993 "Power, inequality, and the accomplishment of gender: An ethnomethodological view." In *Theory on Gender/Feminism on Theory*, ed. Paula England, 151–174. New York: Aldine deGruyter.

West, Candace, and Don Zimmerman
    1987 "Doing gender." *Gender and Society* 1:125–151.

Williams, Christine
    1995 *Still a Man's World: Men Who Do Women's Work*. Berkeley: University of California Press.

Williams, Joyce E., and Karen Holmes
    1981 *The Second Assault*. Westport, CT: Greenwood Press.

Zimmer, Cathy
    1988 "Tokenism and women in the workplace." *Social Problems* 35:64–77.

CHAPTER 8

Policing Woman Battering

Kathleen J. Ferraro

The definition of woman battering as a social problem in the 1970s initiated debate about how to control and prevent violence between intimates. Feminists have argued that the control of intimate violence depends on fundamental restructuring of gender relations and the empowerment of women. Mental health professionals have promoted therapeutic intervention for offenders and victims of domestic violence. Most experts agreed that battered women need more legal protection (Hart et al., 1984; Schechter, 1981; Stanko, 1985; Taub, 1983; Walker, 1985; U.S. Commission on Civil Rights, 1978). The police are the "front line" of the official response to battering. Past research shows that police did not arrest men who battered their wives, even when victims were in serious danger and directly asked officers to arrest (Berk and Loseke, 1981; Black, 1980; Brown, 1984; Davis, 1983; Parnas, 1967). Activists in the battered women's movement saw failure to arrest as tacit support for battering, contributing to the inability of women to escape violent relationships and in the escalation of abuse to domestic homicides (Police Foundation, 1976).

Since 1976, civil suits, legislation, and policy initiatives have challenged police inaction (Ferraro, 1989). In 1984, the U.S. Attorney General's Task Force on Family Violence recommended that "family violence should be recognized and responded to as a criminal activity" and law enforcement agencies should "establish arrest as the preferred response in cases of family violence" (Hart et al., 1984:10, 17). Advocates for battered women insist that police should arrest men who use violence against their wives and lovers (Ferraro, 1989). This "get tough" stance is supported by legislative changes that expand police power to arrest.

By 1986, six states passed laws *requiring* arrests when probable cause exists and the offender is on the scene. Probable cause is established by the presence of witnesses, visible injuries, or property damage that indicate a crime has been committed. Forty-seven large city police departments had adopted a policy of mandatory or presumptive arrests for family fights by 1986 (Crime Control Institute, 1986). In 28 other states and the District of Columbia, police may arrest for a misdemeanor spousal assault on the basis of probable cause (Lerman and Livingston, 1983). Officers cannot arrest for misdemeanor assaults between unmarried people unless the assault is observed by the officer, an arrest warrant has been issued, or a citizen signs a complaint. The changes in the statutes are a response to the fact that most assaults against wives occur in private settings and fall in the misdemeanor category. Without expanded arrest powers, police cannot arrest batterers unless the assault is felonious or witnessed by an officer. Eighteen states require officers to provide information on legal options and services, and in eleven states police must transport victims to hospitals or shelters. Twenty-nine states also provide for temporary restraining orders, in which courts order abusers to stay away from their victims (Buzawa and Buzawa, 1985).

The push to arrest batterers enhances police power to arrest, but mandatory arrest policies limit the discretion of police officers to dismiss woman battering as a "civil matter." Policies that require arrest also limit discretion of complainants in that they ignore the wishes of the victim. Many battered women experience ambivalence about pressing criminal charges or fear retribution if they do so (Ferraro, 1988). Yet academic research purports to demonstrate the superior effect of arrest. Sherman and Berk (1984) found that violence was less frequently repeated when arrests were made than when battering incidents were mediated or resolved through physically separating the couple. Their findings have gained widespread recognition in police culture.

While laws and policies regarding woman battering have changed, the police response to battering relies heavily on extra-legal factors in police decision making (Bell, 1985; Berk and Loseke, 1981; Black, 1980; Davis, 1983; Smith and Klein, 1984; Waaland and Keeley, 1985). Observational studies of police work have consistently supported Black's (1971) early finding that the closer the relationship between victim and assailant, the less likely police are to arrest. Thus, even when departmental policies instruct police to arrest, officers continue to rely on victim and offender characteristics in deciding whether a law has been broken.

The response of police in the field to formal rules and policy about battering is embedded in a social context. As Manning (1971:162) notes, a police officer "moves in a dense web of social action and social meanings, burdened by a problematic, complex array of ever-changing laws." To better understand how these extra-legal considerations reduce protection of battered women, we must look at how police work is done. The purpose of this chapter is to examine the web of actions, meanings, and changing laws through which police construct their response to battering. I begin with a description of the emergence of new laws and policies about policing domestic disputes in Phoenix, Arizona. I then outline four dimensions of police response to battering and conclude by summarizing the difficulties of implementing the presumptive arrest policy for domestic violence.

Arizona's Domestic Violence Law and Policy

Most misdemeanors in Arizona result in a citation and release of the offender. In 1980, the state legislature passed a domestic violence bill that: (1) prohibits officers from citing and releasing domestic violence offenders; (2) expands police power to arrest on the basis of probable cause and requires officers to provide information to victims about procedures and available services; and (3) provides for orders of protection that can be obtained through any court, without filing for divorce. The orders provide grounds for arrest if a batterer goes near his victim. Two local judges drafted the bill. They were responding to two county coalitions on domestic violence that were putting pressure on police and courts to do more to protect battered women. In addition, police and lower court judges had complained that their hands were tied by constraints on arrests and by unwilling victims. The authors of the bill were fully aware of the practical limitations of controlling intimate violence through court orders.

The new law went into effect in July 1980. It had very little impact on law enforcement in Arizona. The police departments did not change their arrest policies. Officers had available one more tool for dealing with domestic violence, but did not view the law as an indication that arrests should increase. By 1983, the Maricopa County Task Force Against Domestic Violence, composed primarily of shelter and mental health workers, convinced a state representative that more legislation was required to force police to arrest batterers. A committee formed to draft a bill mandating arrest for domestic violence. The Phoenix Chief of Police, Ruben Ortega, discouraged the group from pressing for the law, promising that he would adopt a mandatory arrest policy and would encourage other chiefs to do so. Police administrators said that the superior court judge heading the family court had made several complaints to Chief Ortega about failure to arrest violent husbands. At the same time, Chief Ortega was appointed to the U.S. Attorney General's Task Force on Family Violence. After traveling around the country listening to testimony about the need to crack down on wife abuse, he returned to Arizona to help implement the recommendations of the Attorney General's Task Force. In May 1984, the Phoenix police department adopted a presumptive arrest policy. It stated that:

> Officers *should* arrest domestic violence violators even if the victim does not desire prosecution. When probable cause exists, an arrest should be made even if a misdemeanor offense did not occur in the officer's presence. (Ortega, 1984:1, emphasis added)

The policy was publicized in the local papers and on television. All police officers received training on the new policy from their sergeants and from members of the domestic violence coalition.

The Phoenix presumptive arrest policy represented only one minor change in an extensive city and county criminal justice system. Other cities in the county did not immediately alter their policies regarding domestic violence, although some since have done so. The city and county prosecutors did not increase prosecutions, and judges did not sentence batterers to jail. The Phoenix police were not supported in their policy shift by correlative changes in other parts of the system.

The police department figures indicate that the rate of arrest at the scene for family fights more than doubled in the second month after the policy was implemented. In 1983, the average monthly arrest rate was 33 percent. In June 1984, it was 67 percent, at which time a clarifying statement emphasized that probable cause was still a requirement for arrest. Officers told us that "ridiculous" arrests were annoying the judges who, in turn, complained to the chief. The chief reminded the officers that the policy did not override the constitutional requirement of reasonable grounds for arrest. This clarification created some confusion among officers. Some told us things were back to normal; others said they were only supposed to arrest in cases where there was serious injury and witnesses. This apparent hedging by the administration undermined the policy's initial forcefulness about the importance of arrest. In July 1984, the official arrest rate dropped to 52 percent, and by August it was 42 percent.

Methods

The Phoenix presumptive arrest policy offered an opportunity to observe the street level response to an administrative crackdown on battering. I asked Chief Ortega for permission to study the Phoenix police, and after some prodding from my college dean, he agreed to grant me entree. I interviewed Chief Ortega, four assistant chiefs, and the detective in charge of family fights to gather administrative perceptions of the policy before beginning ridealongs. Our team of six field observers entered the field in May 1984, three weeks after the presumptive arrest policy was adopted. Two male professors, one female professor, and three female graduate students conducted the observations. The observers rode with officers on ten-hour weekend evening shifts for 44 nights. Phoenix is divided into five districts with separate stations in each. The districts are divided into beats. Officers do not cross district boundaries but may enter unassigned beats within their districts. Three districts were observed. The two districts with the highest concentration of low income and transient individuals were selected because they represented the highest proportion of domestic violence calls. One district primarily composed of middle-income whites was also observed. Officers were told that we were studying domestic violence and were instructed to respond to as many family fight calls as possible. On many evenings we were assigned to "roving cars," which had no beat boundaries and could respond to family fight calls anywhere in the district.

During the 10-hour shifts, we accompanied officers on every aspect of their duties. During periods in which there was no activity, we questioned officers about the new presumptive arrest policy, their experiences with family fights, and their opinions about the appropriate response. Observers carried yellow pads for recording information and verbatim quotes. Information about police work in general was outlined, but officers' statements about and actions at family fights were recorded in as much detail as possible on the day following observations. At family fight calls we observed the police intervention and spoke with victims whenever possible. When arrests were made, we sometimes went to the station to observe the booking process. In one case, an observer was called to court as a witness to an assault.

In most cases, observers did not attempt to influence police behavior, even when they disagreed with decisions. Observers did not suggest arrest or nonarrest at the scene. When officers signalled completion of the call by saying good-bye to the victim and walking toward their car, I sometimes suggested—consistent with the new statute—that they provide victims with information about services and orders of protection. In several cases I also suggested officers request the services of the on-call mental health team, but only after they began to leave the scene.

We observed the police respond to 69 reports of family fights. Of these, 34 involved married or formerly married couples, 15 involved cohabitees or former lovers, 13 involved neighbors or other relatives, and 7 were false reports. Although twenty of the cases did not involve woman battering, they were dispatched and referred to as family fights by the officers.

Police Response under the New Policy

The intent of mandatory and presumptive arrest policies is to treat domestic violence "as a crime." Thus, officers were supposed to arrest batterers regardless of other characteristics of the situation. That was not what we observed. Out of 69 family fight calls, 49 involved spouses, cohabitants, estranged lovers, or current lovers and fit the definition of battering. Officers made no arrests in 40 of these cases (82%); arrests were made in only 9 (18%) of the battering incidents, in spite of the presumptive arrest policy. In 25 (51%) cases, police used conciliation, which means talking to the people and emphasizing the importance of the relationship over the dispute. Very few cases involved a therapeutic style of social control, and none could be classified as compensatory, in which the officer would attempt to gain redress for the violence inflicted on the victim.

These results were similar to those reported by Black (1980:156) in cases involving married and common law couples: 70 percent conciliatory, 26 percent penal, 2 percent therapeutic, and 2 percent preventative. Black (1980:158) found that for those cases where penal action was taken, 26 percent were arrests. This is quite striking in that Black's observations were conducted prior to the emergence of the battered women's movement and statutory and policy changes in policing battering. The consistency over time attests to the complexity of the police response to battering and the difficulty of altering it.

Department policy is only one factor influencing police decision making at family fights. As Berk and Loseke (1981:342) note, police responses are "rife with situationally determined contingencies." In their research, using police reports, presence of both disputants on the scene, women's willingness to sign complaints, victims' allegations of violence, and male alcohol consumption were all positively correlated with the decision to arrest (Berk and Loseke, 1981:341–42). Our observations suggest that these factors continue to play a major role in decision making even when arrest is the preferred policy.

Officers evaluate each call to decide whether it is really a "family fight." A set of behaviors in one context might lead one officer to arrest, while similar behaviors in another context might lead another officer to take no action. Most of the time officers rejected arrest as an option after weighing certain considerations. However, when they did arrest, they often invoked some of the same considerations. The following categories summarize the considerations impinging on the decision-making process at family fights: legal, ideological, practical, and political.

LEGAL

By legal considerations I mean to emphasize how police think about and use their understandings of the laws and statutes they are officially charged with enforcing. The most obvious instances of these laws being "applied" might be the 9 arrests we observed.

There were two arrests where the police classified as misdemeanor spousal assaults that seemed consistent with the intent of the new policy. In the first case, the couple was married the day before the assault. A neighbor called the police after she saw the husband assault his wife. All three people were sitting quietly at the apartment when we arrived. The couple was Hispanic and lived in a low-income neighborhood. The woman had a deep cut on her forehead and said she wanted to press charges. Police called paramedics to treat the cut, took photographs for evidence of injury, and took the man to jail. With all legal and policy criteria met and a compliant offender, officers did not hesitate to make an arrest.

A second case where the wife was the only victim involved an argument in the presence of a female friend who called the police when the husband threatened his wife with a knife. When police arrived, all three people denied any conflict. Police searched the husband and found a knife. The presence of a weapon satisfied the legal criterion of assault even though the victim and witness said no assault of threat occurred. The officer perceived danger and arrested the man.

In two cases, men were violent in the presence of officers and both were arrested. In the first case, a 65-year-old man was drunk and wrestling with his son. Two male police officers grabbed the man, cuffed him, and loaded him into a back-up police car. In the second case, a man spit on his girlfriend and punched a male neighbor in the mouth. When the officer arrived, the man greeted him at the front door with a raised ball bat. The officer drew his gun, and the man slammed the door in his face. Police subsequently chased and captured the offender, threw him to the floor, tightly cuffed his hands and feet, and carried him to the car.

This case was the only instance where police asked the victim to make a "citizen's arrest." The charges against him were simple assault against a male bystander and spitting at his girlfriend. The officer perceived him as a dangerous character and one who showed a lack of respect for the law. The officer told the observer the assault charge might not hold because the bystander was trespassing; the spitting charge was obviously weak. He therefore instructed the girlfriend to place her foot on the "hog-tied" man's back and say, "I place you under citizen's arrest."

Most of the time, however, the police did not arrest anyone when called to the site of reported domestic violence. One legal ground for this decision is that, at the time of the research, the domestic violence statute did not extend to cohabitants, although the law now has been changed to include them. Of the 15 cases observed involving cohabitants, lovers or ex-lovers, three resulted in arrests. Arrests involving violence in non-married couples did not fall within the purview of the new policy. Presumptive arrest relied on enhanced power to arrest in misdemeanor domestic violence cases. When couples were not married, officers did not consider arrest, even if there were legal grounds for it. For example, it is always possible to arrest if a citizen signs a complaint, but that option was used only once in 69 cases. In that case, the offender was violent to a male neighbor, threatened a police officer, and attempted to escape. In this and the other two cases where an unmarried person was arrested, the high level of danger was more significant to officers than the fact that the new policy did not formally apply. In most cases observed, however, officers did not consider arresting unmarried cohabitees.

In one case, for example, a live-in boyfriend broke down the front door when his girlfriend refused to let him in. He was very drunk, and she did not want to see him, as they were both recovering alcoholics. He tore up their apartment, breaking and destroying her personal belongings. He also hit her in the face, and she had a small cut where her glasses bridged her nose. Three officers arrived at the scene, and the two patrolmen asked their sergeant what to "make" the call. He told them no crime had been committed, except against the landlady for destruction of the apartment door.

Several crimes could have been constructed from these facts, including assault, criminal damage, endangerment, and threatening or intimidating. The officers might have encouraged the woman to sign a citizen's complaint. Either a stranger or a husband committing identical acts would have been defined differently, but the sergeant focused on the cohabitant status of the relationship and decided that no crime had been committed.

Another legal consideration was seen when officers searched for probable cause for arrest. The detective in charge of family fights told us that the presence of visible injuries, property damage, weapons, or witnesses establishes probable cause. The statute permitting misdemeanor arrests based on probable cause authorizes officers to determine whether the situation permits a reasonable conclusion that a crime has been committed. But this determination is, of course, discretionary. For most officers, severe visible injuries or the use of weapons constituted probable cause, but minor injury, property damage, and the presence of child witnesses did not. Officers' interpretations of probable cause undermined the policy because they used a level of evidence high enough for felony arrests. Administrative directives that emphasized the importance of probable cause led many officers to conclude that they had wide discretion in this area.

After receiving the directive about probable cause, one officer said that "things are back to normal." He made no arrests in the three family fights we responded to in one night of observations. In one case, for example, a woman fled her home after her husband beat and choked her. She had taken one child with her, but the other remained at her mother's home where her husband had gone and subsequently assaulted her brother. The husband was drunk and violent, and the woman was afraid he would either hurt the baby or take it away where she could not find them. She had bruises on her neck from the choking, and her mother had witnessed the assault on the brother. They lived in a housing project, and she had to walk three blocks to use a phone to call the police. It was 2:00 A.M. when we arrived on the scene. The officer told her there was nothing he could do. He said the baby was not in danger and that everything was okay. He told her to call if anything else happened. The victim was frightened and believed her husband was "crazy" and capable of serious violence. The officer did not agree and offered her no information or advice except to "call back."

This incident could have met the standards of probable cause. The victim was anxious to press charges, had visible signs of injury, and there were witnesses to the assault on her brother. The man was a few blocks away at his mother-in-law's home, but the officer made no attempt to contact him. He did not suggest that the victim sign a complaint. Legally, his decision not to arrest could be justified by the absence of probable cause as no serious injury or weapons were present. His interpretation of the new policy required these elements for an arrest. But the officer's actions in this case are not what would be expected based on the "get tough" rhetoric or the presumptive arrest policy.

The domestic violence statute specifies the destruction of property, or criminal damage, as a crime. In several cases, women were not physically attacked, but their property was destroyed. These cases included tire slashing, smashed windshields, a waterbed punctured with an ice pick, doors kicked in, and the two cases described above. In all but one case, officers told victims that nothing could be done. The officers said that Arizona is a community property state. Therefore, everything belongs to both people, and one cannot be charged for destroying one's own property. Yet the legislature and courts have recognized that community property means half, not total, ownership. When jointly held property is destroyed, the half not owned is destroyed as well as the half that is. The one case of arrest for criminal damage indicates that it was a legitimate charge if officers wanted to use it.

Legal criteria are not the most salient in police decision making. Presumptive arrest implies that legal standards are the most important consideration for family fights, but in the cases we observed the legal interpretation of events was strongly influenced by other considerations.

IDEOLOGICAL

Ideological considerations are those background beliefs and ideas about battered women and family fights that police officers use to evaluate specific incidents. They include general ideas police have about the people they encounter, specific ideas about family fights, and images of danger. These ideas emerge through police practice, although officers may be predisposed to interpret other people as adversaries. As Manning (1971:156) emphasizes, the occupational culture of police sets the standards for a "good policeman" and prompts the assumptions police officers use in shaping their work.

Police tend to dichotomize the community into normal and deviant citizens (Ferraro, 1989). Normal citizens abide by society's rules through maintaining employment, sobriety, a family, and a modestly clean home. They are heterosexual, white, and speak English. Deviants serve as the "other" for police officers; they are publicly intoxicated or high, homeless, involved in crime, live in run-down houses, have atypical family structures, and/or speak foreign languages. Habitual problems are endemic to their lifestyle.

According to this view, a normal citizen who violates a law responds to police intervention with shame and anxiety. A "normal" wife beater is perceived as situationally deviant, his behavior the product of particular strain or a response to a threatened divorce. Such a man, officers believe, may be deterred by arrest because both violence and arrest are extraordinary and undesirable events for such people. On the other hand, arrest and violence are viewed as routine events for deviant men. Officers on patrol often referred to Mexicans, Indians, gay men, and people in the housing projects as "low lifes," "scum," or "these kind of people." Officers believed arrests were a waste of time and meaningless for these people because violence is a way of life for them. Empirically, middle income, professional men do engage in repetitive wife beating (Weller, 1988). However, representative surveys find higher rates of wife beating among low-income and unemployed men (Gelles and Straus, 1988; Straus et al.,

1980). Police ideology about the types of situations in which violence occurs may be grounded in experience.

In one case, a Hispanic woman who spoke little English approached us at 3:00 A.M. for help as we responded to another call. She complained, through a 14-year-old neighbor, that her husband was drunk, violent, and threatening to take her children away. We found the man intoxicated, sitting among a pile of beer cans. Three small boys sat nearby. The officers (one man and one woman) resolved the problem by walking the woman and children to an apartment a few doors away. They told the woman to call the police if there was any more trouble although she had no telephone or money. The residents were not friends of the woman and were not happy to have her. We left the woman sitting on the porch and walked past the husband who waved good-by to us. The low level of protection provided by this arrangement and the imposition on neighbors did not concern the officers. The male officer expressed frustration at dealing with Spanish speakers and people in the projects.

Police also held stereotypes about battered women. One repeatedly expressed idea was that battered women were likely to drop any charges that might be filed. They often asked for arrest at night when they were angry and then refused to testify or lied about the abuse when later contacted by detectives or prosecutors. The presumptive arrest policy is supposed to take the burden of prosecution off the victim. Still, it is difficult to prosecute an assault when the victim denies it occurred. One officer argued that the policy would lead to more homicides because once women knew arrests would be made they would stop calling the police for help. He said,

> A lot of these people, especially in this district, just want you to do something to stop it for the night. They want us to get somebody to leave. They could do that for themselves, but they want us to do it. If they can't call us, because we'll arrest, then they don't have anybody to help them, and instead of somebody leaving for the night, somebody's going to get killed.

Several officers thought there were fewer reports of family fights because the word had gone out about arrests. However, department figures indicated an increase in calls. Police statistics showed an average of 83 reports a month in 1983. In the first month of the policy, 327 family violence reports were received. The number steadily dropped over the first five months of the policy, but in September there were still 157 calls.

The police believe battered women choose to remain in abusive situations. Most officers believed adult women could leave violent situations if they wanted to. If they stayed with a violent man, it was not the responsibility of police to try to control the violence. An officer expressed this belief in a case involving a young, black woman staying in a run-down motel in a low-income section of town. Her boyfriend hit her, took all her clothes, and left in their car. They had recently moved to town, and she had nowhere to go and no money or clothes. Officers arranged for her to spend the night with others in the motel. On leaving, one officer commented, "This is your typical family fight. They don't really want to do anything." He did not empathize with the woman's lack of alternatives, but rather typified her as willfully choosing an abusive situation.

Officers expressed a range of attitudes toward battered women. At the sympathetic end of the continuum, a female officer, herself a formerly battered woman, strongly supported the new policy. She said,

> What is a woman really supposed to do if she has no job skills and a couple of kids, and he's been tellin' her he'll kill her if she leaves? What is she gonna do? A lot of people can't understand why she stays, but I can really empathize with that. Sure there are a few dingbats that are just so stupid they don't know enough to leave. But I think most women who get beat up really don't have anyplace else to go and they're afraid.

This woman was the only officer who expressed sympathy with the battered woman's situation. Three other female officers mentioned appreciation for the new policy, but the other female officers (15) were either neutral or antagonistic toward the policy. Several female officers openly expressed disdain for family fight calls, citing the danger involved and unwillingness of victims to follow through. One female officer said she believed women who dropped charges should be held in contempt of court.

Male officers also expressed a range of attitudes about woman battering and the policy, but the negative evaluations were more extreme. At the critical end of the continuum, one male officer expressed the belief that a man's home is his castle where he should be allowed to do what he wants. He believed most wife beating was provoked by the woman. He had recently punched a whole in his own living room wall during an argument with his wife. From his perspective, arresting men for destroying their own property was an outrageous infringement on liberty. For officers who view arrests as a waste of time or an illegitimate infringement on private life, presumptive arrest is an illogical policy.

Officers also held implicit images of dangerous situations. For two nights we drove down alleys and kept watch for a man wearing women's clothing who was suspected of rape. Officers believed he was dangerous. Reports of "drive-by" shootings by gangs and gang conflicts were also perceived as dangerous and worth investigating. Certain bars and neighborhoods were described as extremely dangerous, and one bar was singled out for intervention "before somebody gets killed."

Battered women, on the other hand, were usually not perceived as being in dangerous situations. Women cried and shook with fear as they told officers their husbands or lovers were going to hurt them. But repeatedly officers responded with a "call if anything happens," rather than giving them the immediate protection they sought. Everything appeared to officers to be "under control" because they could see no visible signs of danger. To women who were battered and were experienced with their assailants' patterns of violence, the danger was real and frightening, and easy to see. The divergent perceptions of danger held by battered women and police resulted in a minimal effort to intervene in cases which appeared to officers as stable.

PRACTICAL

The statute and policy did not specify the degree of inconvenience and probing required of officers at family fights. So if both husband and wife denied the existence of a fight, or if both accused the other of violence, it was left to the officer's discretion whether intervention of any kind was appropriate.

The policy did not specifically state that offenders had to be on the scene for arrests to be made. Neither did it encourage officers to search for men who had fled. In order for us to observe an arrest, the offender had to have been on or near the scene. In 28 cases (40%) the man was not on the scene at the time of police arrival. Either he had left, or the woman had called from a location other than that of the dispute. In these cases, the officers were supposed to write detective's reports that would allow a detective to follow up the next day. It was not always apparent whether reports were written because several police units were on the scene. Officers with whom we were not riding did not commonly share information about the calls. In cases where our assigned officer was the primary respondent to the call, it was possible to determine whether detective's reports were written. In most cases, they were not.

Although failure to file a report is not a technical violation of the presumptive arrest policy, it does undermine the intent to "get tough." In practice, if the batterer is not on the scene, no punitive action will be taken, even if the woman has left her home to seek safety while her abuser remains at home. In one case a woman called police from her friend's home after her drunken husband smashed her car windshield with a ball and chain and threatened to kill her and her children. She asked the officers to go to her home and arrest him. The officers said they could not do that without a warrant or unless she accompanied them because her home was in another district. The officer told me the woman would not accompany them, but I heard her tell him that she would. They left her at her friend's home, telling her to call if he came around. Whether the policy only applied to cases where the offender was on the scene was irrelevant for the officers. In their view, there was no danger of the violence continuing that night and so the policy was not invoked. The officer said it was a typical family fight and that, although the woman was angry that night, she would cool down the next day and forget about charges. As Davis (1983:275) notes, the police at family fights are concerned with achieving a situational "semblance of order" rather than finding a solution to the larger relational problem.

Arizona domestic violence statute 13-3601 D includes the requirement for officers to inform victims of the procedures and resources available for the protection of victims, namely orders of protection, emergency telephone numbers of the police, and telephone numbers of emergency services in the area. Officers were supplied with domestic violence cards that listed magistrates, shelters, and hotlines along with their phone numbers. In only two of the 69 cases we observed did officers provide this information to victims without being prompted by the observers. Officers did not see providing the victim with information as relevant to restoring order in the situation and so they seldom did it (see Davis, 1983).

Police also had access to a special mental health team on weekend nights. The Family Stress Team was made up of mental health professionals who were on call to respond to mental health problems. Officers stated that the team did good work and was a good resource, but they called them only four times in the 69 cases we observed. When arrests were made, they did not see a need for mental health assistance. As long as the immediate problem was resolved, and order was restored, officers did not consider relevant those options for more long-term solutions, such as calling the stress team or providing the victim with community service information.

In four cases (6%) the problem was defined as "resolved prior to arrival." In these cases either no one answered the door, or someone appeared at the door and told police everything was under control. Officers did not insist on entering the home when the resident requested them to leave. In these situations, there was no complainant, no apparent violence, and thus no problem for the police to handle. In domestic violence situations this response is disturbing, as it is unknown whether the victim is being forced to keep quiet or ask the police to leave.

Officers also spoke about cases they called "mutual combat," where there was aggressive interaction rather than explicit violence. A man physically assaulting a woman who was screaming and yelling at him could be construed by officers as mutual combat, particularly in cases where the woman was intoxicated. Officers said they would not arrest in these cases because it was not possible to determine who was at fault. Directives from the Assistant Chief of the Patrol Division discouraged arrest when both parties were violent at a misdemeanor level. In such cases, it was difficult to get testimony from either party, as they could not talk without incriminating themselves.

Arresting both spouses could also create practical problems of placing children. The police could use local social services to foster children temporarily. This is difficult and time consuming and may be as frightening to children as their father's violence. While some officers explicitly stated that the presence of children would not inhibit them from making an arrest, others recounted instances in which arrests had not been made because they would have had to foster children out.

Although the presumptive arrest policy was intended to remove the decision to arrest from the victim, establishing probable cause is more difficult if a woman refuses to testify to her abuse. Some battered women do not press charges because they love their husbands. But there may be other reasons why arrest would not be in a woman's best interests. In follow-up interviews conducted during a second stage of this research, one victim said she did not want her husband arrested because he had recently obtained a job after six months of unemployment. He might lose his job if he missed a day of work or if his employer learned he had been arrested. Other women worried about immigration authorities and did not want to get too close to the law. Why a woman does not want to press charges may not be clear to the responding officer. But if she unequivocally states that she does not want to press charges, officers may recognize her competence and knowledge of what is best for her. Although the intent of presumptive arrest policies is to shift the responsibility for arrest from the woman to the police, some officers continued to consider the practical consequences of arrest for the victim and her children.

Finally, time is a practical consideration. Since it takes at least an hour to process an arrest, officers are less likely to arrest when they are about to finish their shifts. Moreover, officers view time as a resource to be saved for "important" cases. An arrest makes officers unavailable for other activities during the booking procedure. During this time, officers are off the street, unable to respond to other calls. One officer lamented that once she had been unable to respond to an armed robbery call because she was transporting a woman to a shelter. She implied that the armed robbery was more important and exciting. This was cited by other officers in explaining why they would not transport victims to a safe place. Although time is never sufficient to account for arrest/nonarrest decisions, it combines and probably interacts with legal, ideological, and other practical considerations in shaping an officer's response to a given incident.

INTERNAL AND EXTERNAL POLITICS

In the police department, there is a tension between administrative policy makers and street level actors. Administrators are attuned to professional and community level politics, while patrol officers are attuned to the politics of the street. The presumptive arrest policy was interpreted by officers through their perceptions of administrative motives.

Traditionally, domestic violence is a low status offense. The presumptive arrest policy tried to elevate its importance. But without clear-cut rewards or incentives, officers doubted the political significance of the policy. Some officers believed the policy was just for show, and some said it came from pressure from judges. But most did not know why they were suddenly urged to alter their responses in these cases. Family fights remain low status, undesirable calls for most officers.

One final consideration is the political organization of the housing projects. The projects have committees that officers perceive as "really powerful" and having "a direct line to the chief's office." Officers believe that project residents despise them and that the committees are eager to complain about police misconduct. Graffiti in these neighborhoods suggest that the contempt is not entirely imaginary. Two officers explained that they had been transferred from the projects because of fabricated complaints brought to the chief by the project committee. The belief that the committees had influence with the chief and that people are more than willing to complain about police misconduct was not conducive to a presumptive arrest policy. Officers were hesitant to arrest without sufficient evidence or victim cooperation when they feared retribution from the committees.

Legal, ideological, practical, and political considerations do not exhaust the factors that influenced police decision making at family fights. Sometimes legal considerations voiced in one context were contradicted by actions in another. The process of police responses to domestic violence situations is not entirely rational or accessible to observers. Still, seeing how police took these factors into account in their work helps us to understand how the new law and policy were in fact enacted.

Discussion

The officers in this study did not implement the presumptive arrest policy in a uniform way. The observational data show that discretion persists in spite of well publicized policy changes and training on domestic violence. In part, lack of adherence to the policy can be traced to the confusion produced by policy clarifications after the fact, which was evidence that the chief was "backing off." Publicly, Chief Ortega maintains a "get tough" stance on arresting batterers. Training on the policy did not resolve questions about its political meaning within the department. Officers were free to guess how much importance they should attach to a policy that drastically altered their traditional approach to domestic violence. No explicit incentives were offered for compliance, and no penalties were attached to evasion of the new policy. These were situational problems that may be remedied by a more vigorous, explicit administrative plan to increase arrests. The level of tension and conflict between administrators and patrol officers varies by locale. A department with strong leadership and morale may have more success at implementing a presumptive arrest policy.

On the other hand, these data indicate that each case is evaluated in terms of its relationship to a web of considerations, including legal, ideological, practical, and political issues. Officers can be encouraged to interpret situations in a given manner, but the interpretive process remains tied to these influences. For example, officers may be told to arrest regardless of the victim's wishes, yet still evaluate her recalcitrance in light of the perceived power of the housing project committees or the time taken away from other work. Policy directives did alter police behavior in this study, as evidenced by the two arrests for misdemeanor wife assaults. They did not, however, eliminate the impact of the web of considerations on police decision making.

Information on the factors that discouraged arrests is useful in designing programs to enhance arrests. The legal and political considerations described reflect officers' concerns with what will happen if arrests are made. If they perceive that high standards of evidence are required for prosecution and observe low rates of prosecution, they are likely to see most arrests as a waste of time. Mandatory and presumptive arrest policies implemented in the absence of change in other parts of the legal system will probably have little lasting impact on how police respond to domestic violence. If the official rhetoric about "treating domestic violence as a crime" embodied in the task force recommendations is genuine, changes must occur at the prosecutorial, judicial, and correctional levels in tandem with changes in law enforcement practices.

Concerns about the power of housing project committees suggest that police officers recognize the impact of citizen complaints on their work lives. The recent surge in law suits against police departments may have some impact on street level decision making (Woods, 1986). At the local level, the relationship between police officials and battered women's advocacy groups could have a positive impact on police response. If officers view policies as rhetoric to quiet the "women's libbers," they are not likely to be concerned about the consequences of their street level decisions. However, if they believe that failure to provide adequate protection will result in complaints that include their name and badge number and may lead to disciplinary action, they may be more thorough in their response to victims' complaints. Education and organizing by battered women's advocates can likely influence police perceptions of the power of battered women.

Note

Earlier versions of this chapter were presented at the annual meetings of the American Sociological Association, Washington, DC, 1985 and the American Society of Criminology, San Diego, California, 1985. This research was supported in part by grants from the Arizona State Women's Studies Summer Grant program and the Arizona State University Research Fund. David Aitheide and John M. Johnson were co-researchers on this project and have made significant contributions to this chapter. Kim

Bauman, Nancy Jurik, Gerri Klein, and Kathy Seeley helped in completing this research. I appreciate the cooperation of Chief Ruben Ortega and all the officers who generously allowed us to observe their work. Thanks also to Malcolm Spector and the anonymous *Social Problems* reviewers for their comments.

References

Bell, Daniel J.
 1985 "A multiyear study of Ohio urban, suburban, and rural police dispositions of domestic disputes." *Victimology* 10:301–10.
Berk, Sarah F., and Donileen R. Loseke
 1981 "'Handling' family violence: Situational determinants of police arrest in domestic disturbances." *Law and Society Review* 15:317–46.
Black, Donald
 1971 "The social organization of arrest." *Stanford Law Review* 23:1087–1111.
 1980 *The Manners and Customs of the Police*. New York: Academic Press.
Brown, Stephen
 1984 "Police responses to wife beating: Neglect of a crime of violence." *Journal of Criminal Justice* 12:277–88.
Buzawa, Eva, and Carl C. Buzawa
 1985 "Legislative trends in the criminal justice response to domestic violence." Pp. 124–47 in Alan J. Lincoln and Murray A. Straus (eds.), *Crime and the Family*. Springfield, IL: Charles C. Thomas.
Crime Control Institute
 1986 "Police domestic violence policy change." *Response* 9:16.
Davis, Philip W.
 1983 "Restoring the semblance of order: Police strategies in the domestic disturbance." *Symbolic Interaction* 6:216.74.
Ferraro, Kathleen J.
 1988 "Prosecution of felony assaults against women." Paper given at the annual meeting of the American Society of Criminology, Chicago, IL.
 1989 "The legal response to battering in the United States." Pp. 155–84 in Jalna Hanmer, Jill Radford, and Elizabeth Stanko (eds.), *Women, Policing, and Male Violence*. London: Tavistock.
Gelles, Richard J., and Murray A. Straus
 1988 *Intimate Violence*. New York: Simon and Schuster.
Hart, William L., John Ashcroft, Ann Burgess, Newman Flanagan, Ursula Meese, Catherine Milton, Clyde Narramore, Ruben Ortega, and Frances Seward
 1984 *Attorney General's Task Force on Family Violence*. Washington, DC: U.S. Department of Justice.
Lerman, Lisa G., and Franci Livingston
 1983 "State legislation on domestic violence." *Response* 6:1–28.
Manning, Peter K.
 1971 "The police: Mandate, strategies, and appearances." Pp. 149–93 in Jack Douglas (ed.), *Crime and Justice in American Society*. Indianapolis, IN: Bobbs-Merrill.
Ortega, Ruben B.
 1984 *Operations Digest* No. 84/85:1–2.
Parnas, Raymond
 1967 "The police response to the domestic disturbance." *Wisconsin Law Review* 2:914–60.
Police Foundation
 1976 *Domestic Violence and the Police: Studies in Detroit and Kansas City*. Washington, DC: The Police Foundation.

Schechter, Susan
   1981 *Women and Male Violence: The Visions and Struggles of the Battered Women's Movement.* Boston, MA: South End.
Sherman, Lawrence W., and Richard A. Berk
   1984 "The specific deterrent effects of arrest for domestic assault." *American Sociological Review* 49:261–72.
Smith, Douglas A., and Jody R. Klein
   1984 "Police control of interpersonal disputes." *Social Problems* 31:466–81.
Stanko, Elizabeth A.
   1985 *Intimate Intrusions: Women's Experience of Male Violence.* London: Routledge and Kegan Paul.
Straus, Murray, Suzanne K. Steinmetz, and Richard J. Gelles
   1980 *Behind Closed Doors.* Garden City, NY: Anchor.
Taub, Nadine
   1983 "Adult domestic violence: The law's response." *Victimology* 8:152–171.
U.S. Commission on Civil Rights
   1978 *Battered Women: Issues of Public Policy.* Washington, DC: U.S. Government Printing Office.
Waaland, Pam, and Stuart Keeley
   1985 "Police decision making in wife abuse: The impact of legal and extralegal factors." *Law and Human Behavior* 9:355–66.
Walker, Lenore E.
   1985 "Psychological impact of the criminalization of domestic violence on victims." *Victimology* 10:281–300.
Weller, Sheila
   1988 "Middle-class murder." *Ms.* May:56–61.
Woods, Laurie
   1986 *Resource List: Battered Women: Litigation.* New York: National Center on Women and Family Law.

CHAPTER 9

Emergency Department Responses to Battered Women
RESISTANCE TO MEDICALIZATION

Demie Kurz

Sociologists concerned with the definition and construction of "social problems" and "deviant behaviors" argue that in recent decades a range of problems previously defined in moral or criminal terms have been redefined as medical problems. Some now use the term "medicalization" to describe how the medical profession can label and gain jurisdiction over many areas of life which involve the workings of the body or mind such as drug addiction, alcohol, and aging; birth control, pregnancy, and child birth; and child abuse (Conrad and Schneider, 1980a; Freidson, 1973; Zola, 1972, 1975). Those studying medicalization are particularly concerned with how the medicalization process can depoliticize "social" problems by redefining them as problems of individual pathology (Conrad, 1975; Kittrie, 1971).

This study examines a new area which reformers in the health care system are attempting to medicalize: the area of "battering," or the injury of women by husbands and boyfriends. Attempts to medicalize battering have their origins in a social movement on behalf of "battered women" which began in the early 1970s (Schecter, 1982; Tierney, 1982). The battered women's movement brought to public attention the fact that an estimated 1.5 million wives are injured each year by husbands (Strauss et al., 1980), and 1.5 million single, separated, and divorced women are injured by male intimates (Rosenberg et al., 1985). Supporters from within mental health, social service, and governmental organizations have joined advocates for battered women in bringing about the creation of a nationwide network of shelters and shelter services; legislation in most states increasing police powers and criminal penalties against abusers; government funding for programs and agencies for battered women; and increased data collection on the issues by public and private research organizations (Attorney General's Task Force, 1984; Dobash and Dobash, 1979; Schecter, 1982; Tierney, 1982). The battered women's movement and supporters in the health care system are now calling for the health care system to aid in the identification of battered women and their referral to appropriate sources of help.

From within the health care system, the Surgeon General of the United States (Koop, 1982, 1984), the American College of Physicians (1986), selected state and local health officials (New Jersey Department of Community Affairs, 1985), and a national network of nurses are among those calling for the health care system to play a role in addressing this problem. They argue that health care personnel should "diagnose" the battering "syndrome," consisting of specific injury and behavior patterns, and intervene on behalf of battered women. Some reformers have published articles in medical journals urging health care personnel to identify battering, and describing symptoms and signs of battering (Campbell and Humphreys, 1984; Finley, 1981; Goldberg and Carey, 1982; Greany, 1984; Klingbeil, 1986; Loraine, 1981; Petro et al., 1978). Others are holding conferences (Rich and Burgess, 1986) and developing protocols for use by health care personnel to identify battering (Helton, 1986). Reformers have succeeded in putting into place approximately 100 initiatives at the state and local levels to train hospital staff and other health care personnel about battering.[1]

Reformers argue that intervention in the health care system can result in the timely referral of battered women to sources of help, thus preventing further injury, and in the documentation of injuries on medical records for use by individual women and for the purpose of collecting statistics. They note that the potential benefit of reform is great in that large numbers of battered women come to the health care system. A survey of women in Texas estmated that 360,000 women had at some point in their lives required medical treatment because of abuse (Teske and Parker, 1983). Another study of battered women found that 80 percent of the women went to their physician for a battering injury (Dobash and Dobash, 1979). Stark et al. (1979) found that 19 percent of women trauma patients who came to the hospital emergency departments they studied were either confirmed as or very likely to have been battered.

The efforts of these groups are similar to those of earlier claims-makers who "discovered" specific injury patterns which they claimed were caused by child abuse (Pfohl 1977). Child abuse reformers succeeded in having the identification of child abuse accepted as a legitimate medical concern and in passing legislation requiring the mandatory reporting of child abuse by physicians. The efforts to promote reporting on battering are more recent and less extensive than in the case of child abuse. Unlike child abuse, there are no medical specialties which lay claim to the problem of battering, nor is it expected that there will be legislation mandating that physicians report each individual case of battering. However, a few states have mandated the reporting of statistics on battering, and there is debate on other ways the health care system can help to stop battering (Rich and Burgess, 1986; Koop, 1984).

Since many current efforts are of a voluntary nature and since most future efforts will also require the cooperation of clinicians, it is essential to understand how clinicians will respond to battering. This chapter reports on a participant observation study of responses of emergency department (ED) staff to battered women in four hospitals. In three of the hospitals there were one-time efforts to educate staff about battering and to encourage them to identify it. In the fourth hospital, due to the efforts of a reformer who believed in intervention with battered women in EDs, there were ongoing intervention efforts with staff to encourage them to view battering as a problem for medical attention, identify it, and make referrals. I compare the responses of ED staff in these two sets of EDs and analyze the factors which account for a greater response to battering in the fourth ED.

This study has implications both for our understanding of medicalization and for our understanding of the ED response to battering. Those studying medicalization typically focus on how medical professionals readily define emerging concerns as medical problems that belong within their professional domain (Conrad and Schneider, 1980a; Zola, 1972, 1975). Some argue further that, due to sexist attitudes in the medical system, women's problems are particularly likely to be "medicalized" or appropriated by the male medical establishment (Dreifus, 1978; Ehrenreich and English, 1978; Ruzek,1978). In contrast, the medical staff I studied saw efforts to respond to battering as detracting from the proper performance of their work, not enhancing it. I further demonstrate that staff resistance to battering may be influenced by prevailing views of women, but that they are influenced more by other factors.

One previous study also suggests that health care personnel are reluctant to respond to battering. Based on an extensive review of medical records, Stark et al. (1979) found that staff in a New Haven hospital do not identify battering as such, but instead respond to battered women's psychosocial problems—e.g., depression, drug abuse, suicide attempts, or alcoholism—although the women's ED records indicate that these problems arose after the onset of battering. Stark et al. attribute this inclination to overlook battering to staff's adherence to the current medical paradigm, which does not view social factors as significant elements of medical problems. Whereas Stark et al. relied only on medical records, I present more direct, observational evidence on the reactions of ED staff to battered women.

Methods

I used the following methods to collect data in four hospital EDs in a large metropolitan area: observations of interactions between battered women and staff; informal interviews with ED staff; and a review of medical records. The staff at each hospital ED during each eight-hour shift generally included one or two physicians, four or five nurses, and one or two orderlies or technicians. One or two interns were occasionally present as well. The staff members in all the hospitals are primarily white, the physicians primarily male, and the nurses primarily female. The patients represent a wide range of ethnic and class backgrounds.

Observers, who were graduate students in sociology and social work, followed the cases of all female trauma patients seen by health care professionals during different shifts. The observations extended over five months in two of the hospitals and two months in the other two.[2] A woman was considered battered if (1) the observer heard the woman, or someone accompanying her, say that she had been injured by her husband or boyfriend, or (2) a staff member told the observer that the woman, or someone accompanying her, said she had been injured by a husband or boyfriend. Based on this definition, interactions between 104 battered women and ED staff were observed during this period.

Observers followed as much of the interaction between staff and women as possible and then immediately interviewed staff about what transpired in the interaction—that is, what was said and done, what physical diagnosis was made, whether the staff thought battering had occurred, and what the staff's impression of the case was. Observers took verbatim field notes on all the interactions. Because of confidentiality agreements it was not possible for observers to speak directly to the female trauma patients.

During the informal interviewing observers questioned as many ED staff as possible about whether they saw battered women, what they were like, how they compared to other patients, or what staff thought could be done for them. Medical records of female trauma patients were reviewed for the same time period as the observation.

ED Staff Responses to Battering

In this section I describe responses to battered women in the three EDs where staff had some knowledge of battering, but where there were no ongoing efforts to have ED staff respond to battering on a systematic basis. ED staff were informed about battering at meetings in which staff from the research project explained the purpose of the project: to understand more about battered women who come to EDs and to determine what EDS could do for battered women. Research staff presented battering as a problem which could be medically identified in the ED and for which there were appropriate referral sources. At the meeting, observers told ED staff that they were leaving cards in the ED with the telephone numbers of three hotlines for battered women, although from that point on observers did not mention the cards to staff. The fact that ED directors had allowed these activities to take place was an indication to ED staff that the directors had granted some legitimacy to this issue. On the other hand, at no time did ED or hospital administrators set up procedures for identifying battered women or give any other indication that they viewed the issue as a priority.

Informally, staff knew about battered women from having seen them in the ED. Based on a record review, an average of one woman per day comes to each of these hospitals with injuries inflicted by husbands or boyfriends.[3] All staff who were asked about battered women expressed awareness of "these women." ED staff do not usually use the term "battered women," but refer to "the woman who was hit/beaten by her husband/boyfriend."[4] A major reason for staff's awareness of the presence of battered women is that in 75 percent of the cases the battered women volunteer that they have been injured by a husband or boyfriend. In the other 25 percent of the cases, it becomes known because a relative or the police tell the cause of the injury.

In the following section I describe the three major responses to battered women in the three EDs: "positive," "partial," and "no response." I describe the nature of the interactions in these categories and the reasons staff gave for their responses. Observers questioned as many staff members as possible about particular cases. All staff members were willing to describe the cases if they had time, and approximately half volunteered reasons for their responses.

POSITIVE RESPONSES

In 11 percent of the cases staff take a woman's battering seriously and view it as legitimately deserving of their time and attention. In addition to giving a battered woman medical treatment, staff note battering on the case record, speak to the woman about what happened, her current circumstances, her safety, and attempt to provide some assistance or give the card with hotline numbers. What distinguishes these responses from others is that staff attempt to follow through with a battered woman and ensure that when she leaves, something has been done for her. One nurse talked at length with a woman, and then arranged for her to talk with a policeman who had recently come to the ED. Several others tried to call hotline numbers and shelters, and waited for return calls if necessary. Some arranged to talk to women alone, who then told them they were battered.

The fairly small number of staff members involved in these interactions do not respond to all battered women in this way; their responses are contingent on several factors. First, staff respond to women they see as "true victims." The women have to be polite, have no discrediting attributes, and, in addition, staff members have to feel that some unfortunate event has happened to them. Staff members see women as "true victims" when they perceive them to be in immediate physical danger. As one medical student said,

> She wants to talk to someone about what to do and where she can go. It has happened five or six times before though she does not seem to have been seriously injured, but I mean this is pretty serious. He pulled a knife . . . she is really in a quandary as to what to do now.

Another resident said:

> Well, when I asked her today if she passed out last night when this happened, she said no. But then she said that two weeks ago, she passed out when he tried to strangle her. I couldn't believe it—this is really sick.

Secondly, staff members feel sympathetic towards women who say they are taking action to leave the violent relationship. Some women mention that they have contacted the police in order to press charges; some express their strong interest in leaving the relationship; some have already contacted an abuse agency or state their intention to do so; and some express strong interest in contacting hospital social services. One physician spoke approvingly of a patient who said: "He has beaten me the first time and this will be the last time." Staff have a genuine feeling for the predicament of these women.

Thirdly, if staff believe the woman has a pleasant personality, this influences how legitimately deserving of their time and attention they feel she is. In one ED many staff commented sympathetically about a particular woman. As the physician said:

> I told her completely off the record "you can do better." I mean she looks good, she seems to be nice. She shouldn't have to put up with that stuff. Do you know what that fool did? She was in here Wednesday night and that fool was telling her I want to get out of here. I mean he's nothing but a bastard. She doesn't need that.

A PARTIAL RESPONSE TO BATTERED WOMEN

In 49 percent of the cases, staff makes a "partial" response to the battering side of a case. They do similar things as those staff in the first category, such as asking the woman about her situation, giving her a card with the hotline phone numbers, calling the hotline numbers for the woman, or trying to arrange transportation home for the woman. However, staff members' involvement in these cases is brief and has a routine quality, and they do not typically think of different things they might do for a battered woman. They give a woman a small amount of their time, but give higher priority to other cases. Thus, the response may or may not be appropriate for that woman's condition. Staff may lose track of a woman who says she is in danger, or give extra time to a woman who does not appear to be in immediate danger.

In half of these cases, staff members gave reasons for their partial responses while describing their interactions with these battered women. The factor they mention most often is that the women are not responsive. In a few cases they described them as "not interested." An attending physician said directly to a couple: "So you don't want to talk about it," to which they replied, "That's right."

For the most part staff describe "unresponsive" women as "evasive," or purposely vague and inconsistent in describing how they were injured. In 16 percent of all cases in all four EDs, staff describe the women as evasive, hiding something, or unwilling to talk. In such interactions the women may say their injury was due to an accident. For example, one woman with a facial injury said only that she had been in a car accident. According to the nurse, "She wouldn't say a thing. She was completely non-communicative. I couldn't even get a history." The nurse initially believed the woman, "although it didn't really fit for a car accident. Her lip was split and that was all." The nurse, upon hearing that the woman's husband was waiting for her, went to speak to him. He immediately volunteered that the injury had occurred during an argument.

A staff person will become particularly irritated if he or she suspects battering, takes the time to ask the woman, and the woman will not give an answer. In one case, a nurse asked a woman with a broken jaw what she had been struck with. The woman replied, "a hand." The nurse then asked the woman if she had been struck by a "significant other," and the woman did not reply. The nurse offered the woman a card with phone numbers of battered women's agencies and asked her if she needed shelter. The woman said no, but that she would keep the card. The woman was admitted to the hospital with a broken jaw.

The second factor that staff mention in describing their interactions in cases of partial response is that the battered women have a condition which makes interacting with them difficult. Staff say these women are "AOB" (Alcohol on Breath), have taken drugs, act in ways staff believe are "crazy" or "inappropriate," or are "fighters." Staff describe 24 percent of all cases in all four EDs in terms of these stigmatized qualities.

Women who have been drinking are generally assumed to be upset, vague, and difficult to understand. One badly beaten woman, with a high blood alcohol level, told four different stories about how she had been beaten. The following exchange reveals the typical staff attitude towards battered women with "AOB."

> OBSERVER: What is your impression of this case?
> NURSE: Somebody beat the shit out of her.
> OBSERVER: Is it hard to nurse for these cases?
> NURSE: She had "AOB," Do I feel sorry for her? No, I feel like if somebody drinks, at least they have control over that part of it.
> OBSERVER: Does it make your job harder?

> NURSE: Well, yes. For example, she can't remember what happened. Is that from the alcohol or the concussion? And she is dizzy—that could be from drinking too. Also, when people drink they let it all out. She is upset and maybe because of the alcohol it is more extreme.

Women labeled "AOB" are assumed to be all alike—unable and unwilling to cooperate with staff—although a review of "AOB" cases showed that over a third of these women became more cooperative and willing to talk in the ED as the effects of the alcohol wore off. Staff members perceived drug cases in a similar manner to "AOB" cases. When women act in a bizarre way, staff label them "crazy," express intense dislike for them, and view them as a waste of time. One "crazy" woman wouldn't stop talking, said inappropriate things, and would not sign her forms. Another talked about killing herself and her husband, and then stole valium from the ED.

A third aspect of these cases that staff members mention is the belief that they cannot help or produce "results" with these women. Staff develop an attitude summarized by the statement, "There's nothing much we can do." While staff can give a woman a card with the phone numbers of the battered women's hotlines, they do not know if their efforts will result in the woman's using the hotlines or getting help in some other way. Some staff would also like to be able to help a battered woman get into a shelter, but this is difficult to accomplish. As one nurse said, "There are so few shelters and so few vacancies that when we make a referral it's very difficult to find a place." On one occasion a woman wanted shelter and a staff person called the hotlines. No one answered.

STAFF DO NOT RESPOND

In 40 percent of the cases staff do not respond to the battering side of a case. The reason staff members most often give for not responding is the same reason given for "partial responses"—the women are "evasive." The second reason staff members give for "non-response" also parallels reasons for a "partial response": that the women have a stigmatizing trait—they are "AOB," have used drugs, or act "crazy." Third, staff members say they are sometimes too busy to respond. As one nurse said, "She had two bruised eyes. I had no time to spend with her. I was too busy." A doctor told the observer, "We couldn't get any more information about her. We were too rushed this morning."

The fourth reason staff members give for not responding is that they do not view battering as a legitimate medical concern. They question women patients about the cause of their injuries strictly to diagnose and treat their physical problems; once they ascertain, for example, that a woman was struck, staff do not ask who struck her. As one physician said, "I did not ask anything about her social situation. I only asked about how he hit her with the prong of the fork." Even if a woman volunteers the information about what happened to her, it is ignored.

> NURSE: She has epigastral pain—tingling in her hands—that could be from hyperventilation. She has been upset about her husband . . . she was crying the whole time. She did not sleep last night.

> OBSERVER: Did you ask if her pains were connected with this situation?
> NURSE: It is not necessary. Since it could be coronary you have to be careful—she is in the age group. But I think it is emotional. She could even have been hyperventilating in her sleep.
> OBSERVER: Do you see any direct links between her pain and her upset?
> NURSE: Not really. She does not report any stabbing pain.
> DOCTOR: She strikes me as being very upset. She says she had a fight with her husband. But we can not let that cloud our analysis.

Also, some staff view battering as a personal problem and define an inquiry about battering as an invasion into the patient's affairs. As one surgeon said, "It is none of my business who hit her. I am just here to treat her." One person mentioned a possible additional reason that staff do not respond. This staff person did not want to be legally responsible for bringing up the subject of battering, although she had no information about her legal liability. One staff person also mentioned fear of retaliation by a man if she got involved in a battering case.

NEGATIVE STEREOTYPES OF BATTERED WOMEN

In describing particular cases, staff members state that the demeanor of the women—their "evasiveness" and disruptive behavior—is a primary factor preventing their addressing the battering side of a case. In 40 percent of their interactions, staff members encounter women they believe possess "troublesome" traits. However, it is clear that ED staff believe the number of such women is higher. When questioned about their views of battered women generally, staff members indicated that battered women are a source of frustration, and some staff members held these women personally responsible for the batterings they received:

> It is difficult to feel sorry for these women as they have a choice to leave the situation (nurse).

> Why do anything for people who do not take responsibility for themselves? What good does it do when they won't come in and do something for themselves. Last night we had a battered woman. It took five hours for her to be convinced to come in by neighbors (cardiology resident).

When staff see a woman leave the ED with an abuser, this reinforces their view that the women are irresponsible. They remember these incidents:

> It is ridiculous because the women go back. We see it all the time. They are in the examining room. The man has gouged out her eye or stabbed her or something like that and she is in the ER and gets mad because we won't let the guy in (physician).

Others come to view battering as an inevitable problem of these women's social class.

> She is a blue collar worker. These people come from neighborhoods where husbands beat up their wives all the time. There is nothing much to say—it is a clear case (intern).

> I know battering takes place in middle class families but I do not associate it with middle class people such as myself. . . . I have only seen cases in [a poor section of the city). There it is a way of life, one comes to expect that type of behavior and learns to live with it (physician).

> Well, it is normal for a woman to fight with a man in this area. What are you going to do about those women? . . . That is the culture in this area (nurse).

Occasionally staff members describe the problem as due to women's traits. They use popular negative social characterizations of women and battered women to describe the source of the problem. As one nurse said:

> A lot of women do things to provoke a man. Probably most of them do. I know there are some real crazy women around here.

Thus, many staff members treat battered women as "deliberate deviants" (Lorber, 1975), who have actively or willfully caused their own condition. Lorber demonstrates that medical personnel do not think that "deliberate deviants" are worthy of their time and attention. Staff members form this stereotype of battered women despite the fact that a great variety of battered women come to the ED—e.g., women who are about to take action to change their situation, those who are actively thinking about what to do, or those who are afraid or unwilling to change their situation.

MEDICALIZATION EFFORTS IN ONE ED

This section describes the efforts of a physician assistant in the fourth ED to have other staff members identify and refer battered women. The physician assistant had begun to identify battering cases on her own, and then had made herself knowledgeable about it. She believes the battering aspect of a case is a legitimate medical concern and compatible with her own role. She refers to battering as a "syndrome" with distinct medical symptoms, and urges others to "diagnose" the condition. This physician assistant believes it is necessary to understand that battering is the cause of the injury in order to treat the injury physically, to see the related physical and social effects, and to take some preventive measures to ensure that it will not happen again. She argues that the fact that battering is "chronic" makes it a legitimate concern for the ED because women will repeatedly come back for treatment unless it is stopped.

In addition, the physician assistant is able to have productive encounters with women who are "evasive," "AOB," and "troublemakers." She views these behaviors not as illegitimate, but rather as behaviors expected of those under the stress of battering. For example, the physician assistant talked to one angry battered woman—who other staff members defined as a "troublemaker" that they wanted out of the ED as soon as possible—with a sympathetic tone. The woman began to respond calmly to the physician assistant and to reflect on her situation. From time to time the physician assistant did find a battered woman to be trouble, such as a woman who claimed to be uninterested in anything about battering. However, this physician assistant believes that most battered women are not trouble.

The advocate made several changes in her ED. First, she developed and received approval for a file card system which all staff were to use to note the battering cases they identified. These cases would then be referred to the physician assistant or the ED social worker who was concerned about battering. The ED director put treatment of battering into the official ED manual, and also allowed the physician assistant to conduct training sessions on battering for new residents and interns.

As a result of the physician assistant's efforts, there was a much greater likelihood of "positive" responses to battered women in this ED. Forty-seven percent of the cases were in the "positive" category as opposed to 11 percent from the other three EDs. This high number of "positive" cases was mainly due to the actions of a group of eight ED staff members including a physician, several nurses, and a social worker. These staff members, influenced by the physician assistant, responded to battered women in a manner similar to her. They not only identified battering and referred the women, but briefly talked to the women and told them they didn't deserve such treatment. In a quarter of these cases the women were perceived to be "AOB," drug users, or "evasive," and yet staff members still responded in a "positive" manner.

The one difference between the advocate and other staff members is that the latter expressed frustration in several cases where they felt there was nothing they could do for the women. In a few cases the women had received help from the battering agencies but had returned home for lack of alternative places to live. Staff members also expressed frustration in a few cases where the women appeared to be "repeaters." As one nurse who helped many battered women said: "I mean now that she is here I want to give her good care. But it's just going to happen again."

In 21 percent of the cases in this ED, in contrast to 49 percent in the other three EDs, staff made a "partial" response. Their response was categorized as "partial" because they took only one action—they filled out cards for the physician assistant's card file system. However, even this response was somewhat different from those in the other three EDs because these staff members did not view filling out a card as "trouble"; they accepted the identification of battered women as part of their role. Interestingly, the attitudes of staff members towards battered women in cases of "partial" response were similar to those of staff in the other three EDs. In half the cases the women were "AOB," used drugs, or were "evasive." Staff members were not anxious to spend time with these cases; they wanted to fill out a card for them and send them along as soon as possible. As one nurse said, "I think she's a little drunk and a little crazy. She says he threw her through three rooms. She's not like the women with no place to go."

Thirty-two percent of the cases in this ED fell in the third category, "no response," as compared to 40 percent in the other EDs. Staff members here gave reasons for their nonresponsiveness that were similar to those mentioned by their counterparts in the other EDs. In half these cases, the women were "AOB" or had used drugs. As one nurse said, "She said she was on drugs as soon as she took her coat off. After that I wasn't even interested." In the other half of these cases, staff do not respond to battering because they did not think the women were interested; because they themselves were too busy or forgot to inquire about battering; or because they didn't see the social aspects of battering as part of their medical responsibilities.

Discussion

I have described two sets of responses to battered women in EDs. In the three EDs with a minimal educational effort about battering, three factors affect staff response to battered women. First, staff respond to and form their images of battered women based on their evaluation of the women's demeanor. They respond positively to women who appear as "true victims" and with dislike to those seen to be "evasive" or possessing a stigmatized status such as "AOB." Second, staff feel there is not much they can do about battered women. Third, they don't believe that battering is a legitimate medical problem. Staff members' responses have significant consequences for women. Those staff who respond to women in a "partial" manner spend less time with women and may or may not find out the facts of their cases, determine whether they are in danger, or document battering on the medical record. Staff in the "non-response" category may ignore battering. In the case of women with "stigmatizing" traits, staff may not "see" battering at all. This is consistent with the conclusion of Stark et al. (1979) that staff diagnose and treat battered women not as battered, but as suffering from depression, drug abuse, suicide attempts, or alcoholism.

Staff members focus on demeanor—women's perceived lack of responsiveness and their stigmatizing qualities—because they feel these qualities determine whether and how they will be able to interact with battered women. There are few ways for ED staff to measure the success of their work, and they feel particularly unsure about "results" with battered women. Staff find those who seem like a "true victim" easiest to identify and help, and they find those who are "unresponsive" or "evasive" or have other stigmatized qualities to be trouble.

The second and third factors affecting staff's lack of response—that they feel that there is little they can do, and that they don't see this as a legitimate medical problem—mean that staff feel that responding to battered women detracts from their "real" work. This, combined with their view of many battered women as trouble, results in staff viewing their treatment of battered women as a kind of "dirty work" (Hughes, 1971). As Roth (1972) and Sudnow (1967) have shown, ED staff consider those cases which are life-threatening and qualify as "real" emergencies as most legitimate and worthy of their time and attention; other cases are seen as belonging in medical clinics. Staff do respond to battered women whom they perceive to be in "serious" danger. These cases qualify as "real" emergencies and fit the most valued, "heroic," aspect of the medical role. However, while many injuries due to battering are serious, they are seldom life-threatening. Furthermore, staff define battered women as "social" cases in which the women are responsible for their condition. Thus, in the majority of cases staff believe dealing with battered women is "dirty work," work which detracts from their ability to carry out their role, work which is symbolically degrading.

In contrast, the advocate in the fourth ED views her efforts to help battered women as "honorable work" which is central to her conception of her treatment role.

A small number of other staff members also adopt and practice her orientation toward battered women. The majority of staff members accept the advocate system as legitimate, apart from whether or not they believe the women themselves are legitimate candidates for assistance. This is because the referral system enables the majority of staff members to be less concerned with demeanor. It makes them feel they have a clear, simple task—to get the information for the card—and that they are therefore less dependent on the woman's demeanor. Also, staff members are assured of some result or measure of success—a referral—and thus are not left with the sense, as in the other EDs, that there is "nothing they can do."

However, even with an advocate and a referral system, many staff members continue to view the evasive and stigmatized cases as trouble. Staff members' negative perceptions of women's demeanor still contribute to "partial" responses or "non-responses" in many cases. Staff members who respond "positively" have less difficulty with demeanor, but sometimes they question whether they are actually accomplishing anything with battered women.

Some feminist writers argue that sexist attitudes strongly affect the response of the health care system to women and that medical professionals are eager to "medicalize" women's issues, or appropriate these issues for their own uses (Dreifus, 1978; Ehrenreich and English, 1978; Ruzek, 1978). While I found that attitudes towards women were a factor in staff responses, the main reason staff members were not interested in appropriating battering was that they felt it difficult to make a successful intervention in such cases. One could argue that gender is still a major factor in ED treatment—that if women were more valued by the health care system, medical personnel would define the problem of battering as important. But then we need to reconceptualize more precisely how sexism affects the response to battered women. To do this we need further study of which of women's conditions become medicalized and which do not.

This study demonstrates the importance of looking at the role of clinicians in interpreting and carrying out concepts of medicalization originating from other advocates. First, it suggests a need to look at how conceptions of demeanor and trouble shape clinicians' responses to certain conditions. In theory, medicalization is supposed to mean that moral judgments, or attitudes of "badness" (Conrad and Schneider, 1980a) are replaced by concepts of illness; but this may not always be the case. Second, as Conrad and Schneider (1980b) note, medicalization takes place on three levels—conceptual, institutional, and interactional. This study shows the possibility of an appearance of medicalization on one level while moral judgments prevail on another, thus suggesting a need for more study of the relationship between different levels of the medicalization process.

Conclusion

What does this study suggest about the medicalization of battering in the future? The stereotypes of "troublesome" women and the individualistic orientation toward battering held by ED staff members are consistent with the position that these women should be referred to mental health services for treatment of their personal "problems." Accordingly, "medicalization" could come to mean referral to mental health professionals. An American College of Physicians (1986) position paper recommends that physicians refer battered women to social workers and mental health services. Whereas health care professionals may not intervene directly in cases of battering, they may be willing to serve as referral agents in a medicalized system that redefines battering as a problem of mental health.

However, at least in theory, advocacy or referral systems could develop strong connections with the battered women's movement and its programs. The physician assistant in this study was strongly oriented toward referring women to battered women's services rather than to the mental health system. The National Coalition Against Domestic Violence (1985) provides materials on battering for health care personnel and urges them to train health care personnel about battering. Some health care reformers advocate working closely with shelters and hotlines sponsored by the battered women's movement (Rosenberg et al., 1985). Yet, it goes without saying that, in practice, the medical system has avoided close connections with popular movements (Freidson, 1973).

Thus, this study suggests that the orientation of advocacy and referral systems will be important in determining the course of the medicalization of battering. Those reform groups which mount the most extensive efforts to institute advocacy and referral programs will be able to shape the medical response to battering. However, in the absence of institutionalized advocacy and referral efforts, the response of the health care system to battering will not be long-lasting and medicalization will not take hold.

Notes

The research for this chapter was supported by NIMH Grant MH37180-02. The author thanks Howard S. Becker, Bruce Birchard, Michelle Fine, Carole Joffe, Judith Lorber, and Evan Stark for comments on previous drafts.

1. Evan Stark, Nov. 16, 1986: personal communication.
2. In two of the hospitals there were two observation periods. The first was from December 1981 to February 1982; the second, from October to November 1982. Three observers spent three five-hour shifts per week in the ED or 15 hours each, for a total of 45 hours a week. In the other two hospitals there was a period of observation for two months, April and May 1983, and only two observers.
3. In the record review of female trauma cases collected during the course of the study, 7 percent of the cases were coded as "positive" for battering. These were cases where ED staff had indicated on the medical record that a woman was injured by her husband or boyfriend. Ten percent of the cases were coded as "suggestive" for battering. These were cases where a woman had been assaulted, but no assailant was recorded on the record. Thus, 17 percent of the female trauma cases are either "positive" or "suggestive" for battering. This is equivalent to one woman per day coming to each of these hospitals with injuries inflicted by husbands or boyfriends.

These figures are similar to those of Stark (1984). Using a slightly different coding system, Stark (1984) found that 10.6 percent of the cases were "positive." In 8.7 percent of these cases, where a full trauma history was taken, assault by a male intimate was recorded on the record, and an additional 2 percent were listed elsewhere in the record. Stark categorized 5.9 percent of the cases as "probables" (woman was assaulted, but no assailant was recorded, nor was a mugging recorded on the record), and 2.2 percent as "suggestives" (the recorded etiology of the injury did not seem to account adequately for the injury and there was contradictory information, such as woman fell downstairs and got two black eyes).

4. I use the term "battered women" throughout the chapter as a short-hand term for "women injured by husbands and boyfriends." The term originated with the battered women's movement and names a social problem. My use of the term here is not meant to suggest that the view of battering as a social problem is uniformly defined or widespread.

References

American College of Physicians
   1986 "Position statements of the American College of Physicians." *Philadelphia Medicine* 82:496.
Attorney General's Task Force
   1984 *Attorney General's Task Force. Final Report.* U.S. Department of Justice, September 1984.
Campbell, Jacquelyn, and Janice Humphreys
   1984 *Nursing Care of Victims of Family Violence.* Reston, VA: Reston Publishing.
Conrad, Peter
   1975 "The discovery of hyperkinesis: Notes on the medicalization of deviant behavior." *Social Problems* 23:12–21.
Conrad, Peter, and Joseph W. Schneider
   1980a *Deviance and Medicalization: From Badness to Sickness.* St. Louis: C.V. Mosby.
   1980b "Looking at levels of medicalization: A comment on Strong's critique of the Theses of Medical Imperialism." *Social Science and Medicine* 14A:75–79.
Dobash, R. Emerson, and Russell Dobash
   1979 *Violence against Wives.* New York: The Free Press.
Dreifus, C.
   1978 *Seizing Our Bodies: The Politics of Women's Health.* New York: Vintage.
Ehrenreich, Barbara, and Deirdra English
   1978 *For Her Own Good: 150 Years of the Experts' Advice to Women.* Garden City, NY: Anchor.
Finley, Britt
   1981 "Nursing process with the battered woman." *Nurse Practitioner* 6:11–13, 29.
Freidson, Eliot
   1973 *Profession of Medicine.* New York: Dodd, Mead & Company.
Goffman, Erving
   1963 *Stigma.* Englewood Cliffs, NJ: Prentice-Hall.
Goldberg, Wendy, and Anne L. Carey
   1982 "Domestic violence victims in the emergency setting." *Topics in Emergency Medicine* 3:65–76.
Greany, Geraldine D.
   1984 "Is she a battered woman?" *American Journal of Nursing* 84:725–27.
Helton, Anne S.
   1986 *Protocol of Care for the Battered Woman.* Houston, TX: Texas Woman's University.
Hughes, Everett C.
   1971 *The Sociological Eye.* Chicago: Aldine.
Kittrie, Nicholas N.
   1971 *The Right to be Different: Deviance and Enforced Therapy.* Baltimore: Johns Hopkins University Press.
Klingbeil, Karil S.
   1986 "Interpersonal violence: A hospital based model from policy to program." *Response* 9:6–9.
Koop, C. Everett
   1982 Family Violence: A Chronic Public Health Issue. Lecture to the Western Psychiatric Institute, Pittsburgh, November 9.
   1984 Testimony. Presented to the Attorney General's Task Force on Family Violence. Sacramento, February 15.

Loraine, Kaye
    1981 "Battered women: The ways you can help." *RN* 44:23–28.
Lorber, Judith
    1975 "Good patients and problem patients: Conformity and deviance in a general hospital." *Journal of Health and Social Behavior* 16:213–25.
National Coalition Against Domestic Violence
    1985 *Medical/Hospital Intervention and Domestic Violence.* Washington, DC.
New Jersey Department of Community Affairs
    1985 *Domestic Violence: A Guide for Emergency Medical Treatment.* Division on Women.
Petro, Jane A., Patricia L. Quann, and William P. Graham
    1978 "Wife abuse: The diagnosis and its implications." *Journal of the American Medical Association* 240:240–41.
Pfohl, Stephen J.
    1977 "The 'discovery' of child abuse." *Social Problems* 24:310–23.
Rich, Robert F., and Ann W. Burgess
    1986 "NIMH report: Panel recommends comprehensive program for victims of violent crime." *Hospital and Community Psychiatry* 37:437–39.
Riessman, Catherine K.
    1983 "Women and medicalization: A new perspective." *Social Policy* 14:3–18.
Rosenberg, Mark L., Evan Stark, and Margaret A. Zahn
    1985 "Interpersonal violence: Homicide and spouse abuse." Pp. 4916–37 in J. Last (ed.), *Public Health and Preventive Medicine,* Twelfth edition. East Norwalk, CT: Appleton Century Crofts.
Roth, Julius, A.
    1972 "Some contingencies of the moral evaluation and control of clientele: The case of the hospital emergency service." *American Journal of Sociology* 77:839–55.
Ruzek, Sheryl K.
    1978 *The Women's Health Movement: Feminist Alternatives to Medical Control.* New York: Praeger.
Schecter, Susan
    1982 *Women and Male Violence.* Boston: South End Press. Stark, Evan
Stark, Evan
    1984 *The Battering Syndrome: Social Knowledge, Social Theory, and the Abuse of Women.* Unpublished Ph.D. dissertation, SUNY, Binghamton, NY.
Stark, Evan, Anne Flitcraft, and William Frazier
    1979 "Medicine and patriarchal violence: the social construction of a 'private' event." *International Journal of Health Services* 9:461–93.
Straus, Murray A., Richard J. Gelles, and Suzanne Steinmetz
    1980 *Behind Closed Doors: Violence in the American Family.* New York: Anchor.
Sudnow, David
    1967 *Passing On: The Social Organization of Dying.* Englewood Cliffs, NJ: Prentice-Hall.
Teske, R. H., and M. L. Parker
    1983 *Spouse Abuse in Texas: A Study of Women's Attitudes and Experiences.* Huntsville, TX: Criminal Justice Center, Sam Houston State University.
Tierney, Kathleen J.
    1982 "The battered women movement and the creation of the wife beating problem." *Social Problems* 29:207–20.
Varvaro, Filomena F., and Patricia G. Cotman
    1987 "Domestic violence: A focus on the emergency room care of abused women." Pittsburgh: Women's Center and Shelter of Greater Pittsburgh.
Zola, Irving K.
    1972 "Medicine as an institution of social control." *Sociological Review* 20:487–504.
    1975 "In the name of health and illness: On some socio-political consequences of medical influence." *Social Science and Medicine* 9:83–87.

CHAPTER 10

The Social Construction of Deviance

EXPERTS ON BATTERED WOMEN

Donileen R. Loseke and Spencer E. Cahill

During the 1970s, women's movement activists succeeded in focusing public attention on the topic of wife assault.[1] While the phenomenon itself was not new, contemporary feminists were the first to argue that wife assault was not merely a private trouble but a social issue as well. They asserted that public attention and resources were required in order to assist the immediate victims of this social malaise, "battered women."

While the feminist ideals underlying the movement for battered women suggested that victims of wife assault could be the only "experts" regarding their problems (Ridington, 1977–1978; Segovia-Ashley, 1978; Warrior, 1978),[2] ironically, but not surprisingly, the movement was accompanied by the emergence of experts on battered women.[3] By the late 1970s, these self-identified experts were speaking on behalf of battered women to the media, in government hearings (U.S. Commission on Civil Rights, 1978; U.S. Congress, House of Representatives, 1978), and in legal proceedings (Jones, 1980:2963). A diverse group, these experts share neither a common vocabulary of discourse nor a common ideological perspective; some but not all explicitly state an allegiance to the feminist ideals underlying the movement for battered women.[4] They include academics (sociologists, psychologists, legal scholars), social service providers (social workers, nurses, lawyers, shelter workers), political activists, and journalists. Their claims to expertise are based on either intellectual study (Dobash and Dobash, 1979), academic journal articles (Bass and Rice, 1979; Ferraro and Johnson, 1983; Gelles, 1976; Hofeller, 1982; Langley and Levy, 1977; Morgan, 1982; Pagelow, 1981a, 1981b; Roy, 1977; Truninger, 1971), practical experience in social service provision (Fleming, 1979; Hendrix et al., 1978; Pizzey, 1979; Rounsaville, 1978; Shainess, 1977), or some combination of the three (Hilberman, 1980; McShane, 1979; Walker, 1979, 1983).

Despite this diversity, the experts on battered women share a fundamentally important belief. As members of what Berger and Berger (1983:38) call the "knowledge class," these experts believe that their understandings should be used to educate and assist those who are less knowledgeable and fortunate. Among experts on battered women, this belief in the necessity of expert intervention in others' everyday matters is reflected in their common, overriding concern with a particular issue: why do battered women remain in relationships with abusive mates? This question has been the explicit and almost sole concern of two books (Pagelow, 1981a; Walker, 1979), four academic journal articles (Bass and Rice, 1979; Gelles, 1976; Ferraro and Johnson, 1983; Pagelow, 1981b), and five chapters in larger works or edited volumes (Davidson, 1978; Dobash and Dobash, 1979; Langley and Levy, 1977; Martin, 1976, 1979).

This chapter also considers the question "why do they stay?" However, we focus not on the behaviors of battered women per se, but on the experts. We look at how, by both asking and answering this question, the experts have constructed a new category of deviance: battered women who remain with their mates.[5] Three interrelated questions are also addressed. First, we analyze the question itself to see what asking it implies about battered women. Second, we examine the general character of the experts' responses to this question. Third, we consider the quality of the evidence offered by the experts in support of these responses. Finally, we suggest an alternative vocabulary for battered women's motives.

Sociological Implications of the Question

The question "why do they stay?" implicitly defines the parameters of the social problem of battered women. By asking this question, the experts imply that assaulted wives are of two basic types: those who leave their mates and those who do not. Not only are possible distinctions among assaulted wives who remain with their mates implicitly ignored, but so too are the unknown number of assaulted wives who quickly terminate such relationships. By focusing attention on those who stay, the experts imply that assaulted wives who remain with their mates are more needy and deserving of public and expert concern than those who do not. In fact, some of the experts have explicitly defined battered women as women who *remain* in relationships containing violence (Ferraro and Johnson, 1983; Pizzey, 1979; Scott, 1974; Walker, 1979).

Moreover, the experts' common and overriding concern with the question of why assaulted wives stay reveals their shared definition of the normatively expected response to the experience of battering. To ask why assaulted wives remain with their mates is to imply that doing so requires explanation. In general, as Scott and Lyman (1968) have noted, normatively expected behavior does not require explanation. It is normatively unanticipated, untoward acts which require what Scott and Lyman term an "account." By asking why battered women stay, therefore, the experts implicitly define leaving one's mate as the normatively expected response to the experience of wife assault. Staying, on the other hand, is implicitly defined as deviant, an act "which is perceived (i.e., recognized) as violating expectations" (Hawkins and Tiedeman, 1975:59).

In other words, once the experts identify a woman as battered, normative expectations regarding marital stability are reversed. After all, separated and divorced persons are commonly called upon to explain why their relationships "didn't work out" (Weiss, 1975). It is typically marital stability, "staying," which is normatively expected and marital instability, "leaving," which requires an account. However, as far as the experts on battered women are concerned, once wife assault occurs, it is marital stability which requires explanation.

In view of the experts' typifications of relationships within which wife assault occurs, this reversal of normative expectations seems only logical. Although research indicates that the severity and frequency of wife assault varies considerably across couples (Straus et al., 1980), the experts stress that, *on the average*, wife assault is more dangerous for victims than is assault by a stranger (U.S. Department of Justice, 1980). Moreover, most experts maintain that once wife assault has occurred within a relationship it will become more frequent and severe over time (Dobash and Dobash, 1979), and few believe that this pattern of escalating violence can be broken without terminating the relationship.[6] It is hardly surprising, therefore, that the experts on battered women define "leaving" as the expected, reasonable, and desirable response to the experience of wife assault.[7] Staying, in contrast, is described as "maladaptive choice behavior" (Waites, 1977–1978), "self-destruction through inactivity" (Rounsaville, 1978), or, most concisely, "deviant" (Ferraro and Johnson, 1983). For the experts, battered women who remain with their mates pose an intellectual puzzle: Why are they so unreasonable? Why do they stay?

To ask such a question is to request an account. Experts who provide answers to this question are, therefore, offering accounts on behalf of battered women who remain with their mates. According to Scott and Lyman (1968), two general types of accounts are possible: justifications and excuses. A justification is an account which acknowledges the actor's responsibility for the behavior in question but challenges the imputation of deviance ("I did it, but I didn't do anything wrong"). An excuse, on the other hand, acknowledges the deviance of the behavior in question but relieves the actor of responsibility for it ("I did something wrong, but it wasn't my fault").

Clearly, these different types of accounts elicit different kinds of responses. If the behavior in question is socially justifiable, then the actor was behaving reasonably, as normatively expected. The actor's ability or competence to manage everyday affairs without interference is not called into question (Garfinkel, 1967:57). In contrast, excusing behavior implies that the actor cannot manage everyday affairs without interference. Although the behavior is due to circumstances beyond the actor's control, it is admittedly deviant. By implication, assistance from others may be required if the actor is to avoid behaving similarly in the future. In order to fully understand the experts' responses to battered women who remain with their mates it is necessary, therefore, to determine which type of account they typically offer on behalf of such women.

The Experts' Accounts

Experts on battered women are a diverse group. This diversity is reflected in the emphasis each expert places on various accounts, in the number of accounts offered, and in how series of accounts are combined to produce complex theoretical explanations. Despite such diversity, however, there is a sociologically important similarity among the experts' accounts. None of the experts argues that "staying" is justifiable. "Staying" is either explicitly or implicitly defined as unreasonable, normatively unexpected, and, therefore, deviant. By implication, the accounts offered by the experts are excuses for women's deviant behavior, and they offer two basic types.[8] Battered women are said to remain with their mates because of external constraints on their behavior or because of internal constraints. In either case, the accounts offered by the experts acknowledge the deviance of staying but relieve battered women of responsibility for doing so.

EXTERNAL CONSTRAINTS

Almost all contemporary experts on battered women maintain that staying is excusable due to external constraints on women's behavior (Dobash and Dobash, 1979; Freeman, 1979; Langley and Levy, 1977; Martin, 1976; Pagelow, 1981a, 1981b; Pizzey, 1979; Ridington, 1977–1978; Roy, 1977; Shainess, 1977).

> Why does she not leave? The answer is simple. If she has children but no money and no money and no place to go, she has no choice. (Fleming, 1979:83)

Clearly, such accounts are based on the assumption that battered women who stay are economically dependent upon their mates. If a woman has no money and no place to go, she cannot be held responsible for the unreasonable act of staying. She has no choice.

Although this excuse is the most prevalent in the literature on battered women, further elaboration is necessary. In its simplest form, such an account can be easily challenged: What about friends, family, the welfare system, and other social service agencies? In response to such challenges, experts must offer accounts which will excuse women for not taking advantage of such asistance. Experts meet these challenges with at least two further accounts of external constraints. First, experts claim that most battered women are interpersonally isolated. Even if they are not, family and friends are said to typically blame women for their problems instead of providing assistance (Carlson, 1977; Dobash and Dobash, 1979; Fleming, 1979; Hilberman and Munson, 1977–1978; Truninger, 1971). Second., experts claim that social service agencies typically provide little, if any, assistance. In fact, experts maintain that the organization of agencies (bureaucratic procedures and agency mandates to preserve family stability) and the behavior of agency personnel (sexism) discourage battered women who attempt to leave (Bass and Rice, 1979; Davidson, 1978; Dobash and Dobash, 1979; Higgins, 1978; Martin, 1976, 1978; McShane, 1979; Pizzey, 1979; Prescott and Letko, 1977; Truninger, 1971). In other words, the experts maintain that battered women can expect little assistance in overcoming their economic dependency. According to the experts, the excuse of economic dependency should be honored given the additional excuses of unresponsive friends, family, and social service agencies.

Although the external constraint type of excuse acknowledges that staying is unreasonable, it relieves battered women of the responsibility for doing so. Battered women who remain with their mates are portrayed as "more acted upon than acting" (Sykes and Matza, 1957:667). The implication, of course, is that women would leave (i.e., they would be reasonable) if external constraints could be overcome. The experts provide a warrant, therefore, for intervention in battered women's everyday affairs. In order to act reasonably and leave, battered women must overcome the external constraint of economic dependency, which they cannot do without the assistance of specialized experts.

Despite the prevalence of external constraint accounts in the literature on battered women, most experts consider such excuses insufficient. Instead of, or in addition to, such accounts, the experts maintain that battered women face a second type of constraint on their behavior. Although few contemporary experts argue that women stay because they enjoy being the objects of abuse, that they are masochistic, the experts do maintain that battered women face various "internal constraints."[9]

INTERNAL CONSTRAINTS

Some experts have proposed that biographically accumulated experiences may lead women to define violence as "normal" and "natural" (Ball, 1977; Gelles, 1976; Langley and Levy, 1977; Lion, 1977). Likewise, according to some experts, women define violence as a problem only if it becomes severe and/or frequent "enough" (Carlson, 1977; Gelles, 1976; Moore, 1979; Rounsaville and Weissman, 1977–1978).[10] If violence is not subjectively defined as a "problem," then women have no reason to consider leaving.

For the most part, experts have focused their attention on documenting internal constraints which are said to prevent women from leaving their mates even when violence is subjectively defined as a problem. Experts suggest two major sources of such internal constraints: femininity and the experience of victimization.

To many experts, the primary source of internal constraints is the femininity of battered women. Attributes commonly regarded as "feminine" are automatically attributed to battered women, especially when these characteristics can conceivably account for why such women might remain with their mates. For example, women who stay are said to be emotionally dependent upon their mates (Dobash and Dobash, 1979; Fleming, 1979; Freeman, 1979; Langley and Levy, 1977; Moore, 1979; Pizzey, 1979; Roy, 1977); to have a poor self-image or low self-esteem (Carlson, 1977; Freeman, 1979; Langley and Levy, 1977; Lieberknecht, 1978; Martin, 1976; Morgan, 1982; Ridington, 1977–1978; Star et al., 1979; Truninger, 1971); and to have traditional ideas about women's "proper place."[11] In isolation or in combination, these so-called feminine characteristics are said to internally constrain women's behavior. According to the experts, women find it subjectively difficult to leave their mates even when violence is defined as a problem.

Internal constraints are also said to follow from the process of victimization itself. According to the experts, battered women not only display typically feminine characteristics, but they also develop unique characteristics due to the victimization process. For example, some experts have argued that once a woman is assaulted she will fear physical reprisal if she leaves (Lieberknecht, 1978; Martin, 1979; Melville, 1978). Other physical, emotional, and psychological after-effects of assault are also said to discourage battered women from leaving their mates (Moore, 1979; Roy, 1977). Indeed, battered women are sometimes said to develop complex psychological problems from their victimization. These include the "stress-response syndrome" (Hilberman, 1980), "enforced restriction of choice" (Waites, 1977–1978), "learned helplessness" (Walker, 1979), or responses similar to those of the "rape trauma syndrome" (Hilberman and Munson, 1977–1978). A symptom common to all such diagnostic categories is that sufferers find it subjectively difficult to leave their mates.

As with external constraint excuses, these internal constraint accounts also acknowledge the deviance of remaining in a relationship containing violence while, at the same time, relieving battered women of responsibility for doing so. They function in this way, as excuses, because the various internal constraints attributed to battered women are identified as beyond their personal control. Clearly, battered women are not responsible for their gender socialization or for the physical violence they have suffered. In other words, both external and internal constraint accounts portray battered women who stay with their mates as more acted upon than acting. What women require, "for their own good," is assistance in overcoming the various barriers which prevent them from acting reasonably. Thus, both types of accounts offered by the experts on behalf of battered women who stay provide grounds for expert intervention in these women's everyday affairs.

As Scott and Lyman (1968) have pointed out, the criteria in terms of which accounts are evaluated vary in relation to the situation in which they are offered, the characteristics of the audience, and the identity of the account provider. In the present context, the identity of the account provider is of particular interest. When experts provide accounts which implicitly serve to promote their right to intervene in others' affairs, an important evaluative criterion is the quality of supportive evidence they offer. Experts who speak on behalf of others are expected to do so on the basis of uncommon knowledge. If, therefore, the evidence which the experts offer in support of their accounts for why battered women stay fails to confirm the expectation of uncommon knowledge, then their claim to be speaking and acting on such women's behalf is open to question.

The Evidence for Experts' Accounts

How do experts obtain their knowledge about the experiences and behavior of battered women? In order to explore the experts' claim to uncommon knowledge, we address three questions: From whom is evidence obtained (the issue of generalizability)? By what means is evidence obtained (the issue of validity)? How consistently does the evidence support the accounts offered (the issue of reliability)?

GENERALIZABILITY

Experts on battered women claim to have knowledge of the experiences and behavior of women who remain in relationships containing violence. Yet, while there is general agreement that many battered women suffer in silence, with few exceptions the experts have studied only those assaulted wives who have come to the attention of social service agencies, many of whom have already left their mates.[12] Women who contact social service agencies have decided that they require expert intervention in their private affairs, and there is good reason to believe that such women differ from women who have not sought assistance.

The decision to seek professional help is typically preceded by a complex process of problem definition, and this process is invariably more difficult and of longer duration when the problem involves the behavior of a family member (Goffman, 1969; Schwartz, 1957; Weiss, 1975; Yarrow et al., 1955). Regardless of the nature of the problem, this definitional process seems to follow a fairly predictable pattern. Only as a last resort are professional helpers contacted (Emerson and Messinger, 1977; Kadushin, 1969; Mechanic, 1975). Since it is primarily the experiences of women who have reached the end of this help-seeking process which provide evidence for experts' accounts, the generalizability of this evidence is questionable.

VALIDITY

When not simply stating their own perceptions of battered women, experts obtain their evidence in one of two ways. They sometimes question other experts and they sometimes directly question women. Clearly, others' perceptions, whether expert or not, are of uncertain validity. However, even the evidence based on battered women's responses to the question "why do you stay?" is of doubtful validity.

To ask a battered woman to respond to this question is to request that she explain her apparently deviant behavior. This leaves her two alternatives. She can either justify her staying ("I love him"; "he's not all bad"; "the kids need him") or she can excuse her behavior. Since experts have predefined staying as undeniably deviant, it is unlikely that they will honor a justification. Indeed, some experts on battered women have explicitly characterized justifications for staying as "rationalizations," accounts which are self-serving and inaccurate (Ferraro and Johnson, 1983; Waites, 1977–1978). Given the experts' presuppositions about the behavior of "staying" and the typical desire of persons to maintain "face" (Goffman, 1955), it is likely that the only accounts the experts will honor—excuses—are subtly elicited by the experts who question battered women. If this is so, then the experts, by asking women why they remain with their mates, have merely constructed an interactional situation which will produce evidence confirming the accounts they offer on women's behalf.[13]

It is hardly surprising, therefore, that the experts on battered women offer remarkably similar accounts of why women stay. This is particularly visible in the evidence which supports the external constraint accounts. By almost exclusively interviewing women who turn to inexpensive or free social service agencies and then constructing an interactional situation which is likely to elicit a particular type of account, experts practically ensure that their presuppositions about external constraints are confirmed.[14] In brief, the validity of the experts' evidence is doubtful.

RELIABILITY

Relying primarily on evidence from interviewing and observation, the experts on battered women offer amazingly similar accounts of why women remain. There are, however, many ways to obtain evidence. The question at hand is whether evidence gained from interviewing and observation is similar to evidence obtained using other methods.

If the economic dependency (external constraint) excuse is to avoid challenge, it must be supplemented by the additional excuses of unresponsive friends, family members, and social service agencies. Yet, evidence to support these supplementary external constraint excuses is less than overwhelming. In fact, some evidence undermines the excuse that social service agencies and providers discourage battered women from leaving their mates. Pagelow (1981a) found little relationship between her measures of "agency response" and the amount of time battered women had remained with their mates. Hofeller (1982) found that many battered women self-reported being either "completely" or "somewhat" satisfied with the efforts of social service agencies on their behalf.[15]

As with the excuse of unresponsive social service agencies, available evidence conflicts with various internal constraint accounts offered by the experts. For example, available evidence does not support assertions that battered women hold traditional beliefs about "women's proper place," or that these beliefs internally constrain women from leaving their mates. Walker (1983) reports that battered women perceive themselves to be less traditional than "other women," and the results of experimental studies conducted by Hofeller (1982) and Rosenbaum and O'Leary (1981) indicate that women who have not been victims of wife assault hold more traditional attitudes than women who are victims. Moreover, Pagelow (1981a) reports that her measures of "traditional ideology" did not help explain the length of time battered women remained with their mates.

The experts have also maintained that the low self-esteem assumed to be common to women in general is exacerbated by the process of victimization, producing a powerful internal constraint on the behavior of battered women. Yet in their now classic review of research evidence regarding sex differences in self-esteem, Maccoby and Jacklin (1974:15) labelled as a popular myth the commonsense deduction that "women, knowing that they belong to a sex that is devalued . . . must have a poor opinion of themselves." Contrary to this commonsense deduction, sex differences in self-esteem have rarely been found in experimental studies, and when they have, women's self-esteem is often higher than men's. In addition, at least two studies contained in the literature on battered women refute the statement that battered women have lower self-esteem than women who have not experienced assault. Walker (1983) found that battered women reported their self-esteem as higher than that of "other women," and Star (1978) found that shelter residents who had *not* experienced wife assault scored lower on an "ego-strength" scale than residents who had been assaulted.

In short, the evidence provided to support expert claims about battered women is, by scientific standards, less than convincing. In fact, it appears as if the experts' accounts are presupposed and then implicitly guide both the gathering and interpretation of evidence. In constructing their accounts, the experts have employed the commonsense practice of automatically attributing to individual women (in this case, battered women) sets of traits based on their sex. As females, battered women are automatically assumed to be economically and emotionally dependent upon their mates, to have low self-esteem, and to hold traditional attitudes and beliefs. Methodologies which might yield conflicting evidence are seldom used, and when seemingly conflicting evidence is uncovered it is often explained away. For example, Walker (1983:40) implicitly argues that battered women have an inaccurate perception of themselves. She interprets the finding that battered women consider themselves to be in control of their own behavior as a "lack of acknowledgement that her batterer *really* is in control" (emphasis added). Likewise, Pagelow (1981a) discredits seemingly conflicting evidence by challenging her own measures; the presupposed accounts are not questioned. In other words, the interpretive force of the "master status" of sex "overpowers" evidence to the contrary (Hughes, 1945:357). What the experts on battered women offer in support of their accounts for why women remain is not uncommon knowledge, therefore, but professional "folklore" which, however sophisticated, remains folklore (Zimmerman and Pollner, 1970:44).

This does not mean that evidence which conflicts with the experts' accounts is itself above question. On the contrary, the generalizability, reliability, and validity of conflicting evidence is also problematic. For example, both Pagelow (1981a) and Star (1978) used paper and pencil tests, and both studies were primarily concerned with residents of shelters in urban southern California. Likewise, Walker's (1979, 1983) findings are based primarily on clinical records of an unrepresentative group of women, and evidence regarding self-esteem is primarily derived from experimental studies involving only college students.

The sociologically intriguing issue is not, however, the "truthfulness" of accounts. In a diverse society, a variety of different vocabularies of motive (Mills, 1940) are available for making sense out of the complex interrelationships between actor, biography, situation, and behavior. Under such circumstances, "what is reason for one man is mere rationalization for another" (Mills, 1940:910). Any attempt to ascertain battered women's "true" motives would therefore be an exercise in what Mills termed "motive-mongering." What is of sociological interest is that the experts' accounts are not based upon uncommon knowledge but upon commonsense deductions best described as folklore. Clearly, this should raise questions about both the experts' claim to be speaking on battered women's behalf and their claim to have the right to intervene in such women's private affairs.

Given the experts' claim to be speaking and acting in battered women's "best interests," the sociologically important issue is the relative plausibility of the particular vocabulary of motive used by the experts. According to the experts, their primary concerns are the condemnation and elimination of wife assault, tasks which are likely to require specialized expertise. The vocabulary of motive which supports this agenda is one of highlighting "constraints" on women's behavior which must be overcome in order for them to behave reasonably—that is, in order for them to leave, But such a vocabulary is not the only plausible way to make sense of women's behavior.

An Alternative Vocabulary of Motive

Prior to the 1970s, the problems of battered women received little attention. In contrast, the contemporary experts have portrayed women as little more than victims. The tendency has been to define both battered women and their relationships with their mates almost exclusively in terms of the occurrence and effects of physical and emotional assault. Battered women are simply defined as assaulted wives who remain with assaultive mates (Ferraro and Johnson, 1983; Pizzey, 1979; Scott, 1974; Walker, 1979), and their relationships are portrayed as no more than victimizing processes. Such a focus leads to what Barry (1979) has termed "victimism," knowing a person only as a victim. One effect of the victimism practiced by the experts on battered women is that possible experiential and behavioral similarities between battered women and other persons are overlooked. It is simply assumed that the occurrence and experience of assault clearly distinguishes battered women and their relationships from individuals in cross-sex relationships which do not contain violence. However, even a cursory review of the sociological literature on marital stability and instability suggests that, at least in regard to their reluctance to leave their mates, battered women are quite similar to both other women and to men.

This literature consistently indicates that marital stability often outlives marital quality. Goode (1956) found that such stability was only sometimes due to the obvious, objective costs of terminating the relationship ("external constraints"). Contrary to predictions that relationships will terminate when apparent "costs" outweigh apparent "benefits," it is not at all unusual for relationships to be sustained even when outsiders perceive costs to be greater than benefits. Although experts on battered women have argued that leaving a relationship means that a woman's status will change from "wife" to "divorcee" (Dobash and Dobash, 1979; Truninger, 1971), a variety of family sociologists have noted that terminating a relationship is far more complex than is suggested by the concept of "status change." Over time, marital partners develop an "attachment" to one another (Weiss, 1975), a "coercive bond" (Turner, 1970), a "shared biography" (McLain and Weigert, 1979). As a result, each becomes uniquely irreplaceable in the eyes of the other. Such a personal commitment to a specific mate has been found to persist despite decreases in marital partners' liking, admiration, and/or respect for one another (Rosenblatt, 1977; Weiss, 1975). Battered women who remain in relationships which outsiders consider costly are not, therefore, particularly unusual or deviant.

Moreover, the sociological literature on marital stability and instability suggests that the process of separation and divorce, what Vaughan (1979) terms "uncoupling," is typically difficult. One indication of the difficulty of this process is the considerable time uncoupling often takes (Cherlin, 1981; Goode, 1956; Weiss, 1975). It is also typical for a series of temporary separations to precede a permanent separation (Lewis and Spanier, 1979; Vaughan, 1979; Weiss, 1975). In brief, the lengthy "leaving and returning" cycle said to be characteristic of battered women is a typical feature of the uncoupling process. Further, the guilt, concern, regret, bitterness, disappointment, depression, and lowered perception of self attributed to battered women are labels for emotions often reported by women and men in the process of uncoupling (Spanier and Castro, 1979; Weiss, 1975).

Although the experts attribute unusual characteristics and circumstances to battered women who remain with their mates, the reluctance of battered women to leave can be adequately and commonsensically expressed in the lyrics of a popular song: "Breaking up is hard to do." It can also be expressed in the more sophisticated vocabulary of sociological psychology: Individuals who are terminating intimate relationships "die one of the deaths that is possible" for them (Goffman, 1952). The sociological literature on marital stability and instability does suggest, therefore, an alternative to the vocabulary of battered women's motives provided by the experts on battered women. Because a large portion of an adult's self is typically invested in their relationship with their mate, persons become committed and attached to this mate as a uniquely irreplaceable individual. Despite problems, "internal constraints" are experienced when contemplating the possibility of terminating the relationship with the seemingly irreplaceable other. Again, if this is the case, then women who remain in relationships containing violence are not unusual or deviant; they are typical.

Some experts on battered women have reported evidence which supports this alternative characterization of the motives of women who remain. Gayford (1975) reports that half of his sample of battered women claimed to be satisfied with their relationships, and Dobash and Dobash (1979) note that, apart from the violence, battered women often express positive feelings toward their mates. Moreover, Ferraro and Johnson (1983) report that battered women typically believe that their mates are the only person they could love, and Walker (1979) reports that battered women often describe their mates as playful, attentive, exciting, sensitive, and affectionate. Yet, because of the victimism they practice, experts on battered women often fail to recognize that such findings demonstrate the multi-dimensionality of battered women's relationships with their mates. Indeed, some of these experts have explicitly advised that battered women's expressions of attachment and commitment to their mates not be believed:

> The statement that abused wives love their husbands need not be taken at face value. It may represent merely a denial of ambivalence or even unmitigated hatred. (Waites, 1977–1978:542)

> The only reasons the woman does not end the marriage are dependence—emotional or practical—and fear of change and the unknown. These are often masked as love or so the woman deludes herself. (Shainess, 1977:118)

Such expressions of commitment and attachment are justifications for why a person might remain with their mate. To honor such a justification would be to acknowledge that staying in a relationship which contains violence is not necessarily deviant. In order to sustain their claim to expertise, therefore, the experts on battered women cannot acknowledge the possible validity of this alternative, "justifying" vocabulary of motive even when it is offered by battered women themselves. In other words, the experts discredit battered women's interpretations of their own experiences. The justifications offered by battered women are reinterpreted by the experts as merely "symptoms" of the Stockholm Syndrome (Ochberg, 1980), of an "addiction" which "must be overcome" (Waites, 1977–1978), or as the "miracle glue" which "binds a battered woman to her batterer" (Walker, 1979:xvi). By reinterpreting the justifications of battered women in these ways, the experts sustain their claim that such women require the assistance of specialized experts.

Conclusions

This case study of the social construction of deviance by a group of experts illustrates how members of the knowledge class create a new clientele for their services. In effect, experts discredit the ability of a category of persons to manage their own affairs without interference. The actors in question are portrayed as incapable of either understanding or controlling the factors which govern their behavior. In order for them to understand their experiences and gain control over their behavior, by implication, they require the assistance of specialized experts. Because the category of actors which compose such a clientele are characterized as unreasonable and incompetent, any resistance they offer to the experts' definitions and intervention is easily discredited. For example, battered women's attempts to justify staying with their mates are often interpreted by the experts as further evidence of such women's unreasonableness and incompetence. Experts are able to sustain their claims to be speaking and acting on others' behalf, therefore, despite the protests of those on whose behalf they claim to be speaking and acting.

We do not mean to suggest that experts' potential clientele do not benefit from experts' efforts. For example, the experts on battered women have played a major role in focusing public attention on the plight of the victims of wife assault. In doing so, they have helped to dispel the popular myth that these women somehow deserved to be assaulted. In turn, this has undoubtedly encouraged the general public, the police, the courts, and various social service agencies to be more responsive and sensitive to the needs of such women. Yet, battered women may pay a high price for this assistance.

The experts on battered women define leaving one's mate as the normatively expected, reasonable response to the experience of wife assault. By implication, staying with one's mate after such an experience requires explanation. In order to explain this unreasonable response, the experts have provided accounts, that is, ascribed motives to battered women which excuse such deviance. As Blum and McHugh (1971:106) have noted, "observer's ascription of motive serves to formulate . . . persons." In offering accounts on behalf of battered women who stay, the experts propose a formulation of the type of persons such women are. For example, the experts characterize this type of person as "oversocialized into feminine identity" (Ball and Wyman, 1977–1978), "bewildered and helpless" (Ball, 1977), "immature" and lacking clear self-identities (Star et al., 1979), "overwhelmingly passive" and unable to act on their own behalf (Hilberman and Munson, 1977–1978), and cognitively, emotionally, and motivationally "deficient" (Walker, 1977–1978). Moreover, these women are described as suffering from either the "battered wife syndrome" (Morgan, 1982; Walker, 1983) or the "adult maltreatment syndrome" in Section 995.8 of the International Classification of Diseases. They are "society's problem" (Martin, 1978). Clearly, the categorical identity of battered women is a deeply discrediting one. As Hawkins and Tiedeman (1975) have noted, such typifications of persons by experts often have significant, practical consequences. The experts' descriptions of such "types" often serve as "processing stereotypes" which influence the perceptions and responses of social service providers. Indeed, Loseke (1982) documented how the experts' typifications of battered women served as a processing stereotype which influenced workers' perceptions and service provision at a shelter for battered women.

In summary, once a woman admits that she is a victim of wife assault, her competence is called into question if she does not leave. She is defined as a type of person who requires assistance, a person who is unable to manage her own affairs. As a result, the experts on battered women have constructed a situation where victims of wife assault may lose control over their self-definitions, interpretations of experience, and, in some cases, control over their private affairs. In a sense, battered women may now be victimized twice, first by their mates and then by the experts who claim to speak on their behalf.

Notes

1. Consistent with the literature under review, we use the terms *marriage* and *wife* in a purely sociological, rather than legal, sense. *Marriage* refers to any continuing, cross-sex relationship and *wife* to a female participant in such a relationship.
2. For a history of the feminist-identified battered women's movement see Schechter (1983).
3. Straus (1974) has argued that three social factors combined in the 1970s to bring the topic of family violence to the attention of academics: the emergence of a politically vocal women's movement, public concern about all forms of violence, and the decline of consensus models of society.
4. See Wardell et al. (1983) for a discussion of disagreements among those who state an allegiance to feminist ideals.
5. See Morgan (1981), Wardell et al. (1983), and Stark and Flitcraft (1983) for discussions of how experts have shaped public understandings of the phenomenon of wife assault.
6. There has been little systematic study of the possibility of change in relationships. Walker (1979) reports that her pessimism is based on clinical experience. See Coleman (1980) for a more optimistic prognosis.
7. Of course, this commonsense deduction is also based on the common, although often unspoken, assumption that humans are "rational actors." If the basis of human motivation is a desire to maximize rewards and minimize costs, then why would a battered woman remain in such an obviously "costly" relationship?
8. A third type of explanation for why victims of wife assault remain with their mates is seldom found in the literature on battered women and, therefore, will not be reviewed here. This type of explanation is based on a systems theory analysis of family interactions. Straus (1974) suggests the empirical applicability of such an approach, and Denzin (1983) provides a phenomenological foundation. Erchak (1981) used this approach to explain the maintenance of child abuse, and Giles-Sims (1983) has used this to explain the behavior of battered women.
9. Theories focusing on feminine masochism have been proposed by Snell et al. (1964) and Gayford (1975). Waites (1977–1978) suggested that the "appearance" of masochism results from "enforced restriction of choice." Most experts argue that the concept of masochism is not applicable to battered women (Breines and Gordon, 1983).
10. Empirical testing of the association between leaving and childhood experiences has not confirmed this theory (Pagelow, 1981a; Star, 1978; Walker, 1977–1978). Likewise, empirical testing of the association between leaving and "severity/frequency" has also not supported the theory. See Pagelow (1981b) for a complete discussion.
11. "Traditional ideology" includes such beliefs as: divorce is stigma (Dobash and Dobash, 1979; Langley and Levy, 1977; Moore, 1979; Roy, 1977); the children need their father (Dobash and Dorash, 1979); the woman assumes responsibility for the actions of her mate (Fleming 1979; Langley and Levy, 1977; Martin, 1976); or feels embarassed about the family situation (Ball and Wyman, 1977–1978; Fleming, 1979; Hendrix et al., 1978).
12. Exceptions are Gelles (1976), Hofeller (1982), and Rosenbaum and O'Leary (1981), who included matched samples of persons not receiving services, and Prescott and Letko (1977), who used information from women who responded to an advertisement in *Ms.* magazine.
13. The situation is more complicated when women who have left are asked why *did* you stay? Or, as Dobash and Dobash (1979:147) asked: "why do you think you stayed with him as long as you did?" In such situations, the question asks women to retrospectively reconstruct their personal biographies based on their current circumstances and understandings.
14. However, Rounsaville (1978) found that "lack of resources" did not distinguish between women who had left and women who had not left.

15. The "satisfaction" of victims with social services varies considerably by the type of agency (Hofeller, 1982; Prescott and Letko, 1977).

References

Ball, Margaret
    1977 "Issues of violence in family casework." *Social Casework* 58(1):3–12.
Ball, Patricia G., and Elizabeth Wyman
    1977–1978 "Battered wives and powerlessness: What can counselors do?" *Victimology* 2(3,4):545–552.
Barry, Kathleen
    1979 *Female Sexual Slavery*. New York: Avon.
Bass, David, and Janet Rice
    1979 "Agency responses to the abused wife." *Social Casework* 60 (June):338–342.
Berger, Brigitte, and Peter L. Berger
    1983 *The War over the Family*. New York: Anchor.
Blum, Alan F., and Peter McHugh
    1971 "The social ascription of motives." *American Sociological Review* 36 (February):98–109.
Breines, Wini, and Linda Gordon
    1983 "The new scholarship on family violence." *Signs* 8 (Spring):490–531.
Carlson, Bonnie E.
    1977 "Battered women and their assailants." *Social Work* 22 (November):455–460.
Cherlin, Andrew J.
    1981 *Marriage, Divorce, Remarriage*. Cambridge, MA: Harvard University Press.
Coleman, Karen Hooves
    1980 "Conjugal violence: What 33 men report." *Journal of Marital and Family Therapy* 6 (April):207–214.
Davidson Terry
    1978 *Conjugal Crime*. New York: Hawthorne.
Denzin, Norman K.
    1983 "Towards a phenomenology of family violence." Paper presented at the meetings of the American Sociological Association. Detroit, August.
Dobash, R. Emerson, and Russell Dobash
    1979 *Violence against Wives: A Case against the Patriarchy*. New York: Free Press.
Emerson, Robert M., and Sheldon L. Messinger
    1977 "The micro politics of trouble." *Social Problems* 25 (December):121–134.
Erchak, Gerald M.
    1981 "The escalation and maintenance of chid abuse: A cybernetic model." *Child Abuse and Neglect* 5:153–157.
Ferraro, Kathleen J., and John M. Johnson
    1983 "How women experience battering: The process of victimization." *Social Problems* 30 (February):325–339.
Fleming, Jennifer Baker
    1979 *Stopping Wife Abuse*. New York: Anchor Books.
Freeman, M. D. A.
    1979 *Violence in the Home*. Westmead, UK: Saxon House.
Garfinkel, Harold
    1967 *Studies in Ethnomethodology*. Englewood Cliffs, NJ: Prentice-Hall.
Gayford, J. J.
    1975 "Wife battering: A preliminary survey of 100 cases." *British Medical Journal* 1:194–197.

Gelles, Richard J.
   1976 "Abused wives: Why do they stay?" *Journal of Marriage and the Family* 38(4):659–668.
Giles-Sims, Jean
   1983 *Wife Battering: A Systems Approach*. New York: Guilford Press.
Goffman, Erving
   1952 "On cooling the mark out: Some aspects of adaptation to failure." *Psychiatry* 15 (November):451–463.
   1955 "On face-work: An analysis of ritual elements in social interaction." *Psychiatry* 18 (August):213–231.
   1969 "Insanity of place." *Psychiatry* 32 (November):352–388.
Goode, William J.
   1956 *After Divorce*. Glencoe, IL: Free Press.
Hawkins, Richard, and Gary Tiedeman
   1975 *The Creation of Deviance: Interpersonal and Organizational Determinants*. Columbus, OH: Charles E. Merrill.
Hendrix, Melva Jo, Gretchen E. LaGodna, and Cynthia A. Bohen
   1978 "The battered wife." *American Journal of Nursing* 78 (April):650–653.
Higgins, John G.
   1978 "Social services for abused wives." *Social Casework* 59 (May):266–271.
Hilberman, Elaine
   1980 "Overview: The 'Wife-beater's wife' reconsidered." *American Journal of Psychiatry* 137 (November):1336–1346.
Hilberman, Elaine, and Kit Munson
   1977–1978 "Sixty battered women." *Victimology* 2(3,4):460–470.
Hofeller, Kathleen H.
   1982 *Social, Psychological, and Situational Factors in Wife Abuse*. Palo Alto, CA: R. and E. Associates.
Hughes, Everett
   1945 "Dilemmas and contradictions of status." *American Journal of Sociology* 50 (March):353–359.
Jones, Ann
   1980 *Women Who Kill*. New York: Holt, Rinehart and Winston.
Kadushin, Charles
   1969 *Why People Go to Psychiatrists*. New York: Atherton.
Langley, Roger, and Richard C. Levy
   1977 *Wife Beating: The Silent Crisis*. New York: Pocket Books.
Lewis, Robert A., and Graham B. Spanier
   1979 "Theorizing about the quality and stability of marriage." Pp. 268–294 in Wesley R. Burr, Reuben Hill, F. Ivan Nye, and Ira L. Reiss (eds.), *Contemporary Theories about the Family*, Volume 1. New York: Free Press.
Lieberknecht, Kay
   1978 "Helping the battered wife." *American Journal of Nursing* 78 (April):654–656.
Lion, John R.
   1977 "Clinical aspects of wifebattering," Pp. 126–136 in Maria Roy (ed.), *Battered Women: A Psychosociological Study of Domestic Violence*. New York: Van Nostrand.
Loseke, Donileen R.
   1982 "Social movement theory in practice: A shelter for battered women." Unpublished Ph.D. dissertation, University of California, Santa Barbara.
Maccoby, Eleanor Emmons, and Carol Nagy Jacklin
   1974 *The Psychology of Sex Differences*. Stanford, CA: Stanford University Press.
Martin, Del
   1976 *Battered Wives*. San Francisco: Glide Publications.
   1978 "Battered women: Society's problem." Pp. 111–142 in Jane Roberts Chapman and Margaret Gates (eds.), *The Victimization of Women*. Beverly Hills, CA: Sage.

1979 "What keeps a woman captive in a violent relationship? The social context of battering." Pp. 33–58 in Donna M. Moore (ed.), *Battered Women*. Beverly Hills, CA: Sage.

McLain, Raymond, and Andrew Weigert
1979 "Toward a phenomenological sociology of family: A programmatic essay." Pp. 160–205 in Wesley R. Burr, Reuben Hill, F. Ivan Nye, and Ira L. Reins (eds.), *Contemporary Theories about the Family*, Volume 2. New York: Free Press.

McShane, Claudette
1979 "Community services for battered women." *Social Work* 24 (January):34–39.

Mechanic, David
1975 "Sociocultural and social-psychological factors affecting personal responses to psychological disorder." *Journal of Health and Social Behavior* 16(4):393–404.

Melville, Joy
1978 "Women in refuges." Pp. 293–310 in J. P. Martin (ed.), *Violence and the Family*. New York: John Wiley.

Mills, C. Wright
1940 "Situated actions and vocabularies of motive." *American Sociological Review* 5 (December):904–913.

Moore, Donna M.
1979 "An overview of the problem." Pp. 7–32 in Donna M. Moore (ed.), *Battered Women*. Beverly Hills, CA: Sage.

Morgan, Patricia A.
1981 "From battered wife to program client; The state's shaping of social problems." *Kapitalistate* 9:17–40.

Morgan, Steven M.
1982 *Conjugal Terrorism: A Psychological and Community Treatment Model of Wife Abuse*. Palo Alto, CA: R. and E. Associations.

Ochberg, F. M.
1980 "Victims of terrorism." *Journal of Clinical Psychiatry* 41:73–74.

Pagelow, Mildred Daley
1981a *Woman-Battering: Victims and Their Experiences*. Beverly Hills, CA: Sage.
1981b "Factors affecting women's decisions to leave violent relationships." *Journal of Family Issues* 2 (December):391–414.

Pizzey, Erin
1979 "Victimology interview: A refuge for battered women." *Victimology* 4(1):100–112.

Prescott, Suzanne, and Carolyn Letko
1977 "Battered women: A social psychological perspective." Pp. 72–96 in Maria Roy (ed.), *Battered Women: A Psychosociological Study of Domestic Violence*. New York: Van Nostrand.

Ridington, Jillian
1977–1978 "The transition process: A feminist environment as reconstructive milieu." *Victimology* 2(3,4):563–575.

Rosenbaum, Alan, and K. Daniel O'Leary
1981 "Marital violence: Characteristics of abusive couples." *Journal of Consulting and Clinical Psychology* 49(1):63–71.

Rosenblatt, Paul C.
1977 "Needed research on commitment in marriage." Pp. 73–86 in George Levinger and Harold L. Raush (eds.), *Close Relationships: Perspectives on the Meaning of Intimacy*. Amherst: University of Massachusetts.

Rounsaville, Bruce J.
1978 "Theories in marital violence: Evidence from a study of battered women." *Victimology* 2(1,2): 11–31.

Rounsaville, Bruce, and Myrna M. Weissman
1977–1978 "Battered women: A medical problem requiring detection." *International Journal of Psychiatry in Medicine* 8(2):191–202.

Roy, Maria
 1977 "A current survey of 150 cases." Pp. 25–44 in Maria Roy (ed.), *Battered Women: A Psychosociological Study of Domestic Violence*. New York: Van Nostrand.
Schechter, Susan
 1983 *Women and Male Violence*. Boston: South End Press.
Schwartz, Charlotte Green
 1957 "Perspectives on deviance: Wives' definitions of their husbands' mental illness." *Psychiatry* 20(3):275–291.
Scott, Marvin B., and Stanford M. Lyman
 1968 "Accounts." *American Sociological Review* 33 (Decerber):46–62.
Scott, P. D.
 1974 "Battered wives." *British Journal of Psychiatry* 125 (November):433–441.
Segovia-Ashley, Marta
 1978 "Presentation of Maria Segovia-Ashley." Pp. 98–107 in U.S. Commission on Civil Rights (ed.), *Battered Women: Issues of Public Policy*. Washington, DC: U.S. Commission on Civil Rights.
Shainess, Natalie
 1977 "Psychological aspects of wifebattering." Pp. 111–118 in Maria Roy (ed.), *Battered Women: A Psychosociological Study of Domestic Violence*. New York: Van Nostrand.
Snell, John E., M. D. Richard, J. Rosenwald, and Ames Robey
 1964 "The wifebeater's wife." *Archives of General Psychiatry* 11 (August):107–112.
Spanier, Graham, and Robert F. Castro
 1979 "Adjustment to separation and divorce: An analysis of 50 case studies." *Journal of Divorce* 2 (Spring):241–253.
Star, Barbara
 1978 "Comparing battered and non-battered women." *Victimology* 3(1,2):32–44.
Star, Barbara, Carol G. Clark, Karen M. Goetz, and Linda O'Malia
 1979 "Psychosocial aspects of wife battering." *Social Casework* 60 (October):479–487.
Stark, Evan, and Anne Flitcraft
 1983 "Social knowledge, social policy, and the abuse of women: The case against patriarchal benevolence." Pp. 330–348 in David Finkelhor, Richard J. Gelles, Gerald T. Hotaling, and Murray A. Straus (eds.), *The Dark Side of Families*. Beverly Hills, CA: Sage.
Straus, Murray A.
 1974 "Forward." Pp. 13–17 in Richard J. Gelles, *The Violent Home*. Beverly Hills, CA: Sage.
Straus, Murray A., Richard J. Gelles, and Suzanne Steinmetz
 1980 *Behind Closed Doors: Violence in the American Home*. New York: Anchor.
Sykes, Gresham, and David Matza
 1957 "Techniques of neutralization: A theory of delinquency." *American Sociological Review* 22 (December):664–669.
Truninger, Elizabeth
 1971 "Marital violence: The legal solutions." *Hastings Law Journal* 23 (November):259–276.
Turner, Ralph
 1970 *Family Interaction*. New York: John Wiley.
U.S. Commission on Civil Rights (ed.)
 1978 *Battered Women: Issues of Public Policy*. Washington, DC: U.S. Commission on Civil Rights.
U.S. Congress: House of Representatives
 1978 Research into Violent Behavior: Domestic Violence. Hearings before the Sub-Committee on Domestic and International Scientific Planning, Analysis and Cooperation of the Committee on Science and Technology. 95th Congress, 2nd Session. January 10–12. Washington, DC: U.S. Government Printing Office.
U.S. Department of Justice
 1980 *Intimate Victims: A Study of Violence among Friends and Relatives*. Washington, DC: U.S. Government Printing Office.

Vaughan, Diane
   1979 "Uncoupling: The process of moving from one lifestyle to another." *Alternative Lifestyles* 2 (November):415–442.

Waites, Elizabeth A.
   1977–1978 "Female masochism and the enforced restriction of choice." *Victimology* 2(3,4):535–544.

Walker, Lenore E.
   1977–1978 "Battered women and learned helplessness." *Victimology* 2(3,4):525–534.
   1979 *The Battered Woman*. New York: Harper and Row.
   1983 "The battered woman syndrome study." Pp. 31–48 in David Finkelhor, Richard J. Gelles, Gerald T. Hotaling, and Murray A. Straus (eds.), *The Dark Side of Families*. Beverly Hills, CA: Sage.

Wardell, Laurie, Dair L. Gillespie, and Ann Leffler
   1983 "Science and violence against wives," Pp. 69–84 in David Finkelhor, Richard J. Gelles, Gerald T. Hotaling, and Murray A. Straus (eds.), *The Dark Side of Families*. Beverly Hills, CA: Sage.

Warrior, Betsy
   1978 *Working on Wife Abuse*. 46 Pleasant Street, Cambridge, MA: privately published manual.

Weiss, Robert
   1975 *Marital Separation*. New York: Basic Books.

Yarrow, Marian Radke, Charlotte Green Schwartz, Harriet S. Murphy, and Leila Calhoun Desy
   1955 "The psychological meaning of mental illness in the family." *Journal of Social Issues* 11(4):12–24.

Zimmerman, Don, and Melvin Pollner
   1970 "The everyday world as a phenomenon." Pp. 80–104 in Jack Douglas (ed.), *Understanding Everyday Life*. Chicago: Aldine.

Part III

FEMINIST ACTIVISM AND SOCIAL CHANGE

CHAPTER 11

The Battered Woman Movement and the Creation of the Wife Beating Problem

Kathleen J. Tierney

Wife beating has received increasing attention in recent years, not because it has become more widespread, or because the public has become more concerned, but because social movement organizations (SMOs) have effectively mobilized resources to aid battered women. This chapter discusses the background of the social movement to combat wife beating and examines factors responsible for its growth and impact. The emergence and development of the movement illustrates how professional social movements mobilize resources from outside sources such as government agencies (McCarthy and Zald, 1973) and, in effect, "produce" a social problem.

History of the Movement against Wife Beating

Chiswick Women's Aid, the first widely publicized shelter for battered women, was established in London, England, in 1971. One of its founders, Erin Pizzey, furthered awareness of the problem through speaking tours and a book entitled *Scream Quietly or the Neighbors Will Hear* (1974). By 1980 there were approximately 150 shelters in England sponsored by the National Women's Aid Federation, serving mainly poor and working-class women and their children (Johnson, 1981). Due to agitation by Pizzey, other activists, and sympathetic politicians, two British parliamentary committees investigated wife beating, and a law giving broader protection to battered women was passed in 1976.

In the United States, the organized response to the problem of wife beating has focused on the provision of shelter and crisis services. Several early programs became prototypes for later efforts. Rainbow Retreat, opened in Phoenix, Arizona, in 1973, is believed to be the first U.S. shelter for battered women. Haven House in Pasadena, California, began sheltering battered women in 1974. Originally restricted to helping women beaten by alcoholic husbands, these two pioneer shelters have since opened their doors to battered women in general. Two other early shelters, La Casa de las Madres in San Francisco and Transition House in Cambridge, Massachusetts, were models of feminist, grass-roots shelters.

Other movement groups have become influential beyond their local communities. In 1972, Women's Advocates, Inc. established a hotline in St. Paul, Minnesota, to provide telephone crisis counselling to battered women; group members later informally sheltered victims in their own homes. In 1975, Maria Roy, a social worker, began a Hotline in New York City called Abused Women's Aid in Crisis (AWAIC). This group opened a shelter in Manhattan in 1976. Roy herself helped launch other New York groups working on behalf of battered women and later edited a book on the subject (1977). The Wife Assault Task Force, begun in 1975 by the Ann Arbor, Michigan, chapter of the National Organization for Women (NOW), sponsors a local shelter and has produced manuals for groups interested in setting up shelters or providing counselling for battered women (Fojtik, 1976; Resnick, 1976).

Feminist organizations began emphasizing the wife beating problem in the mid-1970s. NOW formed a National Task Force on Battered Women/Household Violence at its eighth annual conference in October 1975, to raise public consciousness and promote shelters. Del Martin, a coordinator of this task force, wrote an influential book called *Battered Wives* (1977). Late in 1977, the National Women's Year Conference in Houston passed a resolution urging action on the local, state, and federal levels to establish programs for battered women. Efforts quickly gained momentum. New York City NOW chapters formed their own task force in early 1976, as did other local chapters, and many shelters and crisis services were started in communities around the country in the next few years. Most began as community-based groups of concerned individuals; members were almost exclusively women and frequently persons familiar with wife beating through their professions.

Estimates of the number of groups currently serving battered women in the United States vary, but by all accounts, assistance for battered women has improved dramatically since 1975. *Ms.* (1976) listed 20 sources of assistance; Davidson (1978) listed 65 shelters in 26 states and the District of Columbia; the U.S. Commission on Civil Rights (1978) named over 300 shelters, hotlines, and groups acting as advocates for battered women with the police, the courts, and housing and public assistance agencies. *U.S. News and World Report* (1979) reported that more than 170 shelters opened in the United States between 1975 and 1978.

The movement against wife beating includes a variety of organizations with different ideological orientations and complex patterns of support. While some groups are primarily feminist, many characterize themselves as mental health or social service organizations. Funding sources for anti-wife beating groups include churches and traditional women's service organizations such as the YWCA; federal agencies, especially the Law Enforcement Assistance Administration (LEAA) and the Department of Labor, through Comprehensive Employment Training Act (CETA) programs; state and city governments; private foundations; local voluntary fund-raising campaigns such as the United Way; and individual fund-raising projects. Many shelters, hotlines, and related services use volunteers. However, activists also favor the use of paid staffs, because of the continuous demand for crisis assistance and security. Staff salaries and housing expenses make sheltering costly and necessitate a constant focus on fund-raising.

Programs for battered women are becoming increasingly distinct from other support services. Whereas battered women services in the past may have been provided by suicide or mental health crisis hotlines, rape crisis centers, organizations aiding families of alcoholics, or homes for transients, now independently operated battered women's organizations are the norm. The increased recognition of wife beating as a social problem and the involvement of professionals in the provision of services are two major factors in this trend.

Since 1975, the movement has made substantial headway in three areas, besides emergency shelter: legislation, government policy and programs, and research and public information.

LEGISLATION

Students of the U.S. justice system note that criminal charges by wives against husbands, while possible in theory, have been practically impossible to pursue in all but the most brutal and flagrant cases. Civil remedies such as protective orders and restraining orders have also proved ineffective as sanctions against wife beating.[1] The movement has encouraged legislation to broaden protection for battered women by increasing the criminal penalties for battering, strengthening civil protections, and making it easier for women to file charges against their assailants. By 1979, more than a dozen states had passed such laws; by 1980, 45 states and the District of Columbia had made special legal provisions for cases of wife beating (Kalmuss and Straus, 1981). Although law enforcement agencies, prosecutors, and the courts may still be reluctant to intervene in wife beating cases, these laws make it more difficult to ignore wife beating, clarify the legal rights of victims, and raise the costs of wife beating for assailants who are charged. Ohio, Florida, Montana, California, and Pennsylvania have also imposed special surcharges on marriage licenses to raise funds for shelters.

Efforts to pass federal laws have not been as successful. Two domestic violence bills were sponsored in Congress in 1977; neither became law. In 1978, the Domestic Violence Assistance Act was defeated. In 1980, the Domestic Violence Prevention and Services Act was withdrawn when its supporters realized they did not have the votes to overcome a Senate filibuster.

GOVERNMENT POLICY AND PROGRAMS

U.S. government agencies have either established new programs for battered women or extended existing programs to better address the problem. The LEAA put several million dollars into combatting family violence in the last half of the 1970s. Early LEAA assistance was channelled through Victim Witness Assistance Programs and dispute-settlement programs such as the Neighborhood Justice Programs (McGillis and Mullen, 1977; Viano, 1979). In 1979, however, LEAA tripled its allocation to $1 million a year, specifically for domestic violence programs, and agency officials publicly decried the growing incidence of wife beating (*New York Times*, 1977). The Special Programs Division of LEAA funded 14 family violence projects in 1978 and 17 in 1979; the majority were for battered women.

Other government agencies began supporting battered women groups at about the same time. In May 1978, the Department of Labor instructed regional administrators to direct local governments to fund programs for battered women under Titles I, II, and VI of the Comprehensive Employment Training Act (U.S. Commission on Civil Rights, 1978). Subsequently, CETA helped staff many shelters. Starting in 1977, ACTION, the federal volunteer agency, provided for staff support through the VISTA program and made funds available through its mini-grant program. ACTION also funded technical assistance centers in each of the 10 Department of Health and Human Services (then Health, Education, and Welfare) districts; centers distributed information on how to assist battered women. Federal "Title XX" funds (Public Law 93–647), given to states for social services, are frequently used for "protective services," to prevent abuse and neglect of children and adults. Shelters and services for battered women receive "Title XX" funds (U.S. Commission on Civil Rights, 1978; Johnson, 1981), largely because local anti-wife beating groups pressured social service administrators to view battered wives as prime candidates for protective services. Other federal agencies and programs funding services for battered women include the Community Services Administration and the Office on Domestic Violence, created by the Department of Health and Human Services in 1979.

RESEARCH AND INFORMATION

Sources of information on the causes of wife beating and how to combat it have proliferated. The National Institute of Mental Health began funding research into family violence in the early 1970s.[2] The Office on Domestic Violence also funds research projects and publishes a monograph series on how to set up programs and lobby for battered women (National Clearinghouse on Domestic Violence, 1980). The U.S. Commission on Civil Rights (1978) held a national conference on policy issues regarding wife beating in January 1978. The National Coalition Against Domestic Violence was one product of the conference. The Center for Women Policy Studies in Washington, D.C., has, since 1976, published a monthly newsletter on domestic violence programs and policy called *Response*, with funds from LEAA. In the same year, the Washington-based Feminist Alliance Against Rape began publishing a magazine on violence against women; called *Aegis*, the magazine frequently features articles on wife beating. These national activities and information sources are complemented by numerous local programs in communities throughout the United States.

Factors Affecting the Growth and Impact of the Movement

In less than ten years, wife beating has been transformed from a subject of private shame and misery to an object of public concern. The movement that has been instrumental in this transformation provides an example of how social movements can construct social problems and successfully mobilize resources.

How long-standing injustices are brought to the attention of the public and its leaders through the efforts of interest groups, pressure groups, and social movements has become an increasingly important area of sociological research. Recent literature[3] suggests that the public definition of a social problem and the official solutions proposed are products of interaction and negotiation among established and emergent groups, organizations, and interests—all of whom may define the problem and solutions differently. In contrast, both common sense and older sociological views see an increase in social concern with an issue as the result of an increase in the problem or rising demands for solutions.

A complementary body of work stresses organizational characteristics and resource mobilization as important factors in the careers of social movements. Unlike classical treatments of social movements that emphasize social disorganization, social change, and the development of grievances, this perspective focuses on social solidarity and preexisting structural arrangements as conditions for the development of movements (Oberschall, 1973, 1978; Tilly et al., 1975). The resource mobilization approach views the proliferation of social movements in the United States as one outgrowth of an affluent way of life, in which an increase in discretionary income and discretionary time can be used to support movements. The trend toward professional organization and outside support for movements is another important theme in this literature. Professional movements are characterized by: (1) full-time leaders and the chance for careers in movement work; (2) separation between supporters (those providing funds and resources) and beneficiaries; and (3) patterns of support from established sectors in society, such as foundations, government, and the media (McCarthy and Zald, 1973). McCarthy and Zald (1973:20) argue that: "The professional social movement is the common form of recent movements and presents a sharp departure from the classical model." The resource mobilization perspective suggests that groups working on issues congruent with the priorities of established institutions are likely to obtain support from outside sources.

Neither classical grievance theories of social movements nor what Chauncey (1980) terms "objectivist" views of social problems explain why wife beating emerged as a social problem in the 1970s, or why activists have gained so much support. Contrary to the assumption that social concern precedes the development of a movement (Blumer, 1951; Morrison, 1971), the battered women movement did not ride a wave of public sentiment demanding solutions to the problem. The public has shown indifference—even tolerance—toward this form of violence. Before the mid-1970s, major social institutions, community organizations, and the media were silent on the problem. The movement could not use data from research on the incidence, causes, and consequences of wife beating to support its claims, because such information was not available when the movement began. Sociologists acknowledge their own lack of attention to violence in the family; until recently, overt physical conflict among family members was viewed as rare or deviant (O'Brien, 1971; Steinmetz and Straus, 1974). The occasional sociological discussion of husband-wife violence gave the impression that it is confined to the working class (Komarovsky, 1964). Sociologists have recently begun to contend that wife beating is not only approved by our culture (Gelles, 1974; Straus, 1974, 1977) but also common at all levels of society (Straus, Gelles, and Steinmetz, 1980).[4]

As an alternative to a grievance-based approach, the development of the movement can be studied by looking at the structure and strategies of groups working against wife beating and at how resources were mobilized. The movement's growth and the "production" of the wife beating problem can be attributed to three factors: the preexisting organizational base for the movement, the movement's flexibility, and the incentives for sponsors to provide resources.

THE PREEXISTING ORGANIZATIONAL BASE

The battered women movement was built on the structural foundations of preexisting organizations of feminists and groups in the social work, mental health, and legal professions. Groups in both the "older" and the "younger" branches of the feminist movement (Freeman, 1975) became involved in the battered women movement: the former through NOW and other reform organizations, and the latter through grass-roots, antihierarchical battered women refuges that stressed peer support, self-help, and opposition to patriarchy. Preexisting social networks aided the movement in several ways. First, they provided common frames of reference and rationales for participation in the new movement.[5] Second, they provided co-optable networks (Freeman, 1975)— ongoing chains of interaction among persons likely to adopt and promote the idea of a movement to aid battered women. Preexisting networks facilitate the growth of a movement because time, effort, and momentum do not have to be invested building consensus and establishing links among potentially interested parties. Third, the networks provided experienced people to act as movement leaders. While not full-time activists, many women involved in organizing the battered women movement had considerable previous experience working on other women's issues. Many were professionals with experience working in organizations and developing social programs. As in other professional social movements (McCarthy and Zald, 1973), women from the social work and mental health fields often worked for the movement as part of their own professional activities. This occurred at both the national level and in local communities, where professionals played a large role in mobilizing resources for the movement (Tierney, 1979).[6]

MOVEMENT FLEXIBILITY

The battered women movement is flexible in both its structure and its goals. The movement has the type of structure Gerlach and Hine (1970) characterize as segmentary, polycephalous, and reticulate. Movement organizations range from those with a national scope, to local organizations with influence at the state, regional, and national level, to those that operate mainly on the local level. Groups are linked to each other, to feminist organizations, and to established organizations through overlapping memberships, professional ties, and lines of sponsorship. There is no central umbrella organization that decides priorities, strategies, or tactics for the movement. While this form of organization may at first seem to be a handicap, it is in fact an advantage, because a decentralized, loosely articulated structure enables a movement to adapt to local conditions and effectively mobilize resources (Gerlach and Hine, 1970; Judkins, 1979). In part because of its varied ideological base, the movement's goals have been flexible. It has pursued a number of different strategies, including efforts to make the laws, the police, and the courts more responsive to victims; counselling aimed at equalizing power in the violent relationship; and perhaps most widespread, providing crisis shelter and support services for battered women and their children.

The sheer number of battered women needing help, and the nature of their problems, are other reasons the movement has remained flexible. Because so many battered women sought help when the movement first emerged, the scope of the problem became apparent, enabling the movement to approach many different organizations for support. Furthermore, the broad range of problems encountered by victims—including legal, financial, and health concerns—has provided a rationale for almost any potential provider of resources to "invest" in the problem. The ability to contact a variety of potential sponsors is crucial to the success of a movement, because the number and strength of its ties with outside organizations enhances its potential to mobilize resources and thus its power (Aveni, 1978).

INCENTIVES FOR SPONSORS

The battered women movement cannot rely on help from the victims it aids. Beaten women, whether at home or on the run, need much and can give little. An essential task in soliciting resources has been stimulating interest in the problem and providing mutually beneficial exchanges between battered women's groups and their sponsors. The mass media have played a crucial role in promoting this co-operation.

The Role of the Media

The media paid little attention to the wife beating problem until the latter half of the 1970s. The *New York Times* is a case in point. I searched the *New York Times Index* for references to wife beating between 1970 and 1978. I checked the following subject headings for references to the problem: assaults, battered wives, divorce, domestic relations, families and family life, marriages, violence, and women. There was not a single reference to wife beating as a social or community issue from 1970 to 1972. The only references to violence against wives occurred in news reports of assaults and murders in which the victim was incidentally identified as married to or living with her assailant. In 1973, a Federal Bureau of Investigation statistic linking police fatalities to domestic disturbance calls was reported. In 1974, again only one article appeared; it noted that New York City police and courts discourage battered women from pressing charges. In 1975, five relevant articles appeared: three dealt with the lack of police and legal co-operation in wife beating cases, one reported on a conference on battered women, and another described a NOW march protesting violence against women.

More intense coverage of the problem by the *New York Times* began in 1976. Seven articles appeared that year, and for the first time the newspaper began discussing innovative approaches to combatting wife beating, including shelters. Late in 1976, the newspaper began extensive coverage of a class-action suit filed by the Litigation Coalition for Battered Women against New York City's police department and family court, charging them with failing to provide protection for abuse victims (*Bruno v. Codd*, 1977). In 1977, 44 references to the battered women problem appeared in the *New York Times*. The articles discussed such topics as: hotlines to provide services to victims; new and proposed legislation; newly opened shelters; public hearings and conferences; and the trials of battered women who killed their assailants. Nineteen references appeared in 1978. For the first time, "Battered Wives" began appearing as a separate topic in the index, evidence that the *New York Times* had come to view previously disparate facts about wife beating as elements in a common theme.[7]

Similar trends can be seen in popular magazine coverage of wife beating. Until the mid-1970s, "domestic violence" meant riots and terrorism, so far as U.S. mass circulation periodicals were concerned. Davidson (1978), a journalist who writes on wife beating, was unable to interest popular magazines in stories about battered women before movement activity highlighted the problem. Sketchy coverage began in 1973, when *Newsweek* ran one story on Chiswick Women's Aid and *Society* devoted some space to the problem. *Ms.* ran an article on the London shelter in June 1974, the same month *Ladies Home Journal* ran a story on wife beating. By 1978, articles had appeared in numerous publications, including *Science Digest, Good Housekeeping, America, Vogue, Mademoiselle*, and the major U.S. news magazines.

CBS television aired a series on wife beating on its morning news in 1975. NBC's "Weekend" ran a segment on the problem in the spring of 1976. Perhaps due to extensive news coverage of legal cases involving wives who killed their husband-assailants, several television dramas on the subject appeared in 1977 and 1978. Network news stories and dramas led to expanded television coverage in many cities, as local news team supplemented the network perspective by providing information on local efforts to stop wife beating.

According to Downs (1972), the public's belief that a domestic crisis or social problem exists is not the result of a change in "real" conditions in society, but reflects a cycle of increasing interest in the problem. Wife beating possesses all the attributes Downs claims are necessary for this "issue attention cycle": (1) It is not a problem that directly affects the majority in society. (2) The same social arrangements that oppress its victims also benefit powerful interests in society (i.e., those social arrangements and aspects of culture based on the continuing subjugation of women). (3) The public might ignore the problem in the absence of dramatic media treatment. Media interest was crucial to the growth of the battered women movement, because issues that pass through the issue attention cycle typically obtain more resources than those that do not.

Wife beating was a good subject for the media. It was a "new" problem for the public, although certainly not for its victims. It was controversial. It mixed elements of violence and social relevance. It provided a focal point for serious media discussion of such issues as feminism, inequality, and family life in the United States—without requiring a sacrifice of the entertainment value, action, and urgency on which the media typically depend.

Media attention was, in turn, an asset to the movement. Coverage first gave the movement visibility. Then, groups used media interest and the public concern that resulted to recruit support. Finally, wife beating came to be seen as a social problem: authorities began to recognize and respond to the conditions the media described (Fishman, 1978), and established organizations began to perceive new needs and potential constituencies. Movement pressure, combined with media attention, created a climate in which organizations already inclined to offer support to battered women could do so—and obtain benefits in return.[8]

Incentives to Sponsors

Incentives to support the new movement were subtle and diverse. Some sponsors probably believed that they could change or increase their own clientele by supporting anti-battering groups (Levine and White, 1961). Battered women and their children—the "clients" of the movement—were evidently attractive to those sponsors interested in supporting moderate (as opposed to "radical") feminist programs and to organizations that typically worked with more stigmatized clients. A representative of a mental health organization explained the agency's decision to fund a shelter for battered women, rather than other programs, in terms of the sponsorship's benefit to the funding agency:

> The shelter gives us publicity. . . . It is the kind of program that captures the imagination of the community, based on honest-to-God, real need. It's a little harder when the client you're dealing with has been in the state hospital for twenty years, is bizarre in appearance and dress, trying to find a place to live in the community. Because of the kind of visibility and acceptability the shelter gives us, we can in turn pay off for those clients who are not as acceptable. So there is mutual payoff. . . . It helps if mental health clients are seen as people who look all right, who might have the same problem. (Personal interview)

The positive, progressive image some sponsors could gain through supporting battered women groups—and by extension, victimized women—was one reason they invested in the movement.

The hypothesis that sponsors anticipated gains when they gave resources to the movement is supported by evidence that some sponsors volunteered support for anti-wife beating programs. One group applied for a CETA grant, only to be told by a CETA official to increase its request. It did so, got what it asked for, and received even more funding the following year (Tierney, 1979). In another case, the Community Services Administration, a federal agency, asked a coalition of anti-wife beating groups in Massachusetts to submit a proposal for $100,000. Assured of funding, the coalition applied for and received the grant in 1978. Objecting to some of the agency's policies, the coalition later tried to give back the funds, but the agency made policy exceptions for the group rather than take the money back (Andler and Sullivan, 1980).

Some government agencies became involved with sponsorship to encourage or discourage particular forms of response to the problem. For example, the Neighborhood Justice Programs, forerunners of later LEAA programs in the family violence area, were designed to reduce the number of cases in the criminal justice system and to cut case-processing costs. The LEAA's battered women programs perform the same function: rather than ending up in court, cases of wife beating are "referred" to shelters and other programs (Johnson, 1981; Morgan, 1981). Unlike many groups in the battered women movement, LEAA did not take the position that law enforcement agencies or the courts should provide remedies for battering. An LEAA official stated that this is a job for the whole community:

> the approach recommended is called "comprehensive" because it foresees the need for interaction with local service agencies and community-based groups. By concentrating its resources on the role of the justice system, *LEAA does not imply that the part which criminal justice agencies play in the resolution of family violence should be enlarged.* (Niedermeyer, 1978:178; emphasis added)

Another LEAA official stated that the criminal justice system cannot respond to the wife beating problem:

> Advocates for battered women will have to understand that the criminal justice system has nothing inherent in its structure or function that would lead it to make battered women cases a priority. . . . Advocates will have to understand the dynamics of social action and political pressure that lead the criminal justice system to allocate resources to certain areas not because such allocation is good or wise but because, somehow, it becomes expeditious or necessary. (Schudson, 1978:369–370)

LEAA sponsored movement activities to insure that their work was not disrupted by demands generated by the movement and to structure the organized response to the problem in ways that were in line with their own interests.

Direct government involvement in the formulation of the wife beating problem, while significant, was not as great as in cases such as the War on Poverty programs of the mid-1960s (Ferrari, 1975). Although there have been no comprehensive studies of decision-making by government sponsors, movement activists believe that support from the social welfare sector for the battered women movement stems from moral entrepreneurship, an interest in capitalizing on feminist issues, and the more general goal of maintaining the family unit (Klein, 1979; Martin, 1977; Warrior, 1978). Johnson (1981) describes sponsor involvement in the movement as a type of "professional enterprise" that enables sponsors to move into new domains as "old" social problems decline.

As Freeman's (1975) account of the policy impact of the women's liberation movement suggests, collaboration between movements and established organizations is an exchange relationship. Government agencies benefit from co-operating with SMOs. Movement pressure supports claims by sympathetic parties within agencies that a particular problem should be addressed. Movement groups provide valuable information to interest government and legislative personnel on the nature and scope of a problem that is gaining media attention. Working with SMOs can both promote sponsor interests and be a source of publicity and legitimacy for sponsors seeking to show concern for emerging issues.

Conclusions and Implications

Judged by common sense and some sociological criteria, the battered women movement has not been successful.[9] It has neither eliminated wife beating, nor brought about a full-scale institutional response to the problem. Large numbers of victims still await help; others, like many members of the public, are still not aware of the movement's work.

Nevertheless, the movement has achieved several important goals in a relatively short time. The plight of beaten women, once socially invisible, is now the subject of public discussion. For the first time, battered women have been singled out as a special population that needs a range of services. Funds and other material resources have been obtained by anti-wife beating groups. Government agencies and task forces have been established, new laws have been passed, and community organizations are making explicit efforts to aid battered women.

This chapter has emphasized mutually beneficial exchanges between movement groups and sponsors as the key to successful resource mobilization by SMOs. The mass media have played an important role in this process in the battered women movement, by giving visibility to movement groups and broadening public awareness of wife beating. Preexisting organizational ties and structural and ideological flexibility also helped the movement mobilize resources. Control of resources is a source of power, and the movement used its influence not only to aid victims, but also to lobby for legislative and policy changes designed to reduce the future incidence of wife beating.

As movements grow, they are often co-opted by official organizations; this pattern is characteristic of both social problem movements (Mauss, 1975) and professional movements that lack a broad membership base (McCarthy and Zald, 1973). While it is too early to accurately forecast the consequences of co-optation for the battered women movement, I foresee two trends:

First, the trend toward conventional, social service-oriented programs that is already evident will continue, and the emphasis on feminist concerns will decline. Influential sponsors, including federal law enforcement and social welfare agencies, have directed the movement away from "radical" programs that challenge society's patriarchical values and advocate large-scale social change. The fact that much of the movement's support comes from the social welfare sector explains, in part, why obtaining services for battered women is increasingly taking precedence over other objectives. Parallels can be seen in the official response to child abuse: medicine and the helping professions took the lead in defining the problem and providing solutions (Pfohl, 1977). Similarly, the wife beating problem will likely become increasingly "medicalized," professionalized, individualized, and de-politicized (Conrad, 1975; Conrad and Schneider, 1980). Programs for battered women are already beginning to identify tensions in the marriage relationship, rather than patriarchical values or social inequality, as the source of wife beating; to give "therapy," often to the woman alone, since she is the "client" of the program; and to emphasize the maintenance of the marriage as a therapeutic goal (Johnson, 1981). The nature of the relationship between program personnel and the victims of battering may also be changing: the latter are increasingly defined as "clients" of anti-wife beating "agencies."[10] Both the trend toward medicalization (Pastor, 1980) and sponsorship of battered women programs by the criminal justice sector may divert wife beating cases from the courts. Thus, despite new laws to protect battered women from husbands and live-in companions, there may be fewer arrests and convictions as law enforcement agencies exercise the option of referring victims (or assailants) to domestic violence programs. Whether this is in the best interests of the victim is an open question. Battered women are typically the weaker, less advantaged parties in domestic conflict; as such, I believe they would benefit from stronger controls on assailants. It seems doubtful that substituting counselling programs for legal sanctions will help battered women.

Second, outside support should change the character of the battered women movement itself. Groups with goals, ideologies, and modes of functioning that are compatible with those of the broadest range of potential supporters will gain resources. Conventional, social service-oriented organizations staffed by professionals, with relatively limited goals, will ultimately come to speak for the movement. My comparative study (1979) of several battered women SMOs suggests that sponsors favor groups that operate like social service agencies and that avoid projecting a militant image. Grass-roots feminist groups acknowledge that sponsor preferences are affecting the balance of resources in the movement, as well as their own ways of functioning:

> Perhaps the greatest issue facing our movement is cooptation. We recognize the need to rely on traditional institutions to keep our shelters operating. However, these institutions have political structures and goals that are antithetical to ours. . . . These agencies do not understand the social or political context of battering. . . . They are run with hierarchical structures whose purpose is to maintain themselves, not to provide any real services or social change.
> As they make money available to battered women's groups, they are more likely to fund organizations that share their politics and bureaucratic systems. This will mean that research, academic and traditional social service groups will be more likely to get the money rather than feminist organizations operating with a grass roots orientation. They will also try to turn us into more traditional models structurally and politically, and in terms of the goals of our services. . . .
> As we accept money from these sources, we will also be subject to their requirements, many of which are contrary to our own goals. (Andler and Sullivan, 1980:14–15)

Together, these two trends suggest that future organized efforts to control wife beating will be moderate, reformist, and cast in the traditional social service mold.[11] Radical feminism, self-help, self-defense, and similar principles will become less visible themes of the movement. Ultimately, because the growth of the battered women movement has depended on media attention and the resulting support by outside organizations that prize novelty and innovation in the programs they support, movement groups can expect a gradual erosion of resources as the interest of the media, politicians, and professionals inevitably wanes.

Notes

This chapter was prepared with the help of a post-doctoral traineeship from the National Institute of Mental Health (USPHS Grant MH 14583). The author thanks John M. Johnson, Tahi Mottl, Mildred Daley Pagelow, and E. L. Quarantelli for their comments.

1. See Field and Field (1973) for a comparison of the disposition of assault charges between strangers and those involving spouses. See Eisenberg and Micklow (1977) for an overview of legal issues in wife beating.

2. Much of the sociological research on family violence conducted during the 1970s was undertaken by the Family Violence Research Program in the department of sociology at the University of New Hampshire, with funding from the National Institute of Mental Health (Family Violence Research Program, 1979).

3. This extensive literature concerns both social problems in general and the production of specific social issues. Blumer (1971) conceptualized social problems as the product of collective behavior. His formulation was followed by those of Spector and Kitsuse (1973) and others in what has been termed the "perceptionist" view of social problems (Chauncey, 1980). Mauss (1975) discusses the social construction of several major social problems, including alcoholism and mental illness, stressing the role of social movements and professional interest groups in mobilizing public and governmental concern. See also Platt (1969) on wayward children, Pfohl (1977) on child abuse, Duster (1970) on drug abuse, and Rose (1977) on rape.

4. This shift in emphasis illustrates the complexity of the process of social problem formulation and resource mobilization. At one level, emphasizing the "classlessness" of wife beating reflects the movement's growing awareness of how heterogeneous the problem really is. At another level, increasing acknowledgement of violence in middle-class marriages is partly a consequence of movement work: the movement has encouraged middle-class women to speak out about violence in their marriages. At still another level, arguing that social class is not a major factor in wife beating is also part of an effort to create a new image of the battered woman as typical of women in U.S. society and as deserving of support.

5. At least three ideological orientations can be identified: feminism; civil rights and legal advocacy; and the human service/community mental health ideology. These orientations are reflected in the range of helping strategies advocated by anti-wife beating groups.

6. Kalmuss and Straus (1981) found that the existence of local feminist groups was a more important predictor of programs for battered women throughout the United States than several other variables they measured, including per capita income, political liberalism, the level of individual feminist sentiment, and the existence of domestic violence legislation at the state level. They maintain that grass-roots groups are important, not only because they conduct local programs, but also because they indirectly affect policy by pressuring policy makers and documenting the need for services for battered women. Kalmuss and Straus (1981:10) conclude, as I argue here, that "given the number and diversity of pressing social problems, public response to a particular issue depends on the existence of an interest group or coalition of groups that exert pressure for the solution of that problem." However, I believe they over-emphasize the importance of feminist organizations in the movement and misjudge the importance of the battered women problem to the feminist movement. Wife beating was only one of a number of concerns for both the "older" and the "younger" branches of the movement. In the older branch, NOW and other moderate organizations were pressing for changes in several areas that were important to their constituencies, including salary equality for women and passage of the Equal Rights Amendment. Small grass-roots groups in the younger branch played a role in the movement, but they also had other concerns besides wife beating, and their chronic funding problems limited their visibility and influence. Surveys taken in the late 1970s show that less than one-half of the battered women shelters in the United States were founded by feminist groups or are explicitly feminist in orientation (Johnson, 1981).

7. This pattern is similar to the one documented by Fishman (1978) in his research on media contributions to "crime waves."

8. See Gitlin (1980) for a good discussion of movement-media symbiosis.

9. Movements may be considered successful if they survive, increase their membership or member commitment, affect public policy, affect public attitudes, or result in social changes consistent with their objectives (Gamson, 1975; Turner and Killian, 1972). 1 employ a definition of success that

is compatible with the resource mobilization perspective. Like established organizations, SMOs can be assessed from what Molnar and Rogers (1976) term a "system resource" perspective (in contrast to "goal attainment"). Thus, social movements can be evaluated on how successful they are in mobilizing resources. I believe the battered women movement has accomplished a great deal by simply putting the problem of wife beating on the public agenda.

10. See Joffee (1978) on abortion counselling before and after the legalization of abortion, and Ahrens (1980) for an analysis of a shelter's work with battered women before and after the shelter began receiving public funds.

11. The idea that control by the environment results from exchange between an organization and its environment is common in the literature on organizations. Aveni (1978) notes that SMOs linked to a number of established organizations through sponsorship, overlapping memberships, and similar ties are more likely to be more moderate or "mainstream" than those with fewer ties. Piven and Cloward (1977) discuss the ways in which originally militant and disruptive movements have been "tamed" through their ties with government agencies and other sources of outside support.

References

Ahrens, Lois
    1980 "Battered women's refuges: Feminist co-operatives vs. social service institutions." *Aegis: Magazine on Ending Violence against Women* (Summer/Autumn):9–15.

Andler, Judy, and Gail Sullivan
    1980 "The price of government funding." *Aegis: Magazine on Ending Violence against Women* (Winter/Spring): 10–15.

Aveni, Adrian A.
    1978 "Organizational linkages and resource mobilization: The significance of linkage strength and breadth." *Sociological Quarterly* 19:185–202.

Blumer, Herbert
    1951 "Collective behavior." Pp. 167–222 in Alfred M. Lee (ed.), *Principles of Sociology*. New York: Barnes and Noble.
    1971 "Social problems as collective behavior." *Social Problems* 18:298–306.

Chauncey, Robert L.
    1980 "New careers for moral entrepeneurs: Teenage drinking." *Journal of Drug Issues* 10 (Winter):45–69.

Conrad, Peter
    1975 "The discovery of hyperkinesis: Notes on the medicalization of deviant behavior." *Social Problems* 23:12–21.

Conrad, Peter, and Joseph W. Schneider
    1980 *Deviance and Medicalization: From Badness to Sickness*. St. Louis: C. V. Mosby.

Davidson, Terry
    1978 *Conjugal Crime*. New York: Hawthorn Books.

Downs, Anthony
    1972 "Up and down with ecology—The issue attention cycle." *Public Interest* 28:38–50.

Duster, Troy
    1970 *The Legislation of Morality*. New York: Free Press.

Eisenberg, Sue, and Patricia Micklow
    1977 "The assaulted wife: Catch-22 revisited." *Women's Rights Law Reporter* 3:138–161.

Family Violence Research Program
    1979 Program information packet, including bibliography and description of fellowships available. Department of Sociology, University of New Hampshire, Durham.

Ferrari, Art
  1975 "Social problems, collective behavior and social policy: Propositions from the war on poverty." *Sociology and Social Research* 59:150–162.
Field, Martha H., and Henry F. Field
  1973 "Marital violence and the criminal process: Neither justice nor peace." *Social Service Review* 47: 221–240.
Fishman, Mark
  1978 "Crime waves as ideology." *Social Problems* 25:531–543.
Fojtik, Kathleen
  1976 "Wife beating: How to develop a wife assault task force and project." Pamphlet. Ann Arbor: Ann Arbor–Washtenau County National Organization for Women.
Freeman, Jo
  1975 *The Politics of Women's Liberation.* New York: McKay.
Gamson, William A.
  1975 *The Strategy of Social Protest.* Homewood, IL: Dorsey Press.
Gelles, Richard
  1974 *The Violent Home: A Study of Physical Aggression between Husbands and Wives.* Beverly Hills: Sage Publications.
Gerlach, Luther P., and Virginia H. Hine
  1970 *People, Power, and Change.* Indianapolis: Bobbs-Merrill.
Gitlin, Todd
  1980 *The Whole World Is Watching: The Mass Media in the Making and Unmaking of the New Left.* Berkeley: University of California Press.
Joffee, Carol
  1978 "What abortion counselors want from their clients." *Social Problems* 26:112–121.
Johnson, John M.
  1981 "Program enterprise and official cooptation in the battered women's shelter movement." *American Behavioral Scientist* 24:827–842.
Judkins, Bennett M.
  1979 "The black lung movement: Social movements and social structure." Pp. 105–129 in Louis Kriesberg (ed.), *Research in Social Movements, Conflicts and Change.* Volume 2. Greenwich, Conn.: JAI Press.
Kalmuss, Debra, and Murray A. Straus
  1981 "Ideological and social organizational factors associated with state and local response to domestic violence." Paper presented at the annual meeting of the Academy of Criminal Justice Sciences, Philadelphia, March 11.
Klein, Dorie
  1979 "Can this marriage be saved? Battery and sheltering." *Crime and Social Justice* 12 (Winter):19–33.
Komarovsky, Mirra
  1964 *Blue-Collar Marriage.* New York: Random House.
Levine, Sol, and Paul E. White
  1961 "Exchange as a conceptual framework for the study of interorganizational relationships." *Administrative Science Quarterly* 5:555–601.
Martin, Del
  1977 *Battered Wives.* San Francisco: Glide Publications.
Mauss, Armand
  1975 *Social Problems as Social Movements.* Philadelphia: J.B. Lippincott.
McCarthy, John D., and Mayer Zald
  1973 *The Trend of Social Movements in America: Professionalization and Resource Mobilization.* Princeton, NJ: General Learning Press.

McGillis, Daniel, and Joan Mullen
 1977 *Neighborhood Justice Centers: An Analysis of Potential Models.* Washington, D.C.: Department of Justice, Law Enforcement Assistance Administration.

Molnar, Joseph J., and David L. Rogers
 1976 "Organizational effectiveness An empirical comparison of the goal and system resource approaches." *Sociological Quarterly* 17:401–413.

Morgan, Patricia A.
 1981 "Constructing images of deviance: A look at state intervention into the problem of wife battery." Paper presented at the annual meeting of the American Sociological Association, Toronto, Canada, August 24–28.

Morrison, Denton
 1971 "Some notes toward theory on relative deprivation, social movements, and social change." *American Behavioral Scientist* 14:675–690.

Ms.
 1976 "Battered wives: Help for the victim next door." 5,2 (August):95–98.

National Clearinghouse on Domestic Violence
 1980 Domestic Violence Monograph Series, Numbers 1–4. Washington, D.C.: U.S. Office on Domestic Violence.

New York Times
 1977 "L.E.A.A. is tripling funds to aid battered wives." September 5:6.

Niedermeyer, Jeannie
 1978 "Presentation to U.S. Commission on Civil Rights." Pp. 176–178 in *Battered Women: Issues of Public Policy.* Proceedings of a consultation sponsored by the U.S. Commission on Civil Rights, January 30–31. Washington, D.C.: U.S. Commission on Civil Rights.

Oberschall, Anthony
 1973 *Social Conflict and Social Movements.* Englewood Cliffs, NJ: Prentice-Hall.
 1978 "Theories of social conflict." Pp. 291–315 in Alex Inkeles (ed.), *Annual Review of Sociology* 4. Palo Alto, CA: Annual Reviews, Inc.

O'Brien, John
 1971 "Violence in divorce-prone families." *Journal of Marriage and the Family* 33:692–698.

Pastor, Paul, Jr.
 1978 "Mobilization in public drunkenness control: A comparison of legal and medical approaches." *Social Problems* 25:373–384.

Pfohl, Stephen J.
 1977 "The 'discovery' of child abuse." *Social Problems* 24:310–323.

Piven, Frances Fox, and Richard Cloward
 1977 *Poor People's Movements: Why They Succeed, How They Fail.* New York: Random House.

Pizzey, Erin
 1974 *Scream Quietly or the Neighbors Will Hear.* Short Hills, N. J.: Ridley Enslow Publishers.

Platt, Anthony
 1969 *The Child Savers.* Chicago: University of Chicago Press.

Resnick, Mindy
 1976 Wife beating: Counselor Training Manual No. 1. Ann Arbor: Ann Arbor-Washtenau County National Organization for Women.

Rose, Vicki McNickle
 1977 "Rape as a social problem: A by-product of the feminist movement." *Social Problems* 25:75–89.

Roy, Maria (ed.)
 1977 *Battered Women: A Psychosociological Study of Domestic Violence.* New York: Van Nostrand Reinhold.

Schudson, Charles Benjamin
 1978 "The criminal justice system as family: Trying the impossible for battered women." Pp. 365–370 in *Battered Women: Issues of Public Policy.* Proceedings of a consultation sponsored by the

U.S. Commission on Civil Rights, January 30–31. Washington, D.C.: U. S. Commission on Civil Rights.

Spector, Malcolm, and John I. Kitsuse
1973 "Social problems: A reformulation." *Social Problems* 21:145–158.

Steinmetz, Suzanne, and Murray A. Straus (eds.)
1974 *Violence in the Family*. New York: Dodd, Mead.

Straus, Murray A.
1974 "Cultural and social organizational influences on violence between family members." Pp. 53–69 in Raymond Prince and Dorothy Barrier (eds.), *Configurations: Biological and Cultural Factors in Sexuality and Family Life*. Lexington, Mass.: D.C. Heath.
1976 "Sexual inequality, cultural norms, and wife-beating." *Victimology* 1:54–76.

Straus, Murray A., Richard J. Gelles, and Suzanne K. Steinmetz
1980 *Behind Closed Doors: Violence in the American Family*. New York: Anchor/Doubleday.

Tierney, Kathleen J.
1979 "Social movement organization, resource mobilization, and the creation of a social problem: A case study of a movement for battered women." Unpublished Ph.D. dissertation, Department of Sociology, Ohio State University, Columbus.

Tilly, Charles, Louise Tilly, and Richard Tilly
1975 *The Rebellious Century, 1830–1930*. Cambridge: Harvard University Press.

Turner, Ralph, and Lewis M. Killian
1972 *Collective Behavior*. Englewood Cliffs, N.J.: Prentice-Hall.

U.S. Commission on Civil Rights
1978 *Battered Women: Issues of Public Policy*. Proceedings of a consultation sponsored by the U.S. Commission on Civil Rights, January 30–31. Washington, D.C.: U.S. Commission on Civil Rights.

U.S. News and World Report
1979 "Battered families: A growing nightmare." January 15:60–61.

Viano, Emilio C.
1979 *Victim Witness Services: A Review of the Model*. Washington, D.C. : U.S. Department of Justice, Law Enforcement Assistance Administration.

Warrior, Betsy
1978 *Working on Wife Abuse*. Pamphlet, Cambridge, Mass.: Betsy Warrior, 46 Pleasant St.

CASE CITED

Bruno v. Codd, 396 N.Y.S.2d. 974, 1977.

CHAPTER 12

Identity, Strategy, and Feminist Politics

CLEMENCY FOR BATTERED WOMEN WHO KILL

Patricia Gagné

The feminist battered women's movement has been widely credited with creating public awareness of wife abuse as a social problem, establishing safe places for victims of intimate violence, working to eliminate gender bias in the law, and creating equal protection for battered women (Davis 1988; Dobash and Dobash 1992; Schechter 1982; Tierney 1982). Most studies of the battered women's movement of the 1970s and 1980s were grounded in resource mobilization theory (see McCarthy and Zald 1973, 1977). While the early developments in resource mobilization focused on availability of resources and the ability of activists to organize them, a subsequent strand focused on the social and political context as an opportunity for action (Jenkins 1983). Most analyses of the battered women's movement have taken the first approach, focusing on shelters as social movement organizations (but see Schechter 1982). As a result of the focus on shelters, as opposed to an examination of activists agitating for change in other arenas, analysts have argued that the movement has been, or is in danger of being, coopted (Ferraro 1983; Johnson 1981; Schechter 1982).[1]

Resource mobilization theory is grounded in theories of liberal democracy, which narrowly define politics as separate from civic society, personal life, and social movements (Acklesberg 1988; Ferree 1992). With its narrow and rigidly defined conceptualization of social movements, resource mobilization theory is problematic in the examination of women's movements, primarily because it is based upon a white, middle class, masculine (or liberal democratic) tradition of personal and civic life and participation in politics (Ferree 1992). That is, it assumes that activists are people outside of institutionalized positions of authority. It overlooks the liberal feminist goal of placing women in key political positions and other careers where they will work to create social change, excludes the radical feminist concept that the personal is political, and obviates an examination of acts of "everyday resistance" (Collins 1990).

Feminists have challenged the tenet that institutionalized politics are separable from personal life or activism (Acklesberg 1988; Alonso 1992; Cassell 1977; Elshtain 1981; Evans 1979; Kauffman 1989; Morgen and Bookman 1988; Mouffe 1992). Similarly, post-modern, critical, feminist, and new social movement theorists have argued that a merging of political and non-political spheres of life has taken place in post-industrial societies (Acklesberg 1988; Alonso 1992; Bernstein 1985; Elshtain 1981; Foucault 1979; Habermas 1985; Melucci 1980; Morgen and Bookman 1988; Mouffe 1992; Offe 1985; Taylor and Whittier 1992; Touraine 1985). Therefore, an examination of the feminist battered women's movement that is based upon liberal democratic assumptions will overlook the activism that has taken place in nontraditional arenas (such as the work place), institutional politics, or personal relationships and will obscure examinations of activists' efforts to create a political and cultural context conducive to movement success.

Drawing on a case study of the 1990 decision by then Ohio Governor Richard Celeste to grant clemency to 26 women who were incarcerated for killing or assaulting abusive intimate partners or stepfathers, this chapter examines the strategies and tactics used by feminists in the battered women's movement to lay the groundwork for and establish a clemency review process. I have chosen to focus on the Ohio movement for the following reasons: It was the first multiple clemency decision of its type; it was directly influenced by feminists in the women's and battered women's movements; to date, it has resulted in the largest number of women being released from prison at one time; and finally, it appears to have set a precedent that was followed by similar decisions by three other governors, and by feminist organizing efforts in 17 other states. By examining this event in light of social movement and political theories that challenge the assumptions of liberal democratic theories, my goals are to: (1) document an historical event that might otherwise be lost; (2) challenge the notion that the battered women's movement was coopted in the 1980s; (3) identify movement tactics that worked in an environment relatively conducive to change; (4) hypothesize about strategies and tactics that might work in a less hospitable era; and (5) conceptually expand our understanding of what constitutes activism.

Methods

The data for this chapter come from 45 intensive, semi-structured, tape recorded interviews with members of the Ohio battered women's movement and key informants in state government.[2] I used a snowball sampling method, beginning with First Lady Dagmar Celeste, who was involved in the women's and battered women's movements from the 1960s and who was influential in promoting women's prison reform and the clemency review. In addition to Dagmar Celeste, my sample included members of her staff, many of the founders of the battered women's movement, the governor, cabinet members, aides to the governor and cabinet, employees of the Ohio Department of Rehabilitation and Correction, members of a statewide network of direct service providers, former members of three support groups for incarcerated battered women, defense attorneys, judges, feminist and pro-feminist Ohio legislators, and 12 of the 26 women who were granted clemency.[3] I transcribed all of the interviews verbatim.

All of the never-incarcerated activists and authorities in my sample were middle-class professionals, and all but three, two women and one man, were white. Of the clemency recipients I interviewed, seven were African American and five were white.[4] Seven of them worked in blue or pink collar jobs, two received Aid to Families with Dependent Children, and three collected Supplemental Security Income. Although many never-incarcerated activists discussed efforts to diversify the movement, my sample suggests that in Ohio they were predominately white and middle class, working to expand the movement to include an ethnically and socioeconomically diverse population.

I analyzed the data using principles of analytic induction and grounded theory (Charmaz 1983; Strauss and Corbin 1990) and triangulated interview data with archival materials.[5] I have also drawn upon an extensive collection of newspaper and magazine articles from Ohio and the national press and video recorded television talk shows and news magazines on which the women who received clemency appeared.

Historical Overview of the Movement

The Ohio battered women's movement emerged out of the larger women's movement, with early activism concentrated in Columbus and Cleveland. The roots of the later clemency movement were based predominately in Cleveland, with community ties later expanding throughout the state. In Cleveland the movement began in 1974 with women from a wide array of feminist organizations uniting through an organization they called Women Together to confront the issue of woman abuse.[6] Similar to national trends (Schechter 1982), the Ohio movement incorporated diverse tactics. While working to change the legal system, these feminists established organizations that would provide temporary refuge from violence, run exclusively by and for women. In 1975 Women Together founded a hotline, and in December 1976 it opened the first shelter for battered women in the State of Ohio in the home of then Lieutenant Governor Richard Celeste. When it was founded, the shelter was committed to social change, with services based on feminist principles of self-help and empowerment.

Despite efforts to provide them with alternatives, women frequently and repeatedly returned to violent and abusive partners. By the late 1970s, feminists at Women Together, like those doing similar work throughout the United States, began to understand that battered women experience a range of post-traumatic psychological responses to abuse, similar to those of victims of other types of violence or trauma (see Browne 1993). Subsequently, the psychological response of battered women became reified as "battered woman syndrome," a subcategory of post-traumatic stress disorder (Walker 1984). Interestingly, in the course of trying to create social change, the focus perceptibly shifted to trying to explain why battered women fail to leave abusive partners. In trying to address this question, a debate ensued among feminists and mental health workers as to the potential merits and problems of categorizing as a mental disorder what many feminists labeled a *normal* response to fear and an *appropriately* angry response to abuse (see Browne 1987; 1993; Schneider 1986). Although many women left abusive relationships or successfully ended violence through other means, some responded to ongoing or accelerated abuse by killing or trying to kill their partners. In many states, when they went to trial such women found they were restricted from introducing testimony about the abuse they had endured or their resulting states of mind. In trying to address these women's needs, some activists and scholars advocated the use of expert testimony to explain battered woman syndrome to juries. This strategy would introduce evidence of past abuse and challenge the gender biases of self-defense law by explaining the woman's state of mind at the time of the offense (see

Gillespie 1989). Feminist legal scholars raised potential problems in the use of battered woman syndrome. They argued that it could be used against women who did not neatly fit pre-established criteria and had the potential to become another example of the tendency to label women's normal angry responses as mental illness (Browne 1993; Schneider 1986; see also Chesler 1989 and Schur 1984). While the desirability of working to admit expert testimony was debated, individual state courts and legislatures varied in their willingness to recognize battered woman syndrome, permit evidence of past abuse, or allow expert testimony. As the legal debate about battered women's responses to violence was beginning to unfold, the Ohio movement became directly involved in it when a former shelter resident shot and killed her abusive common law husband. In 1978 Women Together, in conjunction with the woman's lawyer, decided to challenge existing law by trying to introduce battered woman syndrome expert testimony at trial.

At the time, battered woman syndrome had little scientific merit or legal recognition, and the decision turned out to be a costly one in Ohio. The trial court refused to allow the testimony, and in 1981 that decision was upheld by the Ohio Supreme Court (*State v. Thomas* 1981 66 Ohio St. 2d S 1).[7] Despite this major setback, activists remained committed to challenging the law and improving their own and society's understanding of the trauma experienced by battered women. The case became symbolic of the Ohio movement's dual focus on gender inequities in the law and women's response to abuse.

By the early 1980s, most Women Together founders left the shelter to establish professional careers, which they viewed as a means of advancing the feminist agenda. Many had become frustrated with the limitations and defeats they experienced as outsider challengers. The strategy they adopted was to infiltrate and appropriate the institutions they sought to change. For example, one founder, who had worked for ERA America in addition to her other feminist activism, explained her decision to run for elected office by saying:

> I was in every state when [the ERA] was defeated. . . . That's when I decided to run for the legislature. I said, "I can do this better than these turkeys. This is not a problem."

Founders became legislators, judges, victim advocates, expert witnesses, government administrators, doctors, counselors, and professors. In 1982, many became activists within the administrative branch of state government when Celeste was elected to his first term as governor.

As movement founders left the shelter, a new cohort of feminists and mental health professionals took over Women Together, and the shelter vacillated between the models advocated by each group (see Davis 1988), ultimately devising an approach that incorporated elements of both. In 1989 a network of feminist shelters—the Ohio Domestic Violence Network (ODVN)—was formed to re-establish the movement's emphasis on social change. That year ODVN worked to pass House Bill 484, an attempt to overrule the *Thomas* decision. While ODVN lobbied from outside the House and Senate, movement founders worked within the legislature and administration, laying the groundwork for clemency. In March 1990, the Ohio Supreme Court reversed itself in the case of *State v. Koss* (1990 49 Ohio St. 3d 213).[8] In August HB 484 was signed into law.

While HB 484 was being debated, the Celeste Administration began to work to implement the clemencies. For several years, Dagmar Celeste had been visiting women on death row at the Ohio Reformatory for Women (ORW), where she became involved in prison reform and numerous aspects of inmates' lives. Sometime during the mid-1980s, she first raised with the governor the issue of a large scale clemency for battered women. His staff reviewed the issue and reported back that there was no precedent for such an action. The matter was subsequently dropped until 1989 when the first lady and her staff began to press the issue. That year the governor ordered research to determine the number of women incarcerated for crimes related to battering and to document the existence of battered woman syndrome among Ohio's female inmate population.[9] In December 1989 he ordered that a clemency application and review process be established.[10] One hundred fifteen women applied, and in December 1990 26 were granted clemency.[11]

In light of these events the question remains: How was such a controversial decision made at a time many analysts have labeled postfeminist (Bolotin 1982; Friedan 1985; Stacey 1987; Steinem 1983) and when the national and state political contexts were increasingly conservative? Further, for social movement scholars and activists, the more important question is: Given the conservative backlash against women and the increasingly punitive incarceration models, which of the Ohio movement's tactics have the greatest likelihood of resulting in success in politically hostile settings? To address these questions, I examine the context of the Ohio clemency decisions, the way the issues were presented to authorities, the strategy and tactics used by activists in this movement, and the role of politically established persons in carrying out the movement's mandate.

Creating Opportunity

Resource mobilization theorists contend that the context in which a social movement occurs is an important component in its emergence and success (Jenkins 1987; McAdam 1982; Morris 1984; Piven and Cloward 1977; Tilly 1988). Because of the assumption that movements react to opportunities provided, there has been little examination of their efforts to alter the political structure or climate. Nonetheless, this is what the Ohio battered women's movement did.

THE CONTEXT

In 1982 Richard Celeste was elected governor by a decisive majority. His success was due, in part, to the recession and high unemployment that had hit the state, particularly in the "rust belt," and to a strong anti-Republican sentiment. Voters were liberal on economic, but not social, issues. To fight against further erosion of jobs and the decline of schools, voters elected Democrats to office across the board. In 1986 Celeste ran for re-election against James Rhodes, a candidate who had already served four terms as governor (in two, two-term periods). At that time, Ohio's economy was on the rebound, and again voters elected Celeste to office by a decisive margin. In neither term was Celeste elected on social issues, nor did he campaign on them strongly. While he had the legal authority to grant clemency to whomever he chose, he lacked a political mandate on left wing or feminist social issues. Although he had received the backing of activists advocating for social change, his staff understood the political risks of being too socially progressive, and they worked to protect him from such demands.

When he took office in 1983, the governor provided Dagmar Celeste with a staff and office space in the State House and depended on her to get involved with many of the issues affecting Ohio citizens. She called upon feminist colleagues and friends, many of whom had helped found the women's and battered women's movements, to help her create a "First Lady's Agenda." Some of those women served in the "First Lady's Unit," but more were selected by the governor to serve in cabinet and sub-cabinet level positions as directors of government agencies and in a variety of other positions. During the second term, these women organized the Women's Interagency Task Force, a network of feminists representing governmental departments and agencies. The Task Force met on a regular basis to discuss social policy as it related to women, review what agencies were doing about women's issues, provide an annual review of the governor's budget from a feminist perspective, and coordinate efforts on behalf of women throughout the state. The result was more efficient mobilization of a feminist community, which increased its influence throughout the state. With backing from the Task Force, as the term progressed, the First Lady's Unit increased pressure on members of the governor's staff who thought certain issues "too controversial" for the governor to address.

Feminists created support for clemency by raising public, judicial, and legislative awareness of gender biases in self-defense law and by pressing for change. In 1989 ODVN and feminists in the legislature pressed the passage of HB 484, despite well-organized opposition from conservative legislators and prosecutors. At the same time, feminist therapists, expert witnesses, and advocates worked to educate judges and Supreme Court justices about battered woman syndrome and its role in domestic homicides. By passing HB 484 and doing the background work that led to the *Koss* decision, they helped to create a context in which clemency reviews could be justified, particularly for women who, according to the law in 1990, had not received fair trials. Feminists developed the context of opportunity the governor needed, but more work had to be done to put the review process in place.

Emergent Frames and the Rhetoric of Wife Abuse

Collective action frames are dynamic efforts by movements to "package" an issue by creating a sense of injustice and attributing blame for it to a particular social group or agent (Snow and Benford 1992). In an informal sense, the movement creates a theory about the source and solutions to the problem and presents it to the public and/or authorities. On a larger scale, master frames are more abstract theories that guide the discourse of movements within the social movement sector (Snow and Benford 1992). Like theories to a paradigm, the collective action frames of individual movements are likely to adhere to the discourse of the larger master frame.

The master frame of the movements of the 1960s and early 1970s focused on structural and cultural inequality, with goals such as equal rights, justice, and freedom from oppression. When the battered women's movement first emerged in the mid-1970s, the cycle of protest that had begun in the 1950s was reaching the end of its heyday (Jenkins 1987). When the battered women's movement became well established in the late 1970s the cycle of protest was in decline (Jenkins 1987) and the anti-feminist, pro-family backlash was gaining momentum (Crawford 1980; Faludi 1991). At the same time, mental health professionals began to reframe battered women's issues in non-oppositional terms and to encroach on the movement (Johnson 1981; Schechter 1982). By the end of the 1970s, the majority of shelters were non-feminist in orientation (Ferraro 1983; Johnson 1981). At the same time, the master frame of that cycle of protest had begun to shift toward personal development, and many radical feminists began to turn toward a cultural or eco-feminist analysis. Whereas radicals were social constructionist in orientation and sought to eliminate the sex-class system, cultural and eco-feminists based their discourse on essentialist premises, with a focus on elevating women's inherent virtues and putting greater emphasis on women's spiritual growth (Echols 1989). In Ohio, the battered women's movement shifted from a focus on gender equality to one of difference, incorporating elements of a debate that has been going on for more than a century.

ALTERNATIVE VISIONS AND OVERLAPPING DISCOURSE

To bring about social change, a movement must create an alternative vision of the world (Dobash and Dobash 1992). But, to enhance their chances of mobilizing potential participants and achieving their goals, activists must develop a collective action frame that agrees, in whole or in part, with something the public already believes. Alternatively, the movement must convert the public to its collective action frame, a strategy that is likely to require greater resources and more time (Klandermans 1992). In movements where there are no pragmatic repercussions for holding out, ideological purity has fewer consequences. However, where individuals' lives are endangered or when people are in prison, time is of the essence. In Ohio, activists incorporated cultural and eco-feminism's emphasis on gender differences and spiritual growth with their goal of social and structural change. As the movement's collective action frame shifted, the First Lady's Unit's goals were presented in the language of recovery and peaceful families—a frame they believed to be culturally resonant with mainstream society (McAdam 1994)—but the goals of personal empowerment, the elimination of gender biases in the law, and the eradication of violence against women remained. For example, among feminists working in the legislature and through the courts, recognition of women's psychological response to ongoing, severe abuse was framed in terms specific to women. Feminist lobbyists and legislators pointed to the fact that women rarely kill, unless they are under extreme duress. Relying on assumptions that women are less violent and less able to protect themselves, and arguing that police had refused to help many of the women who had been convicted of killing their partners, feminists argued that legal recognition of women's response to battering was warranted.[12]

Resources and opportunities are central to social change, particularly when movement goals are dependent on the development of collective consciousness and identity

(Buechler 1990). Prison support and educational groups were an important part of the movement for clemency, but it took the work of non-inmate feminists to get them established at the Ohio Reformatory for Women (ORW). To mobilize the resources needed to establish such groups for battered women, feminists frequently framed demands in terms such as "peaceful families," "recovery," and "spiritual growth." In 1989 Dagmar Celeste became involved in efforts at ORW to build a chapel so that church services and recovery groups could be expanded. In a series of memoranda[13] among her, the governor, their aides, and officials at the prison and in the Department of Rehabilitation and Correction, the governor and first lady referred to the need to provide every inmate with an opportunity for "spiritual growth" and the chance to "recover from addiction." ORW added "support" and "educational" groups for battered women, as well as numerous additional recovery groups. These groups provided a "woman-space, a space free from male intrusion where women could ... nurture each other and themselves" (Jagger 1983:270). As a manifestation of radical feminism, these groups provided a place where women could practice the skills and strengths they were forbidden to use in abusive relationships and patriarchal society and develop alternative ways of perceiving reality and reacting to their circumstances (Jagger 1983). In short, they functioned very much like consciousness raising groups of the 1960s and 1970s, with strikingly similar results. As women participated in groups for battered women, they began to understand the social forces that had shaped their lives. Most entered their groups believing they deserved to be punished for their crimes, but as consciousness of the patriarchal context of their lives was raised, a politicized collective identity emerged among them and they began to work for clemency. As incarcerated women came to believe they deserved to be released, it was incumbent on non-inmate feminists to help them get their cases reviewed. To do that, feminists worked as "ideological outsiders" within the government and its agencies.

Feminist Strategy and the Tactics of Personal Politics

Similar to Collins's (1986) analysis of black female intellectuals' creative use of their own marginality within academic institutions, feminists in the Ohio battered women's movement were ideological outsiders within the institutions they sought to change. There they adopted and modified a strategy of "self-limiting radicalism," challenging the tenets of liberal democracy but accepting the legitimate existence of the state and capitalist economy (Cohen 1985). Activists using this strategy struggle to redraw public and private boundaries by creating democratic public spaces and transforming formerly private domains into social arenas for the renegotiation of identity and other movement demands (Cohen 1985). Similar to the women's movement (Buechler 1990), one of the most important legacies of the Ohio battered women's movement was the creation of a community of informally linked activists, capable of rapid and intense mobilization around specific issues, particularly when it required acting outside of social movement organizations. As movement founders moved into careers, they adopted a strategy I call "insider self-limiting radicalism," by remaining ideologically outside the systems they sought to change. Within state government, they were a minority who worked to advance feminist goals.

FRAMING DEMANDS FOR PRISON REFORM

Had the first lady and members of the network advocated the formation of feminist consciousness raising groups for incarcerated women, it is likely the governor's staff and prison authorities would have resisted their efforts. However, by focusing on "recovery" services they were able to establish groups that became a key factor in creating a social movement community within the women's prison.

CONSCIOUSNESS RAISING AND THE POLITICIZATION OF IDENTITY

The central task of the Ohio battered women's movement in achieving clemency was to create a collective identity among women inmates (see Melucci 1989). All the women I met who had attended educational or support groups for battered women talked about realizing they were not alone in their experiences. They explained how other women in their groups helped them understand how they had been dominated and controlled and how society had failed to help them. For example, when I asked what she had learned in her group, one clemency recipient said:

> By listening to other women [I could see] the control, the isolation, where they want to cut you off from the world, that type of thing. . . . I could relate to how she felt about that, because I went through that, you know? How they want to control your whole life and they don't want you to have any friends and . . . your whole world's just you and the abuser.

In time women began to see themselves as survivors, rather than perpetual victims, and to understand how they came to be controlled, abused, and ultimately trapped in violent relationships.

Talking about their experiences was central in helping the women "reclaim" their definition of self, a step central to the politicization of identity (see D'Emilio 1983; Herman and Miall 1990). Based on my interviews with clemency recipients, activists, and authorities, I found that the importance of reclaiming identity is threefold. First, privately discussing the violent relationship with women who have claimed the identity "survivor" helps the "victim" reinterpret her experiences within the social context and begin to redefine herself.[14] As the victim redefines herself as a survivor, she realizes her strengths and how society has socialized her to be weak, failed to protect her, and blamed her for her own victimization. Second, as the public witnesses the reclaiming and public identification with a previously stigmatized status, old stereotypes and definitions are challenged and the identity is publicly renegotiated and redefined. Third, by publicly discussing and redefining the issues, their private nature is challenged and transformed from a personal to a social problem, deserving of social recompense.

From prison the women carried on a campaign to educate authorities and the public about battered woman syndrome. They told about their experiences with violent and abusive spouses and parents and the injustices they had endured in the criminal justice system. For most these efforts involved letter writing campaigns and meeting with public officials who were frequently brought to the prison by the first lady or feminist legislators. They met with legislators to talk about their experiences, their reactions to abuse, battered woman syndrome, and the need for laws recognizing it. They shared their experiences in closed meetings with the governor's staff and in groups organized to garner media attention, such as a meeting Dagmar Celeste's staff arranged with Miss America. They told their stories on television news magazines and to anyone else who would listen. Their goals were to educate government officials and the public about wife abuse and build public sympathy for their cases. One legislator explained how meeting with the women helped him understand what battered women endure and why it was necessary to change the law and remedy past inequities. He said:

> I wanted to really talk to a real person who's been through this. . . . One woman told me how the windows were nailed shut. When the guy left . . . he took the phone with him and warned her that if she left the house . . . or contacted the authorities, that her children were going to be in serious harm's way. . . . And this had gone on for a decade. So one day, he came home and that was it. . . . He was going to abuse her physically, sexually, too. . . . She shot him dead with a shotgun. And she was in her . . . ninth year of incarceration.

The women's stories matched real lives with the theories and put faces on the statistics. With what they learned in prison, the governor's aides and supporters of HB 484 were able to win the votes of those who opposed the legislation.

As women began to realize there were alternatives to abuse and that their actions could make a difference, they began to resist abuses of power in other domains and demand justice. In prison, those who had witnessed or experienced harassment, sexual assault, or unfair treatment by prison employees began to report it and, when possible, testified in court. For example, one woman told me she and a roommate had witnessed the sexual assault of a third woman by a corrections officer. The three made a pact that they would take "no more abuse." After reporting what had happened, they testified against the officer, who was ultimately convicted. Intolerance of abuse continued when the women returned home. There they began to confront their daughters' abusive partners and teach the young women how to protect themselves. Five of the women had decided to avoid relationships with men altogether. One of them explained:

> I have not interacted with men, I mean I have friends, but I have not entertained a relationship . . . I am not ready. . . . I am gonna stay by myself 'cause I cannot tolerate this no more.

Only three of the women I talked with had had problems with men since being released. One, whose entire family was abusive, tolerated the violence because, as she explained, "I know he loves me." A second left a man she had met who had become abusive. The third was very assertive in communicating that she would not tolerate abuse. When her partner pushed her, she had him arrested and pressed charges. When I talked to her, the two were in couples' counseling and recovery groups and were trying to "work things out." Still, she was adamant that although she loved him, she knew she "deserved better than that." These forms of everyday resistance were made possible because women acknowledged that they had been abused and, in the process, learned to protect themselves and help others.

While inmates' actions were central in the transformation of identity, their voices alone were not enough to result in clemency. That goal required activism outside the prison. To accomplish that, the systems by which women had been dominated had to be appropriated and used to their own benefit.

APPROPRIATING AND CAREER ACTIVISM

One outcome of many of the social movements of the 1960s and 1970s was the creation of job opportunities for activists (McAdam 1988; McCarthy and Zald 1973). However, as the "cycle of protest" (Tarrow 1991) wound down for many movements of the period, activists found themselves in an increasingly tight activist job market (McAdam 1988). Nonetheless, the presence of the growing women's movement gave women expanding career outlets for their activism (McAdam 1988). A major distinction between the experiences of men in the new left and feminists is that the former eschew participation in "the establishment," while many feminists have looked upon career success as one potential means of addressing the economic and power inequities between women and men. For example, a 1960s student radical would look upon the offer of a position as judge as an effort at cooptation, while feminists have sought such positions as avenues to reinterpret or change the law.

Feminist activism on the job entails working to advance the goals of the women's movement as part of one's career. Within the Ohio battered women's movement, efforts to institutionalize change ranged from municipal court systems to the Supreme Court, the state legislature, and the Celeste Administration. At the municipal level, feminist judges, attorneys, shelter directors, and other direct service providers worked together to coordinate the police and judicial response to battering. Throughout the state the Governor's Task Force on Family Violence endeavored to understand and coordinate services for battered women and other victims of family violence. Feminist doctors worked to train their colleagues about family violence. Feminists in the Ohio Public Defender's Office were active in supporting legislation and working to educate their colleagues about battered woman syndrome. After *State v. Koss,* the Supreme Court created a task force to educate judges about domestic violence and battered woman syndrome and called upon movement founders who had established themselves in government careers to work with them. Feminist researchers and correctional staff, working to document the presence of battered woman syndrome among Ohio's female inmate population, stood their ground as the integrity of their work was challenged by their supervisors, and they ensured that the cases of all women who were eligible for review made it to the governor's office. Feminists within the First Lady's Unit and in the cabinet worked to educate the governor and his staff about wife abuse.

The battered women's movement has not taken over the Ohio legislature, judiciary, prison system, executive branch of government, or any of the many state agencies feminists work in or run. But feminists used their jobs to achieve their goals. Their unwillingness to leave their convictions at the workplace door brought the movement into the very institutions that would grant legitimacy to the changes they sought to make. It may not be true of all movements, but because identity is central to feminist movements, it is inevitable that as activists gain entrée to new arenas, the distinction between the movement and social institutions will become blurred. Similarly, as women resist oppression in their personal lives, the distinction between the personal and the political will be obscured.

INTIMACY AND ACTIVISM

At the end of my interviews, I asked participants if there was a clear separation in their minds between their activism, their jobs, and their personal lives. All of the women, and all but three of the men,[15] said no. One of the women explained the connections among these facets of her life;

> I think they're all of a piece.... I can't imagine compartmentalizing life....
> You're acting from a core of whoever you are.

When I asked them to give examples of how their activism was carried on in their personal lives, many women described their efforts to negotiate egalitarian intimate relationships. Many referred to their marriages as partnerships that they and their spouses had worked to establish. Others referred to the music they would or would not listen to and the movies they refused to see. Those with children talked about their efforts to rear them to be socially conscious, nonsexist, and non-violent. My data are replete with examples of how women pursued feminist goals in their intimate relationships and home lives. Such acts of resistance, collectively, have advanced efforts to renegotiate women's identities and lives.

POLITICAL PARTNERSHIPS AND EVERYDAY RESISTANCE

Among politicians, there is a precarious separation that has historically been expected to exist between personal and public life. It is almost as if the public expects office holders to be sequestered from their families. Conversations about political issues should, ideally, not take place among family members or between spouses. If they do, either no influence should be exerted or any opinion expressed by the non-office holder should be ignored. Basing their opinions on liberal, non-feminist assumptions about the division that *should* exist between public and private domains, the public resents the privileged access family members have to office holders and demands that the division between public and private be at least symbolically maintained.

As women have continued to become more educated and have their own careers, the likelihood has increased that male politicians will marry women with political opinions, agendas, and goals of their own. The election of feminists to public office is one way the women's movement has worked to achieve its goals. But elected officials are constrained in ways their spouses and family members are not. Partnership politics increases the likelihood that social movements will gain entrée to arenas of official decision making. Therefore, the election of pro-feminist men who share power with their wives is a potential source of entrée to arenas of power and authority for women's movements.

In Ohio, Governor Celeste lent institutional support to his partnership with the first lady by providing her with a staff and offices in the State House. He empowered her to work toward feminist goals by actively seeking her input, instructing his staff to work with her, and including her in high-level meetings. The governor valued her contributions. Nonetheless, while she kept a low profile, working behind the scenes until the last year of their second term in office, Dagmar Celeste's influence did not come without resentment and resistance from the public, the governor's staff, and other public servants. Governor Celeste explained:

> The staff of the governor serves the governor and thinks that anything else that intrudes is just that, an intrusion, and an unwarranted intrusion. That's family, that's first lady, whatever it might be. . . . Here we are doing the business of the state, why do we need to worry about something that the first lady's interested in? And so I think it's fair to say that there was never a wonderfully smooth relationship between the first lady's staff and the governor's office staff.

Despite resistance, the governor insisted that the first lady's concerns be addressed through official channels. Their relationship is an example of Cohen's (1985) concept of self-limiting radicalism. By challenging the separation between their public and private lives, they created "democratic public spaces" accessible to marginalized groups, including incarcerated women and feminists. Dagmar Celeste's unofficial position gave her a degree of freedom not available to the governor. Nonetheless, because she was not elected to office, her efforts were met with resentment and resistance. Dagmar Celeste used the metaphor of a strategic game to explain their relationship and efforts to create social change. She said:

> I've often viewed the role of the first lady as the queen in a chess game. . . . The whole God damn game . . . is built on protecting the king. . . . And what's interesting in chess . . . is that the queen has a lot more mobility than anybody else. . . . She can move up . . . he can't move at all! . . . Chess is not a feminist game, [she laughs] because there's no point in having a queen, except to protect the king. . . . I would make coalitions with people who didn't serve his interests, if they served a feminist interest. And eventually he would come to see that they served his interest, because if he wanted to be what he said he wanted to be as a progressive feminist politician, eventually, it came to serve his interests.

By challenging the expected boundaries between their personal and political lives, the governor and first lady forged a partnership that allowed her to create alliances that played a central role in providing access to and for marginalized groups. As the spouse of an elected official, committed to feminist principles and goals, she provided an arena through which the women's and battered women's movements could achieve their goals. Without the political partnership that existed between the governor and first lady, the networks she facilitated among feminists throughout the state, and her willingness to violate liberal personal and political boundaries, the leadership within state government that was required to bring about the clemency review process would have been missing. While elected officials are important gatekeepers to many social movement goals, spouses have an enormous potential to push that gate open or leave it closed.

Conclusion

Social movements are frequently thought of as outside challenges to systems of authority, a conceptualization that is incomplete when analyzing women's and other new social movements. The assumption underlying the Ohio battered women's movement's strategy was that any separation of the personal from the political was unthinkable. This tenet was the foundation of the creation of wife abuse as a social problem, the empowerment of battered women within and out of prison, and the appropriation of three branches of the government, numerous state agencies, and the correctional system. Feminist identity entails a willingness to challenge established social arrangements, gender relations, and definitions of women, and to apply a feminist analysis to the social settings in which women find themselves and those they wish to enter. As the Ohio battered women's movement's founders left the shelter, they sought careers where they could work more effectively to achieve feminist goals. As they spread throughout the state and infiltrated all branches of government, they held to their feminist analysis of wife abuse and maintained contact with each other. In their personal lives, they sought social change and created partnerships with spouses who sought their input and were amenable to their influence. Through this strategy of infiltrating all three branches of government and violating public/private separations in their intimate relationships, feminists empowered at least one marginalized group to have greater input in the democratic decision-making process. They did this by creating democratic public spaces in arenas previously considered beyond the realm of democracy. The most influential of these spaces were the political partnership between the governor and first lady and the consciousness raising groups at the Ohio Reformatory for Women.

Previous examinations of the battered women's movement have focused primarily on shelters as social movement organizations and have concluded that the feminist principles of the movement have been coopted by mental health professionals. In Ohio I found a well organized network of feminist shelters that worked toward social change on the local and state levels, despite an anti-feminist/pro-family cultural backlash, an increasingly conservative political environment, and efforts by mental health professionals to redefine the issues. While they staffed the "front lines," the majority of activism that made the clemencies possible occurred in arenas traditionally considered outside the domain of social movements.

Because they did not respect the boundaries between public and private, feminists successfully forced a recognition of the social factors that frequently entrap women in violent relationships. As ideological outsiders within the systems they wanted to change, they created a climate more favorable to clemency by framing issues in terms authorities were likely to understand and accept. This rhetorical compromise helped feminists establish a social movement community within the prison. In Ohio, feminists achieved their goals by carrying their activism into their careers and personal lives and by recognizing that political change occurs at the level of individual identity, as it did when women inmates began to advocate for their own clemencies. Feminists could only achieve these goals by resisting individual explanations of wife abuse, focusing on the need for personal transformation and social change, and remaining ideologically outside the systems they wanted to appropriate and change.

In periods that are inhospitable to movement goals, activists must identify strategies and tactics that are most likely to result in the achievement of movement goals. Based on the success of the Ohio battered women's movement, I have identified six tactics that may assist other movements during inhospitable or hostile cycles. First, movements can elect public officials sympathetic to their views and infiltrate positions of authority in order to swing the political pendulum in their favor. Along these lines, they must recognize the increasingly important role of political spouses in providing or denying access to political decision makers and other authorities. Second, movements can work toward social change in every aspect of their personal and public lives, bearing in mind that identity transformation among nonactivists is a powerful potential source of movement growth. Third, movements can work to create democratic spaces in previously private or non-democratic arenas. Fourth, unless they are able to build a powerful coalition, strong enough to challenge authorities and sway public opinion, movements can engage in rhetorical compromise by framing their demands in terms more likely to resonate with authorities and the public. Fifth, movements can work to create coalitions with activists from across the ideological spectrum, finding a role for all groups and coordinating their activities. Sixth, movements can work from within and outside the system, exerting influence on every pressure point and providing access to, and on behalf of, already marginalized groups. If social scientists are to understand the dynamics of social change, we must continue to examine social movements. However, as I have demonstrated in this chapter, an examination of outsider challengers or activism that takes place through social movement organizations or in "public" places gives us only a partial understanding of how change occurs, how demands become institutionalized, and how new challengers arise and infiltrate the systems they wish to change. Further research is needed to examine to what extent these tactics have been used by other activists, in both left and right wing movements.

Notes

My thanks to Angela Browne, Ann Goetting, J. Craig Jenkins, Mark Richard, Joseph Scott, Verta Taylor, Richard Tewksbury, and three anonymous reviewers for their comments on this work. This research was funded by a grant from the Elizabeth Gee Fund for Research on Women from the Center for Women's Studies and a Research Intense Summer Fellowship from the Department of Sociology, both at The Ohio State University, and by a Project Completion Grant from the College of Arts and Sciences at the University of Louisville.

1. Within the majority of articles arguing that the movement has been coopted, the term is generally poorly defined. However, cooptation, as it is discussed in the context of the battered women's movement, generally refers to a shift away from feminist principles of pragmatic assistance, self-help, consciousness raising, empowerment, and nonhierarchical organization to a mental health or social

welfare model that relies heavily on counseling, rigid rules, and bureaucratic organization, and that assumes that the problem is rooted in individual pathology or within a dysfunctional family system. (See Davis 1988.)

2. Although it may appear that part of my research was ethnographic in nature, I was not involved in activism or decision making during any stage of the organizing or clemency review process. My involvement in this project began when then former First Lady Dagmar Celeste suggested to my advisor that someone needed to research the clemency decisions.

3. One of the women died shortly after being released and another has returned to prison. Of the remainder, five did not respond to telephone calls and letters, and four refused to be interviewed, saying they wanted to put the past behind them and get on with their lives. I was unable to locate three.

4. The racial and ethnic make-up of the women who received clemency are as follows; 11 whites, 14 African Americans, and 1 Hispanic.

5. Archival data included all relevant files in the Celeste Administration records, newsletters from early women's movement organizations and the first shelter in Ohio, correspondence and meeting minutes from numerous social movement organizations and government agencies, drafts of legislation, speeches, Supreme Court decisions, court records, notes from prison support groups, and progress reports and historical summaries from government agencies and movement organizations. Archival data were used to verify dates, events, the exact wording of official documents, the interaction of key players, and to fill in the gaps surrounding forgotten or overlooked events.

6. The feminist organizations that emerged in the 1970s were loosely coordinated by an "organization of organizations" (Morris 1984) called WomanSpace. This organization provided resources that expedited the shelter's opening.

7. The grounds cited by the court were that the syndrome was irrelevant and immaterial to the issue of whether the defendant acted in self-defense, that it was within the understanding of the jury and insufficiently developed as a matter of commonly accepted scientific knowledge, and that its prejudicial impact outweighed its probative value (*State v. Thomas* 1981 66 Ohio St. 2d).

8. In this decision, Justice Alice Robie Resnick wrote that "The battered woman syndrome has gained substantial scientific acceptance to warrant admissibility into evidence" *(State v. Koss* 1990, 49 Ohio St. 3d 213). In the decision, she cited numerous feminists' books and articles that documented and debated the syndrome, the American Psychological Association's recognition of it (which had been advocated by feminist therapists and psychologists), and the Ohio Legislature's introduction of a bill that would recognize battered woman syndrome in law as evidence that the syndrome deserved recognition by the court. Several activists expressed the opinion that the court reversed itself because legislation appeared imminent.

9. Two studies were conducted by the Research Department of the Ohio Department of Rehabilitation and Correction. The first found that 203 women were incarcerated for crimes related to domestic violence, with 97 cases identified in which battered woman syndrome was verified or claimed by the inmate (Black 1990). The second involved interviews with 20 women who exhibited traits of battered woman syndrome (Sussman 1990), That study was used to help the parole board and others involved in researching the clemencies understand what battered woman syndrome was. It was later used at a seminar sponsored by the governor and organized by the first lady to teach defense attorneys, judges, and other legal practitioners about the syndrome and has been read by incarcerated battered women seeking to understand their experiences.

10. In the clemency review process, the inadmissibility of battered woman syndrome expert testimony at the time women went to trial or were convicted was the rationale for the clemencies. The governor and his aides did not use the formal psychological definition of battered woman syndrome in their review of women's cases. Rather, they looked for five things: (1) evidence of long term, systematic abuse; (2) evidence of having come to terms with their experiences; (3) behavior while in prison; (4) prior criminal record; and (5) the length of time they had already served, with all women, including those granted clemency, needing to have served at least two years.

11. An obstacle faced by 34 of the women, whom the governor sent back for further review by the parole board, was their failure or inability to fully document their cases.

12. Schneider (1986) has cogently argued that battered woman syndrome relies on stereotypes of femininity and that women who do not fit the criteria of the perfect victim are likely to be harmed by a focus on battered woman syndrome.

13. December 28, 1989, through February 26, 1990. Governor Celeste Files, Series 4124, Box 4, Ohio Historical Society.

14. In groups open only to inmates, women varied in their degree of reclaiming identity, with each helping the others at various stages of the consciousness raising process. In addition to these private group sessions, a seminar was developed by an organization of inmates serving life sentences. At that seminar, formerly incarcerated battered women who killed abusers shared their life experiences with clemency applicants. The overwhelming response from inmates who attended was that the seminar was empowering and that more opportunities like it should be made available to women in prison. (This response is based on program evaluation forms filled out by all inmates who attended the seminar.)

15. Two of those men were authorities, expected to maintain a separation between their personal and official lives. The third was an activist who had worked to establish boundaries between his job, activism, and home life so that he could devote more time to his family.

References

Acklesberg, Martha A.
　1988 "Communities, resistance, and women's activism: Some implications for a democratic polity." In *Women and the Politics of Empowerment*, eds. Ann Bookman and Sandra Morgen, 297–313. Philadelphia: Temple University Press.

Alonso, Ana Maria
　1992 "Gender, power, and historical memory: Discourses of Serrano resistance." In *Feminists Theorize the Political*, eds. Judith Butler and Joan W. Scott, 404–425. New York: Routledge.

Bernstein, Richard J.
　1985 "Introduction." In *Habermas and Modernity*, ed. Richard J. Bernstein, 1–32. Cambridge: The MIT Press.

Black, Maureen
　1990 "Battered Spousal/Woman Syndrome Project: Report." Columbus: Ohio Department of Rehabilitation and Correction.

Bolotin, S.
　1982 "Views from the post-feminist generation." *New York Times Magazine*, October:29–31, 103–116.

Browne, Angela
　1987 *When Battered Women Kill*. New York: The Free Press.
　1993 "Violence against women by male partners: Prevalence, outcomes, and policy implications." *American Psychologist* 48:1077–1087.

Buechler, Steven M.
　1990 *Women's Movements in the United States*. New Brunswick: Rutgers University Press.

Cassell, Joan
　1977 *A Group Called Women: Sisterhood and Symbolism in the Feminist Movement*. Prospect Heights, Ill.: Waveland Press.

Charmaz, Kathy
　1983 "The grounded theory method: An explication and interpretation." In *Contemporary Field Research: A Collection of Readings*, ed. Robert M. Emerson, 109–126. Prospect Heights, Ill.: Waveland Press.

Chesler, Phyllis
　1989 *Women and Madness*. New York: Harcourt Brace Jovanovich.

Cohen, Jean L.
  1985 "Strategy or identity: New theoretical paradigms and contemporary social movements." *Social Research* 52:663–716.
Collins, Patricia Hill
  1986 "Learning from the outsider within: The sociological significance of black feminist thought." *Social Problems* 33:514–532.
  1990 *Black Feminist Thought: Knowledge, Consciousness, and the Politics of Empowerment.* London: HarperCollins Academic.
Crawford, Alan
  1980 *Thunder on the Right: The "New Right" and the Politics of Resentment.* New York: Pantheon Books.
D'Emilio, John
  1983 *Sexual Politics, Sexual Communities: The Making of a Homosexual Minority in the United States, 1940–1970.* Chicago: University of Chicago Press.
Dobash, R. Emerson, and Russell P. Dobash
  1992 *Women, Violence and Social Change.* New York: Routledge.
Echols, Alice
  1989 *Daring to Be Bad: Radical Feminism in America 1967–1975.* Minneapolis: University of Minnesota Press.
Elshtain, Jean Bethke
  1981 *Public Man, Private Woman: Women in Social and Political Thought.* Princeton, N.J.: Princeton University Press.
Evans, Sara
  1979 *Personal Politics.* New York: Vintage Books.
Faludi, Susan
  1991 *Backlash: The Undeclared War against American Women.* New York: Crown Publishers, Inc.
Ferraro, Kathleen J.
  1983 "Negotiating trouble in a battered women's shelter." *Urban Life* 12:287–306.
Ferree, Myra Marx
  1992 "The political context of rationality: Rational choice theory and resource mobilization." In *Frontiers in Social Movement Theory*, eds. Aldon D. Morris and Carol McClurg Mueller, 29–52. New Haven, Conn.: Yale University Press.
Ferree, Myra Marx, and Beth B. Hess
  1984 *Controversy and Coalition: The New Feminist Movement.* Boston: Twayne Publishers.
Mouffe, Chantal
  1992 "Feminism, citizenship, and radical democratic politics." In *Feminists Theorize the Political*, eds. Judith Butler and Joan W. Scott, 369–384. New York: Routledge.
Offe, Claus
  1985 "New social movements: Challenging the boundaries of institutional politics." *Social Research* 52:817–868.
Piven, Frances Fox, and Richard A. Cloward
  1977 *Poor People's Movements: Why They Succeed, How They Fail.* New York: Random House.
Schechter, Susan
  1982 *Women and Violence: The Visions and Struggles of the Battered Women's Movement.* Boston: South End Press.
Schneider, Elizabeth M.
  1986 "Describing and changing: Women's self-defense work and the problem of expert testimony on battering." *Women's Rights Law Reporter* 9:195–222.
Schur, Edwin M.
  1984 *Labeling Women Deviant: Gender, Stigma, and Social Control.* Philadelphia: Temple University Press.

Snow, David A., and Robert D. Benford
  1992 "Master frames and cycles of protest." In *Frontiers in Social Movement Theory*, eds. Aldon D. Morris and Carol McClurg Mueller, 133–155. New Haven, Conn.: Yale University Press.
Stacey, J.
  1987 "Sexism by a subtler name? Postindustrial conditions and postfeminist consciousness in the Silicon Valley." *Socialist Review* 17:7–28.
Steinem, Gloria
  1983 "Why younger women are more conservative." In *Outrageous Acts and Everyday Rebellions*, ed. Gloria Steinem, 211–218. New York: Holt, Rinehart and Winston.
Strauss, Anselm, and Juliet Corbin
  1990 *Basics of Qualitative Research: Grounded Theory Procedures and Techniques*. Newbury Park, Calif.: Sage.
Sussman, Vicki
  1990 "Battered women who commit violent offenses: A study of battered women incarcerated at the Ohio Reformatory for Women." Columbus, Ohio: Bureau of Planning and Research, Ohio Department of Rehabilitation and Correction.
Tarrow, Sidney
  1991 *Struggle, Politics, and Reform: Collective Action, Social Movements, and Cycles of Protest*. Ithaca, N.Y.: Center for International Studies, Cornell University.
Taylor, Verta, and Nancy Whittier
  1992 "Collective identity in social movement communities: Lesbian feminist mobilization." In *Frontiers in Social Movement Theory*, eds. Aldon D. Morris and Carol McClurg Mueller, 104–129. New Haven, Conn.: Yale University Press.
Tierney, Kathleen J.
  1982 "The battered women movement and the creation of the wife beating problem." *Social Problems* 29:207–220.
Tilly, Charles
  1988 "Social movements, old and new." *Research in Social Movements, Conflict and Change* 10:1–18.
Touraine, Alain
  1985 "An introduction to the study of social movements." *Social Research* 52:749–787.
Walker, Lenore
  1984 *The Battered Woman Syndrome*. New York: Springer Publishing Co.

Sources

The chapters in this volume originally appeared in *Social Problems* and are copyrighted by the Society for the Study of Social Problems. These works are reprinted with the permission of the publisher and the authors.

Chapter 1. Diana Scully and Joseph Marolla. "'Riding the Bull at Gilley's': Convicted Rapists Describe the Rewards of Rape." *Social Problems* 32, no. 3 (1985): 251–263.

Chapter 2. Russell P. Dobash, R. Emerson Dobash, Margo Wilson, and Martin Daly. "The Myth of Sexual Symmetry in Marital Violence." *Social Problems* 39, no. 1 (1992): 71–91.

Chapter 3. Carol Brooks Gardner. "Safe Conduct: Women, Crime, and Self in Public Places." *Social Problems* 37, no. 3 (1990): 311–328.

Chapter 4. Robert M. Emerson, Kerry O. Ferris, and Carol Brooks Gardner. "On Being Stalked." *Social Problems* 45, no. 3 (1998): 289–314.

Chapter 5. Kirsten Dellinger and Christine L. Williams. "The Locker Room and the Dorm Room: Workplace Norms and the Boundaries of Sexual Harassment in Magazine Editing." *Social Problems* 49, no. 2 (2002): 242–257.

Chapter 6. Cassia Spohn, Dawn Beichner, and Erika Davis-Frenzel. "Prosecutorial Justifications for Sexual Assault Case Rejection: Guarding the 'Gateway to Justice.'" *Social Problems* 48, no. 2 (2001): 206–235.

Chapter 7. Patricia Yancey Martin. "Gender, Accounts, and Rape Processing Work." *Social Problems* 44, no. 4 (1997): 464–482.

Chapter 8. Kathleen J. Ferraro. "Policing Woman Battering." *Social Problems* 36, no. 1 (1989): 61–74.

Chapter 9. Demie Kurz. "Emergency Department Responses to Battered Women: Resistance to Medicalization." *Social Problems* 34, no. 1 (1987): 69–81.

Chapter 10. Donileen R. Loseke and Spencer E. Cahill. "The Social Construction of Deviance: Experts on Battered Women." *Social Problems* 31, no. 3 (1984): 296–310.

Chapter 11. Kathleen J. Tierney. "The Battered Woman Movement and the Creation of the Wife Beating Problem." *Social Problems* 29, no. 3 (1982): 207–220.

Chapter 12. Patricia Gagné. "Identity, Strategy, and Feminist Politics: Clemency for Battered Women Who Kill." *Social Problems* 43, no. 1 (1996): 77–93.

Index

abortion counseling, 256n10
abuse: alcohol and drugs, 8; legislation against, 207, 208; past, evidence of, 263–64, 276n10; in romantic relationships, 86; of spouse, 81, 195; wife, 2, 3, 86, 266–68. *See also* child abuse
Abused Women's Aid in Crisis (AWAIC), 244
abusive relationships: death/killing and, 7, 9–10, 263, 267, 277n14; ending, 5, 8–9, 45; leaving/remaining in, 211, 214, 223–34, 263
accounts: discrepant, 135–36, 139–41, 147, 150, 154–57; frames and gendered organizations, 169–83, *173*; justificational, rape processing work and, 167–68, 171–83, *173*
Acker, Joan, 170
acquaintances, 1; rape by, 28n1, 134, 135, 146–47, 151, 154; stalking and, 5, 78–79, 83, 85–86, 88, 96, 105n10. *See also* friends
ACTION, 246
activism, 2, 6; battered women's movement and, 9, 243, 244, 247, 252, 261–75; gender and, 271–73; intimacy and, 272; police and, 7. *See also* feminist activism
adultery, homicides due to, 42
advocacy: for battered women, 191, 204, 207, 216, 217–19, 244, 252, 253; civil rights and, 255n5; legal, 2, 255n5; medical, 2; rape processing and, 168, 183; RCC, 172, 174, 175, 181. *See also* victim-witness-advocates (VWAs)
Aegis, 246
AIDS, 66–67, 143
Aid to Families with Dependent Children, 262
alcohol: domestic violence and, 195–99, 201–2; drugs and abuse, 8; drugs and battered women, 207, 209, 212–13, 215, 216, 217, 243, 245; drugs and sexual assault, 133–34, 143, 144, 146, 148, 150, 151, 154; drugs and stalking, 104n1
American College of Physicians, 207, 219
American Psychological Association, 276n8
anger: rape and, 15, 20–21; violence and, 34, 263–64
anticipated peril, 67–70
AOB (Alcohol on Breath), 212–13, 215, 216, 217
appearance, 4; communication and, 58–71, 72n7; of escorts, 61–65
Arizona: battered women's shelter in, 243; domestic violence law/policy, 7, 192–204
arrests: affidavit, for sexual assault cases, 136, 137; for assaults between unmarried people, 191–92, 194–97; battered women and, 7, 191–202; citizen's complaints and, 192, 195–97, 204; injuries and, 191, 194, 196, 197; legislation, 31, 191–204; for probable cause, 191–92, 193, 197, 202; warrants, 192, 201; witnesses and, 191–92, 194, 196, 197

assaults, 1; as crime, 31; definition of, 40; physicians and, 36; prevention of, 63, 64, 67, 68; in prisons, 270; between unmarried people, arrests for, 191–92, 194–97; wife, 223–34. *See also* sexual assaults

attorneys: gender and rape processing, 169, 172, 176, 179, 181; in sexual assault cases, 136–37, 139, 145, 150, 157, 158, 159, 161

Aveni, Adrian A., 256n11

Barrio, Robert, 97
Barry, Kathleen, 231
bars: dangerous, 200; lesbian, 122
battered husbands, 33–34, 36–37, 40–43
Battered Wives (Martin), 244
battered women, 160, 220n4; advocacy for, 191, 204, 207, 216, 217–19, 244, 252, 253; arrests and, 7, 191–204; children and, 243, 246, 249, 251; clemency for, 9–10, 261–79, 276n10; consciousness and identities, 267, 269–71, 274–75, 277n14; danger and, 7, 101, 191, 196, 197, 198, 200, 201, 211, 212, 217, 225; definition/identification of, 40–41, 195, 207–10, 215–17, 224, 231, 234; drugs and alcohol, 207, 209, 212–13, 215, 216, 217, 243, 245; EDs and, 207–19; excuses of, 225–34; experts on, 223–34; external/internal constraints for, 225–30, 232; femininity of, 227, 234; generalizability of, 228–29, 231; health care system and, 7–8, 207–19; hospitals and, 7–8, 169, 192; hotlines for, 210–11, 212, 213, 219, 244, 250; injuries and, 207–15, 219n3; legislation for, 243–46, 249–50, 252–54, 262–75; medicalization and, 207–19, 253; nurses and, 208–9, 212–16; physicians and, 8, 169, 207–9, 211–16, 219; police and, 7, 191–204, 210, 211, 249; referrals for, 208, 210, 213, 218–19; self and, 232, 234, 269; shelters for, 2, 192, 201, 202, 207, 211, 212, 213, 219, 231, 243–46, 249–51, 254, 255n6, 256n10, 263–64, 267, 271, 274, 276n6; as social problem, 191–92, 214–15, 217, 220n4, 223–24, 235n3, 243–54, 261; social services for, 207, 211, 223, 225, 226, 228, 229–30, 234; statistics on, 207–8, 210; stereotypes about, 7–8, 199, 214–15, 218, 234, 269, 277n12; suicides and, 209, 217; syndrome, 208, 215, 263–66, 269–71, 276nn7–10, 277n12; as "true" victims, 8, 211, 217; victimization of, 8–9, 227, 230, 231, 233, 234, 269. *See also* wife beating

battered women's movement, 9–10, 220n4; activism and, 9, 243, 244, 247, 252, 261–75; feminism and, 7, 9–10, 191, 218, 223, 243–44, 246, 248, 250–54, 255nn5–6; feminist politics and identities, 261–75; funding for, 9, 244–49, 251–54, 256n11; growth and impact of, 246–49, 253–54; history of, 9, 243–46; Ohio, 9–10, 262–79; resource mobilization and, 243, 246, 247–54, 255n4, 256n9, 261, 265, 267–68; stalking and, 77; wife beating and, 243–59

Baty, Kathleen, 94, 101
Berger, Brigitte, 223
Berger, Peter L., 223
Berk, R. A., 7
Berk, Sarah F., 195
birth parents, abuse by stepparents versus, 39, 41
Black, Donald, 17–18, 19, 192, 195
Black, Laura, 88, 92–93, 94, 105n14; Farley's letter to, 101, 102; rejection of Farley, 96, 97, 99
Blum, Alan F., 234
Blumberg, Rae Lesser, 16
Blumer, Herbert, 255n3
body idiom, 58
Bordenkircher v. Hayes, 131
Boswell, 114, 115, 118–19
Brownmiller, Susan, 23
Brush, Lisa D., 36
Bureau of Census Crime Victimization Studies, 16

Cahill, Spencer, 8–9
Canada: homicide in, 42–43; sexual symmetry in, 36, 42–43; surveys in, 35
Caringella-MacDonald, Susan, 168
catcalls, 55, 58–59, 71
celebrities. *See* stalkings; *specific celebrities*

Celeste, Dagmar, 262, 265–68, 270–71, 273, 276n2
Celeste, Richard, 9, 262–66, 271, 273, 276n11
Center for Women Policy Studies, 246
CETA. *See* Comprehensive Employment Training Act
Chauncey, Robert L., 247
Cheyenne people, rape and, 17–18
child abuse, 207, 235n8, 255n3; funding for, 246; legislation for, 208; responses to, 253; by stepparents versus birth parents, 39, 41
children, 272: abusive relationships' impact on, 9; battered women and, 243, 246, 249, 251; defense of, 41; domestic violence and, 199, 201, 202; foster, 202; rape and, 137, 149, 151, 154, 163n2; therapeutic programs for, 2; violence experienced as, 34, 235n10
Chiswick Women's Aid, 243, 250
The Chronicle of Higher Education, 15–16
citizens: complaints, 192, 195–97, 204; deviant versus normal, 198
civil rights, advocacy and, 255n5
Clark, Robert E., 105n17
clemency, for battered women, 9–10, 261–79, 276n10
Cloward, Richard, 256n11
Cluss, Patricia, 168
Cohen, Jean L., 273
college women: rapes of, 15, 28n1; self-esteem and, 231; sex and, 121, 122
Collins, Patricia Hill, 268
Combined Insurance, 170
communication: appearance and, 58–71; characteristics, 58–60; episodic, 59, 67; and self in public places, 58–60, 72n7
Community Services Administration, 246, 251
Comprehensive Employment Training Act (CETA), 244, 246, 251
Conflict Tactics Scales (CTS), 3–4, 32–44
Connell, Robert W., 110, 119
Conrad, Peter, 218
consent: rapes and, 25, 167; sexual assaults and, 2, 135, 140–45, 147, 149, 151, *153*, 154–55, 156, 158, 162, 163n2; stalkings and, 92, 104n2
cooptation, 254, 261, 262, 271, 274, 275n1

counseling, 2; abortion, 256n10; for battered women, 244, 249, 254
courts, 2, 35; battered women's movement and, 244, 245, 249–50, 251–52, 253, 263–64, 266, 267, 270, 271, 276nn7–8; domestic violence and, 191–204; gender and rape processing, 167; sexual harassment and, 124–25. *See also* attorneys; judges; juries; prosecutors
credibility: of RCCs, 176; of sexual assault victims, 6, 132, 133, 134, 137, 141, 145, 147–50, 154, 156–57, 161–62; victimizations and, 6
crime: assaults as, 31; fear of, 1, 55–57, 69, 72n4; prevention, 4–5, 55–75, 72n6
criminal justice system: battered women and, 270; on sexual assault, 131–62; victim treatment by, 171; views of rape, 176; on violence, 31; wife beating and, 245, 251–52, 253. *See also* courts; police
CTS. *See* Conflict Tactics Scales
culture: factors in rape, 16–18, 27; gender and, 167, 168; locker room/dorm room, 115, 116–19, 121, 124; of workplace, 5, 109–25, 170–83
Curry, Timothy Jon, 117

danger: battered women and, 7, 101, 191, 196, 197, 198, 200, 201, 211, 212, 217, 225; gender and, 46; police and, 191, 196, 197, 198, 200, 201; race and rape, 23, 24–25, 27; of strangers, 5, 225; violence in response to, 4; for women in public places, 63, 67–70
dangerous offenders, 133
date rape, 2, 15, 22–23, 121; gang, 25; as sexual assault, 141–43, 158
dating: stalking and, 78, 83–84, 93; violence with, 34
Davidson, Terry, 244
Davis, Angela, 28n9
Davis, Murray S., 86
Dellinger, Kirsten, 5
Denmark, homicide in, 42
Denzin, Norman K., 235n8
Department of Health and Human Services, 246
Department of Motor Vehicles (DMV), 91, 105n12
depression, 209

deviance, social construction of, 223–34
deviant behaviors, 144; breaches of civility as, 72n3; normal versus, 8, 56; sociologists on, 207, 247
deviants, 7; battered women as, 215, 223–34
discrepant accounts, 135–36, 139–41, 147, 150, 154–57
discrimination, 55; gender, 5, 125; sex, 125; against women, 114
disgusting behavior, for crime prevention, 66–67
divorce, 35, 235n11; separations and, 8, 83, 232
Dobash, R. Emerson, 233, 235n13
Dobash, Russell, 3–4, 233, 235n13
domestic violence: alcohol and, 195–99, 201–2; Arizona's law/policy for, 7, 192–204; children and, 199, 201, 202; courts and, 191–204; homicides and, 191, 199; hotlines, 201; income and, 194, 198; judges and, 193, 203; legislation, 81, 191–204; as mutual combat cases, 202; police and, 191–204; pressing charges for, 192, 196, 197, 202; programs, 245, 253–54; stalking and, 77; and threats of murder, 199–200, 201. *See also* marital violence
Domestic Violence Assistance Act, 245
Domestic Violence Prevention Services Act, 245
dorm room culture, 120–24
Downs, Anthony, 250
dress. *See* appearance
drugs, 255n3; alcohol and abuse, 8; alcohol and battered women, 207, 209, 212–13, 215, 216, 217, 243, 245; alcohol and sexual assault, 133–34, 143, 144, 146, 148, 150, 151, 154; alcohol and stalking, 104n1; sexual battery and, 163n2
Durkheim, Émile, 124
Duster, Troy, 255n3

EDs. *See* emergency departments, battered women and
egalitarianism, 60, 72n3
Eisenberg, Sue, 255n1
emergency departments (EDs), battered women and, 207–19

emergency rooms (ERs), 7–8; gender and rape processing, 177; nurses/physicians in, 167
Emerson, Robert, 5
England: battered women in, 243, 250; rape in Wales and, 16; spousal homicide in Wales and, 43. *See also* Great Britain
epilepsy, 67, 72n8
ERA America, 264
Erchak, Gerald M., 235n8
erotomania, 78
ERs. *See* emergency rooms
escorts, appearance of, 61–65
Estrich, Susan, 133, 161
excuses, battered women's, 225–34

families: fights, 191, 193–95, 197–201, 203; massacres, 42; rapes by, 2; as social groups, 45; support of, 9; systems theory analysis of, 235n8; violence, 2, 6, 32, 41, 44–46, 191–204, 247
Farley, Richard, 88, 92–93, 94, 105n14; Black, Laura, rejection of, 96, 97, 99; letter to Black, Laura, 101, 102
fear: of crime, 1, 55–57, 69, 72n4; of rape, 56–57, 174–75; of reprisals, 227; response to, 263
Federal Bureau of Investigation, 249
felonies, 137, 145, 163n2
femininity, of battered women, 227, 234
feminism: battered women's movement and, 7, 9–10, 191, 218, 223, 243–44, 246, 248, 250–54, 255nn5–6; gender and rape processing, 168, 170, 171, 183; magazine, 110–12, 119–25; on police, 7; on rape, 16–17, 28n9; in United States, 122; on victimization, 2; on violence, 3, 6
feminist activism, 241–79
Feminist Alliance Against Rape, 246
feminist politics, 261–75
Ferraro, Kathleen, 7, 233
Feshback, Seymour, 15–16
Field, Henry F., 245
Field, Martha H., 245
Fishman, Mark, 255n7
Florida, sexual battery in, 136–62, *138–39, 152–53,* 162nn2–4
following, stalking and, 81–83, 86–92
Ford, David A., 160
Foster, Jodie, 77

frames: gendered organizations and accounts, 169–83, *173*; wife abuse and, 266–68
Freeman, Jo, 252
friends, 1; rape by, 151
Frohmann, Lisa, 131–61
funding: for battered women's movement, 9, 244–49, 251–54, 256n11; for child abuse, 246; government, 2, 207, 243–47, 251–53, 256nn10–11

Gagné, Patricia, 9–10
gangs: conflicts, 200; rape, 3, 24–25
Gaquin, Deirdre A., 35
Gardner, Carol Brooks, 4–5
Gayford, J. J., 233, 235n9
gays. *See* homosexuals
Gelles, Richard J., 31–34, 38–40, 44–45, 235n12
gender: activism and, 271–73; battered women and, 209, 218, 267; biases of laws, 261, 263–64, 266, 276n7; crime prevention and, 57, 59, 62–71; danger and, 46; discrimination, 5, 125; fear of crime and, 1, 55–57, 72n4; intimate violence and women's empowerment, 191; of police and domestic violence, 200; power and, 2; rape processing work and, 6–7, 167–83, *173*; self-esteem and, 230; sexual harassment and, 110–11, 112, 114–15, 121, 124; socialization and, 17, 45; stalking and, 77, 89–90, 93; stereotypes, 175, 182; symmetry in violence, 4, 31–54. *See also* men; women
gendered organizations, frames and accounts, 169–83, *173*
Gentleman's Sophisticate, 110–19, 123–25
Gerlach, Luther P., 248
Giles-Sims, Jean, 235n8
Giuffre, Patti A., 118
Goffman, Erving, 56, 58, 59, 70, 72n3; on contemporary frame analysis, 170; on sexual harassment, 124
Goode, William J., 232
government: funding, 2, 207, 243–47, 251–53, 256nn10–11; hearings, 223
grassroots groups, 243, 248, 254, 255n6
Great Britain, 35; homicide in, 42–43
Griffin, Susan, 20
Groth, Nicholas, 15, 22
Gruber, James E., 111

guns: sexual symmetry and, 34, 39, 43; in United States, 43

Haber, Scott, 15–16
harassment, 104n5; legislation, 81; in prisons, 270; in public places, 56, 57; in workplaces, 5, 109–27. *See also* sexual harassment; verbal harassment
Harrop, John W., 39
Haven House, 243
Hawkins, Richard, 234
health care system, 7–8, 207–19. *See also* hospitals; nurses; physicians
Healy, Suzanne, 98
Herman, Dianne, 17
Hine, Virginia H., 248
Hirschi, Travis, 27
hitchhiking, rape and, 25, 133, 151
Hofeller, Kathleen H., 230, 235n12
Holmes, Karen, 168
Homey, Julie, 162
homicides: domestic violence and, 191, 199; sexual symmetry in, 31, 34, 39, 41–43
homophobia, 111
homosexuals, 24; police on, 198; sexual harassment and, 117–18, 122. *See also* lesbians
hospitals, 2, 34, 35–36, 172, 209–10; battered women and, 7–8, 169, 192; gender and rape processing by, 167, 172, 174, 177, 183; interns at, 209, 215, 216; police and, 174, 177, 192; sexual harassment in, 109. *See also* emergency departments (EDs), battered women and; emergency rooms (ERs); nurses; physicians
hotlines: for battered women, 210–11, 212, 213, 219, 244, 250; domestic violence, 201; rape, 2; suicide, 244
House Bill 484, 264–65, 266, 270
housing projects, 197, 198, 203–4
humor, sexual harassment and, 113–25
husbands, 72n1. *See also* battered husbands
hyper-hetero extreme talk, 117–18

identities, 114, 120; consciousness and battered women, 267, 269–71, 274–75, 277n14; feminist politics and battered women's movement, 261–75
infanticide, 43

injuries: accidents versus battering, 212; arrests and, 191, 194, 196, 197; battered women and, 207–15, 219n3; from rape/sexual assault, 135, 140, 142, 143, 151, *153,* 154, *155,* 156, 158, 159, 162, 163n2; from violence, 46n1
institutions: on sexual assaults, 5–8; on violence, 3, 31, 129–240
interns: at hospitals, 209, 215, 216; at magazines, 114, 119, 121–23
intimacy, 24
intimate partner violence: institutions on, 5–8; men versus women and, 3–4; public awareness of, 9, 243–47, 249–53, 255n3, 255n6, 255n9; research on, 2; strangers versus, 1–2, 5
intimate partners: killings and, 4, 262; sexual assault by, 6, 151, 154, 158; stalking by, 5; strangers versus, 1–2, 5, 158, 160, 162
intoxication. *See* alcohol
"the Invisible Man Routine," 63

Jacksonville Shipyard, 114
jealousy, 45, 100–102, 146
Jensen, Gary, 168
job training, 2
Joffee, Carol, 256n10
Johnson, Allan Griswold, 16
Jouriles, Ernest N., 38
judges: domestic violence and, 193, 203; gender and rape processing, 167, 168, 169, 172, *173,* 179; sexual assault and, 132–33, 137, 156–57, 161
juries: battered woman syndrome and, 263, 276n7; gender and rape processing by, 169, *173,* 176; sexual assault and, 132–33, 134, 136, 150, 151, 156–59
justifications: battered women's, 225–34; for forced sexual access, 17; prosecutors', of case rejection, 131–61, *139;* rape processing work and, 167–68, 171–83, *173;* for rejection of sexual assault cases, 131–66, *139, 152–53;* for sexual assault cases, 146–47

Kalmuss, Debra, 255n6
Kappa calculations, 38, 47n3
Karpos, Mayaltani, 168
Katz, Jack, 105n18
kidnapping, 101–2, 135, 147

killings: abusive relationships and, 7, 9–10, 263, 267, 277n14; intimate partners and, 4, 262
Kitsuse, John I., 255n3
Konradi, Amanda, 175
Koss, Mary P., 15
Krueger, Bob, 83, 101
Kurz, Demie, 7–8

LaBeff, Emily E., 105n17
La Casa de las Madres, 243
LaFree, Gary, 28n9, 134, 151, 161
law enforcement: battered women's movement and, 244, 245, 251–52, 253; gender and rape processing by, 167–69, 171–83. *See also* police
Law Enforcement Assistance Administration (LEAA), 16, 244, 245–46, 251–52
laws: Arizona's domestic violence, 7, 192–204; gender biases of, 261, 263–64, 266, 276n7; for TROs, 192
lawsuits, sexual harassment, 114
LEAA. *See* Law Enforcement Assistance Administration
Lee, John A., 80
legal advocacy, 2, 255n5
legislation: against abuse, 207, 208; antistalking, 77; arrests, 31, 191–204; for battered women, 243–46, 249–50, 252–54, 262–75; domestic violence, 81, 191–204; harassment, 81; rape, 6, 161–62
Leidner, Robin, 170
lesbians, 122, 183
Letko, Carolyn, 235n12
Letterman, David, 77
Litigation Coalition for Battered Women, 249–50
locker room culture, 115, 116–19, 121, 124
Loe, Meika, 109
Lorber, Judith, 215
Loseke, Donileen, 8–9, 195, 234
Lucca, Joseph S., 42–43
Lyman, Peter, 117
Lyman, Stanford M., 224–25, 228
Lystad, Mary H., 35

magazines: on battered women, 246, 250; feminism, 110–12, 119–25; interns at, 114, 119, 121–23; pornography, 5,

110–25; sexual harassment at, 5, 109–25; women in, 4. *See also specific magazines*
Malamuth, Neil, 15–16, 24
Maldonado, Art, 99, 105n14
Mann, CoraMae Richey, 34
Mann, Douglas, 97–98
Manning, Peter K., 192, 196
maquiladora plant, 109–10, 111, 115
Margolin, Gayla, 40
marital violence: causes of, 45–46; sexual symmetry in, 31–54; as social problem, 31, 36
Marolla, Joseph, 3
marriage, 272; domestic violence and, 194–95, 196; sexual abuse in, 16; stability of, 224, 226, 232; as term, 235n1; wife beating and, 253. *See also* divorce; separations; spouses; wedding rings
Martin, Del, 244
Martin, Patricia Yancey, 6–7
masculinity, hegemonic, 110, 119
masochism, 227, 235n9
massacres, family, 42
Mauss, Armand, 255n3
Maxfield, Michael G., 42
McCahill, Thomas W., 169
McCarthy, John D., 247
McDonald's Corporation, 170
McHugh, Peter, 234
McNeely, R. L., 34, 42
media, 247, 249–51, 254. *See also specific media*
medicalization: battered women and, 207–19, 253; of rape, 15–16
men: fear of crime, 1; as fictitious companions, 4, 61–65; income and domestic violence, 198; Neanderthal, 118–19; self-esteem and, 46; sexual needs of, 15, 17, 22–23. *See also* husbands
mental disease/illness, 72n8; angry response as, 263–64; rape as result of, 15; as social problem, 255n3; stalking and, 78, 104n1
mental health organizations: battered women and, 244, 246, 248, 251, 255n2, 255n5, 263–64, 267, 274; domestic violence and, 191, 193, 201
Messner, Michael A., 116
Micklow, Patricia, 255n1
middle-class etiquette, 55, 71
Mills, C. Wright, 2, 231

Ms. magazine, 235n12, 244, 250
murders: domestic violence and threats of, 199–200, 201; rape and, 18, 19, 21, 26, 71, 145; sexual symmetry and, 33–34; stalkings and, 77, 101–2, 104n7, 105n18; suicides, 42, 101–2. *See also* homicides; killings; massacres, family
Murphy, Holly, 100
mutual combat cases, 202

National Coalition against Domestic Violence, 246
National Coalition on Domestic Violence, 219
National Crime Victimization Survey (NCVS), 1–2
National Institute of Justice, 77
National Institute of Mental Health, 246
National Organization for Women (NOW), 244, 248, 249, 255n6
National Violence Against Women Survey, 78–79
National Women's Aid Federation, 243
NCVS. *See* National Crime Victimization Survey
Neighborhood Justice Programs, 245, 251
Nelligan, Peter J., 169
New York Times, 249–50
no-drop prosecution, 7
NOW. *See* National Organization for Women
nurses: on assault prevention, 63, 64, 67, 68; battered women and, 208–9, 212–16; gender and rape processing, 167, 169, 177, 178, 182; on sexual elements of job, 109; stalking, 95

obsession, 104n5; stalking and, 77, 78, 100
ODVN. *See* Ohio Domestic Violence Network
Oerton, Sarah, 122
Office on Domestic Violence, 246
Ohio battered women's movement, 9–10, 262–79
Ohio Domestic Violence Network (ODVN), 264, 266
Ohio Reformatory for Women (ORW), 265, 268, 274
O'Leary, K. Daniel, 38, 230, 235n12
orgasm, rape and, 17, 20, 24

Ortega, Ruben, 193, 194, 203, 205
ORW. *See* Ohio Reformatory for Women

Paeplow, Colleen, 172
Pagelow, Mildred Daley, 230–31
Perry, Brooke, 82, 88, 93, 98, 99
Perry, Luke, 94
Petersen, Danica, 91, 98, 99, 100, 105n14
Pfohl, Stephen J., 255n3
physicians: assault and, 36; battered women and, 8, 169, 207–9, 211–16, 219; child abuse and, 208; gender and rape processing by, 167, 169, 178
Piven, Frances Fox, 256n11
Pizzey, Erin, 243
Plath, Sylvia, 55
Platt, Anthony, 255n3
police, 34, 35–36, 78; activism and, 7; battered women and, 7, 191–204, 210, 211, 249; citizen's complaints against, 204; danger and, 196, 197, 198, 200, 201; domestic violence and, 191–204; feminism on, 7; gender and rape processing, 167–69, 171–83; on homosexuals, 198; hospitals and, 174, 177, 192; rape investigations, 137, 140–41, 143–44, 145, 149, 151; reporting to, 1, 7, 25, 36, 79, 91, 99, 194; safety near, 61, 62; victimization by, 2. *See also* law enforcement
politics. *See* feminist politics
pornography: magazine, 5, 110–25; rape and, 17, 24, 158
post-traumatic stress disorder, 263
Powell, Marlene, 170–71, 172
power, 110; gender and, 2; rape and, 15, 17, 23–24, 27; resource control and, 253; sexual harassment and, 121–23; in violent relationships, 249
pregnancy, 72n8, 207; sexual assault and, 135, 151, 154, 158
Prescott, Suzanne, 235n12
pressing charges: battered women by, 211, 249, 270; for domestic violence, 192, 196, 197, 202
Prince, David, 102
prisons: battered women in, clemency for, 9–10, 261–79; harassment/assault in, 270; interviews of rapists in, 15–30

probable cause, arrests for, 191–92, 193, 197, 202
probation, violation of, 163n6
property damage, arrests and, 191, 197–98, 200
prosecutors: battered women's movement and, 245; gender and rape processing by, 167–69, 171–72, *173*, 175–76, 178–79, 181, 183; justifications, of case rejection, 131–61, *139*; services through, 2; on sexual assault/rape, 6, 131–62. *See also* no-drop prosecution
prostitutes, 24, 25; rape victims as, 135, 144, 148, 150, 151, 154
protection orders: battered women and, 245; domestic violence and, 192–93, 201
Pryor, John B., 111
public places, 60; self in, women and crime, 55–75; stalking and, 87–88, 90

race: clemency and, 262, 276n4; crime prevention and, 57; danger and rape, 23, 24–25, 27; domestic violence and, 194, 196; rape and, 18–19, 22, 23, 28nn9–10, 132, 136, 141, 151, 170; sexual harassment and, 116–17; stalking and, 89; stereotypes and, 58–59, 199
Radford, Jill, 70
Rainbow Retreat, 243
rape crisis centers (RCCs), 2, 244; gender and rape processing, 167, 168, 172, 174, 175, 176, 177, 180, 181, 183
rape processing work: gender and, 6–7, 167–83; justificational accounts and, 167–68, 171–83, *173;* training and, 168, *173*, 178, 180, 182, 183
rapes, 255n3; by acquaintances, 28n1, 134, 135, 146–47, 151, 154; admitters and deniers of, 28n4; as adventure/recreation, 3, 24–25, 27; anger and, 15, 20–21; children and, 137, 149, 151, 154, 163n2; of college women, 15, 28n1; consent and, 25, 167; cultural factors in, 16–18, 27; danger and, 23, 24–25, 27; date, 2, 15, 22–23, 25, 121, 141–43, 158; as dominance over women, 3, 16–24, 26–27; by family members, 2; fear of, 56–57, 174–75; feminism on, 16–17, 28n9; -free societies, 16; gang, 3, 24–25; hitchhiking and, 25, 133, 151; hotlines,

2; as impersonal act, 17, 23–24, 26–27; injuries from sexual assault and, 135, 140, 142, 143, 151, *153,* 154, *155,* 156, 158, 159, 162, 163n2; legislation, 6, 161–62; mass, 18; medicalization of, 15–16; motivations for, 3, 15–27; murder and, 18, 19, 21, 26, 71, 145; pornography and, 17, 24, 158; power and, 15, 17, 23–24, 27; prevention, 2, 27, 28n1, 71, 167; prison interviews of rapists, 15–30; prosecutors on, 6, 131–62; psychopathological view of, 15–16, 17–18, 27; public attitudes toward, 22; race and, 18–19, 22, 23, 28nn9–10, 132, 136, 141, 151, 170; reporting, 28nn10–11, 143–44, 147; as result of mental disease, 15; for revenge/punishment, 3, 17–18, 19–21, 26; risks of, 16; robbery/burglary and, 3, 18, 21–22, 23, 26; scenarios and inferences about victim, 143; self-esteem and, 26–27; as sexual access, 3, 22–23, 26; spousal, 28n6; stereotypes and, 6, 132; strangers and, 6, 20, 25, 56, 133–34, 151, *152–53,* 154–56, *155,* 157–59, 162, 164n9; trauma syndrome, 227; treatment centers, 139, 142; validity and, 19; victims as prostitutes, 135, 144, 148, 150, 151, 154; wife, 2, 20; as word, 28n7. *See also* date rape

RCCs. *See* rape crisis centers
"real" self, 59, 62, 64
"real" victims, 6, 8
relatives: child abuse by, 39, 41; domestic violence and, 194; sexual assault by, 6, 144–45, 151, *152,* 154, *155,* 158, 160, 162. *See also* families
reliability: battered women and, 228, 229–31; and validity of CTS, 37–39, 41, 44
reprisals, fear of, 227
Resnick, Alice Robie, 276n8
Response newsletter, 246
restraining orders, 2, 245. *See also* temporary restraining orders (TROs)
retaliation, violence in, 33, 214
rhetoric of limited competence, 56, 60–70
Rhodes, James, 265
robbery/burglary, rape and, 3, 18, 21–22, 23, 26

Robinson, Lois, 114
Robinson-Simpson, Gloria, 34, 42
Rose, Vicki McNickle, 255n3
Rosenbaum, Alan, 230, 235n12
Roth, Julius A., 217
Rounsaville, Bruce, 235n14
Rouse, Linda P., 51
Roy, Maria, 244

sadism, rape and, 15
safety, 7, 9; public places and rhetoric of limited competence, 60–70
Saldana, Theresa, 77, 78
Salzinger, Leslie, 109–10, 111, 115
Sanday, Peggy Reeves, 16
Schaeffer, Rebecca, 77, 78, 97, 100–101, 105n12
Schneider, Joseph W., 218
schools, 2
Schultz, Vicki, 124–25
Schwartz, Martin D., 36
Scott, Marvin B., 224–25, 228
Scream Quietly or the Neighbors Will Hear (Pizzey), 243
Scully, Diana, 3
segregation, 23
self: battered women and, 232, 234, 269; and communication in public places, 58–60, 72n7; profaning of, 4, 61, 65–67, 70; "real," 59, 62, 64; situated, 56, 58, 60–61, 64–65, 67, 69–71; "true," 64; women and crime, in public places, 55–75
self-defense: crime prevention and, 57, 58, 64, 68, 70, 72n6; law, gender biases of, 263–64, 266, 276n7; violence in, 4, 33, 41, 42
self-esteem: college women and, 231; gender and, 230; men and, 46; rape and, 26–27
self-limiting radicalism, 268, 273
separations: divorce and, 8, 83, 232; stalking and, 83, 94, 97, 106n19; uncoupling and, 106n19, 232
sex: business versus personal, 118–21, 123; college women and, 121, 122; discrimination, 125; as exchange of goods, 17; joking about, 113–25; oral, 142; rough, 149
sexual access: forced, justifications for, 17; rape as, 3, 22–23, 26

sexual assault cases: arrest affidavit for, 136, 137; characteristics and outcomes, 150–51, *152–53*, 154–62, *155*, 163n7; charge reduction for, 137–38; closeout memorandums for, 136–37, 139, 141–42, 145–47, 148–50, 159, 163n6, 164n9; conviction odds for, 132–34, 136, 138, 141, 156, 159–61; dismissal/dropping, 138–40, 148–49, *152–53*, 159–61, 163n6; evidence in, 132, 137, 142, 147, 161; false complaints, 135, 144, 146–47, 149, 154, 158; justifications for rejection of, 131–66, *139, 152–53*; pre-file interviews, 6, 139, 147–49, 160, 161; processing decisions, 133–34; reporting, 135, 140–41, 143–44, 146–47, 154; screening of, 132, 134, 137–38; seriousness of offense, 132, 133; typefications of behavior, 134–36, 141–44; witnesses for, 135, 136, 140, 142, 145, 146, 147, 148, 149, 151, 157

sexual assaults, 3; alcohol and drugs, 133–34, 143, 144, 146, 148, 150, 151, 154; case processing decisions, 6, 133–34; causes of, 2; consent and, 2, 135, 140–45, 147, 149, 151, *153*, 154–55, 156, 158, 162, 163n2; date rape as, 141–43, 158; institutions on, 5–8; location of, 154, 155, 163n8; physical evidence of, 154, 171, 180–81; plea bargains for, 131; pregnancy and, 135, 151, 154, 158; prosecutors on, 6, 131–62; stereotypes and, 6, 132–33, 134, 136, 157–58, 161, 162; as victimization, 1. *See also* rapes

sexual assault suspects: characteristics of, 131–32, 136, 150–51, *152–53*, 154–55, *155*, 163n7; culpability of, 132, 133; guilt in another case, 140, 163n6; relationships between victims and, 132, 133, 134, 135, 140–43, 145–47, 151, 154–55, 158–60, 162, 163n8

sexual assault victims: age of, 23, 133, 154, 156; body language of, 135; characteristics of, 131–34, 150–51, *152–53*, 154–62, *155*, 162n1, 163n7; cooperation by, 132, 133, 137, 139, 147–49, 150, 154–56, 158, 160, 161; credibility of, 6, 132, 133, 134, 137, 141, 145, 147–50, 154, 156–57, 161–62; discrepant accounts by, 135–36, 139–41, 147, 150, 154–57; failure to appear/locate, 147–49, 150, 154–56, 158, 160, 161; lying by, 140, 145–47, 158, 171; moral character of, 134, 143, 151, 154, 156, 161; promiscuity of, 143; as prostitutes, 135, 144, 148, 150, 151; recanting testimony, 139–40, 145–49, 150, *152–53*, 154, 159–61; relationships between suspects and, 132, 133, 134, 135, 140–43, 145–47, 151, 154–55, 158–60, 162, 163n8; risk-taking behavior by, 133–34, 147, 151, 154–56, 159; as runaways, 148, 151, 154; as street persons, 148, 150; ulterior motives of, 135, 136, 139, 144–47, 150, 154–56

sexual battery: drugs and, 163nn2; in Florida, 136–62, *138–39, 152–53*, 162nn2–4

sexual battery cases, 162n2; screening/rejection of, 136–38, *138*, 155

sexual fantasies, 116, 117

sexual harassment, 3; complaints, 121; definition of, 5; lawsuits, 114; at magazines, 5, 109–25; stalking versus, 77; in workplaces, 5, 109–27

sexual objectification, 109–10, 115

sexual symmetry, in marital violence, 31–54

sexually transmitted diseases, 135, 143, 158. *See also* AIDS; venereal disease

shelters, 34, 35; for battered women, 2, 192, 201, 202, 207, 211, 212, 213, 219, 231, 243–46, 249–51, 254, 255n6, 256n10, 263–64, 267, 271, 274, 276n6; as social movement organizations, 261, 274

Sherman, L. W., 7

Shupe, Anson, 34, 36

situated self, 56, 58, 60–61, 64–65, 67, 69–71

Smith, Don, 17

Smith, Dorothy, 182

Smithyman, Samuel, 26

SMOs. *See* social movement organizations

Snell, John E., 235n9

social change, feminist activism and, 241–79

social costs, of sentencing decisions, 133

social groups: dangerous, 133; families as, 45

socialization: gender and, 17, 45; violence and, 45

social movement organizations (SMOs), 243–54, 255n3, 275; shelters as, 261, 274 social problems: alcoholism and mental illness as, 255n3; battered women as, 191–92, 214–15, 217, 220n4, 223–24, 235n3, 243–54, 261; definition of, 207, 247, 255n3; marital violence as, 31, 36; rape as medicalized, 15–16; sociologists on, 207; stalking as, 77–80; violence as, 1–10, 34

Social Problems, 3, 5, 6

social realities, 59, 67

social scientists: on gender of rape processors, 168; on violence, 2

social services, for battered women, 207, 211, 223, 225, 226, 228, 229–30, 234

social stresses, 34

social workers: battered women and, 216, 219; rape processing and, 178

Society for the Study of Social Problems, 3

sociologists: on deviant behaviors, 207, 247; on family violence, 247; on interracial rape, 28n9; on sexual harassment, 109, 124

sodomy, 18

Spector, Malcolm, 255n3

Spohn, Cassia, 6, 162

spouses: abuse of, 81, 195; beating, 32; homicide of, 42–43; stalking by, 78. *See also* husbands; wives

Stagner, Larry, 94, 101

stalkings, 1, 3, 5, 77–108; acquaintances and, 5, 78–79, 83, 85–86, 88, 96, 105n10; celebrity, 77, 78, 82, 88–89, 90, 94, 96, 102, 104nn7–8, 105n13; consent and, 92, 104n2; crime prevention and, 68; dating and, 78, 83–84, 93; drugs and alcohol, 104n1; ex-partner, 78, 96–97; following and, 81–83, 86–92; gender and, 77, 89–90, 93; history of, 79, 85–86; information gathering and, 80, 90–93, 94, 102, 105n14; legislation against, 77; love versus, 78, 80; mental disease/illness and, 78, 104n1; murders and, 77, 101–2, 104n7, 105n18; normal relationships versus, 77, 79–80, 86, 102–3; obsession and, 77, 78, 100; proposals and rejections, 80, 85, 93–100, 102–3; pseudoacquainted, 83, 88, 96; race and, 89; relational, 5, 83–88; revenge, 84–85, 100–102; semi-acquainted, 83; as social problem, 77–80; strangers and, 77, 78, 79, 84–89, 93, 105n10; as term, 82, 85, 103, 104n5; in Texas, 83, 99, 101; unacquainted, 83–84, 86–87, 94; violence and, 77, 79, 81, 84–86, 100–102

Stanko, Elizabeth, 132

Star, Barbara, 230–31

Stark, Evan, 217, 219n3

Steffensmeier, Darrell, 133

Steinmetz, Suzanne K., 31, 33–34, 36, 40–43

stepparents, abuse by birth parents versus, 39, 41

stereotypes: about battered women, 7–8, 199, 214–15, 218, 234, 269, 277n12; gender, 175, 182; race and, 58–59, 199; rapes and, 6, 132; sexual assault and, 6, 132–33, 134, 136, 157–58, 161, 162

Stets, Jan E., 33

Stockholm Syndrome, 233

strangers: danger of, 5, 225; intimate partners versus, 1–2, 5, 158, 160, 162; in public places, 56, 58–60, 62–63, 67–69; rape and, 6, 20, 25, 56, 133–34, 151, *152–53*, 154–56, *155*, 157–59, 162, 164n9; stalking and, 77, 78, 79, 84–89, 93, 105n10

Straus, Murray A., 31–34, 36–40, 44–45; on battered women, 235n3, 235n8, 255n6

street persons, 148, 150

stresses: response syndrome, 227; social, 34. *See also* post-traumatic stress disorder

Sudnow, David, 217

suicides: battered women and, 209, 217; hotlines, 244; murder, 42, 101–2

Supplemental Security Income, 262

Supreme Court: battered women and, 264, 266, 271; sexual assault and, 131

symmetry, in violence, 4, 31–54

Szinovacz, Maximiliane E., 38

television, 250, 270

Teller, Tina, 98

temporary restraining orders (TROs), 79, 81–82, 88, 104n7, 192

testimony: expert, battered women and, 263–64, 276n10; sexual assault victims' recanting, 139–40, 145–49, 150, *152–53*, 154, 159–61

Texas: probation violation in, 163n6; stalkings in, 83, 99, 101
Thoennes, Nancy, 78–79, 93, 104n2, 105n10
Thorne, Barrie, 167, 170
Tiedeman, Gary, 234
Tierney, Kathleen, 9–10
"Title XX" funds, 246
Tjaden, Patricia, 78–79, 93, 104n2, 105n10
Transition House, 243
TROs. *See* temporary restraining orders
"true" love, 80
"true" self, 64
"true" victims, 8, 211, 217

uncoupling, 80, 97, 102–3, 232; separation and, 106n19, 232
United States: crime prevention in, 56–57; feminism in, 122; guns in, 43; homicides in, 31, 42–43; rape in, 16–17, 23; Surgeon General of, 207; surveys in, 31–46
United Way, 244
U.S. Attorney General's Task Force on Family Violence, 191, 193, 204
U.S. Commission on Civil Rights, 244
U.S. Department of Justice, 1
U.S. Department of Labor, 245–46
U.S. National Crime Surveys, 35–36

validity: battered women and, 228, 229, 231, 233; rape and, 19; and reliability of CTS, 37–39, 41, 44
Vandenberg, Leslie, 102
Vaughan, Diane, 102–3, 106n19, 232
venereal disease, 20, 66
verbal harassment, 28n12. *See also* catcalls
victimizations, 1; of battered women, 8–9, 227, 230, 231, 233, 234, 269; credibility and, 6; feminism on, 2; reporting, 1; surveys, 31–44
victims: rape, 135, 143–44, 148, 150, 151, 154; "real," 6, 8; "true," 8, 211, 217
victim-witness-advocates (VWAs), 167, 172, 178–79, 182, 183
Victim Witness Assistance Programs, 245
violence: causes of, 34; definition of, 39–40, 44, 227; feminism on, 3, 6; gender symmetry in, 4, 31–54; injuries from, 46n1; institutions on, 3, 31, 129–240; intentions and, 40–41, 43; prevention programs, 2; reporting, 4, 35–37, 47n2, 194; in retaliation, 33, 214; in self-defense, 4, 33, 41, 42; as social problem, 1–10, 34; socialization and, 45; stalking and, 77, 79, 81, 84–86, 100–102. *See also* domestic violence; intimate partner violence; marital violence
Violence Against Women Act, 2
Virginia: Department of Corrections, 18, 27; spousal rape in, 28n6
VISTA, 246
VWAs. *See* victim-witness-advocates

Waites, Elizabeth A., 235n9
Wales: rape in England and, 16; spousal homicide in England and, 43
Walker, Lenore E., 230–31, 233
Wall, Tara, 172
Walsh, Anthony, 169
Warshaw, Carole, 169
weapons, 34, 41–43; fingernails as, 68; sexual assault and, 151, 154, 156, 158, 159, 162, 163n2. *See also* guns
wedding rings, 61, 63, 72n5
Weir, Julie A., 169
Welsh, Sandy, 111
wife beating, 31; battered women's movement and, 243–59, 255n1
Williams, Christine, 5, 118
witnesses: arrests and, 191–92, 194, 196, 197; for sexual assaults, 135, 136, 140, 142, 145, 146, 147, 148, 149, 151, 157. *See also* victim-witness-advocates
wives: abuse, 2, 3, 86, 266–68; assaults, 223–34; infidelity of, 42; rape, 2, 20; as term, 235n1; violence against, 34–37. *See also* wife beating
Wolfgang, Marvin E., 42, 43
WomanSpace, 276n6
women: advice for finding dates/husbands, 72n1; collective liability of, 19–21, 26; definition of, 274; discrimination against, 114; fear of crime, 1, 55–57, 69, 72n4; interviews regarding crime prevention, 56–69; minority, 57; as property/commodities, 17, 20, 27; psychosocial problems of, 209; rape as dominance over, 3, 16–24, 26–27; self

and crime in public places, 55–75; sexual double standard for, 4 social control of, 55–56, 58, 69–70; traditional ideas about, 227, 230, 235n11; violence as dominance over, 31. *See also* battered women; college women; wives
Women's Advocates, 244
Women's Interagency Task Force, 266
Women Together, 263, 264

Womyn, 110–12, 119–25
workplaces
culture of, 109–25, 170–83
harassment in, 5, 109–27
Wrightsman, Lawrence S., 169
Wyatt, Jason, 99

Zald, Mayer, 247
Zygmunt, Darlene, 98

About the Editors

Claire M. Renzetti is professor of sociology at St. Joseph's University in Philadelphia. She is editor of the international, interdisciplinary journal *Violence Against Women*, coeditor of the *Violence Against Women* book series (Sage Publications), and editor of the *Gender, Crime, and Law* book series (Northeastern University Press). She has authored or edited fifteen books as well as numerous book chapters and articles in professional journals. Her current research focuses on the violent victimization experiences of women public housing residents. Dr. Renzetti is a past vice-president (2001–2002) of the Society for the Study of Social Problems as well as president-elect (2004–2005) of the Society.

Raquel Kennedy Bergen is associate professor and chair of the Department of Sociology at St. Joseph's University in Philadelphia. She is the author of numerous scholarly publications and the books, *Wife Rape: Understanding the Response of Survivors and Service Providers* and *Issues in Intimate Violence*. With Claire Renzetti and Jeff Edleson she edited *Sourcebook on Violence Against Women* and *Violence Against Women: Classic Statements*.